That Fateful Day

An artist's impression of von Richthofen's last flight—painted specially for "von Richthofen and the Flying Circus" by J. D. Carrick.

von RICHTHOFEN AND THE FLYING CIRCUS

Compiled by

H. J. NOWARRA and **KIMBROUGH S. BROWN**
(*Luftfahrt-Archiv, Berlin*)   (*Major, U.S.A.F.*)

Edited by

BRUCE ROBERTSON

Drawings by

WILLIAM F. HEPWORTH, M.S.I.A.

Produced by

D. A. RUSSELL, M.I.Mech.E.

First Published in 1958
New Printing 1976

Fourth (Enlarged) Impression
COYPRIGHT ©1964

HARLEYFORD PUBLICATIONS
ARGUS BOOKS LIMITED
Station Road, Kings Langley,
Herts, England.

Library of Congress Card No. 58-11941
All Rights Reserved
ISBN 0-8168-6395-4

MADE AND PRINTED IN THE U.S.A. BY
AERO PUBLISHERS, INC.   329 W. AVIATION ROAD   FALLBROOK, CALIF.

The Famous Red Triplane

von Richthofen about to land in his Fokker Dr I triplane.

Fokker Dr I 152/17, used by von Richthofen as exhibited in the Zeughaus.

By BRUCE ROBERTSON

Foreword

This book is the work of a team who have for some considerable time formed a study group to investigate Manfred Freiherr von Richthofen and his famous air-fighting formation. In considering the evidence of the group, the reader, who is judged to have an interest in aviation, is advised of certain details of the presentation.

Many German words do not have a direct English equivalent, particularly the specialised words dealing with military organisations. Therefore, rather than attempt approximations, which could be misleading, the German word has been used and indicated by italics. (A Glossary, with explanations of these words is on pages 204–5.)

Where aircraft have been quoted by serial number to effect identity, the number has been presented, as far as possible, in the manner in which it was marked upon the actual aircraft. It is advised, however, that in spite of research, it has not been possible to discriminate between Albatros D V and D Va models by serial identity.

Among the many books in which von Richthofen has been mentioned, are three devoted to 'the Baron' himself. An autobiography, *Der Rote Kampfflieger*, published late in 1917, did not give any mention beyond his fifty-first victory, and because of wartime restrictions, it contained little of military interest. Also, in the light of recent research, it is evident that events were recorded out of sequence. Nevertheless, it was a valuable guide to von Richthofen's own thoughts and feelings.

His first biographer was Floyd Gibbons, who wrote in the lively style of an American journalist. Undoubtedly he conducted much original research for his book *The Red Knight of Germany*, published in 1930, particularly on the identity of von Richthofen's victims, which provided a sound basis for further research. His portrayal of von Richthofen as a 'ruthless killer', however, would seem to be far from the truth.

Some years later, there appeared a well-balanced and interesting account entitled *Richthofen—The Red Knight of the Air*. The author, under the well-known pen-name of 'Vigilant', had already written several books on 1914–18 War pilots.

So far, no full account has appeared of the *Richthofen Geschwader*, but each year brought articles in, and letters to, the aeronautical press. The references to von Richthofen in published works grew to several thousands. However, many did not stand examination. A fairly recent letter in a magazine, by a pilot 'who fought Richthofen', gave a date on which, beyond all doubt, von Richthofen was lying seriously wounded in hospital! As an ex-No. 20 Squadron R.F.C. gunner put it—'my pilot thought every German pilot was von Richthofen'. Captain Brown, asked by an official historian about an account which appeared by him in an American Sunday paper, of the fight in which von Richthofen was shot down, said that he did not read that paper!

My reason for making these points is twofold. Firstly, by way of extending my grateful thanks to the compilers who have given the facts, without being prejudiced in any way by what had been previously published, thus building upon a framework of documentary evidence, reinforced by reliable records, and by the compilers own extensive knowledge. Secondly, to offer some explanation to the reader as to why facts and figures may be found to differ from information previously published. In particular, the views expressed here on Hermann Göring will be found to be at variance with other records. While it would be presumptuous to suggest that the view taken in this book is right and others wrong, the reader is asked to consider several facts. The account of Göring in 1918 given in a popular monthly magazine, appeared at a time when he was a Minister of State of a friendly Nation. Udet's well-known autobiography, covering this period in some detail, was written at a time when Udet held office under Göring. The several works on the *Richthofen Geschwader* written in German were published under the rigid censorship of the Nazi Government, in which, as we well know, Göring held high office.

Apart from the 'permanent members' of the research team, there were many other contributors. In particular, I wish to mention the industry of Mr. Douglass Whetton, who made available his compilations on the life of von Richthofen and the *Richthofen Geschwader*.

I am most grateful for the assistance rendered by the staff of the Imperial War Museum; and, in particular, I wish A. J. Charge, Esq., M.B.E., and J. L. Golding, Esq., to know that their efforts are much appreciated. My thanks are also due to the Air Historical Branch of the Air Ministry who made many documents available for study, and to J. McGrath, Esq. of the Australian War Memorial, Canberra.

I wish also to express my grateful thanks to R. D. Wallis, Esq., B.A.(Cantab.), who has made many valuable suggestions concerning the presentation of the text; to Flight Lieutenant D. W. Tambling for translations from certain German works; to W. M. Lamberton, Esq., and J. M. Bruce, Esq., M.A., for the loan of documents, and to Mrs. P. Stone for transcription work.

The 'Photo-Map' on pages 120–121 was prepared by D. A. Russell, Esq. With the aid of copies of the actual air reconnaissance photographs taken in early 1918 (obtained from the Imperial War Museum) he had them rephotographed to a common scale, and so built up a photographic picture of the whole area over which von Richthofen's last flight—and fight—took place.

For some of the photographs I am again indebted to the officials of the Imperial War Museum; but many of the photographs reproduced in the book are from the personal collections of the complilers. The following sources are also gratefully acknowledged: H. H. Russell, Esq., W. R. Puglisi, Esq., Douglass Whetton, Esq., Frank Yeoman, Esq., and Eugene Dmitrieff, Esq.

Since publication of the first edition of this book in 1958, I am indebted to the following for additional information and/or corrections: Herr Wilhelm Allmenröder, P. L. Gray, Esq., Nicholas H. Hauprich, Esq., and J. B. E. Crosbee, Esq.

London, 1959.   BRUCE ROBERTSON.

About This Book

By **D. A. RUSSELL**, *M.I.Mech.E.*

The Ace of Aces and leader of the most famous air-fighting formation in history, Rittmeister Manfred, Freiherr von Richthofen with his fur flying coat unbuttoned at the top to display the coveted Ordre pour le Mérite; Germany's highest award for gallantry, hanging from a neckband.

This is a book about the 'Ace of Aces' of the First World War and of the famous unit he commanded. A man who a German leader said was worth two divisions, and a unit that became the most formidable air-fighting formation in history. A biography of Manfred Freiherr von Richthofen, colloquially known as the 'Red Knight of Germany', and a history of *Jagdgeschwader Nr. 1*, better known as the 'Flying Circus'. A book that not only tells an interesting story, but one that also will stand for all time as the standard work of reference on von Richthofen and the 'Flying Circus'.

This book is the result of meticulous research by a team of experts in three different countries and it is undoubtably the most revealing and detailed account ever written on the life and death of Manfred, Freiherr von Richthofen. Not only that, but it is the first time that an account of von Richthofen's life has been covered *jointly* with an account of his famous air-fighting formation, *Jagdgeschwader Nr. 1*, colloquially known as his 'Circus'.

Legend has surrounded this famous figure of recent history and much that was untrue has confused the Richthofen story. The French rumour that his red machine was flown by a woman . . . the German propaganda to the effect that the Allies put a price upon his head with a promised Victoria Cross and promotion for the man who brought him down . . . an American biographical dictionary quotation that D. H. Lawrence was his brother-in-law . . . his own officially credited victory reports claiming the destruction of Vickers fighters . . . these are but a few of the myths that research has dispelled.

With so much conflicting evidence and with a wealth of material offered for investigation, the publication of this book was a challenge to the notions that many people held about von Richthofen and his Circus. Since the central character was not only the most famous air ace of all time, but a figure of much controversy, it was inevitable that the first appearance of this book; claiming to be the first full and authentic account of the man himself and of the men he led, should engender a spate of letters to the Press and the publishers, as well as 'hitting the headlines' in certain national papers.

But of all the letters that flowed in, the most valued were those from the few who could really judge the true worth of this book—those surviving airmen who, some forty-odd years ago, flew with, or against, von Richthofen himself. Their unsolicited testimonies completely vindicate the views expressed and actions described here, which, it is freely admitted, are somewhat at variance with previously published accounts. Truth it may be remembered, is sometimes stranger than fiction.

Leutnant Gisbert-Wilhelm Groos, who features in this book, having served under von Richthofen in *Jasta 11*, both before and after that *Jasta* became part of Richthofen's *Jagdgeschwader Nr. 1*, wrote—'This book has met with my unreserved approval both in regard to its content and its exemplary presentation. In my opinion the authors have succeeded in giving an unprejudiced, absolutely correct and truthful picture of Captain von Richthofen and of the fighter pilots of the First World War'.

Leutnant Carl Galetschley, who is shown in Appendix Two as having joined *Jasta 6* of Richthofen's *Geschwader* on August 18th, 1917, wrote—'I have known Manfred von Richthofen personally and I think that the book is a remarkable publication; as truthful as possible and to the point'. Vizefeldwebel Willi Gabriel who was a witness to Richthofen's last days of service wrote—'I liked all parts of the book very much, and indeed it agrees entirely with the historical facts'. This last letter was particularly gratifying in view of a quarrel recorded in the text in detail, between Vfw. Gabriel and the notorious Hermann Göring.

And what of those who fought against von Richthofen and his formation? Inevitable, with the detailed approach,

Manfred von Richthofen being prepared for flight during the winter of 1917-18. The bitter cold of a high-flying patrol made in an open, unheated cockpit was a hazard in itself that necessitated stringent precautions against frostbite and great care was taken in the adjustment of flying kit.

the famous Royal Flying Corps squadron, No. 56, features largely. Wing Commander Gerald C. Maxwell wrote—'I have always longed to know what happened to people like Richthofen and to "see over the other side of the hill". This book gives an incredible amount of information, and as I was in No. 56 Squadron all that time and in Captain Albert Ball's flight up to the time he was killed in May 1917, it is of the greatest interest to me'.

Letters also came from two surviving victims of von Richthofen. Of the detailed account of the shooting down of Bristol Fighter B1251 of No. 62 Squadron, R.F.C., to make von Richthofen's 64th victory, 2nd Lieutenant H. J. Sparks who was wounded and taken prisoner wrote—'I must congratulate all concerned on its detailed accounts. I happen to be the gunner of the machine that "the Baron" claimed as his 64th, and I must say that the report of the scrap is very exact'. Von Richthofen's 80th and last victim, 2nd Lieutenant D. G. Lewis wrote—'Your account of my fight was correct. . . . I had completely forgotten the serial number of the machine in which I was shot down and am pleased to know what it was'.

Perhaps most gratifying of all, was the praise that came from von Richthofen's mother, the Baroness Kunigunde von Richthofen who said that the book not only correctly portrayed her son Manfred's character, but accurately defined the relative dispositions of Manfred and his brother Lothar.

While every possible step was taken to unravel von Richthofen's life, some days have been lost, perhaps for ever, in the fog of war. Rather than surmise episodes that *might* have involved von Richthofen, they were left unwritten in order that the text, as it stands, would be authentic and backed by documentary evidence. Here, however, and on the understanding that this is speculation, I can ask was Richthofen the pilot of a red Halberstadt that Captain Neale and 2nd Lieutenant Lidsey of No. 16 Squadron in B.E.2c 4592 reported dived on their aircraft's tail at 4.25 p.m., February 4th, 1917? And when on March 6th,

The heavy flying suit worn by Richthofen on this occasion necessitated the use of a step-ladder to mount his aircraft. One of his fur boots may be seen on page 140 as it appears today in the museum of the Australian War Memorial at Canberra, together with relics of his Fokker Triplane.

A recent photograph of the Baroness Kunigunde von Richthofen, mother of Manfred von Richthofen. With a few treasured belongings she fled to Western Germany from her home at Schweidnitz in Silesia, as the Red Army swept victorious across Eastern Germany during the winter of 1944-45.

Flight Sergeant Quirk from the same squadron in B.E.2d 5834 was distracted by a white Halberstadt to his front, who was in the red Halberstadt that 'nipped in' behind and shot up the machine before being driven off by the observer's, Captain L. E. Claremont's, return fire? Then ten days later, three red Halberstadts attacked, without success, Lieutenants F. M. Kitto and H. E. Ward in Sopwith 1½ Strutter A967 of No. 43 Squadron. Were these led by von Richthofen?

A number of readers, and indeed reviewers, claimed to have, or to have seen, photographs of von Richthofen other than those shown in this book. That may well be so, for no claim was made that every photograph of von Richthofen was reproduced here. We are certain that never before have such a collection of photographs of von Richthofen been published, and we saw little point in having other different photographs of him if they showed similarity to those included. Also some original photographs of von Richthofen were reserved for the publication *Air Aces of the 1914-1918 War* which is now another 'HARBOROUGH' best seller.

Some readers claimed to have a photograph of von Richthofen dead and suggested its inclusion. We, too, held a copy, but it was decided not to publish it. Apart from the sensibilities of some readers that might be offended, our chief consideration was the feelings of von Richthofen's own mother and youngest brother and sister who are still living and who have, of course, taken an active interest in this book.

After over two years' industrious and continuous research by his team of experts, there has been produced a book of which I can write with the fullest confidence to assure the reader that here is an intensely interesting narrative, copiously illustrated with photographs, drawings and diagrams, to give for the first time the full and authentic 'Richthofen story', and one which will undoubtedly become the standard reference work on the 'Red Baron' and the 'Flying Circus'.

von Richthofen and

	CONTENTS	Page
Colour Plate	von Richthofen's Last Flight by J. D. Carrick	
Frontispiece	Fokker Dr I triplane	2
Foreword	by the Editor	3
'About this book'	by D. A. Russell, M.I.Mech.E.	4
Portrait of Rittmeister Manfred Freiherr von Richthofen		8

CHAPTERS

1 *The Young Manfred* — 9
Family Background—Cadet School, Wahlstatt—Royal Military Academy, Lichterfelde—Home at Schweidnitz

2 *Manfred Goes to War* — 12
A Lieutenant of Uhlans—Equestrian events—Outbreak of War—Across the Polish Frontier—Cossacks—Move to the Western Front—Luxembourg—Belgium—Ambushed by French Troops—Patrols.

3 *Introduction to the German Air Service* — 16
Sport at War—Awarded the Iron Cross (Third Class)—Transfer to the Air Service—Organisation of German Air Service

4 *To the Russian Front* — 18
Air Observer Training—Posting to *Fl. Abt. 69*—Flying on the Russian Front—Count Holck.

5 *With the 'Carrier Pigeons'* — 20
Return to the Western Front—B.A.O.—Early German bombing aircraft—The *Grosskampfflugzeug*—Bombardment of Ostend—The Champagne Front—First success—Oswald Boelcke—Training to be a pilot.

6 *The Example of Oswald Boelcke* — 23
Boelcke's service career—Introduction of Fokker E I—Immelmann.

7 *Taking Wings* — 25
Training at Döberitz—Sport on the Buchow Estate—First success as a pilot—Death of Count Holck—A Fokker monoplane—Verdun.

8 *The Finger of Boelcke* — 27
To Russia again—*Kampfgeschwader Nr. 2*—Bombing the Russians—*Jagdstaffeln*, introduction and organisation—Boelcke selects Richthofen.

9 *First Successes* — 29
Jasta 2—The dicta of Boelcke—First confirmed victory — Victory cups — Early victories—Boelcke killed in an air-collision.

10 *Versus a V.C.* — 32
Trophies and souvenirs — *Pour le Mérite* and Victoria Cross compared—Attacking a formation of B.E.2cs—Awarded the Saxe-Coburg-Gotha Medal for Bravery—A double victory—Fight with Major L. G. Hawker, V.C., D.S.O.

11 *Squadron Commander* — 36
Duty flying—German Air Service policy with fighting aircraft—von Richthofen adopts a red colour scheme for his Albatros—Christmas, 1916—First Pup encountered—German aces score table, December 1916—Appointed to the command of *Jasta 11*—Awarded the *Pour le Mérite*—Allmenröder, Wolff and Schaefer.

12 *Bloody April* — 41
His Albatros changed for a Halberstadt—Shot down near Hénin Liétard—The *Flugmeldedienst*—First encounter with Spads—Red becomes a *Jasta* colour—Attacked, by a B.E.2d!—A visit from Voss—Shaking British confidence in the Bristol Fighter.

13 *Retaliation* — 47
No. 100 Squadron R.F.C.—Douai airfield bombed—*Jasta 11* take up anti-aircraft gunnery.

14 *An Ace Indeed* — 49
The Battle of Arras — A triple victory—Becomes the Fatherland's highest scoring ace—Schaefer's night out in No Man's Land—An epic fight with F.Es.—Albrecht visits *Jasta 11*—A fight with three Spads.

15 *Brother Lothar* — 55
Lothar's fight with Hamilton—Lothar's service career—Ethics and the tactics of the Richthofens—A 'Circus'—New tactics—Lothar's fight with Captain Albert Ball, V.C., D.S.O., M.C.—Lothar wounded.

16 *Jagdgeschwader Nr. 1* — 60
Richthofen at General Headquarters—Meets his Emperor, von Hindenburg and Ludendorff—Bad Homburg and the Empress—Hunting in the Black Forest—Mining of Messines Ridge—British weaknesses—The Albatros D V—J.G.1 formed—Allmenröder killed.

17 *The Ringmaster Falls* — 67
Shot down—To *Feldlazarett Nr. 76*—Kurt Wolff wounded.

18 *Grand Performances* — 70
A spate of casualties—Courtrai—A night victory—Battle of Ypres, Summer, 1917—Mayberry's epic strafing flight—von Boenigk, Kurt Wüsthoff and Werner Voss.

19 *Aces and Others* — 78
Richthofen flies again—*Jasta 11* achieve their 200th victory—German aces score list—Inspection by Ludendorff—Faulty ammunition—The first Fokker triplanes arrive—Victory Testimonials—Richthofen goes on leave—Kurt Wolff killed—Werner Voss's last fight.

20 *The Ace of Aces* — 83
On leave at Gotha—Air Service pay—Richthofen as a personality—Móritz, the Danish hound—Analysis of Air Service recipients of the *Pour le Mérite*—Return to duty—A bad landing—The Battle of Cambrai—J.G.1 moves

the 'Flying Circus'

21 *March Offensive*   91
At Brest-Litovsk—Preparations for the offensive—German aircraft production—Nominal roll of *J.G.1* pilots—A protracted fight with a Bristol Fighter—Further encounters—Offensive opens—*J.G.1* ordered to Awoingt.

22 *The Great Battle*   97
Anticlimax for *J.G.1*—Arrival of Udet—Richthofen's 'Indian Summer'—Lieutenant A. A. McLeod, V.C.—British losses—*J.G.1* operates from Lechelle and Harbonnières—Udet's service career.

23 *That Fateful Day*   102
No. 43 Squadron victims—A 'burnt offering' of sixteen Camels—Award of the Order of the Red Eagle—Richthofen's 'mystery day'—His eightieth and last victory—Fails to return—Reinhard nominated to command *J.G.1*.

24 *Tribute*   106
British communiqué mentions Richthofen—von Hoeppner's message—Richthofen buried with full military honours—Obituaries and newspaper reactions, British and German—Re-interment November, 1925—Later tributes.

25 *Who Killed von Richthofen?*   111
The point at issue—Captain A. R. Brown, D.S.C.—No. 209 Squadron—Lieutenant W. R. May—April 21st—The fight—Brown fires at von Richthofen—The case from ground witnesses—Possibility of Brown having second opportunity to fire—Medical evidence.

25a A final assessment.   122
By D. A. RUSSELL, *M.I.Mech.E.*

26 *Successors and Successes*   126
The new Fokker D VII—Reinhard, service career—Weiss—*Jasta 11* almost non-effective—Changes in colour schemes—Move to Guise—Advance airfield at Beugneux

27 *The Geschwader under Göring*   130
French aircraft encountered—Arrival of Göring—Fritz Friedrichs—Göring's methods—Vizefeldwebel Gabriel defies Göring—*J.G.1* moves back—'Black Day' of the German Army

28 *Last Days of Jagdgeschwader Nr. 1*   135
Reduced strength of *J.G.1*—Casualties—At Bernes—Further moves—Disbandment.

29 *Survival and Revival*   139
Dark days of the 'twenties—Revival in the 'thirties—*Luftwaffe* constituted—A *Richthofen Geschwader* formed—*J.G.2* in World War II.

30 *What Now Remains?*   143
Personal relics of von Richthofen—The fate of 'Old Eagles'—Survivors today.

APPENDICES

I *Lineage and Escutcheon of the Family von Richthofen*   146

II *The Personnel of Jagdgeschwader Nr. 1*   148
A nominal roll with details of all known pilots and/or officers on the staff of *Jagdgeschwader Nr. 1* from inception on June 24th, 1917, to disbandment on November 11th, 1918.

III *Medals and Motors*   152
A photograph and schedule of all Manfred von Richthofen's Medals—A photograph of Capt. A. R. Brown's Medals—Photographs of four German aircraft engines: Argus; Benz; Oberursel and B.M.W.

IV *An Illustrated Review of the Victory Claims of Manfred Freiherr von Richthofen*   153
A review of all Manfred von Richthofen's victory claims with a line drawing of each of the eighty-four aircraft concerned.

V 1/72 *scale six-view engineers' drawings, and articles on the undernoted aircraft, used by von Richthofen and/or the Richthofen Geschwader*

Albatros C I Two-Seater		160
Albatros C III Two-Seater		164
Albatros D II Single-Seat Scout		168
Albatros D III Single-Seat Scout		172
Albatros DV/DVa Single-Seat Scout		176
Fokker D III Single-Seat Scout		180
Fokker D VII Single-Seat Scout		184
Fokker E V/D VIII Single-Seat Scout		188
Fokker Dr I Single-Seat Scout		192
Fokker E I to E IV Single-Seat Scout		196
Halberstadt D II and D III Single-Seat Scout		200
Pfalz D III Single-Seat Scout		204

VI *Glossary*   208
A Glossary of German terms—Approximate Rank Equivalents—German Aircraft Type Designations.

Index   210

MAP

Location of German and Allied Fighter Units on the Western Front as at March 21st, 1918   88

PHOTO-MAP

Aerial Survey of the area over which von Richthofen fought his last fight, with flight path indicated; also those of Captain A. R. Brown, D.S.C., and Lieutenant W. R. May, D.F.C.   120

The 'Baron'

Rittmeister Manfred Freiherr von Richthofen.
Born May 2nd, 1892. Died for the Fatherland April 21st, 1918.

The Young Manfred

CHAPTER ONE

'What is the first duty of an officer?' This question is often posed by members of officer selection boards. The desired reply, if known, is seldom fully comprehended. It is that the first duty of an officer is to his men. Although a duty, rarely has it been exercised more conscientiously than by Rittmeister Albrecht von Richthofen. Sweating with exertion during a winter cavalry exercise, he plunged fully clad into icy waters to rescue from drowning three of the private soldiers of his beloved *Leibkürassier* Regiment. By so doing he jeopardised his life and career. A resultant chill brought on a more serious illness with complications that caused deafness. A medical board pronounced him unfit for further military service and his retirement was both premature and compulsory.

The loss of a career was not a calamity to the Richthofen family, particularly as Albrecht had married a daughter of the wealthy von Schickfuss und Neudorff family. Nevertheless, had his military service not been so abruptly terminated, time and seniority would have brought higher rank. If it was prestige that Albrecht felt he had lost, then he need not have worried. Their eldest son, Manfred, born on May 2nd, 1892, was to make the name Richthofen a household word throughout Germany. And what father would not be content enough to reflect the prestige given to his name by his offspring? Although never betrayed by gesture or intonation, the pride felt when mentioning those simple words—my son—was sufficient reward in itself.

For was not their son Manfred to become the outstanding German name of the First World War? What of Ludendorff, the Chief of Staff of the German armies and of Scheer the Admiral of the German High Seas Fleet? Their names are confined to history books. The *Encyclopaedia Britannica* finds space to write of Ferdinand von Richthofen the explorer, but not of the later family member: Manfred. Yet Manfred became the most discussed personality of that war, and the German military spirit, embittered by defeat in 1918, was later to be epitomised in the name Richthofen.

Manfred grew up in an atmosphere comparable to that of the son of an English country squire at the turn of the century. His pursuits of hunting, shooting and fishing were not dissimilar. There was, however, one important difference in environment. Silesia, once part of that romantic province Bohemia, had been a conquest of Frederick the Great in 1742. An influx of families from Middle Germany soon altered the character of the population but strong Slavic traits survived and were treated contemptuously by the Prussian element. There was not the fanatical hatred fanned by Hitler in the Third Reich, but there was a profound feeling of superiority. That Manfred was haughty at times cannot be denied, but this trait was rarely the subject of complaint, for it was expected of the many Prussian officers that came from a similar environment.

The British cannot, however, be smug about the foregoing remarks, for they at that time treated all foreigners with contempt. Being an insular people they did not come into such close contact with others; that was the difference. They even laughed at themselves for their contempt, perhaps unknowingly through their favourite operas by

With hair style and dress typical of the period—Manfred at the age of two years.

Gilbert and Sullivan.

Manfred did not choose a career. It was chosen for him. His father, no doubt intending that his eldest son should enter a profession that he had been compelled to leave, packed the boy off at the age of eleven to the German Military School at Wahlstatt.

Formerly a monastery, the school offered little more than a monastic existence. The food was of the plainest, the accommodation was sparsely furnished, if indeed a bed and cupboard qualify as furnishings, and the discipline was severe. An early rising was followed by arduous physical training. Not the rhythmic exercises now in vogue, but meticulous drills with dumb-bells and Indian clubs. To ensure the mind did not wander, the hours of study were long and included evening periods.

The young Richthofen was not a good student, but showed a remarkable agility at physical exercises, soon progressing to the vaulting horse, the horizontal bars and the ropes. Accustomed at an early age to climbing in the pine forests of Silesia, he applied this ability to offset his lack of interest in study. Once he had a dangerous fall, sustaining a knee injury that necessitated an operation. Quick to recover, he was soon literally in the run again. Some prizes for athletics came his way, but he was not happy at Wahlstatt. He spoke little of it at home, except, significantly, to advise his youngest brother against a military career.

Cadet schools imbued their charges with Germany's military greatness and inspired the boys in spite of their

Still in typical 'period' clothes, Manfred is no longer the child. Here he is at the age of seven years. Looking at him here, one could hardly forecast that he was to become Germany's most accomplished fighter pilot.

drab methods. About the time of Manfred's training, the Kaiser visited the school's naval counterpart. The Kaiser watched intently the devious ways by which the boys were trained to descend the rigging of their training-ship masts. Some slid down ropes head first, others came down hand over fist, keeping varying postures. Impressed, the Kaiser asked: 'And is there no other way down?' 'Certainly, Your Majesty,' shouted an ardent cadet from the top of a mast—so saying, the boy flung himself eighty feet to the ground. It was not regarded as a tragedy, nor was the boy thought foolhardy. It was considered—magnificent. That was the very term used by the newspapers in reporting the incident.

There was little pride for Alma Mater, and seemingly Manfred nursed a grudge against it. Boys, smarting under some injustice at school, often imagine in their day-dreams that one day they will be in a position to tweak their master's nose. Rarely indeed is their wish realised; but it was achieved, metaphorically, by Richthofen.

Years later, when Germany's national hero, he was pressed to write his own adventures. Early in 1918 his book, *Der Rote Kampfflieger* (The Red Battle-Flyer), was published. It made a fleeting but uncomplimentary mention of his cadet life, and the Commandant and staff of the Wahlstatt school were furious. Manfred's turn had come.

His youngest brother Bolko was rather shocked, for he was a student there at that time. He wrote to his eldest brother, imploring him not to make disparaging remarks about the institution. Whether this was because Bolko had found the pride in the establishment that had escaped Manfred or because he was bearing the brunt of his brother's remarks it is not clear. The statement that Richthofen was the hero of all Germany should perhaps be qualified by the words: 'except by the staff of the military school at Wahlstatt'!

One event stands out during his sojourn at Wahlstatt; that of climbing the tall church steeple in the town together with his friend Frankenberg. The tricky part was leaving a window from inside the tower, to climb outside and hoist themselves above the guttering that projected out around the base of the steeple. Once accomplished, the climb up the outside of the steeple was achieved by using the lightning conductor for purchase. As a souvenir, Manfred tied his handkerchief around the top projection. When he visited Bolko at Wahlstatt ten years later he reckoned that it could still be seen.

Another example of his fearlessness came from home. There was a legend that the garret of his home was haunted. Manfred wished to disprove the ghost and had his bed removed to the garret. He slept very well there, but Mother thought it right he should have a healthy regard for fear. Together, she and his sister crept to his room and, keeping out of sight, threw chestnuts upon the floor. Manfred slept on. They threw more forcibly, whereupon Manfred woke suddenly, grabbed a cudgel he had placed near by for just such an occasion and swished wildly. Mother then put on the light. Manfred was frustrated, but fearless.

He was happier at the Royal Military Academy in Lichterfelde, for which he qualified after passing Cadet School. There he was treated as a potential officer of the Imperial German Army—and a military career was the ambition of most Germans at that time. Indeed the Army was limited only by Treasury funds, for there was no lack of volunteers.

Lichterfelde was but five miles from Potsdam, an important military centre. Apart from garrison troops the *Lehrbataillon* was stationed there, behind the New Palace erected by Frederick the Great. This formation was composed of drafts from every regiment, to ensure uniformity of drill throughout the German armies. From this one detail alone, it may be gathered that the German Army

On their father's estate the Richthofen children spent many happy hours. Manfred, holding reins, with his sister Ilse.

10

was a highly organised and homogeneous force. The Germans were thorough, and Manfred, too, learnt to acquire the methodical and thorough ways associated with Teutonic military teachings.

The drill book, field regulations and standing orders had already been learnt almost by heart. Now came the more interesting studies. Tactical exercises with locally stationed units, military history with Frederick the Great becoming a central figure, military strategy and, inevitably, a close study of the principles of Clausewitz.

For leisure, Potsdam offered the amenities of a large town. If its straight streets appeared monotonous, such regimentation could scarcely be criticised as the design had been the work of that arch-planner, Frederick the Great. Manfred seems to have made few social contacts during those two years there; he worked hard, making the most of his leaves at home.

There is no evidence that Manfred shone above his fellow cadets, but his environment and training no doubt fitted him for the role he was destined to play. That alone does not satisfactorily account for his ability to shoot eighty aircraft out of the sky in combat. The reason for his fighting ability, coupled with his training, was the fact that he was an accomplished shot. Any soldier can be taught to shoot, but Manfred was a natural marksman.

His shooting ability was gained at leisure. During his leave periods at home in Schweidnitz he spent much of his time in the surrounding area with a gun. He was shooting at the age of twelve. Once, on his grandmother's farm, the wild duck were not rising to his liking so he flighted some of the domestic ducks and brought several down. Grandma, soon aware that some of her ducks were missing, charged Manfred with their loss. After a short pause, he plunged straight to the point and confessed his offence. Because of his truthfulness he was soon forgiven. He was never known to have evaded the truth.

There were game birds on the estates, wildfowl along the Weistritz, and the countryside offered martens, otters and foxes. And whatever the English might think, it was not considered un-Germanic to shoot a fox! Manfred was a shrewd hunter; with a keen eye and infinite patience he

Manfred von Richthofen as a cadet; together with his youngest brother Bolko—on sled—and his younger brother Lothar.

Manfred's youngest brother Karl Bolko, is shown here with his father, Major Albrecht Freiherr von Richthofen. Because of his youth, Bolko was unable to follow in the footsteps of his brothers. He is now a successful businessman in Berlin.

stalked his prey. His shots were telling, for with continual practice he knew the right moment to shoot.

The influence of this sport on his career cannot be over-emphasised. Since a fighter aircraft is basically a mobile gun platform, the importance of accurate and timely shooting was paramount. It was a famous pilot of the Second World War, Group Captain J. E. Johnson, D.S.O., D.F.C., who wrote that the outstanding fighter pilots were invariably excellent game-shots. 'The pilot who could hit a curling down-wind pheasant, or a jinking head-on partridge, or who could kill a widgeon cleanly in a darkening sky had little trouble in bringing his guns to bear against the 109s.'* If those words were true of the 1939–45 War, then how much more meaning they had for the 1914–18 War when the speeds of aircraft and game birds were so nearly related.

Manfred was a keen horseman, and earlier biographies have made much of this fact. There was a prevalent idea that good horsemen made good airmen. Upon examination it would appear that it was no more true than to assume that good airmen would make good horsemen. The fact that cavalry officers had a training background and temperament suited for military flying gave a false impression that horsemanship itself was the qualification.

After passing through the War Academy in Berlin, Manfred joined the 1st Regiment of Uhlans—*Ulan-Rgt. No. 1 'Kaiser Alexander III'* at Eastertide, 1911. Uhlans were lancers whose main military roles were scouting and screening. In those days their duties were envisaged as the most dashing in the Service. It suited Manfred very well.

---

* *Wing Leader*, by 'Johnnie' Johnson (Group Captain J. E. Johnson D.S.O., D.F.C.).

11

CHAPTER TWO

Manfred Goes to War

An informal snapshot of Manfred von Richthofen taken on his father's estate during one of his leaves.

Manfred von Richthofen was granted a Lieutenancy in his Uhlan Regiment during the autumn of 1912. Great was his pride as he donned his epaulettes for the first time. To celebrate the occasion his father presented him with a beautiful mare called Santuzza, which he later trained for jumping.

Based in his beloved Silesia with home conveniently near for leaves, those days of peacetime soldiering were undoubtedly the happiest of his life. He entered his horse in sports meetings at Breslau, kept his hand in with a shotgun and entered into the social life of the regimental mess. Life was rosy.

He took his share of tumbles. As Santuzza showed promise, Manfred entered it for a hurdle event at Breslau. All might have been well had he not decided the day before, to try one more round on the barracks exercise ground. At the final and highest jump, Santuzza's feet hit the fence and the mare came down heavily, hurting its shoulder. Manfred was thrown violently forward on to his shoulder, breaking his collar-bone.

On another occasion, hard-pressed for the lead in a cross-country event, he made the mistake of leaping at a low hedge near a river bank, where a standing jump and quick turn was advisable. The impetus of his leap took him forward, down the river bank—and straight into the Weistritz! During 1913, he entered a charger named Blume for the Imperial Cross-Country Race, an event exclusive to officers of the German Army. Galloping over moorland early in the race, his horse caught its foot in a rabbit-hole and again Manfred took a nasty toss. Yet, he remounted in spite of a throbbing shoulder and went on to win the race! It was then found that his collar-bone was again broken and once again he was committed to the enforced inactivity of a military hospital. His zeal for riding, however, was in no way affected. In the summer of 1914 he acquired another horse, Antithesis, which he intended to train for the autumn events—but when the autumn came there were sterner tasks in hand.

There was talk of war, chiefly in the newspapers, but the junior officers and the rank and file thought little of it. If the thought of an enemy to his country crossed Manfred's mind, it was to nations with frontiers upon German territory; the French with whom his country had fought in 1870 or the Russians with their untold millions, the 'Slav menace' of the newspapers. Britain as an enemy could not have crossed his mind; the possibility was too remote.

Germany did little to avert the serious Balkan situation in the crisis month of July 1914, but used the tension and the precautionary mobilisation of Russia as an excuse to march. In Manfred's regiment, consisting of a depot and four squadrons of cavalry deployed in Silesia near the borders of Russian Poland, there had been of late practice mobilisation moves with such monotony that the true state of affairs was not appreciated. Visiting Manfred's mess, Count Kospoth, district resident officer in Silesia, was shocked to find the young officers regaling themselves with oysters and champagne. In vain did he try to impress them with the situation; almost, it could be said, the seriousness of the hour. They paid little heed and, inviting him to join them, tried to convince him that his fears were groundless. Next day they were at war.

Manfred's orders were to take up position near the Polish village of Kielce and to report upon enemy movements. Shortly after midnight on August 2nd he crossed the frontier leading a troop of Uhlans. At this point a river formed the boundary line. The crossing by a bridge was unopposed, much to his surprise, and Kielce was reached during the morning without incident.

There was little danger of the villagers of Kielce going out of their way to report the presence of German troops to the Russians. The Poles had little love for either side. The village priest, however, by virtue of the affinity between the Catholic Church and the Russian Orthodox Church, was a possible security risk. Manfred settled this matter by 'shanghaiing' the priest, locking him up in the campanile of his own church and having the steps hacked away. To make a further impression he threatened the priest with shooting should any villagers betray his troops. However, after four days Manfred released the unfortunate cleric.

Manfred's troop was whittled down as day by day he sent a man off with dispatches. On the fifth night came an alarm. A guard awoke him to report Cossacks in the village street. Thinking that the priest, released the day before, might have revealed their camp, Manfred moved away quickly with his men on foot. Then, re-forming, the troop made their way to the churchyard where their horses were quartered. One side of the churchyard skirted the village street, but the wall had been breached earlier on the opposite side upon Manfred's instructions for just such an occasion. It was a dark night and undetected they quietly departed with their mounts.

Halting his group at a safe distance, Manfred together with a trooper went back to reconnoitre and assess the enemy's strength. He confessed to having a queer feeling as, peering over the churchyard wall, the streets looked to be swarming with Cossacks. Edging along to where their horses had been picketed, he estimated their numbers as not above forty. They were making much noise, and some carried lanterns that must have made the darkness beyond appear all the deeper. Manfred returned to his troop but detailed a watch on the village. Within a few hours his sentinel reported that the Cossacks had ridden away. Nevertheless, Manfred judged it prudent to find a new camp, in case his previous site had been betrayed. Brave as he was, Manfred was usually cautious.

Seven days after setting out, he returned to his base to find he had been reported killed in the fighting around Kalisch. Already the story had spread and his family were receiving condolences. He soon dispelled the rumour.

Now, surprisingly, came orders not to return across the frontier, but to entrain at Breslau. Back in Silesia, he became aware of the upheavals in Europe. On the same day that he had crossed into Poland, German troops had crossed the French frontier in four places and also had violated the territory of Luxembourg. Even then Britain was still not irrevocably committed to war. Then on August 4th German troops marched through Belgium. Britain no longer hesitated; her treaty obligations were clear. It surprised Germany, but the 'Contemptible Army' caused them no great anxiety. To Manfred it meant little, although it was destined to mean so much.

He was not aware of the reasons for his regiment's move; that only three active corps and three reserve divisions were to remain on the Russian front, allowing seven German armies to mass along the Western Front, and so crush France in the six weeks that it was estimated could be allowed before Russia was fully mobilised. Belgium and Luxembourg would be taken in their stride. Then, utilising the efficient German State Railways again, the forces would re-deploy in the East and destroy the Russian armies. Such were the dreams of the German General Staff.

The opening moves were real enough. Caught up in this gigantic re-shuffling of armies, Manfred found himself one of four young lieutenants allotted an old second-class compartment in a commandeered train, conveying men, horses and baggage of the 1st Uhlans. It was a memorable journey through the heart of their beloved Fatherland, under the blazing sun of that beautiful mid-August of 1914. Coming from a front and bound for a front they were treated as heroes whenever the train stopped in populated areas. Regaled and showered with gifts by a population seized with war fever, they responded with tales of their prowess, no doubt with much embellishment. Manfred's friend Wedel attracted a bevy of admiring Fräuleins at each stop by displaying his captured Russian sword. Tactfully he refrained from mentioning he had demanded it from a Polish policeman!

Finding the confines of his compartment too small to share with others, Manfred retired to a luggage van where he could spread his mattress out fully. He slept as soundly as in barracks. Before the train reached its destination, Busendorf, one incident, amusing in retrospect, alarmed the travellers. The train having stopped in a tunnel, a soldier fired off a round from his rifle. Thinking the train was being attacked, other soldiers fired shots wildly along the tunnel. It was some time before the officers could effect a 'cease fire'! An inquiry to find out who had fired the first shot met with no success. The case was soon dropped, however, as they were nearing the front.

De-training at Busendorf, the horses, weak from travel and sweating under the heat, slowed the marching pace northward. The troops soon became aware of leaving Germany by the sullen faces of the population they now encountered. Manfred, noticing an unfamiliar uniform, had the man seized and claimed as a prisoner of war. Whereupon the man protested vigorously, claiming to be an official of the Duchy of Luxembourg and that if he was not immediately released he would complain to the German Kaiser. Not knowing his Government's attitude to Luxem-

Major Albrecht Freiherr von Richthofen and Manfred visit Lothar in Hamburg whilst the latter is convalescing from a hip wound sustained in May 1917. Both brothers are wearing the Pour le Mérite, *Germany's highest award for gallantry.*

bourg he let this policeman go—for such he was. In fact, the German Kaiser and the Reich cared not one whit about the neutrality of Luxembourg. Either the policeman was bravely bluffing, or else he failed pathetically to appreciate that his country was under occupation. Whatever it was, he got the better of Manfred.

Wheeling across Luxembourg, the horses recovered rapidly from their travel sickness. On one day forty miles were covered, with the regiment keeping formation as if on a peacetime exercise. Halting at Arlon after having crossed the Belgian frontier, the horses were rested. Manfred, enthusiastic as ever, took a bicycle and rode to the church to observe the front from the wide view offered from the steeple of St. Donat's. The enemy, however, were still some twenty miles to the westward. Returning to his bicycle he found the tyres punctured. Noticing a gathering of sullen, muttering Belgians near by, he had a good idea who was responsible. Manfred was beginning to realise that not everywhere were the Germans popular.

News reached him that only three miles from Arlon a first cousin, another Richthofen, had fallen a few days previously. Now came Manfred's time to face the enemy. On August 21st he was ordered to move up near Virton.

A few miles away a battle raged; columns of the French 3rd Army ran literally at right angles into the marching columns of the German 5th Army commanded by the Crown Prince of Germany. The Germans soon turned their front and engaged their enemies. At that time the French troops still wore their peacetime uniforms of red trousers, blue tunics and *képis*. Advancing as they had been trained, head down to present a small body target, without regard for the density of opposing fire the leading columns were mown down. The well-known saying of a French general witnessing the charge of the Light Brigade at Balaclava could almost be quoted back: 'It is magnificent, but it is not war.'

The French quickly moved back, and in the hiatus caused by their withdrawal the Uhlans were called forward for their typical role, to find the new dispositions of the enemy. They were split up into sections under officers. Manfred had command of fifteen troopers with orders to report on the presence of the enemy. An unenviable task that meant drawing the enemy's fire to reveal their positions. Leading his men to high ground to observe his patrol area, he was appalled at the sight of forests in which whole armies might be concealed. Indeed, the wooded plateau of the Argonne was regarded by France as one of her natural bulwarks.

Manfred, of course, did not dream of shirking his duty. He was most eager to meet the enemy. The hazards nevertheless were a matter for contemplation, both personally and militarily.

From the bright sunlight of a perfect August morning they trotted warily into the woods, slowing their pace after entering to reduce the jingling of their equipment. Contrary to what has been written, Manfred was not at the head of the file. This, however, implies no criticism of his valour. It was the duty of a German officer to command, not to lead in the literal sense of the word. Since the unfortunate man at the head was most likely to bear the brunt of any attack, it was cold military logic that the position should not be taken by an officer, who was of more value than a private soldier. On the other hand, the British subaltern considered it a point of honour that he should be in the van of the men he commanded. On this approach to leadership, much was made by British wartime propaganda: that the British officer led, but the German officer drove. This was of course nonsense. It is not the object here to assess the relative merits of these military tactics, but to ensure that Manfred is represented as the German soldier he was, and to refute the statements that have been written by those who would have him glamorised as the man who was 'always first in the battle and last out'.

Manfred's troop, moving along a woodland path, became aware of hoofmarks in the soil that suggested a large body of cavalry had recently ridden in their present direction. Excited, Manfred reined in, called his men to a halt and addressed them with stirring words. He was smarting for a fight and he infected his men with his enthusiasm. They increased pace, following up the spoor of the French cavalry. In his haste Manfred was militarily incorrect. His duties were to seek out the strength and

German troops at the Russian Front. 'Motorised units' were then unknown, and the horse was as essential for cook-house transport as for the Uhlans themselves!

A Uhlan, with lance slung, proudly escorts a batch of Russian prisoners to the rear during the early days of the German offensive in Russia.

dispositions of the enemy, not to engage them in battle. At this time, his younger brother Lothar had reached the front with his dragoons and Manfred was intensely jealous lest his minor should distinguish himself first. Manfred dreamed of the chance to prove himself and particularly to win a decoration as visible proof of his prowess. His pride could not bear the thought of his brother coming into more prominence than himself. With this inner compulsion and an undoubted courage, he rode forward with zest until they reached the far side of the woods.

They were trapped! Manfred realised it before the shots rang out, as his leading men stopped at a barricade that blocked their path. To the right was a rocky incline and to the left was meadow ringed with barbed wire. There was but one way—back. Manfred, wheeling his horse round and flinging out his arm to full length brought the forearm curving back until his hand touched his helmet. This was the field signal for 'Close up and follow'. Those behind, not aware of his intention to withdraw, rushed up to close in upon him. Of those in front, two of the horses bolted in panic because of the noise of shots in the defile and rushed at the barricade.

Confusion ensued and only with difficulty could Manfred persuade his troopers that discretion was the better part of valour. In the meantime several fell, and finally the survivors withdrew in disorder. Manfred's own orderly fell at his side and he left the man apparently unhurt, but pinned down by his wounded horse. We cannot condemn Manfred out of hand for leaving his orderly unless more facts are known. The place at which he fell was sufficiently screened from fire to allow the man to extricate himself from under his horse and climb the rocks to a safe hiding-place. Eventually he walked back to his unit.

Manfred's report gave an estimate of 100 men. This was probably a gross over-estimate, not necessarily given to justify the loss of most of his troop, but because a victim of an ambush is very apt to over-estimate the strength of his concealed opponents. The facts most likely are that it was not a planned ambush at all, for had it been it is doubtful if any of his troop would have escaped. Possibly the French were preparing defences and a picket at the barricade engaged the Uhlans. Commenting on this episode Manfred said: 'The enemy had certainly surprised us. They had probably observed us from the very beginning and had intended to trap us and to catch us unawares as is the character of the French.' He was surely not so naïve as to expect the French to give due warning of ambush! Later, such tactics as catching his opponents unawares in the air were to contribute so much to his own fame.

There was no time for reproach, for another task was at hand. Accompanied by another young officer, Manfred rode off again to seek out the positions taken up by the retreating French troops.

On the third night out, the two officers decided to seek rest for themselves, their troop and for their horses. A monastery with ample stabling facilities, and quite close to suspected enemy positions, offered ideal quarters and here they asked shelter. The monks with their traditional and impartial hospitality regarded them not as Germans or Frenchmen, nor yet officers and men; they were God's children, in need of shelter.

During the night, the officers were awakened suddenly by one of their troopers shouting excitedly: 'Sir! The French are here.' Manfred's brother officer, waking reluctantly from a deep sleep, asked how many of the enemy there were. The man didn't know, but said two had been shot dead and the dark night had foiled further observation. Manfred gratefully heard his comrade say: 'Well, call us when there's more.' With that, both went off to sleep again. Refreshed, they departed in the morning after an ample breakfast. Three days later, the bodies of their hosts hung from the monastery lantern hooks. They were suspected of anti-German activities.

Much had happened that night. The French had advanced and passed by the monastery. At dawn they had clashed with German troops and withdrawn again. As Manfred led his troop back, they became aware of retreating French soldiers. Both sides were equally surprised and both refrained from firing. So ended Manfred's last patrol as a cavalry officer.

CHAPTER THREE

Introduction to the German Air Service

Germany's first fighter, the Fokker E I, with 80 h.p. Oberursel rotary engine and one machine gun firing through the propeller arc.

The day of the cavalryman's war had gone. On Manfred's front, the forces of the German Crown Prince, to which his Uhlans belonged, were halted by the French forts at Verdun that guarded the route to Paris, on the positions known as the Heights of the Meuse. Little help could be expected from other sectors, as the French Army had almost stabilised its positions and the British Expeditionary Force, after beating a long but fighting retreat from Mons, had re-formed and attacked with some success.

Along a continuous line from the Belgian coast to the Swiss border, armies were digging earthworks for protection. The German campaign stagnated as trench warfare developed. Although cavalry units were retained by both sides for the break-through that each successive offensive promised in plan, it was never achieved in practice.

Inevitably the cavalrymen were put to other tasks and Manfred became a supply officer. He chafed at the inactivity, resented being a base-officer—'base-hog' in German Army slang—and feared lest his brother should have a better chance to distinguish himself. There was only one consolation, the locality offered good hunting. During his off-duty hours he would often set out for the woods with a shotgun. Noticing some young wild pigs in the course of his shoots, he resolved to bag a worth-while specimen. The weather was ideal for a hunter; frosty, moonlight nights with a sprinkling of snow to show up spoor. Manfred had his orderly build a hide up a tree close to a lake where he had seen the pigs. At nights he waited, cramped and cold, yet fully resolved to get his pig. Several times the moonlight allowed him to follow the movements of a sow which would make its way down to the lake, swim across, and having feasted in a potato field, return.

With deadly accuracy he shot the sow one moonlight night as it scrambled up the bank, but he nearly lost it as it fell back into the water. Manfred rushed in and dragged it out by one of its hind legs. It mattered not that he was cold and wet; he had achieved his kill. He was well satisfied. A man with such patience for the kill could be a deadly enemy indeed!

On another occasion he bagged a boar. For years after his death its head adorned the wall of his study at Schweidnitz. Manfred was a great collector of trophies, as we shall later learn. He already wore the Iron Cross (Third Class) for his cavalry patrols, but since awards in this class of the decoration from its institution in 1813 to the end of 1918 totalled five and half million it was hardly an event of great moment.

Most people in 1914 envisaged a short war, and the Kaiser's encouraging New Year message to his troops in the field assured them that 1915 would bring victory. Manfred fretted with impatience to get into the fight before it would be all over. Several times his thoughts turned to the air as the occasional aeroplane droned over. He must have appreciated the fact that aircraft, not cavalry, were now 'The eyes of the Army'. To be a pilot did not appeal to him overmuch, since, for one thing, the course was long and he considered he might still be in training

Typical of the early equipment of a Feldflieger abteilungen, two fighter aircraft for the protection of the reconnaissance aircraft. In the foreground is a Pfalz E VI; then an Albatros C IV (recco); then a Pfalz E V; and lastly, without wings, an Albatros C I.

16

when the war ended. Another consideration was the general attitude of the Army to pilots, who were looked upon as chauffeurs. At that time the observer was usually an officer and the pilot a N.C.O. Seemingly strange to British methods, it was not unknown for the observer to belay the pilot with a cane if particularly annoyed at a manœuvre!

Manfred put in an application for transfer to the German Air Service in the capacity of an observer. Legends surround the outstanding characters in history, and one of the most persistent concerning Manfred von Richthofen is that his application bore the words, 'My Dear Excellency– I have not come to war to collect cheese and eggs, but for another reason'!

At the end of May 1915 Manfred's application for transfer was approved and he was introduced to the Air Service. Since the narrative from now onwards has that branch of the German Army as its background, it is a convenient time to introduce the reader to that service.

The success of the German Zeppelins before the war had so captured the imagination of the German military authorities that at first there was little interest in aeroplanes as weapons of war. However, in 1910 a flying school was opened at Döberitz, west of Berlin, as part of the famous military manœuvre ground, and the following year two other schools were established, one at Merseburg in Middle Germany and the other at Metz.

By 1913 there had been considerable expansion and the German Air Service was organised into five *Luftschiffer Bataillonen* each consisting of four companies of balloon and airship personnel and four *Flieger Bataillonen* each consisting of three companies of aeroplane personnel. These were controlled by two inspectorates, *Inspektion der Luftschiffertruppen* (Inspector of Airship Troops) and *Inspektion der Fliegertruppen* (Inspector of Aviation Troops). For field service these units were unwieldy and small sections or flights were allotted to Army formations, normally at corps level.

A major administrative fault was that of placing the inspectorates under the *General Inspektion des Militärischen Verkehrswesens* (the Commander of Railways and Transport), which showed a complete lack of appreciation for the role that aircraft should play in warfare. Major Hermann Thomsen, responsible for the tactical use of the Air Service, together with Major Siegert, who was concerned with technical development, succeeded in convincing the German Staff of the need for reorganisation of the Service.

To supervise in the field, a *Chef des Feldflugwesens* (Chief of Field Aviation Service) was then appointed to the General Headquarters Staff, and to each army an officer known as *Stabsoffizier der Flieger* was appointed, holding either a majority or captaincy to control aviation within each army. Until October 1915, tactical control of each unit remained with the Army formation to which it was affiliated, when, by a General Army Order, some measure of independence was given to the Air Service by vesting full operational control of units in the *Stabsoffizier der Flieger* (*StoFl.*), whose rank, shortly afterwards, became that of Commander and the office that of *Kommandeur der Flieger* (*KoFl.*).

Some aspects of administrative control were still integrated with other branches of the Army until March 6th, 1916, when an Order in Council provided for the establishment of a separate control that became confirmed in a General Army Order of November 25th, 1916. This gave the Air Service a place between the Pioneers and the

An Albatros C I, 1915, mainstay of the general duties units. The engine is a 160 h.p. Mercedes. The aircraft carried a single machine gun for the observer, and had a maximum airspeed of 82 m.p.h.

Communications Troops in the order of precedence of the Imperial German Army branches. This service included the *Flug-Abwehr* (anti-aircraft defences), a factor that facilitated confirmation of victories claimed by fighter pilots. Manfred later had good reason to thank this service.

Aviation units in the field were at first divided into flying sections or flights, known as *Feldfliegerabteilungen*, thirty-four of these units being available in August 1914. Normally their establishment was for six aircraft for reconnaissance, photographic duties and artillery co-operation work. Later they were supplemented by two machines for escort work. When, in 1915, the need for more specialised duties was apparent, units for reconnaissance and fighting only were formed, known as *Kampf und Feldfliegerabteilungen*.

These were the first fighting units to be developed, but since they were not fully operational at the time Richthofen joined the Air Service, there is little foundation for those expressed opinions that he was drawn by the thrill of aerial combat. Nevertheless, his later awareness of the possibilities of combat, his avid regard for the teachings of Oswald Boelcke and his final wielding of air-fighting formations provide a theme of air-fighting development that will show not merely the personality of Manfred von Richthofen but also his influence.

CHAPTER FOUR

To the Russian Front

Manfred was one of thirty officers who assembled for a course in May 1915 at No. 7 Air Replacement Section at Cologne—*Flieger-Ersatz-Abteilung Nr. 7* to give it its German title, or, more briefly, *FEA7*. The observers' courses lasted some four weeks and included about fifteen hours of flying training in navigation and map-reading. For the rest of the time there were lectures on military observation, use of air cameras, airmanship and briefly the mechanics of flight and the principles of the internal combustion engine. Observers were not required to pilot themselves, but to have knowledge sufficient to exercise a supervisory control over their pilots. It was not unusual, even on active service, for the pilot to hold a rank no higher than that of lance-corporal.

Determined to do well, Manfred had an early night before the course commenced with air-experience flights. These first flights were to discover the reaction of pupils to flying and to detect any physical weaknesses resulting from high altitudes and movement. After an early rising, Manfred was driven over to the airfield for his first flight, scheduled for 7 a.m. He was quite unprepared for the sensation he experienced, having failed to appreciate the lashing effects of the wind at some 70 m.p.h. in an open cockpit. His helmet, slackly strapped, blew to one side; his muffler came off; his jacket, not buttoned up tightly, billowed out. It was impossible to communicate with the pilot verbally, and in an attempt to use notes the paper was whisked away in the slipstream. Gradually, surprise and discomfort gave way to a feeling of exhilaration as he became used to the noise and adjusted his flying clothing. The sight of Cologne Cathedral below him, looking like a toy, gave him a pleasing sensation of mastery of the elements. Flying was going to appeal to him.

He was sent on to *FEA6* at Grossenhain to complete his training. After that came the exciting moment of receiving his orders for a flying unit. A home posting for administrative or training duties was unthinkable. Apart from that distasteful possibility he knew it would almost certainly be one of the eighteen *Armee Flugparken* that Germany then had in the field. For, unlike the British, the German airparks were holding units for personnel as well as for equipment.

Well satisfied, Manfred received orders to report to a park on the Eastern Front. This suited him better than the West, for he had more of a personal interest. His beloved Silesia was little more than a hundred miles distant. There had always been a fear of Russian invasion, the so-called 'Slav menace', and at that very time the East Prussian town of Memel was in Russian hands. How real this peril loomed in Manfred's mind can be judged by his warning, in letters home to his mother, to bury the family treasures should the Russians break through. The fact that he advised hiding and not removal points to a faith in Germany's eventual victory. At that time few Germans had any doubts on the subject. His mother, some thirty years later, must have had painful memories of his warning as she fled with her treasured belongings, not least amongst them Manfred's souvenirs, before a victorious Soviet Army. As we are only too well aware, the Russians are there still.

It was different in June 1915. A group of German and Austrian armies, under the inspiring leadership of General von Mackensen, flung the Russians back from Hungary and Poland into Russia proper. Manfred was quickly sent forward to *Feldfliegerabteilung Nr. 69*, a unit responsible for reporting enemy troop movements to the 6th Austrian Corps.

To those in Britain who took the parochial view that any action other than on the Western Front was in the nature of a sideshow, the words of John Buchan on the German campaign in Poland during the summer of 1915 could have dispelled any such misconception. Buchan stated that Mackensen's army group was probably the largest German army formation ever assembled under one general and that no less than 1,500 field artillery pieces were used to back the offensive. Manfred was thrilled; he was taking part in a great battle, which, moreover, was a war of movement involving gains of thousands of square miles of territory, and with every step forward the 'Slav menace' receded.

For 'personal transport' von Richthofen often used C-type two-seater aircraft. Here he is seen entering the 'passengers' cockpit of an Albatros C III, prior to returning from a conference with a neighbouring Staffel. *Thus in later service, he used for communication work, a type he had used on operations in 1916.*

18

German troops preparing to advance against the retreating Russians during General von Mackensen's victorious campaign in which Richthofen participated as an observer, with Leutnant Zeumer or Count Holck.

Flying in an Albatros (either a C I, or more probably a B II) with an officer pilot, a Leutnant Zeumer, Manfred flew most mornings and afternoons on reconnaissances behind the Russian lines. Zeumer was suffering from tuberculosis and at that time the medical authorities could advise no cure. He chose to continue flying, caring little whether or not he met death in the air. Yet, apart from Manfred, he was to outlive his comrades in *Fl. Abt. Nr. 69*. Manfred respected this pale-faced, reserved and distant man, but he realised that the two of them did not make the ideal team. When he knew that Count Holck, a well-known German sportsman, was to be posted to the unit as a pilot, Manfred resolved to team up with him. Together they made a daring and formidable pair.

Holck, recognised as a racing-car enthusiast, did not turn up as might have been expected in a rakish Mercedes; his arrival nevertheless was typical of the man. He arrived on foot with his small kit and a dog! The confines of a train compartment on the long and slow journey from Middle Germany were as a cage to this tall, muscular and energetic man. When the train was held up at Jaroslav, he decided to walk on along the railway track in advance of the train. He reached *Fl. Abt. Nr. 69* at Rava Russka after a thirty-mile tramp. Next day the train arrived with his batman and luggage.

Manfred wrote of Holck that the more dangerous an assignment the greater was the Count's enthusiasm for it. Several times Holck's daring nearly cost them both dearly. A particular occasion was over the burning town of Wicznice, where a gigantic smoke-cloud billowed up to several thousand feet in front of the flight path of their Albatros. Holck did not deign to consider a detour but kept straight on. Manfred, realising his pilot's intention, felt nothing but surprise for his companion's daring. Neither had sufficient theoretical knowledge of aeronautics to appreciate the effect of hot air upon aerofoil lift. They awoke suddenly to the practical effects. Their machine, stalled, reeled, then plunged earthwards.

Choked by fumes and almost blinded by smarting eyes, Holck wrestled with the controls. Manfred could do nothing except hang grimly on to his cockpit sides. He recorded that his thoughts during those moments were on the stupidity of facing death so unnecessarily. Then, at 1,500 feet, the machine emerged from the smoke and Holck regained control. They turned for home, but after some minutes the Mercedes engine of their machine started spluttering. The Albatros gradually lost height as the engine revolutions slowed. A forced landing in Russian-held territory, however successfully accomplished, was likely to have dire consequences, for the Russian infantry had little respect for, or knowledge of, the Hague Conventions regarding the treatment of prisoners of war.

Heading in the direction of the German positions, the machine still lost height. Neither of the occupants could recognise their exact position, but by the rifle fire coming up they were painfully aware of still being over enemy territory. There came the point where Holck had to put the machine down and he chose a small meadow by a wood. The machine was wrecked, but both scrambled out unhurt and raced for the shelter of the trees. They were followed by Holck's dog, which was accustomed to snuggle on a fur on the floor of their machine during flight.

Warily Holck and von Richthofen, the latter with their only weapon—a revolver and six rounds—skirted the woods to get their bearings. They ducked back into the trees upon sighting troops wearing caps—the German troops at that time usually wore spiked helmets. Then, with relief, Holck recognised them as grenadiers of the Prussian Guards, hence their caps. Only that day they had stormed and broken through that part of the Russian front. Soon afterwards the headquarters staff of the Guards rode by, and Prince Eitel Friedrich greeted the aviators and arranged for horses to enable them to return to their base. The dog, however, made off—perhaps it had experienced enough of Holck's flying!

Germany was fighting on two fronts, and the Supreme Command had continually to balance the needs of manpower at each front. With a victory in the East, the needs of the West became more pressing. Thus Manfred was ordered again from East to West.

19

With the 'Carrier Pigeons'

CHAPTER FIVE

One of Germany's earliest bombers was the A.E.G. G II, often used along the Channel coast. It was probably on this type of aircraft that von Richthofen snicked one of his fingers.

Count Holck and Manfred Freiherr von Richthofen were posted to the Western Front, but they separated to different units. Manfred, reaching Brussels on August 21st, 1915, after his long journey was delighted at being met by an old comrade; none other than the pale-faced Leutnant Zeumer with whom he had first flown in Russia and who now was serving in *B.A.O.*, the unit to which he, Manfred, was ordered.

B.A.O. was something of a mystery unit. Manfred had been told nothing of its functions. Indeed, few people outside the unit knew, for under strict security measures the Germans were forming their first long-distance bombing units. The title *B.A.O.* stood for *Brieftauben-Abteilung-Ostende*, i.e. Mail Pigeon Unit, Ostend, a mere cover title for its real functions. As Zeumer accompanied Manfred on the train to Ostend, he told of the various aircraft types with which the unit commander, Hauptmann Siegert, was experimenting. Besides some of the first G-type machines, there were ordinary B- and C-type reconnaissance machines adapted for bombing, and even a pusher-type Otto biplane had seen service there. Most of all, Manfred was intrigued with the mention of the *Grosskampfflugzeug* (large battle-plane), but in the event, it failed to satisfy him.

Soon Manfred and Zeumer were again teamed up as observer and pilot, this time in the *Grosskampfflugzeug*. He was not enamoured of the large, slow battle-plane.

There was a personal irritation concerning the aircraft's general design; the proximity of the two whirling propellers to the observer's cockpit positioned between them. Once, when hand signalling to Zeumer to bank to the left to observe his target, one of the blades smacked his little finger. He was compelled to seek medical attention and it caused him to be put off flying duties for a week. Thus did Manfred Freiherr von Richthofen shed his first drop of blood for the Fatherland.

Once, when on a coastal patrol during that summer of 1915, he saw clearly a submerged submarine. He made Zeumer circle the spot several times as his fingers itched to pull the bomb toggles, but he had no means of ascertaining the submarine's national identity. As he reluctantly left the spot, some twelve miles off-shore, one of the two engines misfired and slowed. That could seriously upset stability and Manfred had prospects of a crash into the sea. However, a new steering device was brought into play and the machine reached base safely.

The type of machine and the nature of the steering device have occasioned much speculation, since it was first mentioned by Richthofen in his wartime censored autobiography, *Der Rote Kampfflieger*. Research shows that at the particular period and place the following aircraft types could be considered: A.E.G. G I; A.E.G. G II; Albatros G II; L.V.G. G I and Rumpler G I. Most probably it was an A.E.G. type G I or G II. It is possible that the rudder could be trimmed to compensate for any unbalanced thrust by the engines, even in such an extreme case as one engine

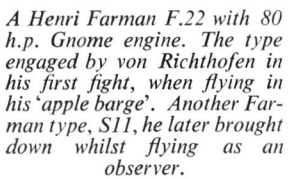

A Henri Farman F.22 with 80 h.p. Gnome engine. The type engaged by von Richthofen in his first fight, when flying in his 'apple barge'. Another Farman type, S11, he later brought down whilst flying as an observer.

stopping whilst the other ran normally. An automatic compensating device was not improbable, since as early as 1913, Glen Curtiss of the U.S.A. had demonstrated in Europe an automatic stabilising device on aircraft in flight.

On the first day of September 1915 Richthofen had his first exchange of shots in the air. Piloted by Zeumer in the 'apple-barge', his appellation for the *Grosskampfflugzeug*, he sighted a Farman of the Royal Flying Corps on reconnaissance. Greatly excited he lifted the safety catch of his automatic rifle and directed Zeumer to close on the enemy machine. The Farman turned quickly and the two machines passed by each other some hundred or so yards apart. Manfred got off

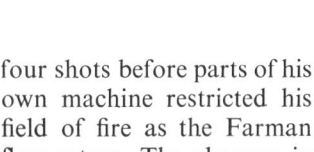
Another experimental bomber was the Halberstadt G I, introduced towards the end of 1915. It was powered with two 160 h.p. Mercedes engines, and had a maximum speed of some 92 m.p.h.

four shots before parts of his own machine restricted his field of fire as the Farman flew astern. The observer in the R.F.C. machine, not quite so much restricted, got in several shots, and holes in the fabric of their aircraft bore testimony to his accuracy. Richthofen signalled Zeumer to turn and meet the enemy again, but, much to his disappointment, the Farman made off.

There were some recriminations over that fight. Richthofen blamed Zeumer's flying and Zeumer blamed Richthofen's shooting. Relations for a time were strained.

At Ostend Richthofen first became aware of the power of the Royal Navy. The airmen off duty made Ostend, the famous Belgian watering-place, their rendezvous. A seafront hotel had been taken over as an officers' club. The beaches lacked their peacetime gaiety, for few Belgians felt disposed to take their holidays under German occupation. German soldiers and sailors had the beaches practically to themselves and they bathed and relaxed there or sipped coffee at one of the seafront cafés. On September 7th, 1915, as Richthofen with some of his comrades were taking coffee they were disturbed by alarm bugles blaring out. A rumour swept round the town that British ships were offshore.

The day had dawned bright, but an early-morning haze hung over the sea. It had shrouded a large naval force of light cruisers, monitors, destroyers, minesweepers and motor-torpedo boats, some eighty ships in all, that had assembled off Ostend shortly after dawn. As the mist cleared and military targets could be engaged without fear of hitting the town, the British commander, Admiral Bacon, ordered the monitors to open fire on installations along the coast, Ostend harbour and the German coastal batteries nearby.

Richthofen and his comrades, having obtained a telescope, made their way up the stairs of their ex-hotel club to watch the 'fun' from the roof. They soon changed their minds and made for the cellar as the twelve-inch guns of the monitors H.M.S. *Lord Clive*, H.M.S. *Sir John Moore*, H.M.S. *General Craufurd* and H.M.S. *Prince Eugène* boomed out. The whine of a ton of metal containing high explosive hurled some few miles through the air was a compelling sound, quite apart from the explosion. After a bombardment lasting half an hour, the British force withdrew; the German coastal batteries were surprisingly accurate and their guns were of sufficient calibre to outrange all but the monitors. German aircraft, too, attacked the force, and the light cruiser H.M.S. *Attentive* was hit by bombs. The British ships did not inflict much damage. Writing of this episode, Richthofen was amused to point out that the only damage done was to the Palace Hotel, built by British capital, but that view was, of course, both biased and expressed under rigid censorship.

On Thursday, September 23rd, the French bombardment opened along the Champagne front and lasted until the dawn of the following Saturday, when the French infantry, in their new horizon-blue uniforms, attacked in force. They stormed the German positions, capturing 150 guns and 25,000 prisoners. A greater gain than Napoleon's famous success at Austerlitz, but here vast field formations were involved, and the German counter-measures in reinforcing the front were effective. One of the major moves was the re-deployment of the Guards Richthofen had met in Russia from the Eastern Front to the Champagne front, and in one of the many minor moves Richthofen was ordered to take his large machine to a unit behind that front.

He flew over the raging battle, but not always in his 'apple-barge', the limitations of which were becoming most apparent. Once he flew with a Leutnant Osteroth in an Albatros, and when about three miles over the French side once again spotted a lone Farman. Osteroth flew alongside to allow Richthofen a clear field for his machine-gun. At first the occupants of the Farman paid no attention

The Fokker E II, an improved version of the E I, was used largely as a trainer to instruct German pilots in the new Eindecker fighters. It was on this type of machine that many future aces were trained to become fighter pilots.

as they were fired upon. Quite possibly they had not noticed the German machine. Not until Richthofen had some trouble in clearing a stoppage did they take evasive action, but Osteroth skilfully kept Richthofen in a good position to fire and eventually he exhausted the 100 rounds available. Then Richthofen excitedly drew his pilot's attention to the enemy machine. It was spiralling down. They followed it with their eyes and watched it fall to earth. Descending they were able to see it had crashed into a large crater, nose first, leaving the rudder sticking out of the ground. Elated, they returned, but as the victory could not be confirmed it was not credited to Richthofen.

On the first day of October 1915 the Richthofen and Zeumer partnership was broken up. They were posted together to *Brieftauben-Abteilung, Metz* (*B.A.M.*), the cover title for Germany's second bombing unit. Later *B.A.O.*, mentioned earlier, and *B.A.M.* became known as *Kampfgeschwader 1* and *2* respectively. Until 1916 they remained the only German bombing units on the Western Front. Both units had a few Fokker monoplanes, then coming into service, allotted for protection duties. It was because Zeumer took over one of these single-seat fighters that Richthofen had to team up with another pilot.

If Richthofen had not given much thought to becoming a pilot before he entrained for his new unit, there is little doubt that he was fully resolved to become one at the end of his journey. Seated opposite him in a dining-car was a young, unassuming officer. One fact about him greatly intrigued Richthofen; he had shot down four enemy aircraft. His name was Oswald Boelcke. Richthofen eagerly engaged him in conversation and asked the inevitable question: 'How do you do it?' Boelcke, a modest man, dismissed the question with a laugh. Then, realising that the question was put in all seriousness, replied that it was a simple matter of flying close to the target, taking careful aim and then, down went the enemy. Richthofen pointed out that he had done just that in his first combat, but the enemy machine continued on its way. The difference, Boelcke answered, was that he flew a Fokker monoplane.

Richthofen was fully resolved to become a pilot, but he was reluctant to leave the front for a full pilot's course. Enlisting Zeumer's aid to teach him and using an old B-type machine that was not required for operations, he spent much of his spare time learning to fly. Just ten days after meeting Boelcke, Zeumer judged him ready for his first solo. Taking off for the first time he circled the field, mechanically following the control movements he had learnt by heart. It was hardly the way to get the feel of the controls, and upon coming in to land he found the machine did not respond in the manner he expected by control movement. It lurched; he over-corrected, and the machine hit the ground and nosed over. Unhurt, Richthofen ruefully extricated himself from the wreckage. Two days later, however, he had the feel of the machine and made several good landings.

The German regulations regarding the training and classification of pilots were even more rigid than either those of the French or British. A pilot could not be classified as such until he had passed a series of examinations by a competent authority. For this, Richthofen had to go to a training unit, but the fact that he had already made solo flights considerably shortened his course. He had hoped to pass his preliminary examination in his field unit under an inspecting officer. This involved flying a series of figures of eight, then landing with a dead engine. After several attempts he eventually satisfied the examining officer, and on November 15th he was sent to Döberitz for further training.

A large German aircraft was flying back to Döberitz and Richthofen was thus saved a long train journey. The proximity of Döberitz to Berlin added interest to his course, and by making friends with a fellow trainee, a Leutnant von Lyncker, he had both company and entertainment. His mother, at this time, visited Berlin and they were able to meet several times. Nevertheless, he gave full concentration to the instruction and prepared early in December for the formidable second examination. The tests were rigid and consisted of fifteen smooth landings as a preliminary. Then came forced-landing tests, where a rocket fired from the ground would indicate that the engine was to be cut and the aircraft landed. Usually this signal was given when the pilot was at a height of about 1,500 feet. Following came a series of longer flights of up to one hour with various loadings.

Richthofen worked hard and passed without difficulty; he was fully determined to follow the example of Boelcke.

The Example of Oswald Boelcke

CHAPTER SIX

Oswald Boelcke, who was to influence so much the life of Manfred Freiherr von Richthofen, was the fourth of six children of a teacher, later professor, of Giebichenstein, near Halle. He was neither a very good child, nor when he expressed a wish to become an officer, a very good pupil. Nevertheless he gained entry in March 1911 to the Prussian Cadets' Corps at Coblenz and in August of the following year he gained a lieutenancy in a communication troop. It was during manœuvres with this unit that he saw his first military flights, which so influenced him that he determined to fly. His hopes were not confided to his parents until mid-1914, when a letter home revealed that he was learning to fly at Halberstadt. On August 15th, 1914, he received his pilot's certificate after being trained and schooled, as he himself put it, on a 'Bristol Taube'.*

He proceeded on September 1st, 1914, to La Ferté, where his elder brother Wilhelm was already in action with *Fl. Abt. Nr. 13*. There he received an Albatros B II, in which he flew with his brother as observer, doing good work on artillery-spotting.

The winter of 1914–15 proved a boring one for Oswald and he sought ways of escaping from the perpetual routine of recognise, photograph and observe. Perhaps the visit of Leutnant Parschau in his Fokker monoplane during November 1914 had turned his thoughts towards a more dashing role. The February of 1915 brought him the Iron Cross (First Class) and towards the end of April he received his chance on posting to the newly founded *Fl. Abt. Nr. 62* at Döberitz, west of Berlin, under Hauptmann Kastner.

At first with *Abt. 62* he flew L.V.G. B II Nr. 308/15, then, when the unit went to the front at Douai, he received one of the first C-type aeroplanes, Albatros C I Nr. 162/15, armed with one machine-gun.

Boelcke took off on June 15th, 1915, for the first time in his new Albatros and by the evening of next day he had made five flights and had become involved in four fights, three with French aircraft and one with an Avro biplane. A few days later, over Liétard with Leutnant von Wuehlisch as observer, he attacked a Morane type L Parasol with his reconnaissance machine. He followed the Frenchmen, attacking them over Valenciennes, using all his experience

Hauptmann Oswald Boelcke, who was to score forty victories before being killed in a flying accident.

to give his observer a good position for firing. After a fight of some twenty-five minutes the Morane crashed to earth. Both Frenchmen, the pilot, Lieutenant Tetu, and observer, Comte Beauvicourt, were killed, the latter falling into his own estate. For this victory Leutnant von Wuehlisch received the Iron Cross (First Class), but as Boelcke had it already he received only congratulations.

This first victory of Boelcke's was his only one with a two-seat machine. At the end of May, the first two Fokker E Is were demonstrated by Anthony Fokker and Leutnant Parschau at the front near Verdun. Afterwards they visited Douai, where Fokker left his machine Fokker E I (factory designation M5K/MG) Nr. E3/15. At that time Fokker pilots were forbidden to fly over the enemy lines lest the machine-gun interrupter device fall into enemy hands. Disregarding this order, on August 19th, 1915, Boelcke shot down a Bristol biplane with his Fokker, but as the machine fell on the enemy's side of the lines he received no acknowledgment. It was about this time that in the course of an off-duty walk he saw a French boy fall into a river. Without hesitating he jumped fully clothed into the water and after considerable efforts succeeded in saving the boy's life.

A new Fokker was available to Boelcke in September, machine Nr. 37/15, with a 100 h.p. Oberursel in place of the 80 h.p. engine of his earlier machine.

---

* The school and factory at Halberstadt was founded by the British and Colonial Aircraft Co. Initial school equipment consisted of Bristol aircraft.

The A.E.G. KI, forerunner of the GI, produced in 1915, was powered with two 100 h.p. Mercedes engines.

23

Introduced in December 1915 the Fokker E III had an Oberursel rotary engine of 100 h.p. and was fitted with a single synchronised machine gun.

On the 18th he achieved his third victory, a Morane.

Towards the end of September, whilst Richthofen was flying the lumbering battle-plane, he won his fourth victory by shooting down one of ten French aircraft that were bombing the railway station at Metz at the very time the Kaiser was scheduled to arrive. Boelcke alone attacked the aircraft, downing his victim at Pont-à-Mousson. His fifth was a Voisin near St. Souplet, and following his sixth victory he was awarded the Knight's Cross of the Order of Hohenzollern with Swords.

On November 9th, 1915, Boelcke was summoned to Supreme Headquarters at Charleville, where he conferred with the *Feldflugchef*, Major Hermann Thomsen. These two men, one concerned with the theoretical, the other with the practical aspects of aerial warfare, collaborated to form a team whose work was to have far-reaching effects. Boelcke gave reports on his experiences in combat, in fighting tactics and on each new aircraft type. Upon these reports, Major Thomsen based his instructions to his fighting units. It is certain that the *Feldflugchef* had a reasonable idea of the requirements of the front, but Boelcke's clear accounts were an invaluable guide. Boelcke, it can be said, was therefore the father and teacher of combat pilots, whereas Richthofen was the man who developed his methods to the highest degree of mastery.

To return to the Boelcke of 1915; in November he was ordered to visit Fokker in Schwerin. There he became acquainted with the new Fokker E IV (M.15). During December he returned to Douai to find *Fl. Abt. Nr. 62* still there, but many changes had taken place.

His eighth victory, a B.E., came on January 12th over Mouscron, north-east of Tourcoing. Landing at *Fl. Abt. Nr. 5*, stationed at Lille, he reported his victory by telephone to his unit and learnt with surprise that Max Immelmann, too, had just gained his eighth victory over Bapaume. Back at Douai, both he and Immelmann were visited by Major Thomsen. During dinner his adjutant rang through the news that both of the intrepid airmen had been awarded the *Pour le Mérite*.

In February 1916 Boelcke was again ordered to *B.A.M.*, then known as *Kampfgeschwader Nr. 2*, which his elder brother, Wilhelm, commanded. Meanwhile he had become an Oberleutnant.

Hauptmann Haehnelt, the officer responsible for German air operations at Verdun, grouped together all Fokkers as a closed fighter force. They were divided into small groups; Boelcke for his group partnered Leutnant Notzke at Sivry, some seven miles behind the front. His task was that of offensive intervention, during the prolonged Battle of Verdun, to reduce the enemy's air superiority. On March 11th he took up position at Sivry and the very next day he claimed two of his opponents.

Leutnant Notzke, Boelcke's comrade, was lost at the end of April, his successor being Oberleutnant Freiherr von Althaus, one of the coming aces. On May 1st another aircraft fell to Boelcke's guns and by the 21st of the month his score had risen to eighteen. A day later he became, by Imperial Order, a Hauptmann, the first time in the Royal Prussian Army that a young man of twenty-five had attained the rank. It was all the more surprising since Boelcke was not a 'von'.

The flying personnel of Fl. Abt. 62. 1, Salffner. 2, Meding. 3, von Mulzer. 4, Oesterreicher. 5, von Schilling. 6, Boelcke. 7, von Cossel. 8, Kastner. 9, Fromme. 10, Immelmann. 11, von Gusnar. 12, von Krause. 13, Hess.

Taking Wings

CHAPTER SEVEN

While Boelcke was achieving fame as Germany's first *Jadgflieger*, Richthofen was grimly determined to learn all he could about flying at Döberitz. Nevertheless he found time for his favourite sport. Not for him the gay city life of nearby Berlin. Whilst brother officers regarded the Fräuleins in the Tiergarten as offering the most attractive sport, Richthofen's preference was for shooting in the country, with wild pig as his quarry. An incongruous alternative that must have led to much leg-pulling.

If his brother officers took their flirtations lightly, Richthofen at least took his pigs seriously. He was willing to wait up all night for the chance of a meeting. Some of his training flights were arranged accordingly. Since the third and final pilot's examination entailed cross-country flights and landings on strange ground, much time was devoted to such practice, and inevitably the trainees used this opportunity to their own advantage. For Richthofen, the Buchow estate was his favourite landing area.

On evenings when the weather permitted, he would fly with a N.C.O. pilot to take the machine back after dropping him off on the estate, where several fields offered suitable landing space. All night he would roam with his sporting rifle, and soon after dawn the N.C.O. would fly over to pick him up, and fly him back to camp. Richthofen seems to have organised this very well, but it was late in the year and the weather was not to be trusted. One night it snowed and it was still doing so at 8 a.m., when his machine was due. Visibility was down to fifty yards and he realised that his pilot would have difficulty in finding the spot. It was more likely that the flight would not be attempted at all. He was musing on the prospect of a seven-mile tramp back to camp when he heard the welcome sound of an aeroplane engine. After some difficulty, the pilot located the ground and came in to land. When he touched down the snow clogged the wheels and the machine skidded to a stop and nosed over, breaking several spars. That was the end of Richthofen's hunting jaunts on the Buchow estate.

Part of the final examination involved several cross-country flights of varying distances. Considerable latitude seems to have been allowed to officer-trainee pilots in fulfilling these requirements, for Richthofen's itinerary was planned to suit himself. First he flew to Schwerin, where Fokker was building the monoplanes which he had resolved to fly. Then he went on to Silesia, landing at Breslau, and on to his home town of Schweidnitz, returning to Döberitz via Lüben. *En route* he made several other landings to meet relatives and friends.

One of his last tests was to attain a height of over 11,000 feet with full war load and to remain above 9,700 feet for at least one hour. That being successfully accomplished, his final test came on a date that suggested that Germany was beginning to take the war very seriously. It was on Christmas Day, 1915.

He joined an active-service unit during March 1916, once more on the Verdun front, and there he flew again in an Albatros, but this time as a pilot. His ambition to fly single-seat fighter aircraft was yet to be fulfilled. In an effort to make his reconnaissance aircraft more battle-

Hauptmann Boelcke with some of his associates at German Headquarters, Charleville. Second from the right is Leutnant Oesterreicher. A photograph taken in August 1916.

worthy he had a machine-gun mounted on the upper wing, fixed so that he could grasp the trigger grip with one hand and fire upwards, an idea that he copied from a captured French Nieuport biplane.

It was unusual at that stage of the war for more than one machine-gun to be carried. Many of his brother officers openly laughed at his device. His observer might well have considered it as poaching upon his preserves. Richthofen, nevertheless, refused to remove it. Although he was the pilot, he was still determined to be a man with a gun; moreover, he sought every opportunity to use it.

A French Nieuport sighted on one of his scouting flights gave him his opportunity. As he approached, so the Frenchman turned away and made off for his own side of the lines. Richthofen gained the advantage by diving to give his machine the extra speed necessary to gain on his enemy, at the same time placing himself to use his upward-firing gun. A few well-aimed bursts hit the Nieuport, which reared up, then fell back, turning over and over.

Both Richthofen and his observer thought the Nieuport pilot was using a ruse, to give the impression that the machine was out of control. Like most German airmen they were somewhat contemptuous, and not a little bewildered, by what they regarded as 'antics' on the part of French pilots. The point was that the French taught and encouraged aerobatics as part of their training, whereas the Germans held the view that aerobatics were of no practical value. However, in this case the Nieuport pilot was not shamming, he was dying. The machine went down still spinning, and as it finally crashed into trees behind Fort de Douaumont, Richthofen's observer clapped him on his shoulder to congratulate him upon his victory. It was not, however, personally credited, as the wreckage fell upon enemy territory and there were no other witnesses. For the wartime Press it was not necessary to be so scrupulous. Richthofen was pleased to point out in a letter to his mother that in the German Army communiqué of April 26th, 1916, stating that two hostile flying machines had been shot down in aerial fighting, one of them fell to his gun.

Four days later he witnessed an aerial drama over the Verdun forts. Richthofen saw that a lone Fokker was attacking three Caudrons. Owing to a strong head wind and insufficient height he could not give assistance and watched as the strong west wind brought another French formation on the scene. The Fokker was forced on to the defensive as the pilot found himself fired upon from several directions. Richthofen, still powerless to intervene, saw the Fokker plunge into a cloud. He sighed with relief, thinking the pilot had sought cover to escape. Not until later did he learn the truth; the machine had plummeted straight through the cloud to earth. The pilot was dead, shot through the head. It was his old comrade, Count Holck.

About that time came his most terrifying experience in the air. His Albatros was wheeled out of a hangar at Metz for a flight back to his unit, although it was evident that a heavy thunderstorm was imminent. Against the advice of more experienced pilots he took off. As he rose it started raining, then it poured in torrents. His goggles were useless in the splashing water so he tore them off. Aware that he was flying into inky darkness he went down low. Only at under 100 feet could he discern the ground, and he was compelled to 'hedge-hop', rising to fly over high trees in his line of flight, a dangerous proceeding in view of the high wind that continuously buffeted his machine. Then lightning flashes around him added to his mental anguish. When it seemed that the storm must at last claim him a break in the cloud appeared. Eventually he reached base, where he was welcomed by an anxious party, warned by telephone from Metz that he had taken off and disappeared into a black cloud! He vowed he would never fly again in a thunderstorm—unless the Fatherland demanded it of him.

At last, after continually worrying his commanding officer, Richthofen was allotted a share of a Fokker monoplane. He flew it mornings, and a Leutnant Reimann afternoons. Both were afraid that each other would cause damage to that famous aircraft type, available in such limited numbers. One afternoon Reimann did not return. His engine had been hit by a bullet and the machine came down in no man's land where Reimann set it on fire to prevent an enemy patrol from learning its secrets. Reimann was uninjured and took shelter in a shell-hole until night, when, under cover of darkness, he crawled into the German trenches.

Another Fokker was allotted and this time it was destroyed in Richthofen's hands. On his third flight the engine stalled when he had gained little height. He was compelled to land straight away. In so doing the machine was completely smashed, but by a miracle Richthofen was unhurt.

There came rumours of another move as the front quietened. The Battle of Verdun had proved a great trial to the Germans. For months waves of German infantry had been hurled in vain against the French forts. French *élan* had never been doubted, but the Germans had expected them to break under sustained attack. They were wrong. *Ils ne passeront pas* (They shall not pass) became the catchword of France, and those words were solemnly regarded by the *poilus*. Verdun was their finest hour. Stand fast they did, during the longest continuous battle in history until the Battle of the Somme, soon to follow. Germany was compelled to break off the battle. There followed a reshuffling of forces and *K.G.2* was directed to the Eastern Front and so Richthofen was sent back yet again to Russia.

On exhibition! A Fokker E III, with 100 h.p. Oberursel engine, which had been brought down apparently intact.

The Finger of Boelcke

CHAPTER EIGHT

Kampfgeschwader Nr. 2 literally rolled across Germany. A mobile unit, housed in German State Railways rolling-stock, its move entailed no great administrative difficulties. Apart from the tedium of long travel there were the comforts of sleeping and dining-car facilities for the officers. But once their destination was reached on the Central Russian Front, the hot, dry, East European summer made the carriages almost unbearable as living quarters, exposed as they were to the sun in a shadeless railway siding.

To take quarters in local villages was unthinkable, as they were little more than collections of hovels. Many had been destroyed in the fighting and most were overrun with vermin and infested with lice. The German airmen were appalled by the lack of sanitation. In one village the whole population, men, women and children, made regular walks to a local marsh which acted as a communal cesspool. The local German military commander, incensed by such a primitive arrangement within the area of his administration, threatened to shoot any villagers using the spot. In the absence of any sanitary arrangements in the village, it proved a short-sighted policy! Such were the conditions.

Richthofen solved the accommodation problem to his satisfaction by camping on the edge of a forest with two comrades, Leutnants Gerstenberg and Scheele. There he mused on the possibilities those giant forests held—wolves, lynx and elk. Living happily, gipsy fashion, he enjoyed many nights hunting in the woods, in spite of bagging only small game.

In the air there was little opposition to fear. The chief danger, as before in Russia, was the possibility of a forced landing amongst Russian troops during flights over enemy territory. Bombing was the main role of his unit, although its title suggested more general work. All *Kampfgeschwader* were in fact renamed *Bombengeschwader* during the following year; i.e. from the general term 'battle formation' to the specific term 'bombing formation'.

His sturdy Albatros C III often staggered into the air with up to 300 lb. of bombs when good targets were offered, and there were plenty in June 1916, as the Russian counter-attack, directed towards Galicia, threatened the railway centre at Kovel, near which his unit was stationed. As Russian units moved across the River Stokhod, so orders came to bomb their pontoon bridges, a task of destruction that appealed greatly to Richthofen. Manœuvring into position to drop his bombs and then circling to allow his observer to pepper the bridge with machine-gun fire, he gloried in watching the ensuing disorder. Troops rushed for the banks to spread out and evade his fire, whilst stampeding horses, some of them dragging limbers, added to the confusion. Richthofen wrote that the half-savage tribes of Asia were even more startled than cultured Englishmen when fired at from above.

Particularly Richthofen delighted in dispersing cavalry by bombing and machine-gunning. Groups of Cossacks would gallop away rapidly in all directions as he opened fire. Germany had undoubted air supremacy on the Eastern Front, but the German and Austrian troops on the ground were at that time hard pressed by the Russian hordes.

An early informal snapshot of von Richthofen in conversation with Hauptmann Carganico, his superior at K.G.2.

Rarely did he see any Russian aircraft in the air, and later, when an ace, he expressed regret that he did not manage to add a Russian machine to his victory score. Chiefly the Russians used aircraft of French design, either supplied direct from France or else built in Russia under licence. A French aircraft unit did operate with the Russians, but strangely, one of the few enemy aircraft to fall into German hands along his part of the front at this time was a French aircraft from the Western Front! A Nieuport piloted by a young French officer had set out from behind the Western Front, dropped propaganda leaflets over Berlin and had then made for the Russian lines. Engine trouble developed and the pilot was forced to descend at Cholm, short of the Russian lines by only sixty-three miles after a 810-mile journey.

Even before Richthofen left for Russia, Boelcke had become a national hero. His deeds in the air were widely reported and they brought him fame. But Boelcke's worth to his Fatherland was not measured only by a victory score. His plans, made in concert with Major Thomsen, the *Feldflugchef*, under the veil of wartime secrecy to reorganise fighting aircraft units, had far-reaching effects upon the course of the air war. In the autumn of 1915, units had been formed to take over fighting duties (see page 17), and escort machines previously allotted to general service units were withdrawn. Thus, *Kampf und Feldfliegerabteilungen* became the first units with specific fighting duties.

At Boelcke's instigation, it was proposed in June 1916 to reorganise these fighting units by integrating them into *Jagdstaffeln*, pursuit flights, often known by the abbreviated form *Jasta*. These units were numbered in straightforward numerical series from No. 1 upwards. *Jasta* Nos. 1 to 7 were formed during August 1916, Nos. 8 to 15 in September and by the end of 1916 thirty-three had been formed. A *Jasta* was the basic self-accounting unit of the Service, corresponding to a British Scout Squadron, although in

27

Taken at the same time as the snapshot on the previous page, von Richthofen as an officer in Staffel Nr. 8 *of* Kampfgeschwader Nr. 2 *on the Eastern Front.*

direct comparison it was smaller. The paper establishment of a *Jasta* in late 1917 was eighteen officer pilots, including the commanding officer, a recording officer, thirty-six air mechanics and personnel with miscellaneous duties, to give a total of 130 officers and men. Authorised equipment was eighteen aircraft, but the actual number held was usually less due to losses and production delays.

Some *Jagdstaffeln* were directly responsible to the Army Aviation Commander, but others were formed into *Jagdgeschwader*, a more or less permanent battle formation consisting of three to four *Jagdstaffeln*. A temporary grouping of an indefinite number of *Jagdstaffeln* was occasionally formed for a major offensive, such a formation being known as a *Jagdgruppe*.

At the very time Boelcke was about to take over his unit at Sivry under the reorganisation, he was, by Imperial Decree, forbidden to fly. The Supreme Command feared lest their national hero should fall. To sweeten what was for him a bitter pill, he was invited to make an inspection tour of the German South-Eastern Front and to confer with Major Serno, the chief German aviation officer with the Turkish Forces.

Whilst on tour, the great Battle of the Somme opened on the Western Front, the magnitude of which may be judged by the sombre fact that on the opening day of the assault, British casualties alone were 120,000 men. In the air British aircraft made continual reconnaissances and spotted for the guns massed along the twenty-five mile front. In vain the Fokkers strove to check them. They had the means but not the inspiration. Immelmann was dead, killed when his machine crashed due to a technical fault, and Boelcke was still away from the Western Front.

Boelcke was therefore recalled with instructions to form and lead a *Jagdstaffel*, with a free hand to select his men. He was then in Bulgaria and he returned via the Russian Front, visiting airfields along the route to find suitable personnel.

When it became known to Richthofen that Boelcke was visiting their airfield near Kovel he was greatly excited. Nothing would please him more than to be chosen. Taking temporary quarters in one of the unit's railway carriages, Boelcke interviewed several of the pilots. Richthofen's heart beat faster as his great opportunity came. As luck would have it, Boelcke remembered his face and recalled their earlier meeting on the train *en route* for Metz, back in *B.A.M.* days.

Boelcke was an excellent judge of men. That day his finger metaphorically pointed to two pilots and events were to prove them worthy of his selection. One was the thirty-seven year old Leutnant Boehme, formerly an officer in the German East African service; the other was Leutnant Manfred Freiherr von Richthofen.

Little time was lost in leaving Russia. As Richthofen took leave of his brother officers, one facetiously shouted to him: 'Don't come back without a *Pour le Mérite*.'

Jasta 1 had been established on August 23rd, 1916 under Hauptmann Zander and seven days later *Jasta 2* was formed, at least on paper, for not a single aircraft had arrived. Amongst the first pilots selected by Boelcke and ordered to the unit were Leutnants Guenther, Hoehne and von Arnim, but before von Arnim could report he had fallen in action with his *Fliegerabteilung*.

On September 1st von Richthofen arrived at Lagnicourt and Vizefeldwebel Reimann reported that same day. A week later came Oberleutnant Viehweger and Leutnant Boehme. These then were Boelcke's chosen, the pilots of Germany's *élite* fighting unit, led by Boelcke himself, the Fatherland's leading fighter pilot.

Left to right: Boelcke, Rachow, the German Crown Prince (son of the Kaiser) and von Brandis, all holders of the Pour le Mérite.

28

First Successes

CHAPTER NINE

When Vizefeldwebel Reimann had reported in to *Jasta 2* at Lagnicourt, he had ferried over from *Jasta 1* the unit's first aircraft, an Albatros D I. Shortly afterwards two Fokker D IIIs were taken on strength and one of these, D III Nr. 352/16, Boelcke used as his personal aircraft. This machine survived him and it was later exhibited in Berlin with the weapons collection of the Zeughaus. It was finally destroyed in 1944—by Allied bombing.

Whilst awaiting the delivery of the rest of the aircraft, Boelcke lectured his pupils on the principles of air fighting as he saw them; rules that stood the test of time and were equally applicable to air fighting in the Second World War. He also found time to fly a few lone patrols, particularly in the clear light of early morning, from which his pupils would await his return with boyish enthusiasm. As he rose to scramble out of the cockpit, they would eagerly scan his chin—the only part of his face not covered by goggles and helmet—for the grimy black smoke-marks indicating that he had used his guns. And if Boelcke had used his guns, then almost certainly he had increased his score. Richthofen wrote that Boelcke almost daily had an Englishman for breakfast.

On September 16th, the *Jasta* received some Albatros D IIs and Boelcke judged his school ready for their first practical exercise. Sunday the 17th dawned bright, developing into a glorious early autumn day. Boelcke took off in the bright sunlight, leading his pupils and headed them towards the lines.

He spotted two formations of aircraft, fourteen machines in all. They were in fact eight B.E.2cs of No. 12 Squadron R.F.C., on a bombing mission with an escort of six F.E.2bs of No. 11 Squadron R.F.C. The B.E.2cs were each loaded with one 112 lb. bomb and four 20 lb. bombs, destined for Marcoing railway station, well behind the German lines. Boelcke did not lead directly into the attack, for the enemy machines were on their outward journey and time was on his side. He put his first rule into effect—try to secure advantage before attacking. Climbing, he gave his formation the advantage of height, enabling them to close in swiftly by diving when the moment for attack came. Then he circled round, placing his group between the sun and the enemy formation, so putting the enemy gunners at the disadvantage of having the full glare of the sun in their eyes as they attempted to sight their guns. Keeping his own men closed up in their station between the enemy and the sun, he followed the British machines. Puffs of smoke rose from Marcoing station and at least one railway wagon was ablaze after the B.E.2cs had dropped their bombs. Inevitably the British airmen, pilots and observers alike, wary as they were, made frequent downward glances to ascertain the damage the bombs had wreaked. It was the moment Boelcke had chosen to attack.

They dived, each with a particular enemy machine in mind. Richthofen chose to attack one of the F.E.2bs, thinking it to be a Vickers fighter, a type which he had been instructed how to tackle. The configuration of a F.E.2b was indeed similar, and considering wartime security measures it is not surprising that enemy aircraft types were

A rare flying shot! Manfred von Richthofen about to land his Albatros D III. It was painted all red and was known by the British as le petit rouge.

often incorrectly identified. He remembered Boelcke's advice not to open fire until the range was close and the enemy machine well in the sights. When within fifty yards he fired at the F.E. from behind, but both the pilot, Second Lieutenant L. B. F. Morris, and the observer, Lieutenant T. Rees, were experienced airmen and they immediately took defensive action. Rees stood up in his cockpit and fired back over the top wing, whilst Morris circled or banked the machine from side to side whenever Richthofen was in the aircraft's 'blind spot', below and behind, where Rees could not fire for fear of shooting the tail of his own machine.

Richthofen broke off the fight, dived into a cloud, but circled round and came back at the F.E. from below and behind. Evidently Rees and Morris did not see him, for their machine kept a steady course. Closing in, he opened fire, spraying the nacelle and engine with bullets. There was no return fire as both occupants had been hit and the engine also had been damaged. He almost rammed the enemy with his Albatros in his eagerness. As he swerved aside, he saw the propeller of the F.E. stop; he watched fascinated as the machine nosed over and went down. Morris, mortally wounded, summoned sufficient strength to control the descent and to bring the machine to a landing close to a German flying field. Richthofen followed the machine down, almost wrecking his machine by a rough landing on a nearby field in his eagerness to view his victim.

He ran to the F.E.2b as others came running up from the airfield. Rees died as he arrived, and Morris, still breathing as he was borne away on a stretcher, was dead on arrival in hospital. Manfred Freiherr von Richthofen had indisputable evidence for his first victory, the bodies of a pilot and an observer, damaged F.E.2b airframe No. 7018 fitted with 120 h.p. Beardmore engine No. 701. He submitted his victory claim No. 1.

There was much rejoicing in the officers' mess of *Jasta 2* that evening. Not only Richthofen but also Boehme and Reimann had each scored. Boelcke, too, had added

Another rare shot—of a rather different kind! Boelcke and von Richthofen talking to Lt. Hœhne seated in the cockpit of a captured D.H.2. This photograph was taken in September 1916.

yet again to his score. His victim, damaged by his guns, crashed and burst into flames when it hit a captive balloon cable in a forced landing. Seven other German aircraft had joined in the fight and altogether six of the F.E.2bs and two of the B.E.2cs had been destroyed. It was no doubt a great boost to morale in the German Air Service. *Jasta 2* in their first operation, in new, untried combat aircraft, had particular reason to be satisfied. Boelcke was delighted with his pupils' performance.

Beer tankards, as presentation pieces, are usual in the military messes of many nations, particularly as mementoes to mess members posted away. Boelcke presented mugs to his officers upon achieving their initial victory and the toast upon such an occasion introduced a mess ceremony that became a tradition. Richthofen, with a hunter's regard for trophies, decided to go one better and present himself with a cup for each successive victory. Accordingly he sent his specification to a Berlin jeweller for a slightly tapering, plain, sterling silver cup, 5 cm. high and 3 cm. in diameter at the mouth, to be inscribed: '1 VICKERS 2 17.9.16.' The '2' implied a two-seat aircraft.

The next day the weather changed and anxious though *Jasta 2* were to repeat their success, they did not get the opportunity. On the 19th, however, the clouds lifted and they were up in time to completely thwart an attempt by No. 11 Squadron F.E.2bs to carry out a reconnaissance of German positions behind Ginchy, where the British 6th Division had recently made some territorial gains. Boelcke shot to pieces in the air one of the escorting Moranes of No. 60 Squadron R.F.C.

Apart from being in command of the *Jasta*, Boelcke remained the teacher. He analysed the results of each fight, pressing home his dicta: Always keep your eye on your opponent and don't let him deceive you by ruses—Try to get behind your opponent to attack—If you are yourself dived upon do not try to evade the onslaught, but turn to meet your opponent. The last rule was wise advice to novices, liable to be out-manœuvred in evasive action by a more experienced pilot. In turning to face the enemy, the meeting would be on more equal terms.

Richthofen's second chance came the following Saturday, when *Jasta 2* engaged the Martinsyde Elephants of No. 27 Squadron R.F.C. Although built as single-seat scouts, the Elephants were unsuited for their intended role, being slow to respond to their controls. They were used as bombers at that time by virtue of their long range. Their defensive armament, consisting of a forward-firing Lewis gun mounted on the centre section of the top wing and a rearward-firing Lewis gun mounted along the fuselage side with no sighting arrangements, was hardly a match for a manœuvrable Albatros, with twin Spandau guns firing forward through the propeller arc. Richthofen, side-slipping into position behind a Martinsyde, had little difficulty in bringing it down. One of his comrades collided with one of the Martinsydes and his machine crashed to earth; the Martinsyde, with a severely damaged wing, nevertheless flew back to its base.

After landing, Richthofen set off in a car to view the wreckage of his victim. From the remains he extracted a piece of fabric, bearing the number G.W.174, which he took to be the number of the aircraft and wrote it as such in his official report. As the number bears no relation to serial numbers allotted to Martinsyde Elephants, it is thought to be the part-number of a component built under sub-contract by the Grahame-White Aviation Company. The piece of fabric was Richthofen's souvenir; for a trophy, the order went again to the Berlin jeweller for a cup similar to the first, with the inscription: '2 MARTINSYDE 1, 23.9.16.'

Richthofen's third victim was his first to fall in flames. He was not a little shaken by this ghastly sight, and in a letter to his mother told how his heart beat more quickly as he witnessed his adversaries, whom he had so recently glimpsed for the first time, plunge down from 12,000 feet enveloped by flames from burning petrol. There was hardly anything recognisable of the F.E.2b or its two occupants, yet afterwards he poked around the wreckage, hopefully searching for a souvenir and eventually departing with a battered number plate.

His nerve remained steady, although he was acutely aware of the dangers he was running; for in one month's fighting five out of the unit's ten aircraft had been lost. Nevertheless he was, if anything, more keen than ever to seek combat. Air fighting gave him the familiar thrill of the hunt, and certainly he had a collector's mania for souvenirs and trophies. He had the will to win, and his method was that of a skilful hunter who studies his quarry. He went to very considerable trouble to collect souvenirs, all of which he packed carefully, and had despatched to his home at Schweidnitz. For guidance and leadership in those days of his early successes, there could be no commander with greater understanding and experience than Oswald Boelcke.

Richthofen was scoring on the average of once a week. His fourth victory was, as he remarked in his report, a new type not previously observed. It was in fact a B.E.12, which fell to him at 9 a.m. on October 7th, after he had fired 400 bullets at it from behind, killing the pilot by a shot through the head. This time the wreckage of the machine was little damaged and he was able to cut away the fabric bearing the airframe serial number—6618—from the fin. This he pinned up on the wall of his hut; the first of a large collection.

An Albatros D III with 160 h.p. Mercedes engine. Aircraft No. D789/17, finished in red, was flown by von Richthofen.

In spite of deteriorating weather during October, his next victory, another B.E.12, came only three days later over the shattered town of Ypres, and yet another B.E.12 fell to him on the 16th of that month.

There was some indignation by Richthofen over his next claim, a B.E.12 that he shot at on October 25th as it was returning over the British lines. It was not accredited to him, as a claim for the same machine was also submitted by a Halberstadt pilot from *Jasta 5*, who had been flying nearby, and who claimed to have brought the machine down by a burst of fire from 1,000 yards range. A ridiculous and childish assertion, as Richthofen himself wrote in protest. There was some delay before this contested

At his home at Schweidnitz there was for many years a 'Richthofen Museum'. Here were displayed trophies collected and sent home by von Richthofen. At the top right is the serial cut from Major Hawker's aircraft.

victory was considered, and by that time Richthofen's seventh and eighth official victories had been substantiated. His contested B.E.12 became therefore claim No. 6A. It remained an unconfirmed claim.

Boelcke's own score still mounted: No. 21 a F.E.2b, No. 22 another F.E.2b, Nos. 23 and 24 Sopwiths and by October 1st he had gained his thirtieth victory. He still remained the teacher, describing all the enemy types with which he came into contact. He brought a F.E.2b down little damaged, for instruction and demonstration as he put it. He was by no means a consoling commander; he demanded much and received his due. He was strict, but always human. The evidence of Richthofen's memoirs, Boehme's letters and Udet's book is that all who came into contact with him, officer or soldier, believed him their friend. Helmuth von Zastrow, his administrative officer, wrote: 'Never is a man by his friends or a commander by his men so liked as Boelcke.' Nowhere could such words be found of Richthofen, when he had his own command.

When Richthofen had made his sixth claim by October 17th, Boelcke shot down his thirty-fifth. His fortieth and final was won on October 25th when a B.E. went down burning south-west of Serre. Boelcke became more earnest every day and was strained with overwork. He was ordered on leave, but refused to go. The weather was more than bad. October 28th dawned rainy and cloudy and proved a grey day, yet he made four flights before noon and one later at 4.45 p.m., when a call came from the infantry for assistance. *Jasta 2* took off and a fight developed with British single-seaters. It happened that Boelcke and Boehme were chasing the same enemy aircraft, when another British machine, harried by Richthofen, crossed their line of flight. Both were forced to bank, and during this quick movement their aircraft touched; Boehme's undercarriage rent Boelcke's upper wing on the port side. His aircraft plunged down. So died Germany's first great fighter pilot.

At the funeral in the Cathedral of Cambrai, Manfred Freiherr von Richthofen carried Boelcke's orders in front of the chest with Boelcke's remains. Among the many flowers and tributes were two laurel wreaths, one dropped from the Royal Flying Corps, and one brought by four captured British officers under Captain Wilson, R.F.C., from the prisoner-of-war camp in Osnabrück. Boelcke was honoured by friend and foe alike.

CHAPTER TEN

Versus a V.C.

Introduced about mid-1916 the Fokker D III was Anthony Fokker's first really successful biplane, and although few were produced it was used by Boelcke. Later a D IV was produced, essentially a D III, but with a more powerful engine (160 h.p. Mercedes).

The thunderclap of the fateful October 28th, 1916, died away, but the war continued relentlessly, leaving little time for mourning. Leutnant Stephan Kirmaier took over command of *Jagdstaffel Nr. 2*, and the fact that in the following month, November, *Jasta 2* could under his leadership claim twenty-five victories, was evidence that he was a worthy successor to Boelcke. Then Kirmaier too, fell, losing his life in a combat before that month was out. He was followed by Hauptmann Walz, who led until June 9th, 1917. During that time the young guard of pilots grew up. Names such as Bernert, von Tutschek, Voss and von Richthofen were on the first rung of the ladder of fame. Fittingly, their unit was, by Imperial Decree, renamed *Jagdstaffel Boelcke*.

Saddened as Richthofen was by the loss of his respected leader, he was as eager as ever to fly. November came in wet, giving little opportunity; but bright intervals on the 3rd, the day of Boelcke's funeral, gave him the chance of a patrol before leaving for the ceremony. Flying with two of his comrades, a lone F.E.2b was observed at the relatively low altitude of 5,500 feet. They dived on the unfortunate machine and after a brief exchange of fire it plummeted down. The aircraft fell near to the lines and the wreckage came under heavy artillery fire, denying Richthofen the chance of collecting souvenirs. At least he could reward himself with a trophy and another order was written to the Berlin jeweller.

Trophies and souvenirs, avidly collected as they were, took second place to decorations. It was much in his mind that both Boelcke and Immelmann had received the *Ordre Pour le Mérite* after achieving eight victories and he now had seven. The *Pour le Mérite* was perhaps the most coveted of German decorations, being the highest award for an individual act of gallantry. As such, it was comparable to the British Victoria Cross and the American Congressional Medal of Honor. To win the *Pour le Mérite* was undoubtedly Richthofen's highest ambition. However, in strict confidence, the German General Staff were reconsidering the 'yard-stick' of eight victories in view of increasing air activity. The offensive spirit that the Royal Flying Corps had maintained during the great Somme battle had been achieved only at great cost in men and material. No less than 190 of the 782 aircraft that they had written off during the period July 1st to November 17th fell into German-held territory and were, in the main, shared amongst the victory scores of German pilots. There were thus too many potential candidates under the existing criterion if the award was to retain its value. It was, therefore, decided to double the qualifying figure of eight.

One of the early successful German aircraft of the 1914-1918 War, the Albatros D II—here shown with a 160 h.p. Mercedes engine—was much used by Jagdstaffeln including Jasta 11.

The B.E.2c was the backbone of Corps Squadrons of the R.F.C. in the early war years. Persistent as their pilots were, in their duties of reconnaissance and registering for gun batteries, over the German side of the lines, they often became easy prey for German fighters. In defence, the observer (gunner), located in the front cockpit, had a restricted field of fire.

In these respects the award differed in comparison with Allied decorations. There was no rigidity with such an award as the Victoria Cross. Britain's top-scoring ace, Major E. Mannock, who achieved seventy-three victories, did not live to receive the Victoria Cross, which was posthumously awarded to him after the war.

Richthofen knew nothing of this. Hopefully he set out on November 9th for an encounter that would lead to his eighth victory. By a remarkably strange coincidence, he did receive a decoration as a direct result of that flight— but not the *Pour le Mérite*. On this occasion he was flying with a particular friend, the boyish, eighteen-year old Leutnant Hans Imelmann (not to be confused with Max Immelmann), who had five victories to his credit. A friendly rivalry existed between them to increase their own scores. Together they scoured the skies. Soon they spotted a large formation, B.E.2cs with three other formations of protecting fighters flying above them, in the manner of Richthofen's first encounter. The B.E.2cs, loaded with bombs, held a steady course with 'an impudent assurance', as Richthofen put it. At first it appeared as if the bombers were making for the airfield at Lagnicourt, but they altered course some two miles short, dropping their bombs around a sugar factory at Vraucourt that was used as an ammunition dump.

Shortly after the British machines had crossed the lines they had been harried by German aircraft. Over Vraucourt village the attacks intensified and altogether some thirty German aircraft were involved. It developed into the largest air battle ever fought up to that time. Two of the escorting D.H.2s of No. 29 Squadron R.F.C. were engaged by persistent adversaries, who fought them down to a low altitude, before giving them the *coup de grâce*. The F.E.2bs of the experienced but long-suffering No. 11 Squadron R.F.C. held their own very well and resolutely fought their way back. Only one of their machines was lost. Manfully controlled by a wounded pilot carrying a dead observer, that F.E. gradually lost height. It cleared the German front line by only a few feet and actually crashed in 'No Man's Land'. The pilot escaped into the British side.

Richthofen and Imelmann made for the bombers, the slow B.E.2cs, flying in two formations of six aircraft, consisting of a flight each, drawn from Nos. 12 and 13 Squadrons R.F.C. B.E.2c No. 2502 of No. 12 Squadron, lagging behind the rest of the flight with engine trouble, carried no observer to protect its tail. Whilst the pilot tried to bring his movable Lewis gun to bear on to a German machine on his left, Imelmann opened up at almost point-blank range from behind. As the startled pilot banked steeply away, Imelmann raked the fuselage side with fire. The B.E., with some of its control wires shot away, turned over; the Lewis gun dropped from its mount, falling to earth. From 6,000 feet the B.E. spun down, straightening out at only 800 feet. Still close on its tail, Imelmann gave it another burst of fire, to persuade the defenceless pilot to land. This he did, overshooting the village green hurriedly selected. Coming down by a road, his machine ran into a heap of picks and shovels of a German working party. The troops were even more startled when the British pilot, realising the hopelessness of his position, made the best of a bad situation by poking his head out of the cockpit and saying: '*Guten Morgen!*'

Another of No. 12 Squadron's B.E.2cs, No. 2506, was Richthofen's victim. It was a strange coincidence that this machine, constructed at the same time as No. 2502 by Wolseley Motors Ltd. at Birmingham, should fall at the same time and place. Richthofen as usual attacked from the rear, aiming at the occupants. Kill the man with the gun became a stratagem of his. He imagined an observer slumped in his cockpit, riddled with bullets. The pilot banked from side to side and each time the fuselage was raked by his pursuer's guns. He nosed the machine down, hurriedly selecting the largest field to land. His escape from the resulting crash landing, uninjured, was all the more remarkable since his bomb-toggle controls had been shot away and the aircraft still carried a 112 lb. bomb!

Both B.E.s had crashed not far from Lagnicourt. After landing, Richthofen and Imelmann set off together in a car to collect the usual souvenirs. Richthofen's victim proved to be inaccessible by road. As it was a mild day, he threw his cap into the car and unbuttoning his tunic, strolled across the fields to view the remains. Dragging his boots through the thick mud he found it warm going and he removed his tunic and loosened his collar. Muddy and

A pleasing photograph of von Richthofen, in which he is shown wearing his highest decoration the Pour le Mérite, *a Maltese Cross in blue enamel edged with gold.*

dishevelled, he was rather concerned to observe a group of immaculately dressed staff officers inspecting the wreckage. With a soldierly instinct he buttoned his collar, but before he could make himself presentable as an officer he was recognised as an aviator and engaged in conversation about the fight. Disconcerted at the realisation that one of the officers, youthful though he was in appearance, wore the dress of a general, he was nevertheless greatly interested in hearing an account of the fight as witnessed from the ground. He left with a piece of fabric cut from the B.E.2c's fin bearing its number. Not until that evening, when he was called to the telephone, to receive the news that he had been awarded the Saxe-Coburg-Gotha Medal for Bravery, did he realise that the youthful general had been His Royal Highness the Grand Duke of Saxe-Coburg-Gotha. It had been the general's impression that the B.E.2cs had his headquarters as their target and that Richthofen, in shooting one down, had performed a direct service to his august self.

It was eleven days before Richthofen scored again, but as if to make up for his usual once-a-week victory he downed two enemy aircraft in that one day, November 20th. An F.E. and a B.E. His first came at 9.40 a.m. during a routine flight with four other members of the *Jasta*, when they attacked an F.E.2b above the low clouds. The F.E. dived, they followed it down. As it descended below

D.H.2 single-seater fighters on Beauval aerodrome, Fourth Army Aircraft Park, 1916.

the cloud base, Richthofen metaphorically fastened on to its tail and dispatched it with 300 rounds from his Spandau guns. During the late afternoon he destroyed one of the few B.E.12s still employed on operations. Some confusion has existed over these two scores since his B.E.12 was credited first and became his ninth official victory, whereas chronologically it was his tenth.

A double event called for a celebration and something special in the way of a memento. At first he thought of ordering a double-size cup for a double success, but upon reflection he decided that a cup of double size should signify every tenth victim. Such was his confidence in the future. With some satisfaction he learnt that he was cited for the *Hohenzollernschen Haus Orden mit Schwerten* (Order of the House of Hohenzollern with Swords), but he still coveted the *Pour le Mérite*.

So far, Richthofen had held the advantage over his opponents by his careful tactics and by virtue of his Albatros D II's superior speed and manœuvrability over the aircraft of his adversaries. By attacking two-seaters from behind and slightly below, Richthofen gave the enemy gunners little opportunity to return fire effectively. The gunners had, in fact, been the target for his opening shots of the 300 or so rounds it was taking to effect each victory. Thus far, his successes over single-seater scouts had been confined to B.E.12s and a Martinsyde Elephant, both unsuited for a fighting role. His real test as an air fighter came three days after his double victory.

'Knights of the Air' is rather a hackneyed phrase beloved by writers of air-fighting fiction. It is not, however, altogether inappropriate to the duel that was fought on November 23rd, 1916, over the shattered battlefield grimly known as the 'blood-bath of the Somme'. One of the duellists was a German of noble birth, shortly to receive his Fatherland's highest award for gallantry; the other contestant was an Englishman, who already wore the purple ribbon of the highest reward for bravery that his Motherland could bestow—the Victoria Cross.

Major Lanoe G. Hawker, V.C., D.S.O., late of the Corps of Royal Engineers, was not only a man of outstanding gallantry but also a man of no mean technical ability. Several mechanical aids to aerial gunnery had been introduced at his instigation, including the ring gun-sight.

34

Fur-lined thigh boots, a later general issue to British flying personnel, were first made to a specification submitted by Hawker. As a pilot he had great skill and ever greater daring. His V.C. was awarded for routing three enemy aircraft in one engagement and the D.S.O. for bombing the Zeppelin sheds at Gontrode. When the first British squadron to be completely equipped with fighter aircraft, No. 24, was formed, no better choice for a commanding officer could have been made than Major Hawker.

The D.H.2s of No. 24 Squadron R.F.C. were not strangers to the *Jagdstaffel Boelcke*. It was in attacking a machine of 'C' Flight of that squadron that Boelcke had become involved in his fatal collision. On this occasion it was four machines from 'A' Flight, led by Captain J. O. Andrews, with the commanding officer, Major Hawker, flying as an ordinary member of the patrol. Andrews, upon sighting five Albatros biplanes shortly after crossing the lines, immediately led his formation in pursuit.

The Germans were quite willing to fight, but as they were at a slightly lower altitude they turned away to secure advantages, not only in height but to lure the British machines farther over the German side of the lines. During this time, one of the D.H.2s developed engine trouble and the pilot had to turn back. Hardly had he dropped from the formation when another D.H.2, No. 5925, one of the oldest D.H.2s in service, had similar trouble and dropped back. The squadron was experiencing an unfortunate spate of engine trouble at that time, two of their finest pilots having been lost when cylinders blew out and severed the tail booms of their aircraft.

Hawker and Andrews flew steadily on. They each singled out an Albatros, Hawker making for Richthofen's machine. As Andrews took up position behind his intended victim, he was himself 'jumped' from behind and a stream of bullets hit his engine, causing it to misfire and lose revolutions. He then wisely dropped from the fight, and zigzagging to spoil the aim of any follower, made for the lines, landing safely at Gillemont. Hawker was on his own.

Not for the first time did Hawker find himself outnumbered, but for some reason there was apparently no interference in the ensuing duel. It is not impossible that the other Germans deliberately refrained from joining in, as a man-to-man duel was at times respected, although not nearly so often as air fiction would suggest. Richthofen's companions may well have lost sight of the two contestants, or they may have been chasing Andrews. There is, too, the possibility that uppermost in their minds was the danger of collision by intervention, as evinced by Boelcke's accident. Perhaps even more to the point, Richthofen would not have wished for assistance; his victory score was the chief consideration. That his comrades well knew.

Richthofen, awakening to the fact that Hawker was on his tail, banked away as Hawker gave his first burst of fire from his Lewis gun. Banking round sharply, he tried to turn fully on to Hawker's tail. They both circled round and round, each trying to get the other in their line of fire. After circling several times to the right, without apparent advantage to either, one of them broke away. The other swiftly followed and they commenced their circling again, this time to the left. Richthofen found that the D.H.2 made a trimmer turn than his Albatros, but his machine had the

Major Lanoe G. Hawker, V.C., D.S.O., who was von Richthofen's eleventh victim, had himself scored nine victories before being killed on November 23rd, 1916.

advantage of speed and rate of climb. Still turning they lost height from some 8,000 feet down to 3,000 feet.

So tight was their circling that they were separated by only some 250 yards in diameter. Banked steeply as they were, they could see into each other's cockpit. Once Hawker actually waved. Richthofen knew he was up against no novice; he knew, too, that soon the British pilot must break off the fight to return to the British side of the lines before his fuel was exhausted. It may well have been part of Richthofen's tactics to force the fight down, so denying Hawker the advantage of height on his return journey against the prevailing west wind. Richthofen knew that when the moment to break came he would have an opportunity. Time was on his side.

Hawker knew only too well his fuel limits. Suddenly he broke off and went into a series of loops. At this juncture Richthofen was out-manœuvred and he was disconcerted by several bursts of fire that came uncomfortably close. Hawker was getting in bursts of fire during the brief moments that Richthofen's machine came into his sights. During such aerobatics, however, careful aiming was not possible; for which very reason Richthofen never adopted, but scorned, such tactics. The analogy, to his mind, was that of the skilled marksman against a trick shot.

Then Hawker broke off completely in an attempt to regain his own lines. Zigzagging to avoid his adversary's fire, he dived still lower to gain speed. Richthofen followed closely, firing as opportunities were presented. He was an experienced pursuer, to which ten victories made in this manner bore testimony. Hawker, straightening out at only 100 feet above the ground, and still zigzagging, neared the lines. Richthofen's guns then jammed and it seemed his foe would escape. They were cleared, and one of the bullets from his next burst struck Hawker in the head. He fell dead, only a short distance from the British lines.

Richthofen had expended some 900 rounds of ammunition during the fight. As a trophy, he managed to have Hawker's Lewis gun extricated from the wreckage. For many years after his death it hung over the door of his bedroom at Schweidnitz.

CHAPTER ELEVEN

Squadron Commander

Leutnant Kurt Wolff, a leading member of Jasta 11, achieved the not inconsiderable score of 33 victories. In the background are two serial numbers cut from two of his victims' aircraft, a Bristol F.2A and F.E.2B No. 7691.

Richthofen's opportunities to score were limited largely by the late autumn weather restricting flying. As a matter of routine, a pilot was not usually detailed for more than one patrol a day. Such detailed flights were to a schedule prepared by *KoFl* of the army concerned, to cover the army front by at least one patrol during daylight hours, weather permitting. *Jadgstaffeln* were each expected to operate for three consecutive hours. To effect this, they were usually divided into two flights known as *Ketten*. Depending upon the serviceability of aircraft, the strength of each flight on patrol would vary from three to six aircraft.

The first flight would take off at the start of the three-hour spell appointed by *KoFl*. If the front was quiet they would return after ninety minutes and the second flight would then take off straight away. If the front was active, the first flight would remain on patrol until their fuel situation made it prudent to return. In that case, the second flight had standing orders to take off after 100 minutes of the duty period had elapsed.

All pilots had to stand by during their unit's duty period to act as reliefs or reinforcements as required. After it was over they stood down. The period could be any consecutive three hours during daylight. Outside that time, pilots were free to leave the airfield, but they were expected to fit in various supervisory duties in connection with the operation of their unit. They were encouraged to make additional flights, and with morale high in early 1917 little encouragement was needed. Many pilots, like Richthofen, sought the opportunity of increasing their scores. However, such additional flights had to constitute an organised *Kette*. Lone operational flights were not usually permitted, two aircraft being considered the minimum tactical unit for pitting against the enemy. Richthofen's ability had not passed unnoticed by his new commander, and in consequence he was frequently detailed to lead routine flights and often nominated leader for the volunteer flights that he instigated.

The leader, as well as flying in front, usually flew slightly below the others, in order that his followers could observe his hand signals. It was the leader's responsibility to decide whether or not to attack, and the methods to be employed. Once he had led into the attack, the formation usually broke up and little further tactical control could be achieved. The followers, usually flying in echelon or 'V' formation, had to follow their leader's tail as well as keeping an eye on their own.

That December the German Air Service adopted a new policy. Hitherto fighter patrols had been in areas *behind* the German lines. This was changed to *along* the German lines. Thus the German soldier, inclined to malign his Air Service in its apparent absence, could see the Iron Cross in the air. The weather, however, did not provide the best setting for these new tactics. Nevertheless Richthofen was able to delight his field-grey audience and dismay his khaki onlookers on December 11th, when D.H.2 No. 5986 fell to his guns, making his twelfth victory.

Nine days later, heading a flight of five Albatros biplanes, he led them into the attack on a formation of six D.H.2s from No. 29 Squadron R.F.C., winning a resounding victory. Only one escaped unscathed! Four were damaged and withdrew, one of them crashing into the trenches. The other, attacked by Richthofen himself, fell with a dead pilot on to the German side of the lines. Meticulous in their examination of enemy aircraft, the German authorities reported the wreckage as that of machine No. 7927 with Gnome motor No. 30413.

Leutnant Karl Emil Schaefer, another prominent member of Jasta 11; was, like his leader a 'hunter', and was regarded by him as his best pupil. Born December 17th, 1891, he was killed in combat on June 5th, 1917, shortly after taking over command of Jasta 28.

36

That same day, December 20th, 1916, he again scored, defeating a F.E.2b. Several of his flight went for this unfortunate machine, No. A5446, each expending several hundred rounds of ammunition. Convinced that it was his shots that had taken effect, Richthofen in his combat report made it clear that he was foremost of the attackers. The victory was accredited to him as his fourteenth.

Richthofen's self-esteem began to show in another way. He wished his machine to be known, and no doubt feared, by his enemies. In choosing a marking scheme, he decided upon scarlet red, seemingly the most conspicuous of colours, although in actual fact orange can be proved the most conspicuous. Only in such a unit as *Jasta Boelcke* could such a departure from convention have been tolerated at that time, particularly as special dyed and printed fabrics were coming into use for camouflage purposes. Certainly some fighter aircraft were then displaying emblems, but Richthofen's Albatros is the first known instance of an overall colour scheme.

Christmas came, celebrated with festivities that mocked the true spirit of Yuletide. The mess hut was decorated with sprigs of evergreen and even a Christmas tree was procured and erected, contrasting with the grim but colourful decorations—red, white and blue roundels torn from the fabric of fallen enemy aircraft, hung on the walls as trophies.

For Richthofen it was a partial family reunion. His father, recalled to the colours, was then military town-mayor of a small town in North-West France, not far from Lille, which was then the largest French town under German occupation. Together with Lothar, his younger brother, now also a Leutnant in the Air Service, they spent Christmas Day at Lagnicourt. Proudly Manfred showed his

Another prominent member of Jasta 11 was Leutnant Karl Allmenröder, who scored a total of 30 victories. His brother, Wilhelm, who was severely wounded, also served in Jasta 11 during April and May of 1917.

father and brother over the airfield, introduced them to his comrades and demonstrated his Albatros D II, No. 491/16. With it, two days later, he shot down another F.E.2b, for his fifteenth victory.

The Albatros D II and D III biplanes were undoubtedly superior to the contemporary British D.H.2s, of which there were 222 on Royal Flying Corps strength in late 1916. A new British fighter, however, was being introduced. the Sopwith single-seat scout, later colloquially known as the Sopwith Pup.

Richthofen had his first encounter with the famous line of Sopwith fighting aircraft on the fourth day of the New Year, 1917. Unknown to him at the time, it was also his first combat in the air with the Royal Navy. The Senior Service of the British Armed Forces had come silently on to the Western Front scene to assist the Royal Flying Corps units, severely strained by the Somme battle losses. By detaching aircraft from Royal Naval Air Service units at Dunkirk, No. 8 (Naval) Squadron, R.N.A.S., was formed with six each, Nieuport Scouts, Sopwith 1½ Strutters and Sopwith Pups. Based on Vert Galand, the new unit had commenced operations on November 3rd, 1916. So successful were the Pups that the unit's Nieuports and 1½ Strutters were withdrawn and replaced by Pups by the end of the year. During that brief period the Pups had accounted for twenty German aircraft.

Flight Lieutenant A. S. Todd of this new naval squadron, flying a Pup on a lone patrol during January 4th, sighted and boldly attacked three Albatros biplanes. Richthofen, one of the three, watched fascinated when he saw the Pup making for one of his comrades, who took quick evasive action as the British machine manœuvred for position. He judged the enemy machine to have a performance superior to the Albatros and he duly noted this in his combat report, adding: 'Only because we were three against one were we able to detect the enemy's weak points.' It is not at all clear what Richthofen meant by 'weak points', as he did not enlarge upon them. The characteristics of the Pup were its ability to hold its height in combat and its faultless manœuvrability. As McCudden, the famous

Probably the most 'off-the-record' photograph of von Richthofen; this one shows that, for all his grim determination, he had a pleasant smile! He could too, dress informally and he was by no means the 'immaculately dressed Prussian Officer' that some writers have implied.

Displaying his Pour le Mérite *even in flying kit, von Richthofen is here seen talking to Hauptmann Carganico.*

British ace, bluntly put it: 'The Pup would turn twice to an Albatros's once.' There were seemingly no weak points, judged by early 1917 standards. Richthofen, it would appear, was able to shoot this Pup down, not because he found any weaknesses, but because the pilot was preoccupied with two other opponents. Eventually, and almost inevitably, in such a case of three against one in a prolonged engagement, Richthofen got into position behind the Pup and shot it down. From the wreckage he salvaged its number, N5193, marked on the fabric in a white rectangle, bearing beneath it the stencilled words, no longer significant, 'LIFT HERE'. To go with it he ordered cup No. 16.

Now surely the *Ordre pour le Mérite* would be his reward, he thought. Strangely, although the victory scores of German aces were published as at the end of 1916,† the pilots of *Jagdstaffel Boelcke* had been omitted. Kirmaier and Boehme both qualified for insertion, and certainly not least, von Richthofen with the sizeable score of sixteen.

At the same time the reported French scores were given, crediting Guynemer, at the top, with twenty-one victories and Nungesser as running him close with twenty. British scores were not mentioned. The British authorities, being very reticent about such matters, had not issued any statements apart from the occasional citation for awards.

It was cold comfort for Richthofen at that time, when such a high decoration was in the offing, to receive orders to take up command of his own *Jasta*. There was, too, the sorrow at parting from his comrades and having to take up new quarters. For a few days he was rather morose; then came the announcement—on January 16th he was awarded the coveted *Ordre Pour le Mérite*. Manfred Freiherr von Richthofen was headline news. Congratulations poured in from all over Germany. He was a hero; military prowess had always commanded great respect in Germany and it was no exaggeration to say that holders of the *Pour le Mérite* were considered among the most illustrious in the Fatherland.

With a lighter heart he went to Douai to take over his new command, *Jagdstaffel Nr. 11*. He was not at all impressed by what he found. Although the *Jasta* had been in existence several months, so far not a single victory had been scored. Yet the officers looked quite promising and most of them had an impeccable record. They were Leutnants Allmenröder, Bockelmann, Esser, Hinch, Hintmann, Matthof, Mohnicke, W. Plüschow, Scheffer, Wolff and Krefft as technical officer, there were also two N.C.O. pilots, Vizefeldwebel Festner and Sergeant Howe. Richthofen was the inspiration the unit needed. Three officers in particular were to win fame under his leadership: Allmenröder, Wolff and a welcome addition—a Leutnant Schaefer.

Karl Allmenröder, Karlchen (Little Charles) to his intimate friends and comrades of *Jasta 11*, was born on

† The list was as follows:

Hauptmann Boelcke	40*	Leutnant Parschau	8*
Leutnant Wintgens	20*	Oberleutnant Schilling	6
Oberleutnant Immelmann	18*	Oberleutnant Walz	6
Leutnant Frankl	16	Leutnant Baldamus	5
Leutnant Höhndorf	15	Leutnant Fahlbusch	5*
Oberleutnant Berr	10	Leutnant Rosencrantz	5*
Hauptmann Buddecke	10	Leutnant Boenisch	4
Leutnant von Mulzer	10*	Oberleutnant Gerlich	4
Leutnant Dossenbach	9	Leutnant Haber	4
Leutnant Leffers	9	Marineflugmeister Meyer	4
Oberleutnant von Althaus	8	Offizierstellvertr. Müller	4
Oberleutnant Berthold	8	Vizefeldwebel Pfeiffer	4

* Died for the Fatherland.

Publicity accorded to Vickers 'Gunbus' type of aircraft, such as the Vickers F.B.9 illustrated, gave German airmen the erroneous impression that the pusher-type F.E.2bs they were encountering, were Vickers aircraft. Even D.H.2s were described as single-seat Vickers aircraft by Richthofen and others!

May 3rd, 1896, at Wald, near Solingen in the Rhineland. His father was a pastor, but Karl, wishing to enter the medical profession, commenced studies at Marburg. At the outbreak of war he entered a field artillery regiment (No. 62) at Oldenburg. By 1915 he was a Leutnant with his unit, fighting under von Mackensen in Poland. Together with his elder brother, Willy, he had nursed a desire to fly, and both of them managed to train together at the Halberstadt School and to get posted together to *Fl. Abt. Nr. 227*. There the exploits of Boelcke so inspired the younger Allmenröder, when on routine artillery spotting work, that he applied for, and received, a transfer to a fighter unit, reaching *Jasta 11* in November 1916. Richthofen, arriving to command in January 1917, provided him with the inspiration that had been lacking since Boelcke's death.

The thin, bashful and gentle-natured Kurt Wolff was born at Griefswald, in Pommern, on February 6th, 1895. Orphaned at an early age, he was brought up by relatives in Memel, where he was also schooled. Passing his examinations successfully he was accepted as an officer-trainee in *Eisenbahn Regiment Nr. 4* (a railway regiment) at Schöneberg. With that unit he went to war, receiving his appointment as a Leutnant on April 17th, 1915.

Having been successful in transferring to the Air Service in July 1916, he was less successful on his maiden flight. His L.V.G. B II crashed, killing the instructor and dislocating Wolff's shoulder. Like Richthofen, he received his training at Döberitz. One of his proudest moments was taking over an Albatros D II with *Jasta 11*.

Joining shortly after the new commander took over, Karl Emil Schaefer, a Leutnant, was probably Richthofen's best pupil. He too had a hunter's instinct. In fact he had been literally a hunter of men on the ground before he hunted in the air. Straight from high school he had joined *Jäger Bataillon Nr. 10* at Goslar. The term *Jäger* originally meant hunter, and the term was not inappropriate to the *Jäger* battalions of the Prussian Army, which were basically sniper units. Astrologers would say he was eminently suited for this role, having been born, in 1891, on December 17th—a child of Sagittarius, the archer.

After a period of military service he went to France and Britain to study their languages, returning to Germany only three days before the declaration of war. He was called up immediately, joining a reserve *Jäger* battalion at Bückeburg. Then, moving through Belgium into France, he served in the opening engagements of the war. On night patrols, when the front was still nebulous, his knowledge of English and French proved a great asset. By the second month of the war he had received the Iron Cross (Second Class) and promotion to Vizefeldwebel. During the assault on Maubeuge he took 2,800 prisoners with the eighty men under his charge.

von Richthofen rarely smoked, but here he is seen doing so—whilst in conversation with (left) Schaefer, and (right) Wolff.

Early in the war Schaefer was seriously wounded in the upper part of the thigh. When after six months he left hospital, one leg was shorter than the other. Overcoming that difficulty he returned to his unit, becoming a Leutnant in May 1915. His desire to fly came after a further year at the front, spent in a fairly quiet sector opposite the French. After training, he went to the Russian front, flying C-type aircraft, and he transferred to *Jasta 11* on the Western Front in February 1917. Richthofen, reading that magnificent record, knew that he had a good man in Schaefer.

Richthofen knew he had the right material; his job was to mould it. Benefiting from his own instruction under Boelcke, his object was to place his men so that they had a

The Sopwith 'Pup', was regarded generally as the most delightful of the British fighter aircraft to fly in the 1914-18 War. Fully aerobatic, the 'Pup' could hold its own with contemporary aircraft, yet served equally well as a trainer—and indeed in the R.N.A.S. as well as in the R.F.C.

An official photograph of Manfred Freiherr von Richthofen of which, in postcard size, many thousands were sold throughout Germany. Undoubtedly, he was the most famous of the select Pour le Mérite *holders.*

chance to show their mettle. On January 23rd, the very first time he took the air with his new unit, leading seven Albatros biplanes, he was enabled to give a practical demonstration of what he required from them.

Above the trenches near Lens was a flight of single-seat pusher F.E.8s of No. 40 Squadron R.F.C. Richthofen led into the attack. Singling out an enemy machine, he discharged 150 rounds into it from behind at only fifty yards range. The plane went down burning. The pilot falling out of his cockpit, or deliberately choosing to die of concussion rather than by burning, parting from the machine at 1,000 feet. After it hit the ground a heavy pall of smoke rose from the wreckage. As they flew back, frequent flickering bursts of flame could be seen marking the spot of *Jasta 11*'s first victory and Richthofen's seventeenth.

The following day, flying one of the new Albatros D IIIs, Richthofen set off at noon on an offensive patrol with the most junior member of his unit, a N.C.O. pilot. A formation of F.E.2bs was sighted and normally they would have been considered too risky a proposition to tackle with but two aircraft. They stalked the formation, hopefully waiting for stragglers. Then Richthofen saw a chance; the leading machine had got well in advance of the rest of the formation, beyond the protective fire of their guns. Richthofen immediately led his N.C.O. pilot into the attack.

Taken unawares by a blind-spot approach, Captain O. Greig, piloting the leading F.E.2b No. 6937, banked immediately he heard the rattle of Richthofen's guns. He was too late, for a few of the ·311 bullets tore through his legs below the knees. His back, fortunately, was protected by the metallic mass of the Beardmore engine, No. 748, which was damaged and slowly spluttered to a stop. The observer, Lieutenant J. E. MacLenan, jumped up in his cockpit to return the fire, whilst Greig gallantly kept at the controls and manœuvred the machine to MacLenan's advantage. Richthofen dived away as MacLenan fired, then circled round to attack again from the blind spot. Although the F.E.2b, having lost its engine power, was slowly gliding down, Greig nevertheless managed to keep manœuvring the machine into a good firing position for his observer. One of the other F.E. observers, Second Lieutenant A. C. Severs, managed to get in a burst of fire at Richthofen's aircraft, but without immediate results, although, as subsequent events showed, his claim that the enemy machine was forced down was not without foundation.

Richthofen was concerned lest his victim should glide over to his side of the lines, only a mile or two distant. He kept circling round, gaining height; then diving for speed he would swoop down and rise up behind and below the F.E.2b, breaking away again as MacLenan was enabled to bring his guns to bear by Greig's skilful handling. Down to 1,000 feet and Richthofen made a final effort. But this time his wing cracked as he came out of his dive. Immediately reacting, he throttled down to reduce strain and gently took his machine down for an emergency landing. Under the circumstances, he was extremely lucky that the wing did not break.

His victim, having failed to make the lines, glided into a landing a few hundred yards from Richthofen's force-landed Albatros. MacLenan, determined to do his duty to the last, lifted his wounded pilot from the cockpit and dragged him some yards away. Then, striking a match, he threw it on to the petrol seeping from the fuel tank. As he turned away there was an explosion, and with satisfaction he saw the machine was well alight. He then tended to Greig as he awaited the arrival of German troops to accept his surrender.

The fight went on above. The F.E.2bs withdrew to the British side of the lines, reformed and set out again over the German side, where further fighting ensued. They returned with eighteen photographic plates successfully exposed—the object of their mission.

Wishing to have a word with his victims, Richthofen was intrigued to hear from MacLenan that his red Albatros was not unknown, having been noticed several times previously and was referred to as *le petit rouge* by his enemies. On the other hand, he was dismayed at the manner in which he was compelled to withdraw from the fight. Reports have been made that a burst from Mac-Lenan's gun shattered the wing of the Albatros D III, but that is pure conjecture; the words of his combat report stated that his wing had cracked. Richthofen undoubtedly would consider bullets the lesser of the two evils. The true cause almost certainly was a structural failure. That same day two members of the *Jasta Boelcke* lost their lives through a similar failing. One of them had been a friend of Richthofen's, the young Imelmann.

Having supreme confidence in his own prowess, Richthofen was slightly unnerved to realise that his downfall might result from the limitations of a designer, not through any fault of his own. For a time his faith in Albatros products was shaken and he decided upon a change of mount. There was not much choice. The only alternative equal to contemporary Allied fighters was the Halberstadt D II. Richthofen was not unfamiliar with that type, having flown one when with Boelcke's *Jasta 2*. It was, in fact, Boelcke who had chosen the Albatros D I to replace the Halberstadt D II. Nevertheless, Richthofen, for a time, went hunting in a Halberstadt.

Bloody April

CHAPTER TWELVE

Manfred Freiherr von Richthofen with Air Service personnel—a photograph taken at the 'Kaiser Truppenschau' (Kaiser's Inspection of Troops) at Courtrai. On the front rank, left to right, are three holders of the Pour le Mérite; *Paul von Pechmann, Eduard Dostler and Rudolf Berthold.*

The winter weather of February restricted flying and reduced the tempo of Richthofen's scoring; but in spite of an inclement March the tempo again rose, until April brought him the fastest scoring of his career. To his opponents of the Royal Flying Corps, that bitter period was later remembered and referred to as the 'Bloody April' of 1917.

Having changed, temporarily, his usual Albatros for a Halberstadt, Richthofen achieved his nineteenth victory on the first day of February 1917. Flying with Allmenröder at 5,000 feet, he had spotted a lone B.E.2e, apparently engaged upon artillery spotting work. So intent were its occupants upon their duty that Richthofen approached unobserved to within fifty yards before opening fire. The B.E. went down, out of control in a right-hand flat spin, crashing into the barbed wire of the German front-line trenches.

A fortnight elapsed before his next victory, for the winter weather was not conducive to additional patrols and little opposition was encountered on detailed flights. Nevertheless, for the commander of *Jasta 11*, it was a busy time with administrative arrangements. A new system for bringing *Jagdstaffeln* into action was, at that time, mooted. Production of aircraft, particularly their engines, lagged behind the military requirements at the front. To make the most effective use of their limited resources an aircraft warning system was being evolved.

Returning on February 14th from a conference with the *Jasta Boelcke* about the new organisation, Richthofen spotted another lone B.E. This one was at about 6,000 feet over Bois Hugo. Approaching again to within fifty yards of the unsuspecting occupants, he sprayed the fuselage of their machine with his fire until the B.E. went steeply down. The observer was shot dead in the air, and the pilot, with severe head injuries, did not regain consciousness for three days. Although he survived the war, the details of that engagement, which gave Richthofen his twentieth victory, were blotted out for ever from his memory.

That same afternoon, almost over the same spot, he led his *Staffel* into the attack upon five B.E.s. Singling out a particular machine, he disabled the observer with his first 100 rounds. Then, having disposed of the possibility of any effective return fire, he concentrated on bringing it down. Damaged, and emitting smoke, the B.E. lurched into an uncontrolled circling, losing height—but not quickly enough for Richthofen's liking. Anxious, because the 40 m.p.h. wind was in the east and he was already over the British side of the lines, it had to be a quick victory, if indeed it was to be a victory at all. For an acceptable claim, the term 'forced down' did not qualify unless the machine was captured. Since this was over the British side, destruction it had to be. Richthofen fired again and again, until he had the satisfaction of seeing a wing break away and the doomed machine fall burning into the snow, near the British positions at Mazingarbe. It was by then nearly five o'clock, with day rapidly darkening on that wintry evening, and, having parted from his comrades, he lacked witnesses, both in the air and on the ground. Nevertheless, his claim was accepted—his twenty-first.

There was another pause in scoring, but it was soon made up. On March 3rd, flying with Allmenröder, who then had one victory to his credit, B.E.2c No. 4179, downed on February 16th, he shot down yet another B.E.2c. The B.E.s were the backbone equipment of the Royal Flying Corps during the first two years of the war; 'but that they should have remained in service, and indeed in production after that, was something of a national tragedy for the British, measured in the lives of many young men, sacrificed for the sake of standardisation. The B.E.s, hopelessly outclassed, fell easy prey to German fighters'.* The wreckage of the B.E. that Richthofen shot down on March 3rd fell on the British side of the lines. Some days elapsed before the victory was officially confirmed, by which time his twenty-first and twenty-second victories had been won. The B.E., therefore, became his twenty-fourth.

The following morning he had watched his *Staffel* take off without him, but, changing his mind, he ordered his machine out and took off after them. Duty for a *Staffel* commander had conflicting calls, both in the air and on the ground. Apparently in this case it was decided by the task

---
* *Aircraft Camouflage and Markings 1907-1954.*

41

for which he had most zest. Whilst scouting around for his men, he spotted yet again another of the lone, persistent B.E.s engaged on artillery work. This time it was not quite so easy, for his approach was observed and the pilot took evasive action. Turning towards the lines, the pilot alternately banked or dived, in a forlorn hope of escape. Down from 7,500 feet to 3,500 feet, he continued to harass the B.E. until it went into a particularly steep dive, faster than Richthofen could follow, and he lost sight of it. However, a report from an infantry unit at the front gave evidence of an enemy machine crashing and the aircraft was credited as Richthofen's twenty-third. The B.E. actually crashed in no man's land. After nightfall, a British patrol crawled out to find the fate of the occupants—both were dead.

Out of chronological sequence, too, came his twenty-second official victory, actually achieved at 4.20 p.m. that same day. Leading five of his aircraft, he attacked a formation of No. 43 Squadron's Sopwith 1½ Strutters that had arrived on the Western Front only a month before. The inexperience of their crews was doubly evident in that not only was Richthofen upon them before he was detected, but even after firing several bursts the pilot of the machine he was attacking held a steady course. Then, as if suddenly awakening to the fact that evasive action was called for, the machine was banked violently. That sudden turn caused a wing, presumably weakened by Richthofen's fire, to break away. The machine then disintegrated, the wreckage being scattered over a wide area. Only its Lewis guns, Nos. 17500 and 20024, were salvageable.

His next victory, five days later, came during a dog-fight that lasted for thirty minutes after his formation of five Albatros biplanes dived into the attack upon nine F.E.8s of No. 40 Squadron R.F.C. Milling round, manœuvring for advantage, the fight seemed interminable by air-war standards. One by one the F.E.s went out, four shot down and four breaking away damaged. One British pilot,

von Richthofen presenting members of Jasta 11 *to General Ludendorff at Marcke on August 19th, 1917.*

wounded, having broken away to make an emergency landing, had his machine burst into flames before touching down. Just before the moment of impact, he threw himself clear and survived his ordeal.

The fight must have attracted other machines to the scene, for the aircraft that Richthofen dispatched, with an expenditure of only 100 rounds, was a D.H.2. This aircraft has been reported as a F.E.8, but the casualty concerned, Lieutenant A. J. Pearson, was an officer of No. 29 Squadron, flying D.H.2s. It is true that No. 29 Squadron did use two F.E.8s from June 15th, 1916, but it is doubtful if they were still doing service in March 1917. However, the fact that from the charred wreckage the part number AMC3425a was reported to be on the fin, points almost conclusively to the identity as a D.H.2—A.M.C. being the initials of the Aircraft Manufacturing Company who produced the D.H.2.

Although the tempo of Richthofen's scoring was now reaching a crescendo, on that day, March 9th, a decidedly discordant note temporarily shattered its hitherto triumphant progress. His machine was hit. He knew not where but a strong smell of petrol, frightening in its implication and in the resultant loss of engine power, left little room for doubt. With the sickening knowledge that its white vapour usually portended fire—having noticed it as a prelude to the flames that had at times consumed his victims—he switched off his engine and glided down out of the battle. He could then hear easily, above the wind wailing in the wires, the chatter of machine-guns as the fight continued above. Once a machine dropped down, passing near him, enveloped in flames, a grim reminder of the fate that so nearly claimed him, victor of twenty-five fights. Having glided down to 1,000 feet, he searched the ground for a suitable space on which to land, eventually bringing his machine down on to a small field near the mining town of Hénin Liétard. There, after examining his machine, he saw that both his petrol tanks had been punctured and his engine damaged by his opponent's fire.

Two days later he scored again. Having set off on a morning patrol with his *Staffel*, he later found that he was flying alone. Evidently his formation had lost their leader in a cloud. Rather than scour the skies for it, perhaps fruitlessly, he chose the more profitable course of seeking the enemy alone. He was not disappointed. A lone B.E. was up, engaged upon its unenviable task of spotting for the British guns. Richthofen stalked it, manœuvring for position. After attacking it in his usual manner, the B.E.'s fuselage broke in half after some 200 rounds had been discharged. The smoking wreckage fell close to the trenches on the German side, near to the stumps of the shell-shattered trees that formed the so-called forest of La Folie. The rear of the fuselage was sufficiently intact to identify the aircraft as No. 6232 (a B.E.2d built by Ruston Proctor of Lincoln), but the engine was buried deeply in the soggy ground, and as the area was under shell-fire it was not considered worth digging out. Possibly it is still there.

Richthofen's score was mounting; he had twenty-six confirmed victories and every promise of further success. His name was known, and although he was still a subaltern, as a holder of the *Pour le Mérite* his requests carried some weight with the military authorities. He spoke for his brother Lothar, whose transfer to his *Jasta* was arranged.

42

A line-up of Jasta 11 *aircraft at Douai about February or March 1917. von Richthofen's all-red Albatros D III is second from the front. The over-painted cross on the side of the fuselage, and the small white Albatros factory insignia at the top rear of the rudder may be noted. Reference to this aircraft is also made in the caption to the lower photograph on page 49.*

Lothar was inclined to be impetuous, but Manfred ensured, by a talk that was both a request and a command, that his brother should make himself familiar with his machine before attempting to fly against the enemy.

On March 17th *Jasta 11* went out in strength. Every serviceable machine, ten in all, led by Richthofen, took the air. Shortly before 11.30 a.m. he sighted two close formations of nine F.E.2bs with an equal number of Sopwith 1½ Strutters. He led into the attack. Collectively the F.E.s could give a good account of themselves and protect each other's tails. They actually evolved 'ring-a-roses' tactics, forming into a circle if attacked. Singly they were fairly easy to tackle from their blind spot. Richthofen therefore concentrated first on luring a machine out of the formation. This he did; then, attacking from behind, he gave bursts of fire expending 500 rounds, not without effect. One of the tail-booms of a F.E. was severed and another so damaged that the complete tail unit broke away. Then it plunged down, hitting the ground with terrific force, leaving little by which to identify the occupants or the machine. From the maps that were carried, the names Smith and Heanly were assumed. However, the maps were borrowed and the occupants, buried at Oppy near the crash, were in fact Lieutenant A. E. Boultbee and Air Mechanic F. King. Their machine was A5439 (built by Boulton & Paul at Norwich), fitted with Beardmore engine No. 854 and armed with machine-guns Nos. A19633 and A19901. It was the only F.E. lost, but two of the Sopwiths also went down.

Late that afternoon, near Vimy, yet another B.E. fell to Richthofen. This unfortunate machine, which was flying at only 2,000 feet, he dived at from above. Raking it with fire, he broke away quickly, lest other enemy machines, observed overhead, should attack him from behind. As he was not pursued, he came up behind the B.E. After a short burst, it broke up, the wings falling off. The wreckage fell in no man's land, where it was further pounded by shell-fire.

The timely meeting in full strength with the enemy squadron earlier that day suggests that the newly established warning system was functioning well. It was certainly due to that institution, whose primary instruments were field-glasses and the telephone, that Richthofen was enabled to steadily increase his rate of scoring throughout the following April.

This aircraft warning service, known as the *Flugmeldedienst*, formed part of the anti-aircraft defences. It consisted of a series of *Flugwachen* (aircraft observation posts) along the front, reporting to a centre—*Flugmeldestation*. At the centre, one of which was established for each army corps frontage, a *Luftschutzoffizier* (aerial protection officer) would be in direct telephonic communication with the duty officers of *Jagdstaffeln* in his area.

The duties of the new service were to keep all aircraft under observation and to enable timely and effective counter-measures to be taken by anti-aircraft guns or pursuit units. They were also responsible for the recording of all enemy aircraft that descended in their area and for arranging salvage of the remains. By having a log kept of all aerial activity observed, many fighter pilots were able to obtain confirmation of their victories from the *Luftschutzoffiziere* reports. Their task of singling out and reporting the action of an individual machine was considerably eased when distinctive markings were used. This one fact, more than any other, is responsible for the many and varied colour schemes that were adopted for aircraft in *Jagdstaffeln* at that time.

Little flying would have been effected in the exceptionally rough weather that prevailed, had it not been for the persistence of the Royal Flying Corps. The R.F.C. had, at the time, two major tasks of reconnaissance; that of ascertaining the new German positions, resulting from the withdrawal to the Hindenburg Line (*Siegfried Stellung*) by the German troops and of reconnoitring to register enemy batteries in preparation for the Battle of Arras.

Late in the afternoon on March 21st, in a strong wind flecked with snow, several B.E.s crossed the lines at 3,000

B.E.2es of No. 2 Squadron R.F.C. in the early summer of 1917. In contrast to the vivid colour schemes then being adopted by German fighters, British aircraft were in sober khaki-green, enlivened by squadron markings, in this case a white zig-zag. Unusual is the No. 5 of 'C' Flight, expressed in 'domino-fashion' on the fin.

feet. Receiving this piece of intelligence from the *Luftschutzoffizier*, Richthofen, impatient at the enforced inactivity, decided to go up alone. He flew a full hour before sighting the enemy, several B.E.s intent upon their registering, but nevertheless with a wary eye. Several attempts to approach were countered by a quick move away. It was not prudent to follow, since the gunners were quickly aroused and easier game might be found. He stalked one machine flying at under 2,000 feet, using the low clouds as partial cover. This B.E. pilot made the fatal mistake of keeping a straight course after his initial turn towards the lines to escape. Richthofen fired 500 rounds, which could hardly fail to take effect! Only then did the B.E. twist and turn, but those movements were uncontrolled, the occupants being in all probability already dead. The wreckage of this machine, Richthofen's twenty-ninth, crashed on to the British side.

If Richthofen had chosen the easiest victim—and on that day he undoubtedly had—it was no reflection upon his courage. It was his bounden duty. Such a case was clearly put by Lieutenant Marc, the French diarist who compiled the *Notes d'un Pilote disparu*, stating that it was a strict duty to destroy the maximum of the enemy with the minimum of loss, and that the French pilots should employ more freely the methods of Boelcke and Richthofen. That was why Richthofen survived to win fame in his Fatherland, he tempered courage with discretion.

When duty demanded a sterner task, he did not shirk. To be master of his trade, it was essential to obtain the measure of the new aircraft which the Allies were bringing into the Field. On March 24th, when flying with seven of his officers, he left unmolested an enemy formation in favour of attacking two enemy scouts of a type unknown to him, with the object of pitting his machine against one of them, to assess whose machine was best, his or the enemy's.

He found the Spad S.7, for such it was, 'fast and handy' as he put it, but not the match of his machine. It was a long fight. The decisive point came when one of Richthofen's bullets hit the Spad's petrol tank and its engine stopped. As the battle was fought over the lines, the Spad pilot gamely tried to make for the British side. Richthofen, showing mercy, countered this by warning shots. Closely followed, the machine made for a landing on the German side. A good approach was marred by a small shell-hole on the run in, causing it to turn completely over. The pilot, taken prisoner of war, at least had the satisfaction of denying the enemy an undamaged Spad. It was Richthofen's thirtieth victory.

Another French type of aircraft used by the R.F.C. fell to him the following day. Catching up with a formation of Nieuports from No. 29 Squadron R.F.C., he fired at the hindmost machine, stopping its engine and thereby forcing it to land. The machine crash-landed and caught fire.

An Albatros had again found favour with Richthofen, who at the beginning of April was using one of the D III biplanes. Like his earlier machines, he had it finished red over-all, making his presence well known on both sides of the lines. Richthofen was a marked man. Because of this, it was said that his officers prevailed upon him to share the distinguishing colour with the whole *Staffel*. Rumours that the Allies had offered a reward for his death or capture were having some effect. On the other hand, it is said that

The B.E.12 was essentially an interim fighter based on the B.E.2c design. Failing to prove itself in a fighting role it was used from September 1916 on bombing duties. Losses were heavy on either duty and five B.E.12s fell to von Richthofen alone.

44

Originally intended as a two-seater fighter-'recco' aircraft, but later used as a night-bomber, the F.E.2b had a harassed career in 1916. This photograph is of an aircraft of 'C' Flight, No. 22 Squadron R.F.C. and was flown by Lt. R. D. Sherbrooke-Walker pilot, with Lt. C. Smith observer. They were shot down near Bapaume in August 1916 and taken prisoner by the Germans.

Richthofen himself ordered red as the general colour for the *Staffel*, stipulating that whereas his machine should remain all red, the others should each have a distinguishing anomaly in a different colour. The scheme was adopted. That he no longer stood out so conspicuously may have hurt his pride a little, but since achievement mollifies egotism and he was proud of his own *Staffel*, egotism gave way to *esprit de corps*. Red was a grimly significant colour for the battles of that April.

The first day of April was not auspicious; only Vizefeldwebel Festner made contact with the enemy, and that without success. The second day, however, was one of great activity. For Richthofen it started with an abrupt awakening as his orderly, Menzke, shouted, 'Sir, the English are here!' Rising hurriedly from his bed, he actually saw, from the window of his hut, a British machine flying over. Already his pilots were taking off in their red Albatros D IIIs. He grabbed his furs, dressed quickly and took the air a few minutes later. Well behind the rest of his pilots, he feared that the enemy machine would escape him, when he was dived upon and shot at—by a B.E.2d! He turned away quickly, then circled round for a firing position, but his two adversaries, pilot and observer, were not inexperienced. He was denied a sitting target. The pilot dived and rolled to shake him off, losing height in the process. Once, after diving away, Richthofen thought the B.E. was going to land, but keeping at an altitude of only some fifty feet, the machine attempted to reach the lines by hedge-hopping. Richthofen followed, having little opportunity to fire, except when the B.E. rose to clear the trees. Although he too was low, he did not intend to go to the reckless limits of the B.E. pilot, who, before reaching the lines, charged into a block of houses. To the last, the observer was firing his gun. Richthofen was full of praise for their bravery and referred to their attack upon him as 'splendid daring', but he could not understand the logic of their conduct. In reflecting upon the action, he said that the British airmen had shown more foolhardiness than courage.

He was back on the airfield before his men returned; they, joining him at breakfast, and imagining that he had only just risen, were indeed surprised to hear that he had already achieved his thirty-second victory. After breakfast on that eventful day he was visited by an old friend, Leutnant Voss, of the *Jasta Boelcke*, who had twenty-three victories. Next to Richthofen, he was the leading living ace. They chatted for an hour, and when Voss took leave to return to his unit Richthofen offered to accompany him, suggesting that they flew a detour via the Front. They did not expect much activity, since there were dark clouds scudding across the sky. On the way, over Arras, they were joined by Lothar von Richthofen, who, having lost his way, was pleased to recognise Manfred's all-red Albatros and join up.

Just over the British side of the lines was a flight of six Sopwith 1½ Strutters flying in 'V' formation at about 12,000 feet. Richthofen dived upon one of the machines at the tail of the 'V', mortally wounding the observer and shattering the pilot's instrument panel with his opening burst of fire. The Sopwith pilot kicked his rudder over and dived. Richthofen, having anticipated this move, had already dived and was circling round ready to close in again from behind. Another burst of fire tore into the Sopwith and

With a fuselage similar to the B.E.2c and 2d aircraft, the B.E.2e had a completely new wing structure and a modified tailplane, but little extra performance was obtained thereby.

A perfect example of a blind approach from behind and below—a view several R.E.8s presented to von Richthofen. The R.E.8 observer, straining over the side to view the photographer's aircraft, could hardly have used a gun if necessary from that position!

Following quickly upon his promotion to Oberleutnant, that took effect from March 22nd, Richthofen was further promoted that Easter to Rittmeister, a cavalry captain, the title being warranted by his secondment from an Uhlan regiment. There was now a terseness in his manner, for an inner compulsion drove him to achieve two more victories. A wish that it would not have been in good taste to confide to his officers, but they in turn realised well enough the significance of Richthofen's next victories. He had thirty-nine and Boelcke had achieved forty. One more victory and he would be level with the Fatherland's hero. Two more and he would be the Fatherland's highest-scoring airman.

If Richthofen missed his chance on the opening day

Jasta 11 led by von Richthofen shot down six R.E.8s in as many minutes during April 1917. This shows the end of one R.E.8.

of the battle, he was soon aware that opportunities were being presented at low altitudes by British aircraft on contact patrols.

The 10th was a very wild day with driving rain and gales, restricting flying; but the following morning, when the wind had abated, he took off with Wolff. Flying low, they encountered a contact patrol B.E.2c over Willerval. After a few shots from Richthofen, the machine dived into a shell-hole, where its wings broke off. Confirmation of his victory was not readily available. That part of the front was under attack and communication with the defending troops was difficult. His victims were luckier than most. They survived the crash and sheltered from the heavy shelling in an abandoned German dug-out. There they were found later by the advancing British troops. Although they were safe, their unit, No. 13 Squadron R.F.C., was particularly unlucky that day, losing three aircraft and having two others severely damaged.

Richthofen now equalled Boelcke's score, but as he later wrote of Boelcke, but for his accident he might have scored a hundred. That too was Richthofen's wish—a 'century', but first he had to surpass Boelcke's score. Having no claim to submit for the 12th of the month, a day of snow blizzards, he made up for it on the 13th. He scored three victories that day—an achievement referred to by airmen on the other side of the lines as a 'hat trick'; but the Germans were not a nation of cricketers and Richthofen summed it up in his journal as 'the day of his triple victory'.

His first that day was an easy win. Six R.E.8s of No 59 Squadron R.F.C. had set out soon after 8 a.m. from Bellevue to photograph a portion of the German front. Two carried cameras and the others were acting as close escort. To give them further protection, fighter formations from other units were planned to patrol their area. But plans, particularly in war, often go astray. The R.E.8s became the victims of circumstances. Three Spads of No. 19 Squadron detailed for take-off from Vert Galand were some twenty minutes late in starting. They were to have joined up with six F.E.2ds of No. 57 Squadron from Feinvillers, but the F.Es, in the absence of the Spads, went on alone and became involved in fighting, resulting in the loss of two of their number. By a patrol of Bristol Fighters from No. 48 Squadron nothing was seen of the R.E.8s. The final link in the chain of unfortunate circumstances was fatal. Richthofen, leading five of his *Staffel* members, came on to the scene. This was his first encounter with a R.E.8,

50

which he described as a 'biplane—new type body', presumably implying a B.E.2 type with a different fuselage shape. In fact the R.E.8 bore a close resemblance to the B.E.2e, and in a defensive role it was equally as ineffectual. All six R.E.8s were shot down; Richthofen's own victims, men and machine, were burnt to ashes.

Later that morning, flying with an apparent newcomer to *Jasta 11*, one Leutnant Simon, he chased a F.E.2b from No. 25 Squadron returning from a raid on a dump at Wervicq. So accomplished was his method of attack that the observer was not enabled to fire back at him, although the one-sided fight lasted for several minutes. The F.E. eventually crashed into the ground between Monchy and Feuchy.

This line-up showing composite equipment of Albatros D V and D Va biplanes and Fokker Dr I triplanes of Jagdgeschwader Nr. 2 at Toulis, near Laon, 1918, presents a picture typical of Jagdgeschwader Nr. 1, for which, unfortunately, there is no comparable picture in existence.

Flying that evening too, he again arrived at an opportune moment, taking a mixed formation of F.E.2ds and F.E.2bs unawares. Yet again were the R.F.C. victims of circumstances. Having been escorted to their target by six Nieuports of No. 60 Squadron, the F.Es had dropped their bombs on the German detraining station at Hénin-Liétard. Their mission accomplished, the fighter escort had outdistanced the bombing machines on the return flight. Unaware that the Nieuports were no longer in close escort, the pilots and observers in the bombers mistook Richthofen's approaching formation of Albatros biplanes for their own Nieuport escort. They were surprised as the German machines dived into the attack. At that time the F.E. squadron, No. 25, was being re-equipped from F.E.2bs to F.E.2ds, but not until the first week in May was the change-over complete. A few of the older F.E.2bs were still flying, and it was one of these Richthofen singled out as his victim, possibly with deliberation, as he reported it as Vickers (old type), still under the impression that these pusher aircraft were of the Vickers 'Gunbus' series.

The fight ended for Richthofen when, after having raked it with fire, the F.E.2b, No. 4997, glided down and crashed into a house at Noyelle-Godault, killing both occupants. Two F.E.2ds were also shot down by *Jasta 11*.

That night, Richthofen not only had the satisfaction of knowing that he was the Fatherland's leading ace, but he had every reason to be satisfied with his unit, for there were no less than thirteen confirmed victories for his *Jasta*. Next day too they remained in form. During the morning, five Nieuports had begun an attack upon two German two-seater observation aircraft when Richthofen appeared on the scene. His chosen victim could do little to prevent the onslaught; his engine had already failed, damaged by the return fire from one of the German observation machines. Zigzagging to evade, the Nieuport glided down to a landing near Bois Bernard, where the pilot was taken prisoner.

The Royal Flying Corps maintained the offensive, in spite of their losses. While they appreciated

At the top an Albatros D III pilot has landed alongside the wreckage of his victim as Kurt Wolff did for his 33rd victory, and below is the burning wreckage of two machines shot down during his engagement. By no means were all losses attributable to air combats, the B.E.2e (third down) landed due to an engine failure during April 1917, and the D.H.5. (bottom) was a victim of anti-aircraft fire.

the vulnerability of corps aircraft, they did not approve the policy of using close fighter escorts, with the limited numbers of aircraft available. Instead they favoured the use of fighter patrols to sweep the areas in which corps aircraft were operating. This was proved the most effective method, but in seasonable April weather, and in the inclement April of 1917 in particular, clouds would often blanket out visual contact between the protected and the would-be protectors.

During the late afternoon of the 16th, the cloud afforded cover for Richthofen to approach, unnoticed, an artillery spotting B.E., that fell with smoke issuing from it after Richthofen's opening burst. Seemingly the pilot gained control momentarily, for at about 250 feet its dive was checked; then again the machine plunged, hitting the ground on the British side between Bailleul and Cavrelle. The observer was killed and the pilot so severely injured—the base of his skull was fractured—that his broken leg was left untended as he was expected to die within a few days, if not hours. Yet he did live, and by the time he was sent to hospital in England the broken bones had knitted together, but not being properly set the leg was crooked and useless. It had to be rebroken and re-set. Even then it was not satisfactory, owing to a splitting bone, and for a third and final time the leg was set. Although, by the nature of the head injury, all recollection of the fight was blotted out of Lieutenant W. Green's memory, he ever-remembered the consequences of being Richthofen's forty-fifth victory.

For the next few days following there was little activity in the air, due to rain and mist. With an improvement on the 21st, *Jasta 11* were out hunting again. During a flight in the evening, Schaefer lost formation and did not rejoin. The sun had gone down when the others landed and as dusk deepened there was some concern for Schaefer. Anxiety increased after an hour had passed and his fuel limit would have been reached. They sought for news by telephoning aerodromes in the area. The *Flugmeldedienst* could not help as the British advance had disrupted the chain of

Another informal photograph of von Richthofen—again smiling. To the left, cigarette to his lips, is Lt. Loewenhardt.

observation posts sited near the original front. By midnight it was evident that Schaefer would have to be officially reported as missing.

Schaefer, however, although down, was not out. During his flight with the *Jasta* he had noticed a British artillery machine low down. He had dived upon it and destroyed it, drawing heavy fire from the British trenches in the process. Most of the bullets passed harmlessly well to the rear, as the British infantry, trained as they were to fire at stationary or slow-moving objects, had little conception of aiming-off to compensate for the speed of an aircraft. Nevertheless, one shot at least took effect, for a bullet hit his engine and caused it to stop. In the absence of its loud throbbing, he became uncomfortably conscious of whining bullets as he glided down from the relatively low altitude of 600 feet. Landing, he was aware of still being under fire as bullets whipped the fuselage fabric. Hardly had his machine come to a standstill than he had jumped out and dived into a shell-hole. The deepening dusk that had made his comrades so anxious for his safety was his salvation. Not that his ordeal was over, for he was in no man's land. The British, unwilling to risk a patrol in the open while there was still some light, apparently decided to destroy his machine and the sheltering pilot by shell-fire. To his fear of the shelling was added the discomfort of lyddite fumes that made his eyes water. He lit a cigarette to soothe his nerves. Still crouching in the shell-hole he took off his heavy flying coat, to allow freer movement should it be necessary to make a sudden dash for safety.

The shelling ceased as the light weakened. At nightfall, Schaefer was aware that animal life, stunned by the shell-fire of the day, was reawakened. That area had only recently been included in the front because of the British advance, and, as yet, it had not been forsaken by all wild life. Schaefer was pleased to hear the distinctive grating note of partridges around, not because he was an ornithologist, but as an experienced game-shot he knew the warning that these birds could give. When, with startling suddenness, first one, then another, of the birds took off with their characteristic whirring flight, he assumed that an enemy patrol was heading his way. It was time to leave. He crept out of the shell-hole and kept crawling for over an hour in the direction he judged the German lines to be. Hearing voices, he froze, then relaxed as he recognised them as German. Lightly, he hailed.

At 2 a.m. Richthofen was awakened by his orderly, who informed him that Schaefer was safe and required transport. Next morning, at breakfast time, muddy and dishevelled, Schaefer arrived. After breakfast he went to bed. That very afternoon he was in the air again, harrying a B.E. over Monchy. Five days later he left *Jasta 11* to take command of *Jasta 28*. His subsequent service was eventful but brief. On May 1st, when he had reached his twenty-fourth victory, he was awarded the *Pour le Mérite*. Following that he took a short but well-deserved leave to visit his parents in Krefeld. It was to be their last meeting, for he was killed in combat on June 5th, during an engagement with F.E.2ds of No. 20 Squadron R.F.C., after having attained the sizeable score of thirty victories. Such had been his pride in membership of *Jasta 11* that he used in *Jasta 28*, the familiar red-painted finish for his Albatros, with his personal characteristic of black control surfaces. It was in this machine that he died for his Fatherland.

A marked improvement in the weather on April 22nd brought an increase in aerial activity, opening with a series of attacks by the R.F.C. upon German observation balloons along the length of the battle-front. This brought retaliation by German aircraft upon British balloons. Anticipating this, the R.F.C. put up strong fighter patrols.

The long-suffering No. 11 Squadron, allotted a photographic task that morning, were thwarted by two Albatros biplanes. When they tried again in the afternoon, they were assailed by *Jasta 11*. Of the six F.E.2bs that set out, one was brought down on the German side and of the others reaching the British side, four were wrecked on landing. One F.E. pilot had an epic return flight. His observer, mortally wounded, lay slumped over the cockpit side in danger of falling overboard. Grabbing his clothes with one hand, the pilot tried to control the damaged machine with the other. Clearing the front-line trenches by a few feet, the machine burst into flames as it touched down. No sooner had the pilot jumped out and dragged his observer clear, than the F.E.2b received a direct hit from a shell.

One of those wrecked on the British side was Richthofen's own victim. He had chosen to attack the rearmost machine. After his opening burst, it had emitted smoke, testifying damage, but persistently he went on firing until he had expended something like 500 rounds. The pilot was injured in the crash and the observer wounded in the leg. No

Major Albrecht Freiherr von Richthofen with his eldest son —Manfred—on his right, together with other members of Jasta 11. *A photograph taken at Douai in April 1917.*

doubt they owed their lives to the configuration of the F.E.2b, with the engine placed between them and Richthofen's attack from the rear. Although the machine fell near to Richthofen's old aerodrome at Lagnicourt, the area was in British hands due to the German retirement.

With continuing fine weather, the 23rd was another day of intense activity. The R.F.C. patrolled the lines with A.W. F.K.8s, F.E.2bs and R.E.8s while above them flew formations of Spads, Nieuports and the new S.E.5s on fighter patrol; additionally the R.N.A.S. were providing patrols of Sopwith Triplanes. Two British pilots of note also flew that day on roving commissions and both scored. They were the redoubtable Ball and Bishop from Nos. 56 and 60 Squadrons respectively. Yet that day, Richthofen's claim was for the destruction of a lone B.E.2c that had been engaged upon artillery work. The German *Jagdstaffeln*, including Richthofen himself, were not to be drawn. The dicta of Boelcke were too deeply ingrained. If advantages were not to be gained before attacking, then, in the interests of the Service, it was best not to attack at all.

Richthofen, warily avoiding becoming embroiled in unequal combat, sought an easier prey elsewhere. He found it in a B.E. whose occupants failed to notice his approach, allowing him to blast them at close range. Shedding its port wing first, the machine then broke up in the air, to fall, scattering wreckage near Maricourt, just within the German lines. Five days later another B.E. fell to him in similar circumstances.

The following day, by arrangement, Major Albrecht Freiherr von Richthofen arrived at Douai to visit his sons. Perhaps it was sensed that this would be an auspicious day, as his eldest son's score of forty-eight was so near to that significant round-figure of fifty. Watched by their father, his two sons, Manfred and Lothar, took off in company with four others shortly before noon. So perfect were the arrangements that both brothers returned with a victory claim. It is even possible that this was 'stage-managed' to the extent that the Albatros pilots knew from advance intelligence reports of the *Flugmeldedienst* that they would meet three Spads in the area Lens–Le Foret–Noreuil.

For the last five days No. 19 Squadron R.F.C. had provided continuous patrols during daylight hours over the same area. On the 29th their patrols, each consisting of three Spad S.7s, commenced at 5 a.m. The third, consisting of Major H. D. Harvey-Kelly, D.S.O., Second Lieutenant W. N. Hamilton and Second Lieutenant R. Applin, left at 10 a.m.—none returned.

Richthofen was just too late to join in a battle between six silvery-grey Albatros D IIIs from another *Jasta* and three of the new S.E.5s from No. 56 Squadron R.F.C., that had been joined by five F.E.2ds of No. 57 Squadron. The contestants had parted and flown their separate ways, leaving a score of one-all—one Albatros and one F.E.2d. The remaining grey Albatros D IIIs, shortly afterwards, joined up with the red D IIIs of *Jasta 11*. It was then that the Spads appeared; having the advantage of a 1,000 feet in height, they dived down upon the red machines.

Before Major Harvey-Kelly had led into the attack against greatly superior numbers, he had noticed six Sopwith Triplanes of No. 1 (Naval) Squadron R.N.A.S. in the offing and had confidently counted upon their support. This was not lacking, for the Triplanes battled for some twenty minutes with the German formation, sending at least three down out of control, one of which was observed to crash—but they were too late to save the Spads.

Applin, the least experienced of the three, was the first to fall. Hit by fire from Richthofen's machine, that had been banked quickly round to avoid the initial onslaught, his Spad reared up, fell back on its tail, catching fire as it went. It broke up in the air, the pieces falling into a swamp near Lecluse. Harvey-Kelly, too, who had been the very first pilot of the British Expeditionary Force to land on French soil on August 13th, 1914, fell mortally wounded under the fire of Leutnant Wolff. Only Hamilton escaped with his life, being shot down and taken prisoner near Oppy Wood. His victor was Lothar von Richthofen, who, by the rapidity of his scoring, was aspiring to outdo his famous elder brother.

General-Feldmarschall von Hindenburg about to shake hands with von Richthofen, who was on a visit to Field Headquarters. Major Thomsen and General von Hoeppner at right.

54

Brother Lothar

CHAPTER FIFTEEN

Although, when the name Richthofen was mentioned, almost invariably Manfred was inferred, his brother Lothar was already an ace. On the very day, April the 29th, that Richthofen had his conspicuous success of downing four enemy machines, including his fiftieth victim, Lothar shot down two machines to make his 18th and 19th victories.

Lothar's victim that day, in the fight with the Spads, was as related, Hamilton. A seemingly straightforward engagement of pursued and pursuer, was subsequently considerably complicated by conflicting reports. Lothar, writing, perhaps more for effect than record, gave an account of his chase wherein he fired burst after burst, until he had expended all his ammunition, some one thousand rounds. Frustrated, he even contemplated running into the enemy machine! Yet, to dissuade the enemy pilot, who eventually landed in German territory, from setting fire to his machine, he was able to fire further bursts around the Spad on the ground! An obvious explanation—that the inability to fire was due at first to a jam is ruled out by Lothar's own words that he had himself suspected a jam and found it not to be the case. Perhaps he was confusing two separate fights or possibly his story was rewritten carelessly. It is often the case that poor translation further detracts from an account which was not, in the first place, as expressive as could be wished. Particularly inexpressive were the reputed exclamations of Lothar upon finding his ammunition exhausted, which an earlier publisher cautiously quoted as 'Confound!' and 'Damn!'

Even more amazing is Lothar's admission, that when he examined the captured Spad there was not a bullet mark upon it! He would hardly be ready to make such an admission, implying that in his discharge of a 1,000 rounds not one reached its target, unless there was some foundation. Not that it worried Lothar unduly; he was not a scientific fighter like his brother. However, the point at issue is—how then, did Lothar get Hamilton down?

A published report, purporting to be Hamilton's own account does not answer this very well. Hamilton credits the enemy with good shooting, reporting that all his aircraft's instruments and most of its struts and flying wires were shot away! Finally, a hole in his gravity tank immobilised his engine. The impression so gained, that Hamilton was given to exaggeration, is in no way dispelled by his further suggestion that between Harvey-Kelly on Spad A6681 and himself on Spad A6753 they destroyed five of the enemy aircraft. No one can doubt Hamilton's courage in following Harvey-Kelly down in an attack upon a superior number of enemy aircraft known by their red machines as formidable foes. There was, however, little need to exculpate his downfall. Outnumbered, by a formation that included two Richthofens, the consequences were almost inevitable.

Having returned from that fight, Lothar strode quickly to his waiting father, who had been trying to glimpse the fight through a telescope. He reported, 'Father, I have just shot down an Englishman.' Then Manfred too, striding less hurriedly as befitted a Rittmeister and squadron commander, gave similar report. Albrecht was delighted and most proud of his sons. He may well have had a poor opinion of the

Oberleutnant Lothar Freiherr von Richthofen, younger by some two years than his brother Manfred.

enemy airmen and under-estimated the dangers of aerial combat. If so, he was soon to think differently. A fight developed overhead and from it, turning over and over, fell a machine. It bore, not the roundels those watching from the ground had wished to see, but black Maltese crosses. With relief they saw the machine's descent checked as the pilot regained control. It turned for a glide into their own airfield. On an unfamiliar field, the pilot's landing was rough and the machine came to an abrupt stop. The pilot rose to get out, but the gunner remained inanimate. As Albrecht, Manfred and Lothar ran over to the spot, they realised the gunner was dead. The sight, familiar enough to the sons, was new to the father, and served to remind Albrecht that aerial combat was no less fraught with danger than ground engagements.

That afternoon Manfred led five of his men on patrol, but it cannot be recalled whether or not Lothar was one of them. That flight was one of moment, for an encounter with a reconnaissance patrol of four F.E.2bs of No. 18 Squadron R.F.C. gave Manfred the opportunity of scoring his fiftieth victory. His victim put up a stout fight, that won Manfred's praise by the words 'admirable defence'. After he had obtained favourable positions to expend some 300 rounds, the F.E. caught fire in the air, the occupants falling out. A triumphant return from attaining his fifty, was somewhat marred for both himself and his unit, by the loss, in flames, of one of their own number.

In the evening, Lothar was certainly up. Together with his famous brother, they each tackled a low-flying B.E.2d from No. 12 Squadron R.F.C., whilst the rest of their flight circled around. This was the Richthofens' day. Manfred's victim lost its wings and plunged down, catching fire, on to the German side; Lothar's victim, with a dying pilot and wounded observer, crashed on to the British side. They both rejoined formation, where, soon afterwards, they were

Two brothers, two fighters, but two quite different natures. Manfred, ever ambitious, ever eager to be, and remain, the first of all. Lothar, ever in the shadow of the 'big' brother.

set upon by Sopwith Triplanes from No. 8 (Naval) Squadron R.N.A.S., joined by a lone Nieuport. While the Nieuport concentrated on one of the German formation, Manfred got behind it and shot it down in flames. One Sopwith Triplane and one Albatros D III were also destroyed before the contestants broke away. It had been a memorable day for all three Richthofens—Albrecht, Manfred and Lothar.

Manfred was ordered for his much needed and well deserved rest. A Royal Command left no option. The question of who should lead in his absence had to be settled. Allmenröder, the most senior member was on leave, Schaefer was under orders to move and Wolff was too young. Command devolved upon Lothar. At least a Richthofen would still lead *Jasta 11*.

Lothar was born in Breslau on September 27th, 1894, making him Manfred's junior by over two years. His entry to the Army, through high school and the War Academy, brought less hardship than Manfred's progression through cadet school. On the other hand, he experienced nothing of peace-time soldiering as an officer, receiving his lieutenancy at the outbreak of war. Like Manfred, he aspired to cavalry, but whereas Manfred was a light cavalryman—a Uhlan, Lothar was a heavy cavalryman—a dragoon. With *Dragoner Regiment Nr. 4 'von Bredow'*, he took part, as related earlier, in the opening battles of the Western Front.

Moving from West to East, he spent the winter of 1914/15 experiencing the rigours of the Russian Front, showing great forbearance, particularly on one occasion when he carried out a lone reconnaissance. The opposing forces at that time were separated by the wide, navigable River Warta (also known as the Warthe). To assess the strength of the enemy, Lothar swam across the icy water at night and crept along the bank on the Russian side, making mental notes of the enemy's positions and probable strength. Within a short time of rising from the water after his swim back, his clothes had frozen upon him. Yet, he remained on duty, chiefly in the saddle, all next day. Not until evening did he return to his quarters to change.

It was Manfred who prevailed upon him to enter the Air Service. First, Lothar became an observer, seeing active service with *Kampfstaffel Nr. 25*. Such battle flights, each with six C-type biplanes, had a purely offensive role. Lothar went on some thirty or so bombing raids with his unit, an operation that gave him considerable satisfaction, particularly at night, when he took a somewhat juvenile delight at the fireworks produced. Stirred by Manfred's success in *Jasta 2* during the autumn of 1916, he applied for a pilot's course, intending to follow in his brother's steps. It was an opportune moment to change since the *Kampfgeschwader* organisation into which *Kampfstaffeln* were formed, six to each, was then being changed. Already the rigidity of the system had broken down during the Somme battle when units were hurriedly detached and moved as the battle dictated. Under the revised policy, some units were re-equipped with twin-engined G-type aeroplanes, whilst others were formed into *Schutzstaffeln*, flights to afford protection to *Fliegerabteilungen*. The latter was a task for which Lothar had little relish. He need not have worried. His brother, holder of the *Pour le Mérite*, a squadron commander and an ace, had the necessary pull. When Lothar had passed his third examination as a pilot in March 1917, to Manfred's *Jasta 11* he went.

Lothar was carefully schooled by his brother. For a fortnight after arrival at Douai, he was pledged to practice locally and to familiarise himself with his machine and the district. Then he was taken on an offensive patrol by his elder brother who exhorted him to watch the method of attacking, but take no part if a fight developed. That instruction, however, was against Lothar's impetuous nature. When on his third patrol with his brother an opportunity was presented, he took it. Manfred, alarmed at first to see his protégé part company, felt a glow of pride as Lothar rushed at an enemy machine—and shot it down.

Lothar was an outstanding fighter. He served for 77 days at the Front, and in that period of time he shot down 40 enemy aircraft. A unique performance.

56

Lothar's approach to aerial combat differed greatly from Manfred's. It was Manfred himself, who made the analogy of a hunter and a 'shooter'. He, Manfred, was a hunter; once he had achieved a kill his goading instinct was temporarily appeased. Not for some fifteen minutes or so, did he feel the urge to seek further combat. Lothar was the 'shooter'—and remember that the word was Manfred's—who was never satisfied in his quest to shoot down enemy aircraft, as witness the remarkable achievement of twenty victories in his first four weeks of operational service. A unique record. Later, almost regretfully, Manfred remarked that he too, against his instinct, became a 'shooter'.

Prima facie, these remarks would seem to place the Richthofen brothers in a loathsome light, using war as their excuse to play with human lives. They have been condemned by some on that score. This book attempts neither a justification nor a condemnation of their attitudes, but does aim to present an unbiased view. For this reason, some of Manfred's words, since they have been already published, would need some qualification.

No man, unless he be bestial, enjoys killing his fellow-creatures. War demands that men must kill and each one must find his own form of escapism to atone for that grim requisite. The bomber crew, in raiding a town, think of their contribution towards reducing the industrial capacity of the district; not of the possibility that their bombs may have killed or maimed women and children, lest such reflection impair their sense of duty. Some men, and certainly amongst them was Britain's leading ace—Mannock, achieved a blind sense of rage against their foes. Others blinded themselves to the fact that their enemies too, were flesh and blood. Most experienced a natural exaltation at striking a blow at their country's enemies, a sentiment consistent with a sense of duty. To Manfred, a serious hunter, the attitude of the hunt was easily, in fact naturally, assumed. His methods reflected that pretence. When, against his natural feelings, he became a 'shooter', it was because duty demanded that he should kill the enemy whenever possible, not selectively as does a huntsman. The attitudes of the Richthofens differed little from many others on either side of the lines. Condemnation should be reserved for war itself which is the licence to kill, not for its unfortunate pawns.

That the quality of mercy was at times withheld by the Richthofens, in continuing to fire at aircraft already doomed, is true enough. But their bounden duty was to ensure that neither the men nor the machines they attacked, should be of any further use to the enemy. We have the words of a British ace, who, to this end, felt fully justified in shooting a man dangling from a parachute that would seemingly land the man safely in his own territory. Manfred could and did at times show mercy. In subsequent years, three different British pilots were to testify to his mother, that he showed them mercy. Unfortunately, like the generally accepted beliefs that chivalry was widely displayed between the contestants in the aerial engagements of that war, to show mercy was, in fact, the exception—not the rule.

War, vile as it is, has its regulations. For the 1914–18 War they were vested in The Hague Convention* of 1907 (as amended to 1914) which both Germany and the Allies had individually ratified. Since it was an International Agreement, it was, presumably, above national prejudice. By those accepted standards there is no evidence, or even a suspicion, that Manfred or Lothar in any way contravened its articles. Therefore, in the eyes of the world, both may be regarded as honourable men.

The last known photograph of the two brothers to be taken together. As the triplane serial number is obscured by Manfred's left thigh, it is not known whose aircraft it was.

The differing attitudes of Manfred and Lothar caused at times a slight friction to develop between them, as on the occasion of Lothar making his second and third victories in quick succession. Chasing an enemy machine, Lothar's fire caused an explosion and the aircraft took fire. Without awaiting further result or contributing further to its despatch, he immediately switched his attention to another nearby enemy machine, which he also shot down.

After landing, Lothar asked Manfred, presumably with his tongue in his cheek, 'How many did you get?' Manfred replied, 'One', to which Lothar rejoined, 'I got two!' Turning his back on Manfred, he walked away. Manfred was rankled, not so much because Lothar had been more successful than he, but by his brother's cocky manner. He thereupon challenged Lothar's claim, ordering him up to the lines to seek confirmation. Crestfallen, Lothar returned with the wreckage of only one machine confirmed. His claim for two, however, was allowed as it was witnessed by other members of the flight. They had purposely withheld their

---
* The Convention amended still stands under the International Court of Justice which is an integral part of the United Nations Organisation.

Although reputed to be a photograph of Lothar von Richthofen, the helmet and goggles preclude any confirmation.

reports, upon Manfred's instruction, to teach Lothar a lesson.

Apart from differences in the approach to a fight, the one careful in his selection, weighing all the factors, the other rushing in at every opportunity, they also differed in their tactics once the fight was joined. Manfred was horrified at first to see Lothar's machine turn over on its back and plunge, spinning earthwards. As he watched, the machine righted itself and turned into a favourable position to fire at the enemy machine that had followed his down. It was one of Lothar's ruses. He was an exponent of aerobatics and Manfred, we know, was not.

On the day before Manfred left on leave, April 30th, a new German policy was evident to the Royal Flying Corps, who met a massed formation of some twenty machines sweeping over the battle area. This formation comprised flights from *Jasta 3, 4, 11* and *33*. As the red machines of *Jasta 11* were conspicuously present, the formation was soon dubbed 'Richthofen's Circus' by the R.F.C. It should not, however, be confused with the accepted meaning of the 'Circus', which implied the later permanent grouping

Oberleutnant Lothar von Richthofen in his triplane. The method of fairing off the end of the wing tip may be noted. It was not *straight-edged as thought by so many modellers.*

into a *Jagdgeschwader* under Manfred von Richthofen.

The new tactics met with some success. The German formation became embroiled in a series of fights with Sopwith Triplanes, S.E.5s and F.E.2bs. As would be expected, the F.Es proved the most vulnerable and the resultant losses were six British to five German. Although concentrating fighter formations put the Germans in a stronger position for attacking British fighter patrols, their collective effort was thus localised. Hence, the Corps machines on their routine reconnaissance and battery-work had less interference. Never again were losses so high in the R.F.C. 'Bloody April' was over, and, although the R.F.C. were not immediately aware, Manfred von Richthofen was leaving the front on leave.

Instead of an all-red Albatros at the head of *Jasta 11* from May 1st, there was a red Albatros with yellow ailerons and elevators. Yellow, chosen because that was the traditional colour of Lothar's dragoon regiment in which he had first served.

There was considerable activity for the next few days in which *Jasta 11* played so prominent a part that Douai became marked out for special attention by their enemies. Evidently they were becoming set in their flying habits for the Ninth Wing R.F.C., arranged for fighter patrols to cover the Douai area each morning and evening at certain times previously noted as 'peak hours' for activity. For this reason, on the evening of May 7th, eleven S.E.5s of No. 56 Squadron and six Spads of No. 19 Squadron set out from Vert Galand in misty, cloudy weather. Due to the poor visibility there was difficulty in maintaining full formation and they were split up. As they had expected, *Jasta 11* were up and about. Lothar, apparently realising that it was impracticable to fly in full formation, had split his unit into three *Ketten*. Thus there was no great clash of formations, but a series of skirmishes in and out of the clouds.

It was in the ensuing engagement, or rather series of fights, that Captain Albert Ball, V.C., D.S.O., M.C. lost his life. Discounting victory scores as the criterion for fame, Ball with 44 victories was probably the greatest of British air-fighters. Young, unassuming, with no military background, he displayed in the air skill and daring in formidable combination. Seemingly the cold logic of superior numbers made no impression upon him. By quick thinking, sure shooting and faultless manœuvring, he would dash, often alone, into enemy formations and as quickly dive away. But, in that time, he would despatch yet another of his country's foes.

Next to that great controversy of the manner in which Manfred von Richthofen met his death, is the mystery concerning Ball's last fight. For the Germans credited Lothar von Richthofen as being Captain Ball's victor. The German military authorities reported, by wireless that night, that in the course of the day two English* aircraft were downed, one three-decker (triplane) piloted by Capt. Ball being shot down by Leutnant von Richthofen. But herein is the mystery, Ball was not flying a triplane, but a biplane. The difference is fundamental.

Ball in his S.E.5 A4850 had taken off with No. 56

---
* The Germans persistently referred to English where British was intended.

Squadron, eleven strong, but soon reduced to ten as Lieutenant W. B. Melville in A4861 was forced to return with engine trouble. The formation then split; Ball as 'A' Flight Commander remained on patrol along the lines at about 7,000 ft. with Lieutenants G. Maxwell (A8902) and K. J. Knaggs (A8904), while 'B' and 'C' Flights gained height to effect patrol layers at varying heights.

Due to the cloud banks, the flights lost contact. 'C' Flight, led by Captain H. Meintjes (A8900) and consisting of Lieutenants R. T. C. Hoidge (A4862) and C. A. Lewis (A4853) were the first to make contact with the enemy, four Albatros D IIIs of *Jasta 11*—Lothar von Richthofen, Wilhelm Allmenröder, Mohnicke and one other. They flew at each other, then split up and milled round as they each tried to bring their guns to bear. Meintjes went down, seemingly out of control, but he returned to send an Albatros down in similar fashion, but that too, apparently regained control. Becoming hard-pressed again he left the fight with a wounded wrist and the top shot off his aircraft's control column.

Meanwhile 'B' Flight, with Captain C. M. Crowe (A4860) leading Lieutenants R. M. Chaworth-Musters (A4867), A. F. P. Rhys Davids (A4868) and J. O. Leach (A4856) emerged from a large bank of cloud, with A4867 missing. Prior to entering the cloud Musters had been observed to break away as if to attack a machine. He was not seen again by No. 56 Squadron and he was probably the second of the two aircraft subsequently claimed by the Germans. In the clear again, 'B' Flight were attacked by a lone Albatros, red in general colour but with a green fuselage band and red and green wings, which achieved no more success than to scatter the formation.

According to plan, should the squadron get scattered, rendezvous was to be made over Arras. There, Crowe and Leach, after having engaged a lone Albatros, which fell to Leach's guns, joined Ball, Knaggs, Hoidge and Lewis. Before the S.Es could formate, there was further scattered fighting. The light was now very bad and some of the pilots, finding themselves alone, made for home. Capt. Crowe, having his goggles shot away in a fight against a skilful opponent, broke off combat when he sighted five more enemy machines above him. Hardly had he shaken them off than his attention was caught by two Very-lights fired from Ball's machine, the 'tally-ho' signal. Ball was chasing a single red Albatros and after he fired and turned away, Crowe followed up with his guns at close range. This machine had also been attacked by a Spad of No. 19 Squadron, the only one of the six to make contact that evening, and by some Triplanes from No. 8 (Naval) Squadron. Ball returned to the attack and still fighting, the two machines disappeared into a cloud bank.

That was the last seen of Ball from the British side. The fight apparently went on down to low altitude. Like Manfred von Richthofen's end, a claim was put in for Ball by a machine-gun crew positioned in a church steeple and there is some evidence that he might have met his end that way.

This photograph is reputed to show Lothar's crashed aircraft—on March 13, 1918. After being forced down in a fight, he made a good approach for an emergency landing near the airfield at Awoingt, but sideslipped into the ground on the run-in.

Wilhelm Allmenröder stated that he clearly saw Lothar engaged in earnest combat with a British biplane, and he observed that no other aircraft were in the vicinity. He saw too, the British machine rear and then fall, but as Lothar's machine also dived steeply, he tried, without success, to follow. Both machines disappeared into the evening mist and it was nightfall before Allmenröder landed.

Lothar may well have been the pilot Ball was last seen engaging, and the confusion with a Triplane a result of his earlier fight. However, Lothar himself, at the end, was not able to give a coherent account. First he was lost. At a low altitude, the wrong side of Vimy Ridge, he felt his plight desperate. It had been an exhausting engagement. Then he was hit, apparently from the ground. Brave though he undoubtedly was, he had a haemal aversion. With a wound in the hip from which blood was flowing, he almost lost consciousness. More by luck than judgment he regained his own lines, made an emergency landing and fainted. To Manfred, on leave, there came a telegram to the effect that his brother was wounded.

CHAPTER SIXTEEN

Jagdgeschwader Nr. 1

Manfred Freiherr von Richthofen had earlier been given to understand that the German Emperor wished to see him, but when final details were telephoned through to him, late in the evening of April 30th, it left little time for preparation. His attendance was required on May 2nd, and on the day prior to that he was to report to General Headquarters for briefing. It meant an early start on the morrow. Fortunately, an aeroplane had been standing-by for this anticipated occasion—a two-seat D.F.W. C V.

Leutnant Krefft, also due for leave, piloted Manfred, who for once flew as a passenger. Before departing he took leave of his brother, to whom he was entrusting command of his *Jasta*, no doubt cautioning him not to do anything rash. Command, having formally devolved upon Lothar, Manfred took-off into a promising blue sky on that May day, with the prospect of a long leave ahead and with the satisfaction of duty well done. He was on his way to meet the German Emperor, Kaiser Wilhelm II, himself. He was truly famous.

The first stage of the journey, the 200 mile flight to Cologne, was made by way of Namur, Liege and Aix la Chapelle. As clouds, dense at times, were encountered, those towns were necessary landmarks to check their position, lest they should stray off-course over neutral Holland. More easily done than perhaps realised, since the direct line of flight, Douai–Cologne, would cut across the south-eastern extremity of Holland. The ignominy of internment for Germany's leading ace was unthinkable.

At Cologne there was quite a reception. Word of his arrival had been notified in advance by telephone. Public dignitaries accorded him ceremonious welcome and a host of admiring *Fräuleins*, some with bouquets, greeted him in a manner which was anything but formal. Overwhelmed and uncomfortable, Richthofen pleaded a need for rest and retired for a few hours to a local officers' mess.

After a midday meal, they flew on to the Air Service arm of General Headquarters. There, after reporting to an adjutant, he was taken into General von Hoeppner, General Officer Commanding the Air Service, known then as *Kommandierender General der Luftstreitkräfte*, or more briefly—*Kogenluft*, the former title of *Chef des Flugfeldwesens* having been replaced late in 1916.

Following his interview, Manfred toured the Air Service Headquarters, both out of interest and for his own instruction. There was a useful exchange of views, during which time, he met several old comrades, plying the unenviable task of—ink-spilling—to quote Manfred's own expression—evidently the equivalent of our pen-pushing!

The administration was not organised on the conventional lines of Operations, Administration and Quartering as the familiar 'G', 'A' and 'Q', three-prong organisation of British Army formation headquarters. The staff, however, had the usual three-grade staff officers. At the top, the General Staff Officer 1, known simply as *G.1*, acted as deputy to the Commander and was responsible for future plans. *G.2* was concerned with day-to-day matters, preparation for operations, daily situation and state reports, whilst *G.3* dealt with balloon and anti-aircraft units with particular regard to co-ordinating their duties with other arms of the Service.

Equal in status to the General Staff was the Adjutant-General's Department. *A.1*, who dealt with promotions, supply questions and decorations *inter alia*, was the officer who decided the criterion for Air Service recommendations for the award of the *Pour le Mérite*, and was, at that very time, considering the eligibility of Lothar von Richthofen. *A.2* dealt with staff administrative problems and miscellaneous matters that would include

Albatros D Vs. The aircraft but one from the front—D 1177—is one that von Richthofen flew during June 1917. It was in this aircraft that he was shot down and wounded on July 6th, 1917.

60

arranging for Manfred's visit with the Emperor on the morrow. *A.3* was merely an appointment to provide a deputy for *A.2* whose duties often took him away from the Headquarters.

Under those two branches, the General Staff and the Adjutant-General's Branch, were the various departments of the Air Service. To Manfred the most important was Department *FL* (*Flieger*—Aeroplanes), in which, the adjutant was responsible for recording air victories. No doubt the adjutant was interested to meet the man who headed his list. This department was in three sections. With *FLI*, dealing with personnel matters, there was little to discuss, but with *FLII*, concerned with organisation, there was the new policy of grouping *Staffeln* upon which to hold forth. There, it is imagined, the views of the department and those of Manfred were compatible, but with *FLIII*, dealing with all technical matters, there was the vexed question of structural failures to discuss. Less than a month ago, Manfred had the occasion to submit a report, through the Headquarters, on the failure of the wing of an Albatros D III flown by Vizefeldwebel Festner.

The work of other departments held little of direct interest for Manfred, although some did touch upon matters concerning him. Department *FLAK* he had mixed feelings about; for whilst the aircraft warning service was proving most valuable, the tendency to make claims for the guns, when fighter aircraft were involved, was a source of annoyance. In the new Department *H* (*Heimatschutz*—Home Defence), he foresaw a possible drain upon the availability of pilots, but in the event, service on Home Defence provided a rest from operations for pilots of more active units. Department *B* (*Nachrichten und Presse*—Intelligence and Press) had the task of finding out all it could of the enemy air forces, their equipment, organisation and policy, including the records of enemy aircraft shot down. It is not known whether or not they enlightened Manfred that the 'Vickers' he had so often claimed were in fact, F.Es. Not that it much mattered, for the occasion was not to arise again. Later it was to this department that Manfred submitted the MSS of his own book—*Der Rote Kampfflieger*, in order that no secrets would be revealed.

The other departments were rather out of Manfred's sphere, but each had equal status in the Service. There was Dept. *W* (*Wetterdienst*—Meteorological Services), Dept. *LB* (*Luftbild*—Photography and Mapping), Dept. *FEU* (*Feuerschutz*-Anti-fire and other precautionary measures) and Dept *S* (*Sanitäts-Abteilung*—Medical Section) as well as the offices of liaison officers, technical and administrative advisers. Manfred might well be the best-known personality of the Air Service, but his work was but a facet of that organisation.

Having come straight from operations, in an aircraft allowing little luggage, Manfred wore an ordinary field-grey uniform under his leather flying suit, that contrasted with the immaculately dressed staff officers. On the morrow, he progressed to the Emperor, through interviews with Field Marshal von Hindenburg, the Chief of General Staff and his chief assistant—Ludendorff. The one, von Hindenburg, was the figurehead and mouthpiece for the other, Ludendorff, the brain behind the operations of the German Armies. It was indicative of their positions that during

A 'hitherto-unpublished' photograph of von Richthofen.

Richthofen's interviews, Ludendorff's conversation turned upon the most effective way of killing the enemy, whereas von Hindenburg digressed upon the average number of shots necessary to kill a bison!

Evidently the Kaiser had received a brief upon Richthofen for he was congratulated firstly upon his fifty-second victory and secondly upon his twenty-fifth birthday. There followed a birthday present from the Emperor—a bust of the Kaiser himself—hardly a functional gift for an officer at the front! Formalities were by no means over; that evening the ageing von Hindenburg, who nevertheless was to outlive Manfred by nearly two decades, had arranged dinner for him. And for the following day, the Empress had expressed a wish to meet him.

At least the meeting with the Empress would be less formal. It entailed a flight to fashionable Bad Homburg where the Empress was in residence. Krefft flew the D.F.W. C V. and Manfred emerged from the passenger's cockpit to meet the Empress in his flying suit. She displayed interest in his machine and bade Manfred take off and demonstrate. After formalities were over and the Empress and her party had left, Richthofen and Krefft were admired by the population. At last they were free and could please themselves. They rejected many pressing invitations and went their separate ways—Krefft to his home and Richthofen to do some shooting!

Truly Manfred was a hunter. Few men, granted leave from the front, would give second place to home, unless there were a woman elsewhere to embrace. In this case, hunting was Manfred's love and so to Freiburg he flew, to tramp the Black Forest in search of game. It has been reported that he went to shoot capercallie. If so, it was rather a wanton occupation, for it was too early in the year

von Richthofen entering the 'passenger's seat' of an Albatros C IX aircraft he used for personal transport.

for the young birds to have grown and feasted upon the bilberries which give their meat a distinctive flavour, while, the old birds, having grubbed amongst the pines all winter and in the early spring, would have the unpalatable taste of turpentine. Perhaps the end product mattered not to Manfred. For most huntsmen, there must be a sense of service, a 'bag' to be distributed amongst the villagers and even fox-hunting is represented as necessary to keep that wild creature in check. What then did Manfred seek in shooting so early in the year? Boar perhaps; and as for his reason, possibly Cervantes had the answer. For when Sancho asked—'What pleasure can you find, any of ye, in killing a poor beast that never meant harm,' the reply was, 'You are mistaken, Sancho: hunting wild beasts is the most proper exercise for knights and princes; for in the chase of a stout noble beast, may be represented the whole art of war, stratagems, policy and ambuscades, with all other devices usually practised to overcome an enemy with safety. Here we are exposed to heat and cold; ease and laziness can have no room in this diversion. By this we are inured to toil and hardship; our limbs are strengthened, our joints made supple and our whole body made hale and active.' If this then, was Manfred's relaxation, at least he was free, temporarily, from the responsibilities of command and the threat of sudden death. In that alone, it was a holiday.

Meanwhile his mother at Schweidnitz, waited with pride and longing to welcome her famous son. Perhaps it was hard for her to understand why he had not already arrived. However, a letter on the 9th, a week after Manfred had left Douai, told of his excellent sport at Freiburg, the possibility of a tour of other fronts in the manner of Boelcke, his next move to Berlin for some three days to examine new aircraft at Adlershof and then, what his mother most wished to hear, his intention to journey to Schwiednitz. Then came the news, by telegram, that Lothar was wounded, worrying at first, but followed by assurances that it was not serious.

With warm enthusiasm, he was welcomed to his home-town. There, amongst the people he knew and understood, he accepted in good grace the displays in his honour—an official welcome, a demonstration by the local Boy Scouts and the inevitable stream of visitors.

During his stay at home he worked on the drafts of his book, for which he had hired the services of a shorthand-typist. Escorting that young lady from the house one day, he was stopped by two of the local 'busybodies' for a chat. Irritated by the delay and angered by their all too-obvious curiosity as to the identity of the lady, and by their pressing conversation working round to a direct question, he obliged them by presenting the lady as his bride—and then whisked her away down the road. Perhaps his administration of a similar rebuff was responsible for an announcement that appeared later in some Dutch newspapers—that Manfred Freiherr von Richthofen was engaged to Fräulein von Minkwitz, daughter of the Duke of Saxe-Coburg-Gotha's Master-of-Horse! He was the most eligible bachelor in all Germany—but he made light of his opportunities.

But he soon tired of inactivity and was away to take up a promise given during his visit to Headquarters, that he might shoot on the Pless Estates. The attraction there, to Manfred, was bison. Thrilled with such an opportunity he wrote enthusiastically that there were only two places in the world where one could find that almost extinct beast, a preserve in Russia and upon the Pless Estates. Thereby he missed an important link in Wegener's theory of floating continents, for in some of the national parks of North America, bison were reserved. Perhaps to him the name buffalo, applied there to the bison, implied a different species! If he had left the United States out of his calculations

The German Empress receiving von Richthofen at Bad Homburg on May 3rd, 1917.

von Richthofen (in leather flying jacket) in attendance on the Empress (centre). Note the mudguards on the D.F.W. C.V. in which he flew to Bad Homburg.

in that connection, that great Federation could not but have impinged upon his active mind on another matter. The United States had, but a month earlier, declared war upon Germany. There was no immediate effect, but its implications could be presaged. About this time, Manfred confided to his mother, that he could not see the way clear for ultimate victory. A bitter and distressing thought for so devoted a son of the Fatherland. It needed all the more courage to carry on. Perhaps his spirits were later bolstered by the promise of the great offensive planned for the spring of 1918, but there can be little doubt, that he had few illusions about his ultimate fate.

For the moment, his world was an estate where the buffalo roamed and the deer—but not the antelope—played! During the afternoon of May 26th he arrived at the Pless Estate, which had been visited by several of the crowned heads of Europe. Some idea of the magnitude of the estate can be gained from the fact that an hour's drive through part of it was first necessary. Then the party, foresters and drivers, left the road for a short tramp to a hide. Manfred received the treatment of a regal guest and was offered the hide, in an elevated position, from which his Emperor had often fired.

Once in position, the drivers were signalled and the shoot, in theory, was on. The bison, however, were not to be roused. They had not always hurried for crowned heads

The dark dresses of the Empress and her ladies in the photograph above, may be compared with the less formal attire of others who welcomed von Richthofen to Bad Homburg.

and they made no concession to the famous Rittmeister. When a large beast did eventually emerge from the timber, Manfred's keen eyes spotted it before the head forester. It lumbered straight for the hide, giving Manfred the feverish sensation that he experienced in the air when he sighted an enemy machine. Unhurried, the bison moved nearer. At 200 yards range, Manfred contemplated the expediency of firing. But because he wanted a clean kill, he waited, being not a little anxious of his reputation, should he miss. In waiting he lost his chance. The bull, perhaps sensing danger, or being frightened by drivers from behind, turned and rushed off at what seemed a terrific pace. Snorting, it made for the cover of nearby trees without presenting the opportunity for a killing shot.

Another wait, then a second bison, less wary appeared. Manfred fired when the range was about eighty yards. The bison still came on. A second shot, still without apparent effect—and then a final shot that caused the beast to stop in it's tracks, roll over—and die. All three bullets were embedded near the animal's heart. It was not, altogether, wanton destruction, since bison meat is only slightly inferior to beef and would provide a welcome addition to the wartime meat ration of the district.

June came with Manfred still on leave. His *Jasta*, however, were meeting with less opposition. After May 7th, the British thrusts of the Battle of Arras petered out and the main Allied effort was concentrated farther to the north where many R.F.C. units had been redeployed, to prepare for the Battle of Messines. Never had a battle opened in a louder or more awe-inspiring manner. For eighteen months tunnelling companies of the Royal Engineers had sapped under Messines Ridge. At 3.10 a.m., a full hour before sunrise on June 7th, nineteen mines, placed in the tunnels leading under the German positions, were exploded. Four-hundred tons of ammonal went up in under twenty seconds. Before the roar of the terrific explosions had died away, the British artillery bombardment, by over two-thousand guns commenced and the infantry assault by nine divisions opened. Lille was rocked as if by an earthquake and even in London the reverberation was felt.

von Richthofen (centre figure) with Lothar behind him. The sheds in the background are in fact hangars.

In the air the Germans were outnumbered by approximately two to one. There was redeployment and reorganisation in the German Air Service. Manfred was recalled to the front, both to provide a boost to morale and to play his prominent part in the new scheme of grouping certain *Jagdstaffeln*.

His return was not direct. There was more business at Adlershof, presumably in connection with the new Albatros D Vs. From there, he flew over to Krefeld to attend Schaefer's funeral and went onwards as instructed, to report again at Supreme Headquarters at Bad Kreuznach. There he was decorated by the King of Bulgaria with the Cross of Valour, but a more important reason for his attendance, was to confer with Colonel Thomsen on the subject of the new *Jagdgeschwader* scheme. First, he would be allowed a few days to pick up the threads of life on active service.

He arrived back on June 14th, the day Allmenröder received his *Pour le Mérite*, the fourth member of *Jasta 11* to receive that high award. But things were not the same. The old order was changing and he was not altogether happy with the new. Yet another of the old guard passed away three days later when Zeumer died, as he would have wished, in aerial combat, cheating a death from natural causes by only a few months as his condition had got much worse. The promising Vizefeldwebel with twelve victories, Sebastian Festner, had also been killed.

It was up to Richthofen to show that he had not lost his old skill and four days later he scored. He was back in form. Leading his *Staffel* in red Albatros D III *Nr. 789/17*, he attacked an artillery-spotting R.E.8. Firing at point-blank range, he was forced to jerk his control column back and lift his machine to prevent a collision. As he passed overhead, he saw both occupants of the R.E.8 slumped in their cockpits, apparently dead. Their machine fell in uncontrolled circles. Driven by the wind, it fell in a farmyard where the wreckage burned.

Since the main sphere of activity had moved northward, there were few British Corps aircraft required to operate on the Arras Front and *Jasta 11* found few chances to score. They had for once, a marked superiority in numbers, which they exploited by attempting to bait the British fighters and by harassing troops in ground-strafing attacks. Their opponents, however, were not to be drawn; they had the will but not the strength. Not only had that part of the British front been weakened by the redeployment of squadrons northward, but it had been further depleted due to a public outcry in Britain. Fourteen Gothas on the 13th had raided London in daylight, causing loss of life and damage, particularly in the East End. Public opinion was such that the military authorities were compelled to withdraw No. 56 Squadron (S.E.5s) to Bekesbourne, Kent and No. 66 Squadron (Sopwith Pups) to Calais for Home Defence duties.

The Ninth Wing R.F.C. was thereby left with only one fighter squadron, No. 19, whose efficiency was impaired by trouble with the 150 h.p. Hispano-Suiza engines of their Spad S.7s caused by excessive vibration and a defective lubricating system. Major Martinot Legarde of the French *Section Technique* had this matter under investigation, but his provisional advice, not to run the engines beyond 2,100 r.p.m. was a precaution, not a remedy. With that disadvantage, it is small wonder that No. 19 Squadron lost a little of their aggressiveness.

In the absence of local activity, Richthofen received permission to make offensive patrols northward in the Ypres area. Soon afterwards, base was moved from Douai to Marcke, preliminary to the new grouping.

At this stage, Richthofen changed over to an Albatros D V. Flying in *Nr. 1177/17* at the head of six of his machines in the late evening of June 23rd, he led over the Allied lines near Ypres. Sighting a late-flying patrol he headed the attack. His own victim, reported as a Spad, was evidently piloted by a novice, for with Richthofen firing burst after burst at close range, there was no sign of any attempt at evasion. The familiar pattern of events ensued, first a trail of smoke, then the uncontrolled descent, turning over and over until the inevitable crash into the ground.

Richthofen's claim received confirmation as his fifty-fourth, but historians have been sceptical of the claim, for both British and French records show that no Spads were missing that evening. Could Richthofen have been mistaken in the aircraft type? It is certainly true that his knowledge of British aircraft types was limited; he found especial difficulty in identifying the confusing, and indeed inappropriate, designations of the Royal Aircraft Factory—the B.Es., F.Es. and R.Es., but with distinctive French types such as Nieuports or Spads, he was rarely, if ever, in error.

The late evening light has been blamed for the confusion, but at 9.30 p.m. (the advance in German time would then equal British Summer Time) on Midsummer's Eve, the light at 5,000 feet would normally be good. The fact that Richthofen had yet to lead his men back to land before twilight, suggests too, that there was reasonably good visibility.

One explanation has not previously been mooted. The Spad might have been other than British or French! It is known that the Belgians had forty aircraft available at that time, albeit mainly artillery types. They did in fact have a few Spads alloted to them and the Belgian Army held part of the line north of Ypres, which was the region given in Richthofen's claim. This information provides by no means a conclusive explanation, but it does show a new possibility.

With Richthofen in position with *Jasta 11* at Marcke, opposite the active Ypres front, the new, much discussed grouping could be put into effect on receipt of the administrative instructions. The seal of authority came in a series of telegrams over the military telegraph system. Firstly, on June 24th, Telegram *Nr. Ic. 20706* from the Commander of Army Group, *Kronprinz Rupprecht*, gave notification that *Jasta 4, 6, 10* and *11* in the area of *Nr. 4* Army, were established as *Jagdgeschwader Nr. 1* (*J.G.1*) with immediate effect. Then, the following day, a telegram from Air Service Headquarters, *Kogenluft FIII Nr. 62880*, gave the brief, but necessary authority to the commander—Rittmeister Manfred Freiherr von Richthofen appointed commander *J.G.1*.

That day, as if to open the scoring, Richthofen flew with Allmenröder on an offensive patrol. They often flew together. On this occasion each stalked an artillery-spotting R.E.8 and both put in victory claims. The wings of Richthofen's victim broke off under his fire. It fell, a blazing wreck, near Le Bizet. To ensure confirmation, he flew low over the local observation post at La Montagne, waving to the watchers.

A slight delay in confirmation, resulted in that victory on June 25th, becoming officially his 56th, whereas his 55th was in fact achieved the following day. The latter was a bold attack upon two reconnaissance R.E.8s escorted by ten fighters. Before the fighters could take up their protective role, Manfred had cunningly positioned his flight. Their attack was both swift and sure. Richthofen, himself, claimed one of the R.Es. which broke up under his fire. The fuselage crashed into a farm building a few thousand yards east of Zillebeke.

That day, June 26th, *J.G.1* received its charter from *Kogenluft* in a telegram referring to Order *Nr. Ic. 5834-1op* dated 23.6.17 from the Chief of Staff of the Army. The text read—'*Jagdgeschwader Nr. 1* comprises *Jasta 4, 6, 10* and *11* (Stop) The *Geschwader* is a self-contained unit (Stop) Duty is to attain and maintain air supremacy in Sectors of the Front as directed (Message ends).' The final sentence was especially significant. Therein was the intention to deploy the *Geschwader* as the situation in the air dictated. It was to be moved along the front as required. A liberal establishment of transport was in fact allowed to ensure that mobility. The term 'Circus' that the bright colours had evoked from the R.F.C. seemed quite apt!

J.G.1 was centred around Courtrai. At Marcke, Richt-

Left to right: Joachim Wolff, Bodenschatz, von Richthofen with dog, Gussmann, another and Steinhäuser.

Left to right: Festner, Schaefer, Manfred, Lothar, Kurt Wolff.

hofen had his headquarters, together with *Jasta 11*. The other units comprising the *Geschwader*, were at Cuene (*Jasta 4*), Bisseghem (*Jasta 6*) and Heule (*Jasta 10*). On paper, a *Geschwader* had been created. The unit that was to develop into the most famous and the most feared, air-fighting formation in history, was born. But it was only the beginning. There was much yet to be done. In *Jasta 11* there was a sound foundation and the other units each showed promise, but so far there had been little attempt at co-ordinating action between *Jagdstaffeln*. The welding of four individual units into a corporate formation had yet to be effected.

Richthofen chose his subordinate leaders and key personnel with care. Since he himself would spend much time in the air, a dependable adjutant was needed and in Oberleutnant Bodenschatz,* known to Richthofen in *Jasta 2*, he found his man. Having provided well for the administration of his men, he left the care of the machines to Leutnant Krefft, whose appointment was that of technical officer.

Leading a *Staffel* was an exacting task and in an elité formation such as the *Geschwader* a unit commander needed to be something of a paragon. Richthofen saw to it that he was! A shrewd judge of character, he selected his leaders with care—not hesitating to change them if the need arose.

Jasta 11 he left in the young but capable hands of Kurt Wolff. Possibly the command might have devolved upon Allmenröder, had he not been killed the day after the *Geschwader* officially formed. He fell in combat, on June 27th, the victim of a long range shot by a British pilot. His machine at first glided down, but the glide became a dive that ended in a crash between the lines in the Ypres area. The night following a German infantry-patrol brought his body in and Allmenröder was buried at his home-town of Solingen-Wald. He had been devoted to Richthofen. A few days before he fell he wrote these words in a letter to his sister—'You beg me urgently to take leave, but the situation at the front is similar to that at Arras last spring. I would find no rest with you. Richthofen and I fly ever together,

---

* Herr Bodenschatz, happily still living, has been consulted on several occasions in connection with this work.

Jagdgeschwader Nr. 1. 1-3 unknown, 4 von Rautter, 5 Aue, 6 Just, 7 Wolff, 8 Kuhn, 9 Friedrichs, 10 Gussmann, 11 Manfred von Richthofen, 12 Loewenhardt, 13 Bodenschatz, 14 Reinhard, 15 Wenzel, 16 Janzen, 17 Kirschstein, 18 Tüxen, 19 von Gluczewski, 20 von der Osten.

one watching the other. We have many newcomers in the unit and I am one of the few remaining old-hands. You can imagine that he would not like me to go and that at the moment, I would not wish to go.'

Jasta 4 was in the hands of Oberleutnant Kurt von Doering, who, with the relatively low score of three victories, nevertheless had a distinguished military career to warrant his privileged position.

Oberleutnant Eduard von Dostler commanding *Jasta 6* was a Bavarian, born at Pollenstein on February 3rd, 1892. Soldiering was his career and Bodenschatz, an old comrade of his, described him as stocky, solid, broad-shouldered and handsome, well endowed with 'Kommiss'—soldier-like qualities. Before transferring to the Air Service he had served in Pioneer Battalions and after learning to fly at Schleissheim in July 1916, he had served in *Schutzstaffeln 27* and *36*. In the former unit he had shot down the well-known French bomber pilot Capitaine Robert de Beauchamp over Bezonvaux near Verdun in December 1916. Later, having proved his ability as a fighter pilot in *Jasta 34*, he became leader of that *Jasta*. His transfer to the command of *Jasta 6* was at Richthofen's own request.

Jasta 10 had a leader of note in Ernst Freiherr von Althaus, the son of the adjutant to His Highness the Duke of Saxe-Coburg-Gotha. Born in Coburg on March 19th, 1890, he joined a Saxon Hussar Regiment at Grossenhain in 1909, receiving a lieutenancy two years later. As early in the war as January 1915 he had won the highest Saxon award, the Knight's Cross of the Order of St. Heinrich. In the Air Service in 1916 he was famous as a Fokker pilot and had been awarded the *Pour le Mérite*. Meritorious service was behind the brief entry in the *Jagdgeschwader* record book: *6.7.17 Oblt. Frhr. v. Althaus von Jasta 14 zu Jasta 10 als Führer.*

Inspection: 1 Reinhard, 2 Schaeffer, 3 Lothar von Richthofen, 4 Groos, 5 Mohnicke, 6 Wilberg (KoFl.), 7 Meyer, 8 Müller, 9 unknown, 10 von der Osten, 11 Gerstenberg, 12 Manfred von Richthofen, 13 Wilberg's adjutant, 14 Bodenschatz.

66

The Ringmaster Falls

CHAPTER SEVENTEEN

Father and son. Major Albrecht, Frieherr von Richthofen with his famous eldest son, during a visit to the Hospital of St. Nicholas in Courtrai; after his son had received his head-wound in July 1917.

The units soon settled in, but *Jasta 10*, having suffered a number of recent casualties, was for a short time, below establishment for pilots. At Marckebeeke, a chateau was taken over to provide quarters and an officers' mess, and in a requisitioned house, No. 74 Courtrai Street, an orderly room was established. A local watching post was also set up, equipped with a stereo-telescope and a rangefinder.

Notwithstanding the amount of administrative work in hand, Richthofen made time to fly. He was apparently alone, when, on July 2nd, he attacked the foremost of several R.E.8s out on reconnaissance. With his first shots the observer collapsed and shortly afterwards the pilot was mortally wounded. The R.E. fell as Richthofen continued firing at close range until it burst into flames.

But, the new *Geschwader* was hardly organised before Richthofen himself—was shot down! It was on the morning of July 6th. *Jasta 4* had already been on patrol and Kurt Wolff, who had also been up on patrol, was writing out a claim for his thirty-second victory, when a report came from the front of British aircraft. Richthofen himself led *Jasta 11* in the air and headed for the lines, but the sky was clear. They were more than a match for the machines they eventually encountered, six F.E.2ds from No. 20 Squadron R.F.C., but it was no walkover. The F.Es., forming up in a defensive circle, put up a magnificent fight. From a watching post of the *Flugmeldedienst*, an officer likened it to terriers worrying a hedgehog as the machines weaved and pirouetted.

More German machines arrived until some forty were ranged against the F.Es., but help came to the hard-pressed British machines, when four Sopwith Triplanes of No. 10 (Naval) Squadron dropped in. Without loss to themselves, they drove four German machines down, one of which was observed to crash. But the odds against the F.Es. were too great; two fell and of those remaining, one carried a wounded observer.

Gamely, the remaining F.Es. edged over to the British side of the lines. In one of them, piloted by Captain D. C. Cunnell, the observer 2nd/Lieutenant A. E. Woodbridge, had kept up an accurate and spirited fire throughout. He claimed four enemy machines as shot down out of control and in his account of the fight, reported that another spun away—that was Richthofen. The range, some 300 yards, was too distant for accurate fire and Woodbridge, although aiming at the red Albatros D V did not feel justified in claiming it. Richthofen, too, would not have been unduly worried at being fired at from that range.

Nevertheless, Richthofen was hit—wounded in the head. He blacked out and his machine went into a vertical dive, until at barely 500 feet, he regained consciousness and managed to check its descent. Light-headed from shock, he fought against the swooning sensation which again threatened to overwhelm him, realising only too well that at such a low altitude, even a momentary loss of consciousness would almost inevitably lead to disaster. By sheer effort of will he forced his machine down to a landing near Wervicq and staggering from the cockpit, collapsed. His Albatros D V, *Nr. D1177/17*, was badly damaged and for a while he remained still, close by it. Blood flowed from a wound in his head, filling his helmet. His face was white and his eyes were closed. Those first upon the scene feared the worst.

An officer of the *Flugmeldedienst*, Leutnant Schröder, had witnessed the fight from the ground, through a telescope. He had seen Richthofen's machine falter and fall; he saw too, the Albatros D Vs of two of his officers, Leutnant Brauneck and Leutnant Niederhoff, follow their leader down and then circle over the spot where he had crashed. The crash occurred only a mile from Schröder's post at La

von Richthofen, with head bandaged, is visited in hospital by pilots of his newly formed Geschwader. To the left is a recent trophy, the propeller from a British aircraft that had been shot down.

Mortaigne. Schröder, together with a corporal, ran quickly to the spot. Panting, they arrived to find Richthofen lying quite still beside his machine. Taking off his helmet and loosening his collar, they applied a field dressing to the back of his head—a dressing, in a sealed package, was a compulsory item of kit on active service. The corporal was ordered to run to the nearest field telephone and ring for an ambulance. Meanwhile Richthofen had regained his senses. Some local troops having arrived, he was offered a swig of cognac, but wisely he asked for water. It is one of the fundamental rules of first aid that stimulants should not be given where there is bleeding. Richthofen asked to be taken to Courtrai at once.

An ambulance arrived and Richthofen, then in a feverish state, was placed inside. He called alternately for the window shutters to be opened and closed as he felt hot and cold in turn. No doubt he was suffering considerably from the effects of shock, since a wound in the head can have such terrible implications. Reaching Menin, the ambulance turned into an aid post. But Richthofen had his own ideas on where he should receive attention. A doctor was called and Richthofen repeated his request—'I want to go to Courtrai—please hurry.' The doctor, presumably because Richthofen was his senior, shrugged his shoulders and the ambulance moved off again—to Courtrai.

There, he was taken to the St. Nicholas's hospital, administered by the Germans as *Feldlazarett Nr. 76*. It was discovered that a bullet had grazed the left side of his skull, exposing the bone. An anaesthetic was administered and his head was shaved to permit an examination. The bullet had furrowed along the skull and without penetrating had splintered the bone. Careful nursing was needed and his nurse, Fräulein Kätie Otersdorf, proved to be not only capable, but also pretty.

The personnel of *Jagdgeschwader Nr. 1* were stunned by their leader's sudden downfall, but war is relentless. Oberleutnant von Doering was appointed that same day to the temporary command of the *Geschwader*. He supervised several offensive patrols on the morrow and they were attended with considerable success. It was almost as if they were inspired by a spirit of revenge. Elements of *Jasta 4* and *Jasta 11* opened the day with a devasting attack upon a formation of Sopwith Triplanes. The result is summed up in the grim statistical record-book of the formations—11.00 a.m. to Leutnant Wolff his thirty-third victory, 11.05 a.m. to Leutnant Krüger his first victory, 11.10 a.m. to Leutnant Niederhoff his fourth victory. Less than half an hour afterwards, Vizefeldwebel Krebs was destroying an R.E.8 to make his sixth victory. During the afternoon, the *Geschwader* not only repeated their success, but added to it, by obtaining five victories—Oberleutnant Dostler shot down a Sopwith at midday for his fourteenth, Vizefeldwebel Clausnitzer destroyed a Nieuport for his

von Richthofen is visited in hospital by the officer who was destined to succeed him—Oblt. Reinhard.

third, Leutnant Klein gained his fourteenth and Leutnant Anders and Vizefeldwebel Lautenschlager both scored their first victories.

Kurt Wolff, the young leader who had taken Richthofen's place at the head of *Jasta 11*, had opened the scoring that day. His victim had fallen near Comines and he landed alongside to collect a memento, as he, like his predecessor, had a mania for souvenirs. In fact, souvenir-collecting was a craze of that era. Perhaps too, in the case of Richthofen and Wolff, they required something more tangible of their own as evidence, instead of a mere entry in an official book, that was the property of their Fatherland.

Comines and Werwicq, being equidistant from La Mortaigne, Leutnant Schröder again came on the scene, this time strolling. There was little left of Wolff's victim except a charred wreckage, leaving no fabric with a roundel or serial number to collect. Wolff had to be content with the number plate on the blackened metallic mass that had been a Clerget engine. Whilst trying to prise it off, Schröder arrived. They chatted. Wolff learnt that Schröder had got into trouble by leaving his post to go to Richthofen's aid and there was threat of a court-martial. Schröder was assured that Richthofen would see him in the clear—and it was indeed so.

It was a warm day and the exertion of removing the number plate—which incidentally it was Schröder's duty to note—had made Wolff perspire. As if on a picnic, he went to his machine—and pulled out a bottle of mineral water from which he took swigs. In grim contrast, Schröder remarked upon the charred body of the pilot. Wolff then revealed his philosophy to the grim realities of war by the words—'It was either him or me—I would rather it was him.'

The next day brought rain giving all the pilots a rest and not until the 11th was there much aerial activity. It started in the early morning with the R.F.C. raiding Bisseghem, destroying three tented hangars and damaging two machines of *Jasta 6*. In the afternoon, the tables were turned by *Jasta 4* out on a balloon-strafe. Leutnant Klein shot down two kite-balloons within a space of as many minutes, credited to him as his fifteenth and sixteenth victories. A few minutes later Vizefeldwebel Wüsthoff made it three, which was also his personal score. Leutnant Mohnicke too, scored his third victory that day.

There was one casualty that day, none other than Kurt Wolff. He had retired from a fight during the morning after a bullet had passed through his left hand. He was taken to Courtrai, examined, bandaged and put to bed—and in the bed adjacent, was his Rittmeister, Manfred Freiherr von Richthofen.

Klein, who that day had shot down two balloons, was one of the first 'Circus Stars'. He was born in Stettin on January 17th, 1891, one of seven children of a local businessman. He graduated from the Schiller-Real-Gymnasium to the Friedrich-Wilhelm-Realgymnasium and finally to the Technical High School in Berlin-Charlottenburg, where his studies were abruptly terminated by the contraction of war-fever! War came during a vacation and immediately he volunteered and drilled with 34th Infantry Regiment in Stettin. Six weeks later he was transferred to the 210th Reserve Infantry Regiment and with that unit he arrived

von Richthofen with his nurse, Fräulein Kätie Otersdorf in the grounds of St. Nicholas's hospital (Feldlazarett Nr. 76) *in Courtrai.*

on the Western Front early October 1914.

By distinguishing himself in a patrol action, Klein had received promotion to lance-corporal by October 26th and early the following month he was further promoted to sergeant! A lieutenancy was granted in March 1915 and as an officer he remained with his regiment a full year before leaving to train as a pilot at FEA 2, Cöslin. Having passed all his examinations, he went on to train for fighters at Cologne, reaching *Jasta 4*, then under the command of Hauptmann Buddeke, in November 1916.

Flying Albatros D IIs, D IIIs and later D Vs, he saw action over several battle-fronts. It was during the Battle of Arras, on April 4th, 1917, that he scored his first victory, and from that time, he scored steadily. When his Jasta was grouped to form *J.G.1*, he had already scored twelve victories. Coming under Richthofen's eye, he was soon marked as a potential *Staffelführer*, but a week after Richthofen received his wound, Klein too was wounded, albeit lightly, but necessitating his removal to hospital. When he was fit enough to return to active service, Richthofen saw to it that his posting was back to *J.G.1*.

CHAPTER EIGHTEEN

Grand Performances

von Richthofen as a right-marker for the four holders of the Pour le Mérite, at a parade, August 1917.

With two of the star members of the Circus absent, the bright skies of the next day, July 12th, 1917, brought the greatest activity ever in the air up to that time. The R.F.C. admitted that nine of their aircraft fell in the German lines that day, of which, the Circus could claim seven by their performances; four to *Jasta 6* and three to *Jasta 4*. In the latter unit, two members made their initial scores, Leutnant Hübner and Vizefeldwebel Marquardt, but one of their comrades fell, Vizefeldwebel Patermann who, but the day before, had claimed a Spad for his second victory.

The climax came in the evening when the Allies regained their prestige. A large formation of German aircraft had attracted a number of British and French fighter patrols, until some sixty aircraft were engaged, twisting and turning as each one manœuvred, either to gain a position to fire—or to evade the fire of another. Seemingly, they were more skilful at evasion than attack, for the battle lasted a full hour and at the end of it only two aircraft, both German, had been destroyed! Although many of the Allied machines had been hit, all the pilots landed safely. When fighters were ranged against fighters in approximately equal numbers, it was no easy matter to obtain decisive results.

For the Circus, there followed a spate of casualties. On the 13th, Leutnant Klein, the star performer of *Jasta 4* was wounded and three days later, another man of that unit, Vizefeldwebel Clausnitzer was forced down by three British Spad S.7s whilst he was attempting to destroy a kite-balloon. Clausnitzer was taken prisoner, but for another Vizefeldwebel, Krebs of *Jasta 6*, there was no eventual return to the Fatherland; Krebs fell to the guns of Captain G. H. Bowman from No. 56 Squadron. Another black day followed, Leutnant Krüger, with one victory—Sopwith Triplane N6291 destroyed ten days earlier—fell mortally wounded and died in hospital. Leutnant Meyer too, was a casualty, but his wound was slight.

The run of bad luck ended on the 20th with a score of five without loss. One, a R.E.8, was the initial score of Leutnant Walter Stock, or 'Stock Walter' as he appeared in official reports; the Christian name being warranted by the fact that two officers in *Jasta 6* bore that English sounding name. Two other victories were of much greater significance. One was a Sopwith Pup as the initial score of Leutnant Freiherr von Boenigk who was to rise to become a leader, as well as to account for some twenty-six Allied aircraft and the other was the sixth victory of Vizefeldwebel Wüsthoff, whose victim was classified as having flown a 'Sopwith new type'. Thus was the famous Sopwith Camel heralded. At that time only No. 70 Squadron R.F.C. and No. 6 (Naval) Squadron had Camels, but it was scheduled to re-equip all Sopwith 1½ Strutter squadrons and then gradually, as production permitted, the scale increased. Tricky to fly, it was superior in performance to the Albatros D Vs and with it, British pilots were to shoot down more German aircraft than with any other type of machine—in fact 1,294.

But the German Flying Service too, was to receive new equipment. Richthofen himself brought the news to his *Geschwader* of the pending deliveries of Antony Fokker's new triplane, then entering production at Schwerin. Richthofen accompanied by Wolff had visited Marcke from hospital. Both were then up-patients, chafing at their enforced inactivity, but the doctors were adamant. They

Lt. Adam, who shot down a Camel on November 6th, 1917 for his twenty-first victory, was himself shot down by a Camel pilot making his first offensive patrol, nine days later.

With von Richthofen in the centre of a group, this is very much a posed picture for the German Press. Left to right—Schubert, Scholz, Steinhäuser, von Linsingen, Esser, von der Osten, Mohnicke, Lübbert, von Boddin and Gussman.

languished in the hospital by the Lys, occasionally strolling in the *Parc due Peuple* or the *Cercle Musical*. It was not the best of times for either rest or sight-seeing in that ancient town of Courtrai. Although it was in a back area of the front and little had disturbed the tenor of its citizens since 1382, the activity on the Ypres front made it an important base on the German lines of communication. Its station became an important military target and the basing of *Jagdgeschwader Nr. 1* in the vicinity attracted several bombing attacks.

Indirectly, the town had particular significance to Richthofen, for it was the centre of the Flanders flax growing industry, a commodity in increasing demand for aircraft fabric. In general, Germany had to be content with fabric of inferior quality to Courtrai linen, due to disrupted production in the ravaged areas near to Ypres, but for special machines, such as the first production Fokker Dr Is destined for *J.G.1*, the restricted Courtrai linen was used.

Richthofen arrived back at Marcke on July 25th to resume command the next day. His arrival was heralded with a bang, for No. 100 Squadron R.F.C. had started another phase of night-bombing. Five F.E.2bs had set out two nights before and failed to locate the airfield, but on the night of the 25th it was located by one F.E. from which a 230 lb. bomb was dropped, just wide of the hangars.

On one of these attacks, a returning F.E.2b pilot observed that the airfield at Bisseghem was lit up as if for night-flying. There is no record of any *J.G.1* unit attempting night-interception, although, before the *Geschwader* was formed, there is evidence from the ex-telephonist of *Jasta 4*, that during April 1917, Leutnant Klein did achieve a victory

Oblt. Dostler, commanding Jasta 6, who fell to the gunner of an R.E.8 on August 21st, 1917, had previously claimed at least three R.E.8s in his total score of twenty-six.

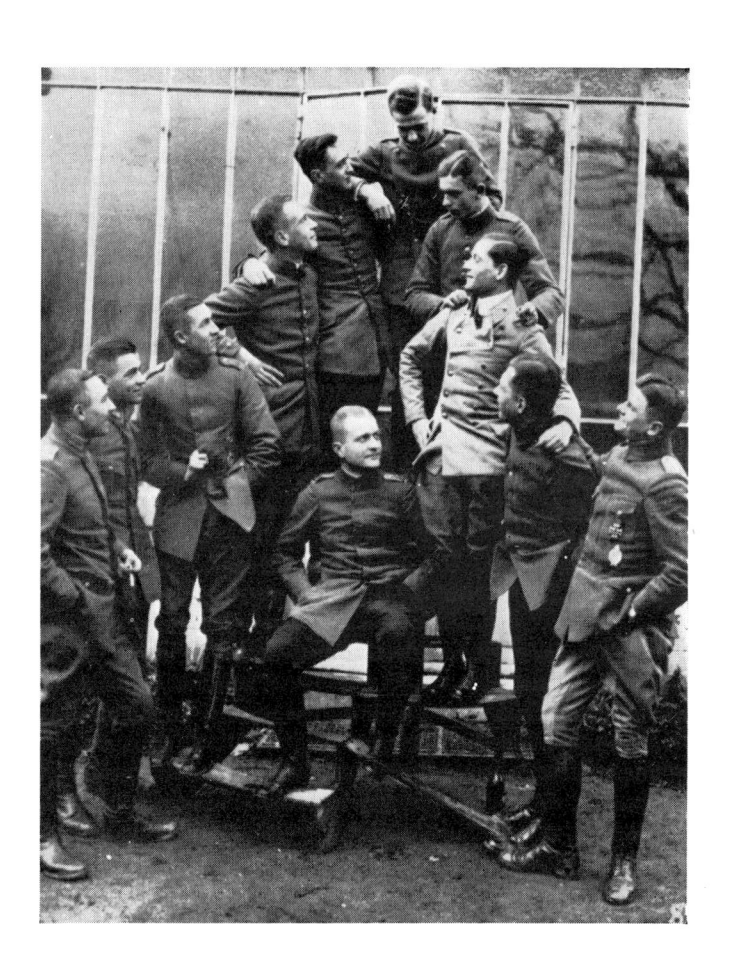

at night. At that time at Douai, *Jasta 4* shared the airfield with *Jasta 11*. When two British bombing aircraft were attacking Douai, Leutnant Klein, without helmet or flying coat, ran to his Albatros and took-off. He was guided by the glow from the exhaust pipes of the bomber's engine, at which he aimed. The bomber, with its engine disabled, went down, suffering little damage in its landing. That is the only known night victory by a *Jagdgeschwader Nr. 1* pilot.

One of Richthofen's first tasks was to be briefed on the formation's activities during his absence. He had been kept in the picture by frequent visitors, but there had been little chance, or indeed encouragement from the hospital staff, to study the situation. July 22nd had been an auspicious day. Eight machines from *Jasta 11* had broken up a formation of six Sopwith 1½ Strutters from No. 45 Squadron, one of which fell to Leutnant Niederhoff and a second to an officer making his initial score, Oberleutnant Reinhard. Another initial-scorer that day was Vizefeldwebel Heldmann, who shot down a R.E.8 over Deulemont.

The leader of *Jasta 4*, Oberleutnant von Doering had scored two, destroying a Spad and a Nieuport.

During the evening of the day on which Richthofen returned a series of air battles developed, until from Polygon Wood about one hundred aircraft could be counted, of which over ninety were single-seat fighters engaged in combat. *Jasta 11* were in action and without achieving any victories, suffered the loss of a veteran, Leutnant Brauneck. The tempo of air-fighting was rising— and it took its toll.

At midday, two days later, another veteran by 1917

The first of the famous Fokker Triplanes to be handed over to the German Air Service: Fokker FI 102/17. It was first flown by A. H. G. Fokker.

standards, fell. Leutnant Niederhoff was shot down. There were two thorns in particular, in the sides of *Jagdgeschwader Nr. 1*. They were Nos. 56 and 100 Squadrons R.F.C. The one attacking by day and the other by night. It was a No. 56 Squadron member, Lieutenant R. T. C. Hoidge, with fourteen victories to his credit, who had killed Niederhoff of *Jasta 11* and it was F.E.2bs of No. 100 Squadron which bombed that unit's base both the preceding and the following night. In the first of these two attacks little was achieved, as only one 230 lb. and two 20 lb. bombs were dropped, but in the second, considerable damage was caused. One 230 lb. bomb, dropped from 1,000 feet hit a hangar and six 20 lb. bombs dropped close to tented hangars, caused damage to aircraft by flying fragments. Another 230 lb. bomb shattered the windows and brought some of the ceilings down in the chateau.

Three days later, July 31st, the Battle of Ypres opened, forcing aerial activity in adverse weather conditions. Richthofen first became aware of the new offensive when the airfield at Marcke was attacked by Martinsyde Elephants of No. 27 Squadron. Six had set out from Clairmarais at 4.30 that morning, carrying 20 lb. bombs. At 10 a.m. six more left for the same objective, accompanied almost as far as Courtrai by a further six directed to Heule. Then at 2 p.m. the attacks on both Marcke and Heule were repeated. In connection with the bombing, fighter patrols by Squadrons 19 (Spads), 56 (S.E.5s) and 70 (Camels) provided cover, lest *J.G.1* should rise to the occasion. They did not. Their five victories that day were easier game; 2 R.E.8s, 1 F.E., a Nieuport making Oberleutnant Dostler's twenty-first victory and a Bristol F2B as Leutnant Hübner's second.

In view of the activity that day it was not a very spirited performance for *J.G.1*, but they had been instructed at mid-morning to stand-by to give support over the lines, in view of the British offensive. The weather too, was partly responsible and also the fact that several of the pilots were attending St. Joseph's Church in Courtrai, where Leutnant Niederhoff's funeral service was conducted. Only two days before they had assembled there to pay their last respects to Leutnant Brauneck.

Certainly the R.F.C. were spirited that day and the Circus's most formidable adversaries, No. 56 Squadron, were out in strength in a new role of ground-strafing, with *J.G.1* bases as their primary target. The report of but one of their pilots typifies their offensive spirit. Lieutenant Mayberry, took off from Estreé Blanche in his S.E.5A at 4.45 a.m. He headed for the lines with little altitude because of low, black clouds, but due to the heavy artillery bombardment supporting the infantry attack just launched, a heavy pall of smoke covered the lines, precluding ground observation. Thereupon Mayberry, still flying low, detoured to the south-east and located Wervicq, focal point of so much aerial activity.

Wervicq, close to the front, with five trunk roads branching from it as well as being a rail junction, could not fail to be a useful landmark for both sides. It also marked the Franco–Belgian frontier, but at the time, that had little territorial significance. Having checked his position, Mayberry then went down to 30 feet and flew along the road to Gheluwe! Such was the devastation in the area, that not one of the poplars, that had once lined the route, remained standing to challenge his progress at that height.

The pilots of No. 56 Sqn. R.F.C. were a thorn in the side of J.G.1, and in particular, Lt. Mayberry shown here in his S.E.5A.

Another view of Fokker FI 102/17. After being flown by von Richthofen it was flown by Kurt Wolff, who crashed in it to his death.

Courtrai was his next landmark and from there he turned north-east to strike at Heule, but two German fighters from the direction of Courtrai headed him off. Mayberry did not want a fight—yet. His machine was carrying four 20 lb. Cooper bombs that he had every intention of placing—selectively. To dissuade the enemy machines from approaching, he fired short bursts from the Lewis gun mounted on his top wing, but the German machines were not to be diverted. He made west to shake them off and then turned back again to Heule.

Circling the airfield, the only activity he could see was a man lighting two smoke fires at one end of the aerodrome, presumably to obscure the sheds from view, but it had little effect. This man concerned seemed not in the least perturbed, and by Mayberry's account, the field appeared otherwise deserted. He soon stirred up some activity, however! After turning to make a bombing run in, he dived over a line of sheds, dropping the first of his bombs, hitting the third shed in line. Figures could then be observed running out of the sheds. Mayberry turned again and aimed his second bomb at another shed, again scoring a hit. Flying over to the far end of the field he tried for yet another shed. Observing smoke pouring out of the side of that one, he presumed his bomb had gone through the roof. Machine-gun fire then opened up from the ground as he turned to drop his final bomb—but when he pulled the toggle nothing happened. He flew straight on and as he came over Courtrai station, he thought it a good place in which to test the release again—the bomb, his fourth and last, fell between a goods train and a building.

Mayberry had got rid of his bombs, but he was by no means finished—he still had bullets. So back to Heule he went, whereupon machine-gun fire again came up at him from the same gun-post, supported by fire from another position. He dived on the first location dispersing the crew, but he could not locate the second. Thinking how best to effect maximum damage he decided to make low runs across the field, firing at the sheds. His first run was at a height of about twenty feet. As he turned for his second run, so he changed the Lewis-gun drum. On his next run he came so low that he felt a bump—he had actually hit the ground! Literally, he was making a ground-level attack! Firing bursts into the mouths of the open-ended sheds, that housed the aircraft of *Jasta 10*, he followed up by zooming over the sheds and flying on to Cuerne, the base of *Jasta 4*!

At Cuerne, mechanics were just wheeling a machine out when Mayberry arrived, coming in low across the field with both guns firing. They wheeled it back again—so Mayberry observed! Leaving the airfield, on his way back, he spotted two men on horse-back and presuming them to be German officers he sent a few shots in their direction and had the satisfaction of seeing the horses bolt. Skirting Bisseghem, apparently without stirring up *Jasta 6*, he shot up a troop of infantry marching along a road. As if that were not enough, he made for a German two-seater aircraft he sighted above him—at 500 feet, just below the clouds. Climbing he got into position behind and under its tail. Aiming upwards with the Lewis gun mounted on the top wing, he discharged almost half a drum, some twenty rounds, into the enemy machine, which evaded by going down in a steep left-hand turn. As it straightened out, Mayberry opened up with his Vickers gun and the machine went down. With precision he gave its fate and location as having crashed just north of the railway, south of the 'g' in Wevelghem! Mayberry circled to observe the wreckage

von Richthofen, standing behind General von Lossberg, listens to Anthony Fokker seated in the cockpit of the triplane which is being demonstrated, and is to be handed over to him as his personal aircraft.

Following von Richthofen's Fokker Triplane FI 102/17 on the production line was Werner Voss's FI 103/17, seen here finished in a silver-blue paint and with a face marked on the engine cowling.

noticing that only one man got out. As a crowd gathered round he went down again with guns blazing. Having dispersed them he continued his belligerent mood by firing at a passenger train steaming into Courtrai, which was a troop detraining station. Not surprisingly he found he was out of ammunition. There was nothing more he could do, so he returned to his base. Such was the spirit of the men Richthofen and his personnel faced. Theirs was no mean task and well they knew it.

The bad weather, rain and storms, continued for four days. Not until August 4th could the *Jagdgeschwader* claim a victory and that in an isolated fight giving Leutnant Hübner his third. The wet, cloying soil of Flanders, the curse of the infantry, made the airfields on the flat country by the Lys, a sea of mud. Few patrols were detailed, but two determined men of *Jasta 4*, who were destined to win fame, braved the elements and both scored. They were Leutnant von Boenigk and Leutnant Wüsthoff.

Oskar Freiherr von Boenigk's determination was to lead him to a generalship in the *Luftwaffe*. Like Richthofen he was born into Silesian nobility and followed the traditional profession of a Prussian nobleman by entering the Army. That was on March 22nd, 1912. As a lieutenant he went to war in 1914 with *Grenadier-Regt. Nr. 11 'King Frederick III'*, sustaining wounds in the first month of hostilities. The following October he was back at the front, taking his part as an infantry officer in the battles of Champagne, Loretto and Arras.

His flying commenced late in 1915, first as an observer. On March 1st, 1916 he joined *Kampfstaffel Nr. 32*, taking part in bombing raids on Dunkirk and along the Western Front. During 1917 he learnt to fly and he was posted to *Jasta 4*.

Kurt Wüsthoff, who was born January 27th, 1898 in Aachen, was the son of music-director, Ferdinand Wüsthoff. At Dresden, where the family later settled, Kurt studied art and his pale, gentle features with soft, dreamy eyes, gave the impression of a sensitive student. Of sixteen years, when war broke out, there was little required of him, although he had passed his examinations and volunteered. When eventually he was accepted for air-training at *FEA6* and passed the tests—he was too young for service at the front. Therefore he was retained as a flying instructor—at the age of seventeen! Pressing for active service when he became of age, he served first at *K.G.1* at Ostend and later saw service in France, Bulgaria, Rumania and Salonica. He joined *Jasta 4* as a Vizefeldwebel obtaining his lieutenancy on August 1st, 1917.

Several replacements arrived at *J.G.1* about that time. From the 4th Army Park came freshly trained pilots to replace casualties; Leutnant Koch and Vizefeldwebel Stumpf to *Jasta 6* and Leutnant Graul to *Jasta 4*. There was also a change in leadership. Oberleutnant Frieherr von Althaus, who less than a month before had been brought in from *Jasta 14*, was posted to give the benefit of his operational experience to *Jastaschule II* (Fighter School No. 2). He had been in action since the beginning of the war and was long overdue for a rest from service at the front. Richthofen, ever careful in his selection of leaders, requested as replacement a Leutnant Voss, who was also from *Jasta 14*. On the last day of July, *Kogenluft* gave authority for the change, posting Leutnant Voss to *Jasta 10* as commander.

It would be a hard matter to decide who was the greater man, Richthofen, or his nearest competitor during his life for the title of leading ace—Werner Voss. If flying and fighting qualities alone were the criteria, then Voss was the most accomplished of the two. He was a born flyer.

Lt. Otto Brauneck, a founder-member of the Geschwader *and victor of nine combats, fell a victim to No. 70 Sqn. R.F.C. on July 26th, 1917. The crude wooden steps by which a pilot mounted his aircraft is worthy of note.*

With Voss as the central figure, this photograph symbolises the partial transition in J.G.1, during August/September 1917, of their aircraft types in service. This involved the fundamental differences in configuration of biplane to triplane, and experience with in-line to rotary engines.

Richthofen, on the other hand, had to work hard to achieve a position that Voss attained almost instinctively. Richthofen was the cold, calculating type, who weighed quickly the chances before engaging in combat. When he attacked, he was putting into effect a pre-conceived plan. If he deviated from a method he found himself in danger. This had just happened and he had received his head wound. A second and last time was when he met his end. Inevitably, Richthofen would be the better known, by attaining the higher score, but he was, too, a born leader, and this could not be said of Voss. Voss was a born fighter.

Werner Voss was the son of a dye-factory owner of Krefeld in the Rhineland. First he served in the 2nd Westphalian Hussar Regiment, nicknamed the 'Dance-Hussars', transferring to the flying service in the August of 1915. Flying at first as an observer he became a pilot in May 1916, serving his 'apprenticeship' at *Jasta 2* under Boelcke's guidance. He began his career as a coming ace by a double victory on November 27th, 1916 and by the following March he had a score of 14. No mean achievement for that early period. A month later he was rewarded with a *Pour le Mérite*.

An example of his dash is evident from an incident that occurred in the spring of 1917, just after the German withdrawal to the Hindenburg Line. He brought down a British B.E. between the lines but there were no witnesses to confirm his victory. Thereupon he landed beside the damaged aircraft, removed a machine-gun and took off over the heads of a British patrol. With such evidence his victory was acknowledged!

von Richthofen's association with Werner Voss began in Jasta Boelcke. This photograph was taken when Voss, still a member of that Jasta, visited Richthofen's Jasta 11, early in 1917. At Richthofen's instigation Voss was later posted to J.G.1.

Voss was a curious fellow with little interest other than aircraft and flying. Whenever possible, wearing an old grey jacket, he tinkered with his aircraft. But, when he flew, it was in his best uniform with silk shirts. He gave as the reason for this, the possibilities of becoming a prisoner, in which case he must be as elegant as possible because of the pretty girls!

Voss started his performance with *Jasta 10* on August 10th by shooting down a Spad for his thirty-fifth victory and leading Unteroffizier Brettel to his second. The skies had cleared and the persistence of the R.F.C. and R.N.A.S. were presenting opportunities for the fighters. However, with the improved conditions, the British bombers were also out and in the early morning a fire had been started at Heule by the twenty 20 lb. bombs that had been dropped. Bisseghem too, in a heavier attack, received some seven 230 lb. bombs dropped by the F.Es. of No. 100 Squadron.

The following day it was the turn of Marcke to receive attack. Early morning a large bomb fell by the telephone exchange, but failed to explode. Like the exchange operators, Leutnant Krefft too, had a lucky escape. As technical officer, he was taking up an aircraft on test when the engine failed. The machine stalled over the airfield and crashed to the ground, crumpling the fuselage and smashing the wings, yet Krefft was able to get out of the wreckage, albeit slightly injured. He could ill be spared, for his efforts to maintain the highest degree of serviceability in the aircraft in his charge were badly needed to ensure maximum performance in the critical battles ahead.

Both sides were making the most of the summer weather and patrols were flown at any time throughout the hours of daylight. On August 12th, Leutnant Stapenhörst claimed a Sopwith at 8.50 a.m. as his initial victory. Oberleutnant Dostler another Sopwith at 3.55 p.m. for his twenty-third victory, and Leutnant Adam as late as 9.10 p.m. that day, scored his eleventh victory.

His Emperor

von Richthofen meets his Emperor. Richthofen with head bandaged through his recent head-wound, salutes the Kaiser who requested his attendance at a review of troops near Courtrai, August, 1917.

His General

von Richthofen meets the Commanding Officer of the German Air Service, General von Hoeppner. The occasion is believed to be during preparations for the great German offensive in March, 1918.

CHAPTER NINETEEN

Aces and Others

Kurt Wolff engages in conversation with von Richthofen after a combat flight from Marcke. In the background are requisitioned Belgian houses used as offices.

Richthofen was still a sick man and he had been forbidden to fly by his doctors. It has been said, that after receiving his head-wound, he was never quite the same again. For the first few weeks he was afflicted with headaches and dizziness. On at least two occasions he returned to hospital at Courtrai for examination and for further bone splinters to be extracted from the wound. As he returned to Marcke via the market place, he would have passed the bronze statue to one of Courtrai's most famous citizens—Jan Palfyn—the inventor of surgical forceps!

He drove himself to work and faced his new responsibilities. The initial onslaught of the British attacks had been stayed; beaten by the low-lying, clayey soil, that, drenched with the continuous rain and pounded by high explosive, formed a veritable morass. But in the air the pressure remained and Richthofen's task was to ensure that *J.G.1* would meet it. At that time, the second week in August 1917, he was strengthened by the addition of *Jasta Boelcke* at Bisseghem, which was placed temporarily under his tactical control.

The week that followed brought several successes, the 14th being a particularly active day. Of *Jasta 11*, Oberleutnant Reinhard scored his third and fourth victories and Leutnant Müller and Leutnant Meyer their first and second respectively. Their cost was Leutnant Joachim Wolff known as the 'boy of *Jasta 11*' to his comrades (and in official reports as Wolff II, to avoid confusion with Kurt Wolff), who was wounded and removed to hospital. Oberleutnant Weigand and Leutnant Löwenhardt of *Jasta 10* both made their second victories and in *Jasta 6*, Leutnant Adam and Oberleutnant Dostler made respectively their twelfth and twenty-fourth victories. But in *Jasta 4* there were no victories to celebrate, instead they suffered the loss of Leutnant Hübner who was seen to crash at Moorslede, having been shot down by Leutnant T. F. Hazell of No. 1 Squadron R.F.C., whose eventual victory score was to rank only one less than that of Captain Albert Ball.

With the better weather, and consequently drier ground, the British re-opened their attack on the 16th with operations around Langemarck. That misty morning with light cloud, Richthofen chose to fly before breakfast. Possibly the fact that the quarters of *Jasta 11* had been bombed soon after 6 a.m. accounted for his early rising. As far as is known, it was his first patrol since receiving his wound. Being far from fit, he experienced dizziness and faintness as his machine rose. Overcoming this nausea by an effort of will, he regained something of his old skill when he later sighted a Nieuport. After stalking it warily, he gained a firing position and sent it to lie amongst the shattered trunks that the map location gave as Houthulst Forest. Then came reaction, his feelings of sickness and dizziness returned. He made straight back to his airfield to rest.

That day, Voss too had scored as indeed he had the day before. Richthofen might yet have to look to his laurels, with this new unit leader so rapidly increasing his score. The official list by *Kogenluft* then stood as follows:†

These were days of moment. The war continued relentlessly and personalities came and went. On August 17th it was the turn of Leutnant Ohlrau of *Jasta 10* to make his first victory in the morning and for Leutnant von der Osten of *Jasta 11* to achieve his first in the evening. That night there was a special ceremony at a party in a local casino, when Richthofen went up to von der Osten and shook him warmly by the hand. It was not only that it was his first victory, it was the two hundredth victory achieved by *Jasta 11*! Six weeks later No. 56 Squadron R.F.C. were celebrating their two hundredth recording of aircraft destroyed or shot down out of control. If the reader should wish to draw

† Rittmeister Freiherr von Richthofen	58	Leutnant Kurt Wintgens	20*
Hauptmann Oswald Boelcke	40*	Oberleutnant Max Immelmann	18*
Leutnant Werner Voss	37	Leutnant Hartmut Baldamus	18*
Leutnant Heinrich Gontermann	34	Leutnant Wilhelm Frankl	17*
Leutnant Kurt Wolff	33	Leutnant Walter von Bülow	17
Leutnant Karl Allmenröder	30*	Leutnant Hans Klein	16
Leutnant Karl Emil Schaefer	30*	Leutnant Walter Höhndorf	15
Leutnant Otto Bernert	27	Leutnant Albert Dossenbach	15*
Oberleutnant Eduard Dostler	26	Leutnant Kurt Schneider	15*
Offizierstellvertr. Max Müller	26	Oberleutnant Rudolf Berthold	14
Leutnant Freiherr von Richthofen	24	Offizierstellvertr. Nathanael	14*
		Leutnant Erwin Boehme	13
Oberleutnant Ritter von Tutschek	23	Leutnant Walter Göttsch	13
		Leutnant Hans Bethge	13

78

a comparison it should be pointed out that No. 56 Squadron had not made their first offensive patrol until April 22nd, 1917. They had achieved their successes in a shorter time, but on the other hand, unit strength of a *Jasta* was only two-thirds that of a British squadron.

Congratulations were received from many sources, and on the morrow the *Jasta* paraded for inspection by General Ludendorff. The General had been badly shaken en route when an engine had run into his special train, overturning the coach in which he was dining with his staff. It was not the least of his misfortunes, for within a few days he lost his stepson, who was shot down over the Channel.

Emboldened by their congratulations, *Jasta 11* through *J.G.1*, ventured a wire to the *KoFl* of the 4th Army, Major Haehnelt, which was in effect a complaint. It pointed out that owing to being ordered on escort work for bombing missions, ground-attack flights, reconnaissance patrols, etc., the pilots were unable to fulfil their most important task of keeping the sky free from enemy aircraft. A return wire pointed out that their efforts were appreciated, without comment upon the implied criticism of policy. The second part of the wire congratulated Richthofen on his latest victory, but exhorted him to have a proper regard for the value of his person and, until he was fully recovered from the effects of his wounding, he should not fly unless it was absolutely necessary.

The fortunes of the personnel of *J.G.1* fluctuated. On August 19th, Eduard, Ritter von Dostler, the Bavarian leader of *Jasta 6*, received the *Pour le Mérite*. Two days later he was reported missing. He was shot down by a R.E.8. of No. 7 Squadron R.F.C., which he was attacking. A report by a British pilot captured a few days later to the effect that Dostler was a prisoner-of-war, proved false. His last resting place is unknown. At the head of *Jasta 6*, Leutnant Adam took over.

On the 26th, Richthofen, disregarding the advice of his superior officer, flew with four members of *Jasta 11* on early morning patrol. Spotting a lone Spad several thousand feet below, he circled round until the glare of the morning sun was to his advantage when he closed in to attack. The Spad dived for cloud to escape, but Richthofen's bullets hit it first. Richthofen was forced to give up pursuit as his own engine was damaged, 'by bad F.B. ammunition', as he wrote in his report. Since the Spad, by Richthofen's

Lt. Erich Loewenhardt, leader of Jasta 10 *and holder of the* Pour le Mérite, *who scored fifty-three victories.*

account, took only evasive action, it is difficult to appreciate how damage to his engine was sustained, unless by his own faulty ammunition. The Spad pilot seemingly had little chance to use his single Vickers gun No. L.1639 and his only other armament was a Colt automatic revolver! It could be that Richthofen was using some of the *Luft Einschiess* explosive ammunition. This ingenious bullet had the nose pierced by a small hole whereby air pressure in flight acted upon a percussion cap, which actuated the striker and so ignited the delay fuse. Explosions, premature to the four-fifth second fuse, were not uncommon.

Richthofen, with his engine damaged, had no alternative but to return. As he came below the cloud, he saw the Spad blow up in the air. Coupled with anxiety over the state of his engine was a re-occurrence of his feeling of nausea; he was not sorry to land after achieving his fifty-ninth victory.

The new triplanes had arrived. On August 28th, Fokker FI 103/17 was allotted to *Jasta 10* and was taken over by Voss. It became his hobby, his pet and indeed his life—his very short life. Second of the production batch was FI 102/17*, taken by von Richthofen himself. It is

Vizefeldwebel Sebastian Festner	12*	Leutnant Hermann Göring	10
Leutnant von Eschwege	12	Leutnant Ritter von Mulzer	10*
Hauptmann Hans-Joachim Buddecke	12	Oberleutnant Hans Berr	9*
Oberleutnant Stephan Kirmaier	11*	Oberleutnant Freiherr von Althaus	9
Leutnant Hermann Pfeiffer	11	Leutnant Gustav Leffers	9*
Oberleutnant Hans von Keudell	11*	Leutnant Otto Brauneck	9*
Vizefeldwebel Freidrich Manschott	11*	Leutnant Adolf Schulte	9*
Leutnant Renatus Theiller	11*	Offizierstellvertr. Wilhelm Frickart	9
Leutnant Hans Müller	11	Leutnant Hans Adam	9
Leutnant Heinrich Bongartz	11	Leutnant Leopold Anslinger	8
Offizierstellvertr. Julius Buckler	10	Vizefeldwebel Fritz Krebs	8*
		Leutnant Albert Dietlen	8
		Oberleutnant Hans Schüz	8
		Oberleutnant Hans Schilling	8*
		Leutnant Otto Parschau	8*

* Died for the Fatherland.

* It is presumed the first aircraft, FI 101, was retained at the Fokker works for testing purposes.

Leutnant Werner Voss, on the right, discusses his new Fokker FI 103/17 with two staff officers.

possible that von Boenigk first flew this machine in service, but there is little doubt that Richthofen was flying it for the first time on September 1st. With it, that day, he achieved his sixtieth, and the easiest, victory of his career, but it was no merit to the triplane—or to Richthofen.

With four of his pilots, he had attacked a lone R.E.8 over Zonnebeke. There was no reaction from the occupants when Richthofen approached almost to within a hundred yards. The observer stood in his cockpit and made no move to use his guns. With only twenty shots Richthofen despatched the R.E. to its doom. He would have been failing in his duty to his Fatherland had he refrained from firing, but he had a good idea why the observer had remained so placid—he had mistaken the new Fokker Triplane for one of the familiar Sopwith Triplanes. Up to that time the Sopwiths had been the only operational triplanes at the front.

Two days later, flying his same triplane, accompanied by five members of *Jasta 11*, including Oberleutnant Reinhard, Leutnant Groos, Leutnant Meyer and Leutnant Mohnicke, he engaged in combat with a patrol of Sopwith Pups. Singling out a machine he found he had chosen a deft opponent, but his triplane proved superior. The pilot, Lieutenant A. F. Bird was a game fighter. Even after being forced down by Richthofen, he used up his ammunition in his descent, by firing at troops on the ground. Then, coming in to land, he deliberately ended his run by smashing into a tree, so as to wreck his machine and so deny it to the Germans.

To Richthofen's combat report were appended a series of testimonials by witnesses of the fight. From the air by three members of his flight and from the ground by an officer of the *Flugmeldedienst*, an officer of an anti-aircraft company, a Vizefeldwebel of an anti-aircraft battery and a report from a balloon company. All the more strange, since there was the material evidence of a prisoner-of-war and smashed airframe B1795 fitted with Le Rhone Type 'R' engine No. 035123. One can only assume that Richthofen had received a slight rebuff, possibly in the form of a request for further confirmation of an earlier victory. Oberleutnant Bodenschatz had the testimonials collected, their correctness certified and submitted to *Kogenluft*. If the supposition is correct, then Richthofen's reaction by superfluous testimony evidently had the desired effect, for he did not supply such written evidence again; presumably because he was informed that it was not necessary.

The day had been a good one for the formation. Leutnant Mohnicke had also downed a Pup and Leutnant Wüsthoff scored twice. Leutnant Adam was proving his leadership by scoring his fourteenth and Richthofen's nearest competitor, Voss, scored this thirty-ninth. There were also four other victories, one each by Oberleutnant

Oskar, Freiherr von Boenigk, like von Richthofen from the Silesian nobility, scored seven victories with J.G.1, but his fame lay in his subsequent service, first as leader of Jasta 21 and later as commander of J.G.2. In all, he scored 26 victories.

80

von Doering, Oberleutnant von Boenigk, Leutnant von Schoenebeck and Leutnant Stapenhorst, at the cost of one casualty—Leutnant Bockelmann wounded.

Next day, September 4th, Wüsthoff again made a double victory, but together with Leutnant Mohnicke's seventh, they were the only victories at the cost of Oberleutnant Reinhard wounded. Voss, however, was undoubtedly the star of the 'Circus' that month. At 3.50 p.m. on the 5th he shot down a British Pup and at 4.30 p.m. a French Caudron. On an evening five days later, he downed two Sopwiths and a F.E. within thirty minutes. His victory the day following brought his score to forty-six. Undoubtedly his thoughts must have been on challenging Richthofen for his coveted title of leading ace—and Richthofen was not at the front to defend his title.

Richthofen had departed on September 6th on belated convalescent leave. Once again Oberleutnant von Doering took over the reins. Older than the rest of the pilots, he was not noted for his aggressiveness, but he was a reliable and capable officer. At that time he had six victories to his credit. To replace Doering at the head of *Jasta 4*, Oberleutnant von Boenigk moved up to the lead. When Richthofen had gone on leave before, Krefft had also been granted short leave; this time, within two days of Richthofen leaving, Krefft was posted away for a course at the Pfalz works.

The *Geschwader* carried on. As an experiment it had proved its worth and a second *Geschwader*, *J.G.2*, formed on August 17th, was then functioning on the German 9th Army's front. It consisted of *Jasta 12, 13, 15* and *19*. There were thus two 'Circuses' on the Western Front at this time.

Richthofen, on leave, daily received a brief on the activities of *J.G.1*. The formation was not without its vicissitudes. No. 56 Squadron R.F.C. was again the chief thorn in its side that September. A patrol of S.E.5As led by Captain James Byford McCudden himself, engaged a patrol from *Jasta 10* in the evening of September 14th. McCudden, who was to become fourth on the list of British aces, singled out Oberleutnant Weigand's machine. Getting beneath its tail he fired upwards with the Lewis gun

Five 'holders' of the Pour le Mérite. *Left to right: Wüsthoff, Reinhard (apparently wearing this Order as a joke) Manfred von Richthofen, Loewenhardt and Lothar von Richthofen.*

von Richthofen (left) chats with a group of Jasta 5 *pilots. This aircraft, with a red and white-striped tailplane, is believed to be that of Hpt. Reinhard's.*

mounted on the S.E.'s top wing. Weigand's Albatros D V spun down, vibrating violently as if some bullets had perforated the cylinders of the engine, causing it to function sporadically. He was able, however, to bring the aircraft under control and land with nothing worse than a light flesh wound and a severe shaking. Leutnant Groos too, had been lightly wounded. In spite of making nearly one hundred flights, *J.G.1* could report no victories that day.

Next day, when fifty-four flights were made, fifty could be dismissed as abortive, three recorded as successful and one notified as a complete loss. The successes were by Leutnants v. d. Osten (his third), Adam (his fourteenth) and Wüsthoff (his sixteenth), who each claimed a single-seat Sopwith; the loss, was the last flight of Leutnant Kurt Wolff, who had, but three days before, received promotion to Oberleutnant.

He had set out flying Richthofen's own triplane, Fl 102/17, accompanied by four Albatros D Vs. In the vicinity of Wervicq he lost contact with his comrades and so flew back and forth along the patrol area hoping to sight them. It was then that a patrol of Camels from No. 10 (Naval) Squadron dived upon him. Almost at the same time, the Albatros D V pilots spotted their leader's machine and hastened to his aid. Too late. Flight Sub-Lieutenant MacGregor in Camel B3833, foremost of the attacking machines, so damaged Wolff's machine, that it spun down, with flames spurting from its engine. Plunging to earth, a petrol tank blew up and the machine disintegrated. So died the young leader. His body was laid in state in St. Joseph's Church, before being entrained for Memel. Kurt Wolff was going home. Richthofen himself wrote an obituary for the Memel newspapers in which he said of Wolff: 'In the history of the *Geschwader* he will live for all times as a model of soldier-like virtue and as an example that could be equalled only by the great.' In Wolff's place, Leutnant Groos took over the lead of *Jasta 11*.

On the 20th, there were further casualties both on the ground and in the air. *Jasta 4* had a N.C.O. and three men killed as well as others wounded by a bombing attack.

Leutnant Werner Voss with Anthony Fokker watches a flying demonstration of a Fokker Triplane circa August, 1917.

Three of their aircraft were destroyed and four damaged. As if to make up for their losses they flew over a hundred *Kreigsflüge*—a word corresponding to the familiar 'sortie' of World War II—and claimed as their victories: two Sopwith (Pups or Camels), one Sopwith Triplane, three Spads and a balloon.

Three days later Voss scored his forty-eighth—and final victory. Before that day was out, he had fallen in a fight that is considered one of the epic combats of that war. On patrol in Fokker FI 103/17, painted to his own colour scheme of silvery-blue, he had attacked a lone S.E.5A. It attracted other aircraft to the scene, first an Albatros, although it would appear that Voss was master of the situation. Then 'B' Flight of No. 56 Squadron, who had just re-formed after shooting down a D.F.W., sighted the combat; their six S.E.5As, led by Captain McCudden, swept into the attack. The fight developed into a general melée with Voss's triplane, skilfully handled, turning, twisting, diving or climbing to elude the fire of the seven S.E.5As swarming around. More Albatros fighters arrived but they were followed closely by a patrol of Spads and four Camels that successfully protected the S.E.5s from their intervention. Only one other German machine got into the fight and that soon disappeared. The Albatros and the Fokker Triplane continued the fight unaided.

Second-Lieutenant A. P. F. Rhys Davids, M.C., flying S.E.5A B525, got in several bursts of fire at the triplane, without apparent effect. Twice he used up a drum of ammunition on his Lewis gun. Not until he was in a diving position to fire his forward-firing Vickers gun and the Lewis did he achieve any result. After that Voss made no attempt to turn, for mortally wounded, his end was near. His triplane slowed and the S.E. almost collided with it. Then slowly down it went, gently gliding westward. Rhys Davids reloaded his Lewis gun and fired again to make sure of his victory, causing the triplane to turn slightly right as it continued its slow, shallow dive and by so doing the S.E. unavoidably overtook it. By the time Rhys Davids had circled round, the triplane had disappeared. Only McCudden saw it finally reach its stalling speed and plunge to earth from less than 1,000 feet.

So died Werner Voss. Of him McCudden wrote: 'As long as I live I shall never forget my admiration of that German pilot, who, single-handed, fought seven of us for ten minutes, and also put some bullets through all of our machines. His flying was wonderful, his courage magnificent, and, in my opinion, he was the bravest German airman whom it has been my privilege to fight.' Leutnant Klein took his place as the leader of *Jasta 10*, being officially appointed to that office on the 27th. Only two days before, *Jasta 11* had received notice of their new commander—Lothar Freiherr von Richthofen, who had at last recovered from his wounds received five months earlier.

Although new leaders were taking over, promotion was relatively slow. It was not uncommon for a *Staffelführer* to remain a Leutnant (2nd Lieutenant), whereas in the R.F.C. each fighter squadron had posts established that allowed a majority in command and a captaincy for each flight leader. However, many of these R.F.C. posts were filled by the granting of acting rank, but in the German Army most of the promotions were immediately substantive. The difference was in the British system of unit establishment compared with the German system of bulk personnel establishment.

For the next few weeks there were few victories to record for the casualties sustained. It was the fate of Oberleutnant Weigand to meet No. 56 Squadron R.F.C., a second time in combat—and on this occasion it was fatal. Four Albatros D Vs of *Jasta 10* had dived upon a lone S.E.5A piloted by Lieutenant L. Barlow of No. 56 Squadron who had set out to intercept a D.F.W. reported in the vicinity of the British G.H.Q.

Barlow's reaction was swift; twisting and turning back, he manœuvred for position and fired from his Lewis gun as an Albatros came into his sights. He watched it spin away, but only for a moment as another Albatros approached head on, to receive the full blast of his Vickers gun. The wings of that Albatros then collapsed, folding back and the fuselage spiralled to earth. As it fell, Weigand's body fell clear and hurtled down. Within two minutes, he was followed by Unteroffizier Werkmeister, who descended in flames, another victim of Barlow's guns. Werkmeister had only arrived in *Jasta 10* on September 23rd, was shot down on the 25th and was buried with Weigand at St. Joseph's Church on the 29th. Such are the fortunes of war. Barlow himself was killed the following February; having been 'rested' from service at the front, he was killed testing a Sopwith Dolphin at Martlesham Heath.

Nine replacement pilots arrived at the *Geschwader* that September, mostly straight from *Jagdstaffelnschule I*, to face the dangers of aerial warfare. They arrived at a time when the leadership of the individual units was changing and the famed commander of the formation was absent. September 1917 was not the best of months for *Jagdgeschwader Nr. 1*.

The Ace of Aces

CHAPTER TWENTY

With Werner Voss dead, there was no immediate challenger for the title of leading ace; Richthofen could, for a while, rest upon his laurels. Not that the remainder of his leave was conditioned by such motives, but rather by the necessity for rest from his onerous duties and by the low condition of his health, due to lack of convalescence. His rehabilitation took a form typical of the man—hunting. Based on Gotha, ducal residence of the Duke of Saxe-Coburg-Gotha—a former Duke of Edinburgh—he stayed at the recently built and impressive Schloss Hotel. Again he was proud of the opportunity of hunting a rare beast—elk. His bag that September, including one large elk, three stags and a buck, was recorded with almost as much enthusiasm as his victory log.

Tangible evidence of these sporting kills could be made absolute by the taxidermist's craft, but the jeweller's task of providing monumental witness to his achievement in war was now limited by the general shortage of metals throughout Germany. No longer was sterling silver available and Richthofen was not prepared to accept an ersatz material. His sixtieth cup was the last.

From Gotha, he went on to Berlin, spending most of his time at Adlershof and then on to his home at Schweidnitz. There he put the finishing touches to his book. With the responsibilities of an eldest son, he wished to provide in some way for his mother in the future, should he be called upon to make the supreme sacrifice; for his father, if he should survive the war, would most surely be retired on the cessation of hostilities. The royalties from the sale of the book were a means of making money with dignity.

Others were not so scrupulous. Many picture postcards of himself were left at the house for him to autograph. He gallantly obliged by signing each and every one with the exception of a hundred that had been presented to the house by a woman. Those he would not touch, not a single one. His mother later learnt what her son had known—the woman was expecting to sell them for one mark apiece!

Richthofen, as Germany's leading flyer, received no gratuity or other monetary reward for his services other than those of the same rank flying under similar conditions. In fact his pay at that time was less than he usually received, since, having been on the non-effective strength of a unit at the front for over a month, his pay dropped by 60 marks (£3) a month. A feature of the Air Service pay scales, judged by British military standards was the special rate for service at the front and the disparity between the pay of senior N.C.Os. and junior officers. However, flying pay of 150 marks (£7 10s.) a month was paid as a fixed sum irrespective of rank. Thus, the flying personnel of a unit at the front would receive pay as follows:

Rank and Approximate British Equivalent	Marks	£	s.	d.
Hauptmann or Rittmeister (Captain)	660	33	0	0
Leutnant (Second-Lieutenant)	460	22	10	0
Feldwebel (Sergeant-Major)	213	10	13	0
Unteroffizier (Corporal)	189.60	9	9	7
Flieger (Private)	165	8	5	0

Those on ground duty would receive 150 marks (£7 10s.)

von Richthofen with Moritz. After von Richthofen was killed, Moritz was looked after by Leutnant Gerstenberg on whose farm he died years afterwards of old age.

less and therefore it left a Flieger of the ground staff with 15s. a month. (The exchange rate was approximately 4 marks to an American dollar.)

When Richthofen was not hunting he relaxed a little uneasily. The social round or gay parties were not of his world. He was not a good mixer and even on short leave, when *J.G.1* personnel could reach Brussels, Richthofen had been observed to be dining at the Hotel Metropole—alone! With women, he seemed to have been almost unconcerned. Those who knew him intimately refute the stories of the special letters he received from 'a lady who has been kept secret'. Rumours arose from the fact that he selected certain letters from his extensive mail to read straight away in private. A very natural action for a man with an extensive mail from his admiring countrymen, to extract for immediate reading, those letters postmarked from home, or addressed in the familiar handwriting of intimate friends.

Most Germans were correct and unemotional in their conduct. The higher a position gained, the greater would be the self-discipline exercised. Laughter and a sense of fun were not absent, but they were not openly expressed. There was too, a feeling that to show emotion, including amusement on occasions, was not consistent with dignity.

Richthofen was more than a German, he was a Prussian of noble birth. He inherited military traditions in spite of an

The Ordre pour le Mérite, a blue Maltese Cross edged with gold, worn from the neck by a black ribbon with a white stripe, interwoven with a silvery thread.

early environment that would provide an interesting study for the modern psychologist. Dressed 'adoringly' as a child with long curly hair, mingling only with friends carefully chosen and restricted to a circle equal in social status, he was flung into the harsh, frugal life of a cadet school whose motto was: 'Learn to obey in order that you may command'. It demanded much of him and he in turn was to demand much of others.

Demanding though he was, he never asked the impossible. He was a leader, showing by an impeccable example what was required. As a *Jagdstaffel* commander we have the witness of a *Jasta 11* member, von Schoenebeck who wrote of Richthofen's careful schooling of new members to his unit. The initial interview, a flying test, criticism, encouragement and above all, example. There were frequent practice flights at ground targets with a fifty-round allowance for each machine. Richthofen himself flew on these flights and often achieved 90 per cent. hits. On patrol, when finally he took his fledglings to fly against the enemy, they were amazed at what he had observed of their own conduct. He saw all and could react correctly. He was a unit commander upon whom men could depend. Later as a *Geschwader* commander, his job was to see that his unit commanders had that same art of skilful schooling.

The dicta of Boelcke were reiterated. They could not be over-emphasised. In particular he was insistent upon a close watch behind when in the air. After a patrol had landed from a combat, he would often inspect the rear of the aircraft for bullet-holes and woebetide the unfortunate pilot if any were found. One offender is said to have pleaded engine-trouble as his reason for landing at another airfield, whereas in reality it was to get the bullet holes in his aircraft patched up before meeting Richthofen! At least one officer was posted for collecting too many bullet-holes from behind!

Scold he did, but what arrogance there had been, had faded. On duty his manner was correct and off-duty he would often acknowledge the salutes of his subordinates with less formality than is usually associated with German military discipline. One officer, Leutnant Schröder of the *Flugmeldedienst*, even described it as a friendly nod. He spoke too, of the shy manner of Richthofen, a defence readily understandable in one who was the focus of all eyes.

Few persons ever shared Richthofen's confidence, except perhaps Móritz—and Móritz was a Danish hound. He had been chosen as a puppy from the litter of a bitch owned by a Belgian, when Richthofen had served with *B.A.O.* at Ostend. Móritz accompanied Richthofen from station to station and from front to front, identifying himself with the Germany Army by accepting only those in field-grey uniforms and barking indiscriminately at French, Belgians and Russians alike, in the occupied territories. As the pet of a commander antics of chasing everything that moved were indulged, but when it extended to the chase of balls upon the billiard table, resulting in the ruination of the cloth, the Mess Committee was faced with a delicate proposition from members. Móritz learnt his own lesson from chasing aircraft on take-off. A whirling propeller blade smacked his thick skull—shattering the blade! Poor Móritz, although badly hurt, survived. Up to then, Richthofen had omitted to have his long ears cut, but since the blade had neatly lopped one off, the other was cut to match.

Strolling with Móritz was one of his off-duty pleasures, although, strangely, he did not approve of Móritz hunting. An activity encouraged by some of the mechanics, who were glad of a rabbit to supplement their rations. What other pleasures Richthofen had apart from his hunting, it is difficult to conjecture. The theatre, seemingly, held little interest for him and as for music, it is believed that he was tone-deaf. He indulged in an occasional cigarette, drank moderately, enjoyed a good discussion and played billiards.

His earlier avid regard of trophies he still retained, but his ambition for decorations was largely mollified by the *Pour le Mérite*. But even that order no longer had the distinction it had once carried, with some thirty awards having already been made. (The *Ordre pour le Mérite* was awarded in the course of the war to eighty-one members of the Air Service, fifty-nine fighter pilots, nine observers, five bomber leaders, three naval pilots, two airship commanders, one balloon-observer and the Officer Commanding and the Chief of Staff of the Air Service.) Whatever the *Pour le Mérite* lost in quality, was compensated for in quantity that October of 1917. As Richthofen travelled back from leave, several principalities bestowed their highest awards upon him.

The Kaiser, the High Command and his immediate superiors, all advised him to have a care for his valuable person and to act in an advisory capacity, rather than to lead in actual combat. But he returned to the front with every intention of flying in action. His reply to their exhortations, which was written, was typical of him: 'I should indeed consider myself a despicable person if, now that I have achieved fame and wear many decorations, should consent to exist as a pensioner of my dignity and to preserve my life for the nation, while every poor fellow in the trenches—who is doing his duty equally as much as I—has to stick it out.' To the front he returned.

There had been relatively little activity for the *Geschwader* during October and the occasional individual victory was barely balanced by casualties. When Richthofen resumed command at midday on the 23rd he became aware of the unfortunate catalogue of events over the past three days. Leutnant von Gerstenberg of *Jasta 11* was badly wounded, having been shot in the lung; Unteroffizier Hardel, wounded in combat, crashed on landing receiving severe concussion and Vizefeldwebel Backmann was missing from patrol. It did not end there. Four days later, Leutnant Müller, flying a Fokker D V, crashed to his death on his own airfield. Even more tragic was the loss of one of the most promising men, again of *Jasta 11*, Vizefeldwebel Lautenschlager. He was shot down by a German C-type aeroplane, the observer of which had mistaken his machine for a Sopwith Triplane.

As related, Kurt Wolff had been killed flying Richthofen's Fokker FI 102/17. It was therefore necessary for Richthofen to select a new machine and he settled upon Dr I 114/17. He flew it, accompanied by Lothar, on the 30th, a rather rough day that restricted the whole *Geschwader* to only six sorties. Noticing that Lothar's machine was lagging behind, he was startled to see it dive steeply down. With relief he noticed the sky was clear of enemy aircraft and he followed anxiously. Lothar was having trouble with his engine and had been forced to make an emergency landing. He made a good run-in and landed safely with a stopped propeller; but Manfred, who followed him in to find out what the trouble was, had one of the wheels of his triplane dip into a hole which brought the machine shuddering and slewing to such an abrupt halt, that it was completely wrecked. Another Dr I 121/17, was lost the following day in more serious circumstances, for with it *Jasta 11* lost yet another of their members, Leutnant Pastor.

Although Manfred had been impressed by the manoeuvrability and climb of the Fokker Triplane, he was well aware that its speed was inferior to contemporary British aircraft except perhaps the Sopwith Pup and the D.H.5. Nevertheless, with it, he felt he could match any of the Allied aircraft types so far encountered, but he was by no means as enamoured with the triplane as is generally believed. He went back to using an Albatros D V. The choice was not wide. Pfalz D IIIs were also in use with the *Geschwader*, but they were deemed inferior to the Albatros D Vs and D Vas. For training purposes a few Fokker D Vs were available, but this type received a bad name after Müller's crash and when Leutnant Tüxen crashed during November in similar circumstances, flying Fokker D V 2642/16, that aircraft type became decidedly unpopular.

The Germans were not so successful in bringing out new and better aircraft types as the Allies at that time, and in the production of standardised models, lack of raw materials seriously hampered output. Although the front was quieter, the R.F.C. continued the offensive in the air, by patrolling over the German side of the lines and with the occasional strafing of German airfields, including those of *J.G.1*. That formation's gravest loss during November was Leutnant Adam, the commander of *Jasta 6*, who was shot down in flames in Albatros D V D5222/17 on the 15th. His place was immediately taken by the senior officer of the unit, Oberleutnant Reinhard. It was particularly galling for the formation, to find out later from a prisoner, that Adam had been shot down by a pilot making his first offensive patrol.

One of the most remarkable attacks of the war was launched that November by the British Third Army. It was the first battle in history in which the tank played a

Scholz, Mohnicke and von Richthofen—with stick—and parachute. The aircraft behind Scholz has its wing leading edges picked out with black and white stripes. These aircraft are of Jasta 11.

A Sopwith Camel which had been forced down in the fighting in October 1917.

notable part—The Battle of Cambrai. In other respects, the method of attack, for a major operation, differed by the lack of obvious preparation; there was no preliminary artillery bombardment or increased reconnaissance by aircraft to suggest an impending attack. The attitude of the staff planners to this operation was epitomised in the introduction to the operation order for the R.F.C. units concerned: 'The essence of the success of this operation is secrecy.' Nevertheless, preparations had to be made, but as unobtrusively as possible. At night train-loads of tanks were moved in, unloaded and the tanks driven off to assembly points and carefully camouflaged with netting.

Certainly the Germans had been lulled into a false sense of security. Alarms and excursions there had been, but a serious attack had never developed on that part of the front. Therefore, when the commander of the only air fighting unit behind the threatened front, *Jasta 5*, received orders to despatch his aircraft to patrol the lines, he was inclined to use his discretion and decide that in view of the heavy morning mist, his aircraft would remain grounded. His Army Corps commander, however, was insistent upon action to the extent of threatening him with court-martial. Thus provoked into preparing for action, the unit found it even before they had all taken-off. Nine Sopwith Camels of No. 3 Squadron R.F.C. appeared out of the mist bent on strafing. One was shot down by a *Jasta 5* pilot who managed to get up, but before the others had gained height, the Camels were away in the mist. Owing to the appalling flying conditions, however, two other Camels failed to return, having crashed into trees.

The mist that had made flying so hazardous, assisted the attackers on the ground. Tanks, looming out of the mist, overran the German forward positions, flattening lanes in the wire defences that had been constructed some fifty yards deep, so allowing the infantry to follow up. According to plan the Hindenburg Line was overrun and the troops moved forward through open country on a seven-mile front. So promising was the initial assault that some Canadian cavalry units were moved forward, to exploit the German withdrawal in traditional role, thus providing an incongruous comparison in military transportation. It was, however, the lack of sufficient troops in tactical support and strategic reserve to exploit the successes that caused the advance to be halted, after an initial check when a canal bridge, vital to the advance collapsed under the weight of the leading tank.

By midday on the opening day of the attack, November 20th, Ludendorff was aware of the seriousness of the German position. He called upon the German 4th Army Commander to release troops immediately for the threatened area. The day following, *Jagdgeschwader Nr. 1*, was ordered to the Cambrai front, to perform a role in accordance with its establishment charter.

KoFl of the German 2nd Army, administering the threatened area, advised *J.G.1* of airfield availability and a march-table was immediately drawn up. *Geschwader* staff and *Jasta 11* would occupy the airfield at Avesnes le Sec. *Jasta 4* and *6* that at Lieu St. Amand and *Jasta 10* that at Iwuy. But there were two major difficulties, the railways were overloaded with the transportation of reinforcing troops and could not move their equipment for several days and the airfields allotted were practically derelict.

The *Flieger-Hallenbau-Trupp* (airfield installation troop) of the 2nd Army could not perform miracles and erect the sheds and facilities required in so short a time, and although the *Geschwader* units carried tented hangars on their war equipment scales, that could have been rushed forward by motor transport, it was refuelling facilities, an armoury and all the various items essential to an air unit at war, which were required. At such times improvisation is as important as organisation. Red tape was swept aside and everything possible was done to get *J.G.1* operational over the Cambrai front.

At Valenciennes was *Jastaschule I*, which, being only a matter of twenty miles behind the front, could serve usefully as a base. Training was temporarily abandoned and the school became an operational airfield, to which *J.G.1* machines flew on the 22nd and seven of their machines later made sorties over the front that day.

There was considerable activity in the air in spite of the inclement weather. German air reinforcements included several *Schutzstaffeln* (see page 56). This was the first time that these units, designed for low-level ground strafing, had been employed in force. With an establishment of six aircraft per *Staffel*, manned chiefly by N.C.O. pilots and gunners, they continually harassed the British infantry in the forward areas. Part of Richthofen's responsibility was to provide protection for these units.

The British too, although they did not employ units with such specific duties, were also using low-flying strafing tactics. The pilots of No. 64 Squadron R.F.C. had been practised in flying low in their D.H.5s in England and after October 14th, when they arrived in France, this was continued in formation.

On November 23rd, particularly heavy fighting had

86

developed on the important high ground near Bourlon and cunningly positioned machine guns, in Bourlon Wood, were holding up the British advance. From 10 a.m. that day relays of British aircraft patrols strafed the area in support of infantry attacks. With the specially trained No. 64 Squadron were No. 68 (Australian) Squadron also flying D.H.5s, No. 3 Squadron flying Camels and No. 46 Squadron in the process of changing its Pups for Camels. Whilst engaged upon this task, the first clash with *J.G.1* occurred. Richthofen had been given overall tactical control of fighter aircraft in the area; in addition to his command of *J.G.1*, he exercised tactical control of the fighter unit *in situ*, *Jasta 5*, and of *Jasta 15* brought up from the south. In the early afternoon, Richthofen himself, in Albatros D V D4693/17, led a fighting patrol over Bourlon Wood, to find D.H.5s actively engaged in close support.

His first shots struck a D.H.5 flying low over the wood, forcing the pilot to make an emergency landing. Following that moral success he next attacked another D.H.5 flying at about 2,600 feet over the heavily contested Bapaume–Cambrai road. After only a few shots that aircraft glided downwards into the south-eastern corner of Bourlon Wood. The pilot, Lieutenant J. A. V. Boddy of No. 64 Squadron went down with severe head-wounds, but he was dramatically rescued by a pilot in somewhat similar circumstances. His rescuer had been brought down in a D.H.5 ahead of the forward British troops, by a direct hit from a shell. After extricating himself from the wreckage, he saw Boddy's machine crash into the trees. Running from a wreckage, to a wreckage, he dragged Boddy out and together they stumbled through the British forward positions, to a dressing station.

The R.F.C. sent out a recovery party to salvage what they could of Boddy's aircraft, since it was not officially missing. As the position was barely tenable by the infantry, salvage was reported as impossible and in consequence airframe No. A9299, with Le Rhone engine No. 101287 War Dept. No. 15883, was struck-off unit charge. Later the wood was captured by a German counter-attack and evidently Richthofen arranged for a snipping of the fabric of this machine as a trophy, for in the Schweidnitz collection was a piece of striped rudder fabric, bearing small numerals consistent with the size of the small D.H.5 rudder with part of the numerals decipherable as ?299. There can be little doubt this was A9299.

The foregoing details are important in view of the opinions that have been expressed and published, that Richthofen's victim that day was Lieutenant A. Griggs of No. 68 (Australian) Squadron. Griggs, a pilot of American birth, gave magnificent support to a battalion of the Royal Irish Rifles, by repeatedly diving down and firing from only some fifty feet upon German machine-gun positions, until he was finally shot down and killed. So memorable was this individual action that it evoked a tribute in the 'In Memoriam' column of *The Times*, inserted by the grateful Irishmen. But his end was not at Richthofen's hands. Griggs flew D.H.5 A9428 and was last seen by one of his brother officers as late as 3.45 p.m. Richthofen's victory claim gives the time as 2 p.m. which, taking into account that German time was one hour in advance of British time (Greenwich Mean Time), would be 1 p.m.

G.M.T. The fact that Boddy left on patrol at 12.40 p.m. and that the serial A9299 was collected later for Richthofen, leaves little doubt that Boddy, not Griggs, was his victim.

Lothar also scored that day. Leading a patrol of *Jasta 11* he shot down a Bristol Fighter of No. 11 Squadron R.F.C. It was significant of the arrival of *J.G.1* that hitherto this British squadron had deemed four machines in formation sufficient for armed reconnaissance, but from that day the number was doubled, and within a few more days trebled.

The bitter fighting on the ground continued. Bourlon village was captured by the British on the 24th and lost to the Germans on the 25th. *J.G.1* continually sent patrols over the area, but they achieved few victories. By that time, staff and base personnel had arrived from the Courtrai area.

If the British attack had been excellently planned, the German measures to contain the assault and then counter-attack were equally as brilliant. On November 30th the German infantry attacked after a severe preliminary bombardment, supported by low-flying *Schutzstaffeln*, which, as the official history points out—tended to facilitate the enemy's success. In vain the British machines tried to emulate the German tactics, by low-flying attack; although in their usual role of fighting, the fighter squadrons held their own.

Again Bourlon Wood became the focal point of aerial activity; one pilot reporting the air above it thick with D.H.5s, R.E.8s, Bristol Fighters and some S.E.5s, with approximately an equal number of German machines. *J.G.1* were hotly engaged. Their first success of the day was a kite-balloon near Ribecourt, that made Leutnant Klein's twenty-second victory. Two D.H.5s fell to *Jasta 11* near the Wood and two Sopwith machines were also claimed.

Richthofen scored too, his sixty-third victory. For the first time he came into close combat with S.E.5s. He was flying, again in Albatros D Va D4693/17, with his brother and Leutnant Gussmann when they were attacked by a formation of ten S.E.5As. In the ensuing melée, Richthofen fired at several of the British machines before his fire took effect when aimed at Martinsyde-built S.E.5A B40, powered with a 200 h.p. Hispano engine No. 1000 W.D. No. 8575, at a distance of just over a hundred yards. The S.E. broke

von Richthofen attends an open-air conference. He is fourth from the right—has his left hand in his pocket.

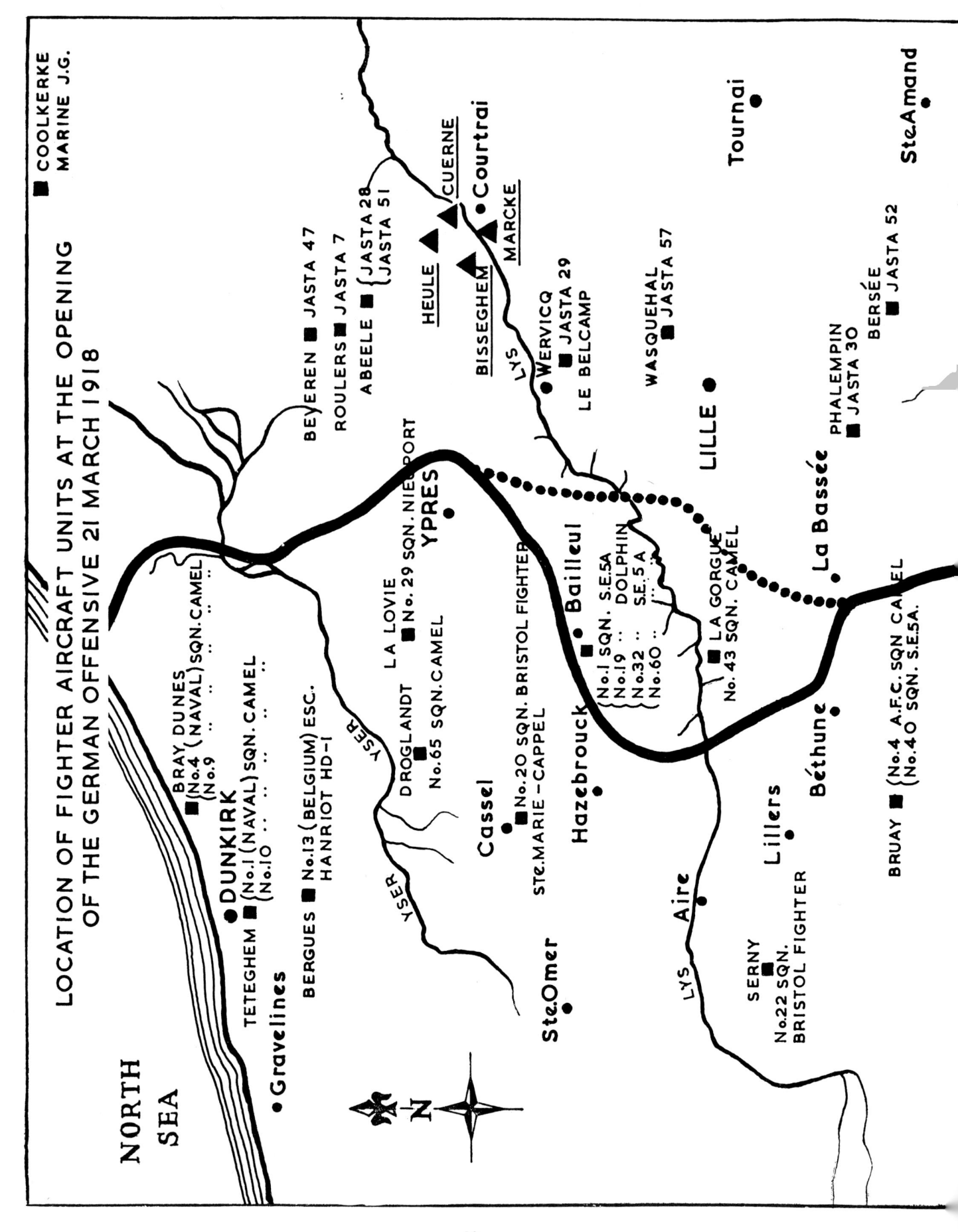

LOCATION OF FIGHTER AIRCRAFT UNITS AT THE OPENING OF THE GERMAN OFFENSIVE 21 MARCH 1918

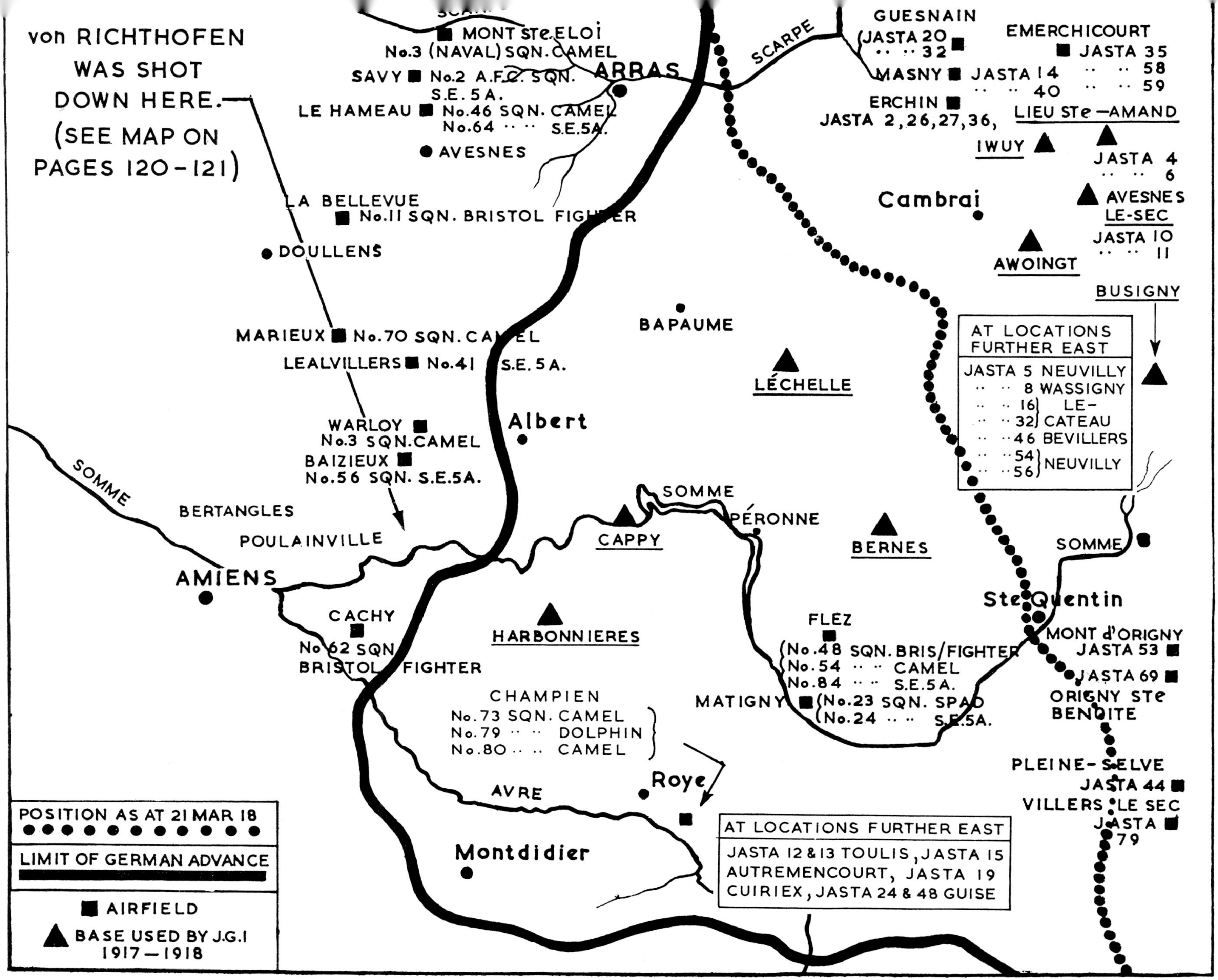
von RICHTHOFEN WAS SHOT DOWN HERE. (SEE MAP ON PAGES 120-121)
MONT Ste ELOI
No.3 (NAVAL) SQN. CAMEL
ARRAS
SAVY No.2 A.F.C. SQN. S.E.5A.
LE HAMEAU No.46 SQN. CAMEL
No.64 .. .. S.E.5A.
AVESNES
LA BELLEVUE
No.11 SQN. BRISTOL FIGHTER
DOULLENS
MARIEUX No.70 SQN. CAMEL
LEALVILLERS No.41 S.E.5A.
WARLOY
No.3 SQN. CAMEL
BAIZIEUX
No.56 SQN. S.E.5A.
SOMME
BERTANGLES
POULAINVILLE
AMIENS
CACHY
No 62 SQN
BRISTOL FIGHTER
Albert
BAPAUME
LÉCHELLE
SOMME
PÉRONNE
CAPPY
BERNES
HARBONNIERES
CHAMPIEN
No.73 SQN. CAMEL
No.79 .. .. DOLPHIN
No.80 .. .. CAMEL
AVRE
Roye
Montdidier
FLEZ
No.48 SQN. BRIS/FIGHTER
No.54 .. .. CAMEL
No.84 .. .. S.E.5A.
MATIGNY
No.23 SQN. SPAD
No.24 .. .. S.E.5A.
SCARPE
GUESNAIN
JASTA 20
.. .. 32
MASNY JASTA 14
.. .. 40
ERCHIN
JASTA 2, 26, 27, 36,
EMERCHICOURT
JASTA 35
.. .. 58
.. .. 59
LIEU Ste-AMAND
IWUY
JASTA 4
.. .. 6
Cambrai
AVESNES LE-SEC
JASTA 10
.. .. 11
AWOINGT
BUSIGNY
AT LOCATIONS FURTHER EAST
JASTA 5 NEUVILLY
.. .. 8 WASSIGNY
.. .. 16 LE-
.. .. 32 CATEAU
.. .. 46 BEVILLERS
.. .. 54 NEUVILLY
.. .. 56
SOMME
Ste Quentin
MONT d'ORIGNY
JASTA 53
JASTA 69
ORIGNY Ste BENOITE
PLEINE-SELVE
JASTA 44
VILLERS LE SEC
JASTA 79
AT LOCATIONS FURTHER EAST
JASTA 12 & 13 TOULIS, JASTA 15
AUTREMENCOURT, JASTA 19
CUIRIEX, JASTA 24 & 48 GUISE
POSITION AS AT 21 MAR 18
LIMIT OF GERMAN ADVANCE
AIRFIELD
BASE USED BY J.G.I 1917—1918

The visit to the Pfalz works at Speyer, December 1917. 1 Lt. Aver, 2 Ernst Everbusch, 3 Hpt. Willy Meyer, 4 Hpt. Muhlig Hoffmann, 5 Lt. Krefft, 6 von Richthofen, 7 Lt. Fritz von Falkenhayn, 8 von Tutschek, 9 Schlegel, 10 Alfred Everbusch, 11 Oblt. Rist, 12 Baierlein.

up in the air and fell in a small wood near Moeuvres, about two miles west of Bourlon.

For the five victories that day, the *Geschwader* lost two men; Leutnant Schulze who was killed in collision with another Albatros and Leutnant Demandt missing from patrol. But thereafter the front became stable almost as if for a winter recess. During the following December the *Geschwader* flew 750 war flights to achieve but five victories, three of them to pilots making their first score, viz. Leutnant Just, Leutnant Koepsch and Vizefeldwebel Barth, whose varied claims were respectively for a balloon, a Camel and a Bristol Fighter. In the grim statistics of war, it was somewhat off-set by the loss that month of Vizefeldwebel Hecht who failed to return from a patrol and Leutnant von Schweinitz who was yet another victim of the inherent weakness of Albatros designs, when his wings collapsed, folded back and the fuselage of his D V, D5313, plunged to earth.

Richthofen had left on December 12th, to visit the Pfalz works at Speyer where he hoped to find a satisfactory replacement design for his out-dated machines. As it was, the Pfalz D III was having a new lease of life in units because production had been increased and availability was the important factor at that time. In particular he wished to receive new equipment before the spring offensive opened. But he was disappointed, the Pfalz Dr I, did not match up to his expectations. Perhaps he felt as Rudolph Stark had, when the latter wrote in his diary—'the Fokker is a thoroughbred, but the Pfalz a cart-horse'.

The Pfalz products, sponsored by the Bavarian government, did not come directly under *Flugzeugmeisterei* control. For that reason, Richthofen and others, were called to the Speyer works to test Pfalz aircraft types instead of to the Adlershof trials. In particular the Pfalz D III equipped most Bavarian *Jagdstaffeln* as well as a number of Prussian units. Personnel for the Bavarian Air Service were recruited and administered separately, but their operational units were placed under German operational control and were numbered in the German series for *Staffeln*. Some Bavarian personnel served in German Air Service units and vice versa.

Apart from major problems, there was a minor problem interesting to note. Bolko, the youngest of the three Richthofen brothers, then a cadet at Wahlstatt, entreated his brother to show himself off at the school. Manfred pleaded that the ground adjacent to the school was not sufficiently dry to attempt a landing, but in the summer he would see what he could do. He was not to get the chance and perhaps he had few illusions about it, for news had arrived of Erwin Boehme's fate, shot down over the vicinity of Ypres, which meant that of the original pilots that had assembled under Boelcke in September 1916, Richthofen alone survived.

Christmas went much as any other day for the war was too intense and the very antithesis of all that Christmas meant. Rain and lack of enemy activity—not Yuletide—restricted flying that day to seven flights. As an occasion for celebration, the awards of the *Ordre pour le Mérite* to Leutnant Wüsthoff on November 27th and to Leutnant Klein on December 5th were matters of greater moment.

So ended 1917 and the first six months of the 'Circus'. While it had proved its fighting worth, it was, so far, by no means an outstanding success, due largely to limitations in both men and machines. The fact that pilot strength was then forty-four, shows that it was 20 per cent. below establishment strength and suggests that *J.G.1* was not staffed at the expense of other *Jagdstaffeln*. Aircraft of better performance were not forthcoming and replacement of aircraft and components was hampered by lack of raw materials. It had been particularly galling to crash three perfectly good Albatros D Vs (D2161/17 damaged, D4628/17 written-off and D5313/17 damaged) in a landing pile-up by *Jasta 11* that December. One machine had slewed on landing and the other had crashed into it, one turning over on to its back. All the pilots, however, escaped with nothing worse than bruises. The morale of the *Geschwader* was their one asset, bolstered by hints, rumours and obvious signs that in 1918 the Fatherland would mount a great offensive.

March Offensive

CHAPTER TWENTY-ONE

The Treaty of Brest-Litovsk was a necessary preliminary to the gigantic offensive that Germany intended to launch early in 1918, in an effort to secure final victory before the telling weight of fresh American troops had arrived in France. By ensuring peace terms with Russia, whose military strength, after heavy defeats, had collapsed following a bloody revolution, thousands of German troops could be released from the Eastern Front for the offensive in the West. This treaty provided not merely a background to Richthofen's destiny, but a phase in his life, for Richthofen was attendant upon the German delegation to Brest-Litovsk.

A more incongruous disparity between parties at a conference table could scarcely be imagined. The German delegation, backed and flanked by a host of officials and military advisers, including the von Richthofen brothers, Manfred and Lothar, conducted themselves with all the pomp and solemnity that Teutondom could offer. In contrast, many of the Russians were unkempt in appearance and disinterested in attitude, except when a political issue occasioned undue vociferation in expounding their impractical theories. Richthofen, we are told, was impressed by one of the women Communists, a Madame Bicenko—it is presumed with her personality, not her doctrine!

Richthofen tired of the protracted wranglings and suspected machinations. He did, however, witness the first stage in which the Ukrainian Republic, refusing to identify itself with the new Government of Russia, concluded a separate peace with Germany. Both he and his brother, off duty, became friendly with Count Czernin, leader of the Austro-Hungarian delegation, whose views on chivalry in air-fighting are not without interest. Lothar, relating his adventures to the Count, told of an occasion when his British opponent had refrained from firing when he was aware that Lothar's gun had jammed. Czernin said he would like to meet that Englishman, for in his eyes he was greater than the heroes of old.

Long before the conference ended—not until March could the Soviets be induced to sign—Manfred and Lothar were away to the forest of Bialowicza, in search of the only big-game hunting Europe could offer—bison and elk. This was the Russian preserve on which he had yearned to hunt, until recently an estate of the fabulous Romanoffs, whose autocracy, already waning, had ceased abruptly under the Bolshevists. In this area, however, the German military authorities were still in power. Setting off in a horse-drawn sledge, the two brothers settled down to an almost primeval existence, trudging through the snow in the deep of the Russian winter, searching for beasts almost extinct.

Meanwhile, on the Western Front, 1918 came in quietly for *J.G.1*. Their first success of the year was a Bristol Fighter on the 4th of January that gave Oberleutnant Reinhard his seventh victory. The following afternoon Leutnant Loewenhardt shot down a balloon behind St. Quentin. It was significant of the impending offensive that their aircraft should concentrate upon shooting down observation balloons to screen the preparations behind their lines.

Probably the best informal photograph of Manfred Freiherr von Richthofen ever taken.

On the 13th *Jasta 11* set out on a balloon strafe in the afternoon, shooting one down to give Leutnant Steinhäuser his second victory, but at the cost of Leutnant Stapenhorst. The latter was set upon by three Spads, who so damaged his aircraft that he was forced to land. According to his own account, after landing, he was set upon by some Cockney artillerymen from a nearby battery and soundly thrashed! Rescued by a party of R.F.C. men he at least commented favourably upon his subsequent treatment in a British prisoner-of-war camp.

Bad weather followed, washing out all flying until the 17th—when one flight was made! On the 18th it was clearing, and over thirty flights were made, one, however, ending in disaster. A young pilot, probably the most junior flying member of the formation, Flieger Riensberg, was shot down in his Pfalz D III 4059/17. Not only from this one instance, but from the researches of the German compiler, it is evident that the best machines, the Albatros D Vs and the Fokker Dr Is were being used only by the best pilots and the Pfalz D IIIs relegated to lesser lights and new arrivals. This selective allocation also appears to have extended to new machines of the same type, those new going to the accomplished pilots. Further evidence to support this

For victory scoring, a balloon destroyed counted equally with an aeroplane. Shown here is a Caquot type kite-balloon, used by an R.F.C. balloon section near Fricourt. The motor-winch is on the right of the picture.

assumption is provided by the fact that Leutnant von Linsingen was severely injured when his Pfalz D III D4223/17 crashed just off the main road through Iwuy.

It has already been observed that *J.G.1* units suffered as any other units in being below their establishment for personnel. Now it transpires that their unit equipment was not to scale at the expense of other units. Only in the selection of personnel, and that only with the sanction of *KoFl*, did the Commander of *J.G.1* have any advantage. Thus, the achievements of the *Geschwader* can only be attributed to the example and leadership they received from Manfred von Richthofen. His effect upon the War in the Air is by no means to be measured solely by his personal victory score. It was more than *Jagdgeschwader Nr. 1*—it was the *Richthofen Geschwader*.

Manfred von Richthofen himself, late in January, was giving the benefit of his experience to the *Prüfanstalt und Werft* at Adlershof, a section of the *Flugzeugmeisterei* (Directorate of Aircraft Production) that dealt with the examination and testing of new airframe and engine types and certain major components. The directorate also arranged, through the Air Service channels, for the attendance of accomplished pilots with experience at the front to make comparison tests on the various prototype aircraft, with a view to ensuring that the most suitable design was committed to production. Lothar, however, went home to Schweidnitz, but Manfred, with the Fatherland making so many calls upon him, could not find the time.

The *Geschwader* carried on. Better weather towards the end of January increased activity, but there were few engagements. On the 30th, Vizefeldwebel Barth, since July 1917 a member of *Jasta 10*, was lost in his Albatros D Va D4565/17. Three days later he was avenged by another member of his unit, Leutnant Kühn, who succeeded in forcing down a S.E.5A near Bouchain. There followed, on February 3rd, a forced landing that caused an adverse technical report on Fokker Dr I 155/17. During a flight piloted by Leutnant Joachim Wolff, the top wing collapsed and only with difficulty did Wolff bring it down under control near Villers Outreaux. The Fokker Triplane was by no means as well liked as is generally believed. Outside *J.G.1* few were still in use. Because of an unorthodox configuration and by the fact that von Richthofen still chose at times to use this triplane, the type achieved an importance out of all proportion to the limited number produced.

Rain restricted activity until February 16th, when Oberleutnant Reinhard shot down a Bristol Fighter over St. Quentin. A significant victory that portended the impending offensive. The R.F.C. had become aware of unusual activity, particularly train movements behind this front, and measures had been taken to increase the establishment of No. 48 (Bristol Fighter) Squadron to enable it to perform regular extended reconnaissances behind St. Quentin. Although this was the area from which the main attack was launched, preparations behind other parts of the front confused British G.H.Q. until two days before, when British Intelligence were able to report where and when the blow would fall. Apart from Reinhard's victory, the only other event of note was that Leutnant Klein had to be taken to *Feldlazarett Nr. 253* with slight injuries after crash-landing Pfalz D III 4283/17.

March was the month of *Der Tag*. Preparations were most evident to the flying personnel of the *Geschwader* as they glanced down during patrols. New support lines, fresh battery positions, supply depots expanding and increased activity on road, rail and canal. The Air Service too was expanded, chiefly by arrivals from the Russian Front. The supply of miscellaneous items of equipment, important to efficiency, was now much better, for in raw materials the Air Service was then second only to the Submarine Service in priority for allocation. A new fighter aircraft type was still sorely needed, but production of existing types had greatly increased. Whereas Germany had built 8,100 aircraft of all types during 1916; 19,400 left the production lines in 1917. Forward airfields were being constructed in anticipation of success and morale in general soared.

The *Geschwader* knew well that the day was near, but so far there had been little increase in their strength. Pilots from the Russian Front had not the training for air-fighting on the Western Front, or indeed the experience with fighter aircraft types. The fighting strength of *J.G.1* was now 43 pilots. These were as follows: *Jasta 4:* Leutnant Wüsthoff *Staffelführer*, Leutnant Dreckmann, Leutnant von Gluczewski, Leutnant Joschkowitz, Leutnant Koepsch, Leutnant Maushake, Leutnant Meyer, Leutnant Rousselle, Sergeant Schmutzler and Leutnant Skauradzun. *Jasta 6:* Oberleutnant Reinhard *Staffelführer*, Sergeant Beschow, Leutnant von Breiten-Landenberg, Vizefeldwebel Hemer, Leutnant Janzen, Vizefeldwebel von Raffay, Leutnant Tüxen, Fw. Lt. Schubert, Leutnant Paul Wenzel and Leutnant Wolff (yet a third Wolff!). *Jasta 10:* Leutnant Klein *Staffelführer*, Off. Stellv. Aue, Leutnant Bender, Leutnant Bohlein, Vizefeldwebel Burggaller, Vizefeldwebel Delang, Leutnant Friedrichs, Leutnant Grassmann, Leutnant Heldmann, Leutnant Kühn and Leutnant Loewenhardt. *Jasta 11:* Leutnant von Richthofen *Staffelführer*, Leutnant Bahr, Leutnant von Conta, Leutnant Esser, Leutnant Gussmann, Leutnant Just, Leutnant Lübbert, Leutnant Mohnicke, Leutnant von der Osten Leutnant Steinhäuser and Leutnant Joachim Wolff; additionally Leutnant Krefft as technical officer was officially on the strength of this *Jasta*.

Thus, as the preparations for the greatest battle of the war neared completion, forty-four men of an average age of just under twenty-three, formed the fighting strength of *J.G.1*. The youngest, Wüsthoff—and a *Staffel* leader at that, was nineteen. The eldest were Schubert and Wenzel, who were 'old men' of thirty. At their head, Manfred von Richthofen was a veteran of twenty-five years.

If the list of names be taken as the parade-state of *J.G.1* on the evening of March 1st, not all would have been shown as available for duty. That morning Leutnant Mohnicke had been shot down and by evening would have been shown as in hospital. As his wounds were severe, he would have been struck off the unit strength within a few days. Leutnant Just too, having been shot in the hand, would be shown unfit for duty. Correspondingly the aircraft state would show Fokker Dr I 155/17, only recently repaired after a forced landing, as once more damaged, and Dr I 110/17 in a similar condition. And then the rains came; for three continuous days, which at least had the effect of conserving life and limb—but only temporarily.

With brighter weather, thirty-eight flights were made and on one of them Leutnant Bahr crashed to his death in Dr I 106/17.

Richthofen's quarters on the airfield at Lechelle, an aerodrome hurriedly vacated by No. 15 Squadron R.F.C., during the German offensive.

After a further respite on the 7th, when bad weather allowed only seven flights, the 8th brought even honours —a French biplane claimed by Leutnant Heldmann balancing the wounding of Leutnant Skauradzun in Pfalz D III 4042/17.

All leave had been cancelled preparatory to the offensive. Lothar von Richthofen had returned and he continued his scoring on March 11th, when a Bristol Fighter, crashing down near Fresnoy les Roye, gave him his twenty-seventh victory. Manfred too, was back, and on the day following the two brothers were together in the same action.

No. 62 Squadron R.F.C. had recently been moved to an airfield behind the British Fifth Army's Front. On March 12th, nine of their Bristol Fighters had set out on an offensive patrol over the Cambrai area soon after 10 a.m. An hour later, Manfred, flying a triplane again, Dr I 152/17, and accompanied by Lothar and Leutnant Steinhäuser had sighted the Bristols and were steadily reaching their height, some 18,000 feet. Warily the three *J.G.1* pilots followed, moving round, to take advantage of the sun, waiting for a suitable opportunity to attack. It came when one of the British pilots dived down upon a German two-seater below, quickly followed by another—No. B1251. Richthofen closed in. As he did so the gunner of B1251 fired into the air—so Richthofen wrote in his report. Actually, in anticipation of action with the two-seater, he was testing his guns!

The test had an unfortunate consequence. As the empty cartridge cases fell away, one lodged between the bottom of the control column—usually known as the joy-stick in those days—and a metal fitting. Frantically the pilot poked with his foot and wobbled the stick in an effort to dislodge it. In so doing he lost height. Meanwhile the first Bristol to dive down was climbing back into the formation, the pilot evidently having realised that there was safety in numbers. This left B1251 on its own—setting the stage ideally for Richthofen's tactics.

von Richthofen engaged in conversation with, it is believed by the stance of the officer concerned, Oberleutnant von Doering.

Richthofen fired and the gunner, Second Lieutenant Sparks, slumped wounded to the bottom of his cockpit. The pilot, Lieutenant Clutterbuck, glancing back and seeing the huddled form of his gunner, realised his defenceless position. Taking advantage of the Bristol's structural strength he power-dived, hoping to outdive his pursuer. At 4,000 feet he pulled out, after noticing several bracing wires streaming aft, that had presumably been shot away. His object then was to make a direct line for home at the fastest possible speed—but he was well over the German side, and due to flapping fabric his machine was not making good speed.

Having been outdived, Richthofen now had the advantage of height to give him the extra speed necessary to catch up the Bristol by a long shallow dive. With the observer apparently knocked out, it was an easy matter to attack from above and behind, diving to sight his guns. Clutterbuck, gamely swerved and even banked round into an about-turn! But Richthofen, persistent as ever, followed closely, firing short, but accurate bursts. Clutterbuck even tried to man the rear guns himself, when Sparks, having regained consciousness, but very weak from loss of blood and in great pain, rose in his cockpit and with hands wet with blood, gripped his guns—and fired. The effort, however, was too much and back he fell again.

Still the Bristol lost height and with Richthofen cross-firing from side to side it is evident he had the advantage of speed.

A demonstration of air-fighting by Bristol Fighters of No. 48 Squadron, showing a position 'blind to the guns' of the defending aircraft.

B1251 was badly shot about and with scarcely a hundred feet in height, Clutterbuck realised the utter hopelessness of his position. It is possible Richthofen realised this too and his final shots were merely harassing fire. Many have questioned the reason for the three-way control to the twin Spandaus on the Fokker Triplane, that allowed individual or simultaneous firing of the two guns. In the case of harassing fire, firing of just one gun would conserve more ammunition than by the absence of individual control, although the primary reason was to conserve ammunition in protracted fighting.

The device was useful for a ruse practised by Richthofen when his adversary had the advantage of an aircraft of greater speed. Hoping that the pilot was inexperienced he would fire at long range, no doubt using single fire to conserve ammunition. If the pursued pilot was inexperienced, he would, perhaps, on hearing fire behind, take evasive action by swerving from side to side—thus reducing his forward speed and so allowing Richthofen to catch up and fire at closer range—with both guns.

In any case, it mattered not to Clutterbuck and Sparks, they at least had the satisfaction of knowing that they had fought their utmost as B1251 touched down and rumbled to a stop with its wheels in a shell-hole. Troops soon converged upon the machine and Clutterbuck and Sparks were led away. The latter, suffering from the effects of his wound, was taken to a hospital, where, a little later, a box of cigars reached him, sent with the compliments of—Manfred, Freiherr von Richthofen.

B1251 was not the only Bristol lost by No. 62 Squadron that day. One of the flight commanders, Captain Kennedy, M.C., had fired a red Very light soon after the German machines had been sighted to give due warning to his flight. Within minutes his machine had burst into flames and both he and his observer had fallen out. Two other Bristols also fell. From the German side, two Bristols were credited to Lothar as his twenty-eighth and twenty-ninth, and one to Leutnant Steinhäuser. In addition, three balloons and a S.E.5. were claimed that day for the twenty-five flights in all that *J.G.1* made. There were no losses.

It would be thought that No. 62 Squadron would have had enough for a time, but they were out next morning and in even greater strength! This time eleven set out for an offensive patrol along a line Cambrai–Le Cateau, whilst two flights of Camels from No. 73 Squadron patrolled a fringing line, in connection with a bombing raid carried out by the D.H.4s of Nos. 25 and 27 Squadrons.

Richthofen had taken off with *Jasta 11* and was joined in the air by two more of his units, until some thirty-five machines, Albatros D Vas and Fokker Dr Is, were concentrated.

The Fokker Dr Is of a Jasta being prepared for take-off. Early in 1918 the Greek cross as shown here, superseded the earlier cross patée shown on the opposite page.

First he shot at a D.H.4, then he left it, a doomed machine, harried by other fighters. Sighting the Camels of No. 73 Squadron above, he climbed to secure an attacking position.

As he watched he saw Camel B5590 turn and attack one of his own machines. Approaching quickly he fired at the Camel, hitting a petrol tank and wounding the pilot, who, in trying to put his machine down near Gonnelieu, crashed just behind the German lines. So died a young man from Nova Scotia.

In a published report, this Camel was reputed to have carried a Lewis gun and a single Vickers gun, which would have been unorthodox armament for a day-fighter Camel on the Western Front. Lest the enthusiasts have been confounded by that account, it can now be definitely stated that B5590 was a standard 130 h.p. Clerget Camel and that its armament has been checked as twin Vickers guns, to the degree of ascertaining that the left-hand gun was Vickers No. C5059 and the right-hand gun Vickers No. A8167.

Having disposed of B5590, Richthofen led on to the Bristol Fighters. Perhaps by their squadron markings, three stripes around their fuselages, he recognised them as his opponents of the day before. With some twenty aircraft following Richthofen, the Bristols were outnumbered. Their leader, Captain G. F. Hughes with Captain H. Claye in the gunner's cockpit, tried to avoid becoming embroiled and skilfully led away with the intention of drawing the German fighters away from the D.H.4 bombers. However, by a mistaken signal, some of the Bristols dropped from formation and a general dog-fight ensued. Captain Claye claimed to have shot down two Fokker Triplanes and several other gunners made claims for enemy aircraft sent down out of control. One of these was evidently Lothar, for his machine was shot about and upon trying to land, he side-slipped into the ground.

His triplane struck obliquely, smashing the undercarriage and shattering the lower wings on the port side. Lothar was thrown violently forward and his face smacked into the dashboard, knocking him out. His injuries were at first thought serious as he was spitting blood, but it was blood swallowed from his facial injuries, a badly cut nose and jaw. Each day his brother visited him in hospital.

They were tense days. The date of the offensive had then been fixed. von Hoeppner, the commander of the Air Service, himself visited the *Geschwader*, meeting many of the pilots on the aerodrome at Avesnes-le-Sec on March 17th. The day following was most auspicious for *J.G.1*. Some forty British aircraft had crossed the lines in flights, forming roughly a quadrangle, and were met by thirty *J.G.1* machines formed up in a loose triangular formation. In the resulting mêlée, nine British aircraft were shot down without loss to *J.G.1*. Amongst those scoring were Leutnant Kirschstein, later to become a famous ace, who was achieving his first victory and Manfred von Richthofen scoring his sixty-sixth.

Richthofen was flying at the head of *Jasta 11* followed closely by *Jasta 6* and *Jasta 10*, when he spotted British formations crossing the lines and making in the direction of Le Cateau. He climbed and led first into the attack upon

von Richthofen with Leutnant Klein, leader of Jasta 10, *who achieved twenty-two victories before his second and serious wounding, early in 1918.*

some Bristol fighters. Both Leutnant Gussman of *Jasta 11* and he made for the same machine and the *coup de grâce* was by Gussman's fire. Flying on to another enemy formation, again Richthofen found one of his pilots attacking the machine at which he was firing. He was evidently not too certain of the type, for he wrote in his report—*scheinbar ein Breguet oder Bristol-Fighter*. In any case, he left it to the other pilot, Leutnant Loewenhardt, who thereby achieved his thirteenth victory.

It might well seem strange now that there was difficulty in distinguishing between two such types as the Breguet 14 and the Bristol Fighter, but it should be appreciated that the pamphlets of silhouettes showing Allied aircraft types, issued to German pilots, were very crudely drawn.

Leaving the two-seaters, he joined in a fight against ten S.E.5As and nine Camels. As a Camel flashed across his sights he fired, scoring hits on both its fuel tanks. The Camel pilot, Lieutenant Ivamy of No. 54 Squadron R.F.C., blinded temporarily with spurting petrol and conscious of Richthofen's impelling firing, nose-dived his machine to lose height for an emergency landing. There was nothing more he could have done. His landing was remarkably good under the circumstances. As his machine rolled to a stop he was aware of many troops running towards him, with rifles at the ready. He could not even destroy his machine. Not that it much mattered, as limitation in numbers and the supply of spares precluded its use by the Germans, and as far as secrets went, the *Flugzeugmeisterei* had already completed a technical evaluation of the Camel from an earlier example captured almost intact—B6290. With Ivamy's Camel, little more was done than removing it to a dump, cataloguing it as Camel B5243 with Clerget No. 35751/W.D. 9400 and stripping it of any copper or brass fittings.

Leutnant Ernst Udet, who became Germany's second highest scoring ace, is shown here when he was leader of Jasta 37, *prior to joining* J.G.1.

Der Tag was near. On the 20th of March, the eve of the offensive, *J.G.1* provided an operational detachment for the advanced airfield at Awoingt. Sealed orders, by then opened, gave *J.G.1* their operational instructions which included a new grouping of *Jagdstaffeln* into two fighting areas—classified simply as Northern and Southern regions of the German 2nd Army Front. In the North Region, *J.G.1* and *Jagdgruppe 2* (*Jasta 5* and *46*) were under von Richthofen and in the other, *Jagdgruppe 9* (*Jasta 3, 37, 54* and *56*) and *Jagdgruppe 10* (*Jasta 16* and *34*) were commanded by Oberleutnant Kohze.

The stage was set. German hopes were high. At 4.45 a.m. on March 21st, the bombardment opened, with a hail of steel, high explosive and gas along the British Fifth Army's Front and part of the Third Army's Front to a depth of twenty miles. Four hours later, the initial infantry assault, for which some fifty-six divisions had been assembled, was launched through the smoke that hung low in the air that misty morning. The greatest battle of the war had commenced.

The Great Battle

CHAPTER TWENTY-TWO

Probably the best known of all Fokker Triplane pictures, but as one that was officially taken by the German authorities, to show von Richthofen's famous red machine in flight, its inclusion is inevitable. This picture, however, is shown in its original state, without the background 'blacked out' as in many previous reproductions.

The German onslaught achieved considerable success at first. Launched so that the main blow would fall against the British Fifth Army, which had less men per mile of frontage than any one of the five British Armies forming the B.E.F., its front and support lines were overrun. Unhelpfully its army commander, General Sir Hubert Gough, was instructed by G.H.Q. to stand firm, but using his initiative, and taking a realistic view of the situation, he conducted, under the circumstances, a magnificent fighting retreat—only to be relieved of his command. Not for many years after was his generalship in that action appreciated and his honour vindicated.

Thorough planning, good discipline and massed infantry were met by British courage and fortitude. Weight of numbers told and the British were forced to give ground. Few tanks were used by the Germans, although it is interesting to note that they formed units of captured British tanks as well as using, in limited numbers, a tank of their own design. Ludendorff, advanced in his ideas upon the use of aircraft, had little faith in the tank. His main reliance was upon trained infantry, and air units, such as *J.G.1*, were conditioned to giving them their utmost support.

The personnel of *J.G.1* had awakened early. They breakfasted to the thunder of guns. As 8 a.m. approached they had expected the call would come for take-off in support of the infantry attack, but no call came. The heavy mist, mingling with the heavier smoke of explosives, precluded any possibility of flying. Dismally they hung about the airfield, becoming very conscious, that for them at least, *Der Tag* was an anti-climax. However, by midday the fog had lifted a little and their 2nd Army report centre gave notice that the R.F.C. had two observation balloons up.

Two *Jasta 10* pilots, Loewenhardt and Friedrichs, took off to deal with them and both reported success on return. Later in the day, a few patrols were flown, but poor visibility restricted action. If *J.G.1* felt frustrated by the fog, it was an asset to the German infantry, whose movements were considerably screened. Both sides, as conditions permitted at intervals that day, concentrated on low-level work to assist the troops on the ground and only one dog-fight developed, that being over Bourlon Wood.

Mist continued to hamper the activities of *J.G.1* until the 24th, when better weather enabled them to make up for lost time by flying over a hundred sorties! In the air-fighting that day, forty-two German aircraft were claimed by the R.F.C., whose losses comprised eleven missing, forty-six wrecked and eight destroyed or abandoned in withdrawals. *J.G.1*, however, claimed only one victim—and that by von Richthofen himself.

Leading twenty-five aircraft in a new triplane, Dr I 477/17, he was involved in a long fight with ten S.E.5As of his oft-encountered enemies—No. 56 Squadron. Singling out C5389, that happened to be piloted by a young American, W. Porter, jnr., his fire severed the interplane struts on one side, causing the mainplanes to be wrenched apart in the slipstream. Thus disintegrating, the components of the aircraft were scattered over a wide area, the engine, Hispano 1050/W.D. 8623, thudding into the ground near Combles, on the British side of the lines. Porter was well avenged that day by a Captain J. L. Trollope of No. 43 Squadron who shot down six aircraft, a record at that time. However, four days later his Camel (C8270 Clerget No. 1263/W.D. 29862) was shot down and he was taken prisoner.

Next day, the 25th, Richthofen was again the only

During the March 1918 offensive, the Germans used a tank of their own design as well as using captured British tanks. Here, a captured German model is being examined at Tank Corps H.Q. Repair Shops, Erin.

J.G.1 member to score, this time a Camel. In common with most R.F.C. fighter units that day, the Camels of No. 3 Squadron were committed to ground-strafing in a desperate effort to stem the German advance. When Richthofen, at the head of five *Jasta 11* men, met them, they were hampered by the carriage of Cooper bombs. Apparently Richthofen hit and despatched Camel C1562 (110 Le Rhône No. 35759/W.D. 9408) before the pilot was sufficiently aware of danger to release his bombs, for explosions were observed taking place in the burning wreckage.

Next morning Richthofen welcomed Leutnant Ernst Udet to *J.G.1*, a posting that he had arranged. A few days before, in pouring rain, he had toured *Jagdstaffeln* in the 2nd Army area. Coming to an airfield near Le Cateau, where *Jasta 37* had moved ready for the offensive, he found their unit commander, Udet, of whom he had good report, engrossed in helping his mechanics to erect tents. Leaving his car on the Le Cateau road, he squelched through the mud. Tapping Udet on the shoulder and making a facetious remark upon the weather by way of introduction, he asked him his victory score. It was nineteen confirmed and one awaiting confirmation. Well satisfied Richthofen then put the significant question—'Would you like to join us?'

And so it happened, that on March 26th, Udet, late leader of *Jasta 37*, flying for the first time a triplane, accompanied Richthofen on an offensive patrol, followed by three *Jasta 11* members, Lt. Gussmann, Lt. Just and Vfw. Scholz. Meeting again low-flying Camels, both Richthofen and Gussman scored against a flight of No. 54 Squadron. Richthofen's adversary was more astute than his previous victim. By skilful flying he sought to escape, but in the end he was blasted from a distance not greater than his aircraft's length—so wrote Richthofen in his report. Whilst falling the machine broke in half, leaving little hope for the pilot.

Within fifteen minutes, in approximately the same area and at about the same height, 2,000 feet, he encountered an R.E.8. Due to the desperate situation, the R.F.C. had been forced to employ even those aircraft on low-altitude work. The instructions at that time to certain R.F.C. units were unequivocal, '. . . very low flying essential . . . all risks to be taken'. This was in some cases carried out to the letter, for the history of the German 8th Grenadier Regiment records at that time an officer being—run over by a British S.E.5! The duty of the occupants of the machine Richthofen was stalking was to report upon German reserve troops; information that No. 15 Squadron has been asked by G.H.Q. to provide. Gamely the observer, aware of the importance of his mission, fired at the approaching enemy machines. Seeing the gunner alerted, Richthofen dived down under the R.E.8 and rose to get off a hundred shots from below and behind, that sent it down in flames, killing the occupants, two young second lieutenants. The wreckage of this R.E.8, B742 (R.A.F. 4A No. 29556/W.D. 12387), a rebuilt machine, continued to burn on the ground.

Richthofen was headline news again. His score stood at seventy. He had achieved victories on three consecutive days and two in one day. Almost a year had passed since he had scored so quickly. He was a new man again, or so it seemed from statistics. It was not so in reality. If, for a time, he achieved the same end, it was not in the same spirit. He was bent on doing his duty to the last and he lived only for that. When not in the air he sought the four walls of his hut. Already Bodenschatz held a sealed grey envelope, deposited by Richthofen, whose handwriting on the front gave the brief instruction—'Should I not return—open'.

Nevertheless, during this period, which has been described as 'Richthofen's Indian Summer', he certainly appeared to be in great form, for on the 27th he scored three victories! His tactics at this time should, however, be taken into account. As leader of a large formation it was part of his duty to detach himself at times from his formation in an engagement and watch his men in action. Opportunities to select victims on the fringe of the fighting would come his way; opportunities that no other pilot would dare take, or could take, with equanimity.

General strategy changed that day. Hitherto, the main object had been to give direct assistance to their own attacking infantry, by ground-strafing defending British troops and by protecting *Schutzstaffeln*. Owing to the determined way in which the R.F.C. had concentrated upon a ground-attack role with their fighters, *J.G.1* was switched to dealing with them. It suited them very well and a record number of sorties, 118, were flown! The British fighters, operating at low altitude and more occupied with the scene below than the dangers from above, were at a disadvantage, quite apart from the limitations imposed upon their machines by the carriage of bombs. Also, although in general along the front, the Allies had numerical advantage in numbers of aircraft to approximately a 3 to 1 ratio, behind the forty-four-mile battle-front the Germans had a superiority of 822 to 645 in actual numbers.

Morale throughout *J.G.1*, and indeed of most German units at the time was high. Certainly it looked as if Germany had a good chance of winning the war. *J.G.1*, to keep pace with the advance, were given a new forward airfield at Lechelle, evacuated only a few days earlier by No. 15 Squadron R.F.C. Major servicing facilities still remained back at Avesnes le Sec. Presumably Richthofen's own mount, Dr I 477/17, was there under overhaul, for when he set out in the early morning on March 27th from Lechelle, with five *Jasta 11* men, he was flying Dr I 127/17.

About 9 a.m. they attacked Camel C8234, that had set out on low-flying patrol. Closing in and firing 150 shots, Richthofen sent it down to splash into the flooded area of the River Ancre.

For a patrol in the afternoon, his earlier triplane, Dr I 477/17, was available. With it, he led again some *Jasta 11* men, making in all a formation of seven triplanes. A No. 20 Squadron Bristol Fighter was approached unnoticed to within 150 feet, when Richthofen opened fire. Flames shot out of the Bristol and as the wing fabric burnt and reduced lift, the dead-weight of the engine, Rolls-Royce 2/Falcon/1265, bore the wreckage down rapidly. Within five minutes, he had attacked another Bristol observed pursuing one of his own machines. There was no return fire and in his report Richthofen stated that the observer's seat was closed and that in all probability it was filled with bombs —which was most unlikely! As the Bristol fell burning into a wood and the reporting service, due to the advance, was unable to identify the wreckage in connection with Richthofen's victory, it cannot be substantiated that there was no observer. Facts point to the pilot of the doomed aircraft being Captain H. R. Child of No. 11 Squadron. If this was so, then Child was scheduled to fly that day with a Lieutenant A. Reeve, seconded from a Canadian Regiment, who was that very day reported as missing.

Whilst Richthofen achieved three victories, the rest of *J.G.1* made up a further ten. Leutnant Loewenhardt, in despatching a D.H.4 made his fifteenth victory and a S.E.5A gave Leutnant Friedrichs his third. Amongst four pilots claiming R.E.8s was Leutnant Udet, who was soon finding his feet in *Jasta 11*. Another pilot, Leutnant Kirschstein, destined to win the *Pour le Mérite*, was involved in a fight that gave one of his adversaries a well-deserved Victoria Cross.

On patrol, *Jasta 10* had been attracted by an action in which a Fokker Triplane, crossing the front of an Armstrong Whitworth F.K.8, B5773 from No. 2 Squadron, had been shot at by the Ack W's observer, Lieutenant A. W. Hammond, and sent spinning down out of control. *Jasta 10* then descended upon the lone A.W. from several different directions, confusing the gunner. The pilot, Second Lieutenant A. A. McLeod, threw the machine about, whilst Hamilton kept up a spirited and well-directed fire. At least three triplanes withdrew, but Kirschstein persisted and went in close. McLeod, manfully taking evasive action was already suffering from five flesh wounds, and the observer too was wounded. They were both still fighting back, when a bullet penetrated the fuel tank and the machine caught fire. A determined man, McLeod clambered out of his cockpit rendered untenable by the heat, and standing on the port lower wing, he endeavoured to control the machine by reaching over from that position. Side-slipping steeply down towards the port side, he kept the flames fanned away from the observer, who continued firing, even though his difficulties were added to by the bottom of his cockpit

A British tank captured and re-captured. One J.G.1 pilot, Lt. Udet, caused a tank to slew and overturn from a railway embankment, after he had made six diving attacks upon it with guns blazing.

Seated on the fuselage of a captured aircraft from No. 10 (Naval) Squadron is Richthofen's own mechanic, Holzapfel. It is said that it is von Richthofen standing by the cowling.

breaking away, compelling him to brace himself against the fuselage sides for support.

Six times the observer had been wounded and as the A.W. crashed to a landing in No Man's Land, he sustained yet further injury. Lying helpless, he was dragged from the wreckage by McLeod, who himself then collapsed through loss of blood. Their troubles were by no means over, for only with difficulty, under German machine-gun fire, were they rescued by British troops. During this time, Kirschstein went on to shoot down a Camel.

Sad to relate, McLeod died of his wounds a week before the Armistice, but not before he had reached his native Winnipeg, Canada. Hammond, after the amputation of a leg and treatment, survived.

Next day Richthofen himself encountered a A.W.F.K.8 and achieved his first and only victory over that type. It is not without interest to note that the letters F.K. stood for Frederik Koolhoven, a Dutch designer with the firm of Armstrong Whitworth and that Richthofen's machine was built under the direction of another Dutchman who had a factory in Germany—Anthony Fokker. Richthofen, that day, was attracted to the A.W. by anti-aircraft shells bursting well below him at 2,000 feet. Still over the German lines, but making in a homeward direction, was the A.W. Cutting off its retreat, Richthofen fired a hundred rounds at it, after which it fell burning.

That victory, Richthofen's seventy-fourth, which caused No. 82 Squadron R.F.C. to lose two young second lieutenants, and a brand-new F.K.8 C8444 with only 100 minutes' flying time—and that probably on delivery flight—fitted with Beardmore engine No. 1559/W.D. 20593, was only one of the squadron's many misfortunes. Their task, typical of many Corps Squadrons in those desperate days, was to supply a continuous contact patrol by at least one aeroplane throughout the whole day, with all other aircraft maintaining the maximum number of machine-gunning and bombing attacks upon the enemy.

Withdrawing to another airfield, they were forced to destroy F.K.8 C3654, that could not be repaired in time. As they left in formation, the engine of C8431 cut and due to the sudden loss of forward speed C8437 crashed into it from behind, bringing both down in such a condition that only their guns were salvageable. The elements, too, were against the squadron that day. Reaching their new airfield, B3302 took off for patrol, but owing to a blustery wind, it was lifted suddenly and it dropped back heavily over the edge of the airfield, smashing its undercarriage. Richthofen, his 'Circus', or indeed the whole of the German Air Service, were by no means the only rigours of the campaign!

Restrictions in the supply of materials and of fuel in particular had hampered the Germans. Now the supply situation was affecting the British, not through production difficulties, but because the supply and repair depots were in danger of being overrun by the German incursion, and their removal to the rear, merely as a safety precaution, would seriously affect supply.

This picture of the squadron leader's S.E.5A of No. 32 Squadron, with a flight of Sopwith Camels in the background, gives a picture symbolic of the British fighter aircraft types facing J.G.1 during the German offensive.

100

Providing an interesting comparison with the picture opposite of a Sopwith Triplane in German hands—a Fokker Triplane in Allied hands.

On the day Richthofen claimed his A.W., March 28th, three victims fell to his men; a Camel to Udet, a Bristol Fighter to Leutnant Weiss and a S.E.5A as the initial victory of Leutnant von Rautter. The only casualty during that momentous period occurred that day, but it was not fatal—Leutnant von der Osten, who was acting leader of *Jasta 4*, was shot down in Albatros D Va D4566/17. His place was taken by Leutnant Janzen.

From then until the end of the month, rain and low clouds curtailed flying. Three pilots, an officer and two vizefeldwebels, were at that time posted to an Air Park. It was significant that all three had served for a relatively long time with the formation and only one of them could claim a single victory. Perhaps, therefore, they were not matching up to the exacting standards required by their leader, although such presumed relegation was less frequent under Richthofen than under later commanders. No doubt because Richthofen was more selective in his recruitment.

On April 1st, 1918, the Royal Air Force was formed by the amalgamation of the Royal Flying Corps and the Royal Naval Air Service. In the Field it had little immediate significance, for the battles were too engaging. That day there was little ground fighting, the attack having at last lost its impetus, but there was much aerial activity, particularly at low altitudes. Early-morning Camels of No. 65 Squadron were out strafing, losing D1811 and D6474 in the process, one falling to a *J.G.1* officer, Leutnant Siemelkamp. The D.H.4s of No. 57 Squadron made three bombing attacks upon Bapaume, losing two of their number (A7401 and A7872), one of which fell to Leutnant Wolff, who also claimed an S.E.5A. Reinhard, recently promoted to Hauptmann, achieved his victory at the cost of another S.E.5A, presumed to be either C5433 or C6351, which were lost that day by No. 56 Squadron. A Bristol Fighter also fell to Vizefeldwebel Hemer. It was not a good day for the R.A.F., who, altogether, lost ten machines over the lines, had thirty-eight wrecked and four destroyed by bombing, when German aircraft followed the F.Es. of No. 101 Squadron back to their base. Of the losses over the lines, *J.G.1* could claim half.

Next day, another advanced airfield was established at Harbonnières. As a temporary measure it was intended to fly their red machines each morning from Lechelle, where quartering and servicing were provided, and to operate from the new airfield during the day, where refuelling and ammunition replenishing facilities were available. Soon after midday, Richthofen, apparently alone this time, was patrolling in Dr I 477/17 when he spotted an R.E.8 flying just below the cloud at some 2,500 feet. After closing in to about fifty yards, the observer became aware of the impending attack. Too late, his fire failed to deter Richthofen, who closed in to ten yards and fired. He was closer still when the R.E. burst into flames. So close, that he witnessed the ghastly sight of the occupants writhing in agony and bending over the cockpit sides to avoid the searing flames. Blazing, the R.E.8 went down, not hurriedly, but uncontrolled. As it hit the ground, a merciful explosion left little doubt that the occupants were beyond further suffering. Again two young second lieutenants had died. This time in an early production R.E.8, A3868 (R.A.F. 4A engine No. 1207/W.D. 4576). Three Bristol Fighters and an S.E.5A made up the day's score of *J.G.1* victories for the eighty-nine flights made.

With the halting of the German advance, it became the turn of the R.A.F. to change their tactics and to concentrate upon the German fighter formations that were sweeping along the lines. *J.G.1*, however, owing to rain and cloud in their area, were able to achieve only one victory, that on April 3rd, when Leutnant von Rautter scored again by shooting down a A.W.F.K.8. Not until the 6th did they get further opportunity. During that time another Richthofen came to *J.G.1*, Leutnant Wolfram von Richthofen, a cousin of Manfred, enrolled in *Jasta 11*.

There were no pilot casualties in action at this time, but Udet, who had been suffering from earache, and had so recently transferred to *J.G.1*, was forced to report sick. With twenty-two confirmed victories, he was already becoming a well-known personality. He had been born at Frankfurt-am-Main on April 26th, 1896. As a young army volunteer, he had been able, due to an understanding with his father, to learn to fly before soldiering and his transfer to the Air Service was thereby facilitated. He first took the Field with *Fl. Abt. 206*. The vicissitudes of his early service brought him through several crashes, condemnation and approbation, to the command of a *Jasta*, and now, having reached *J.G.1*, the height of his ambition, he was admitted on April 3rd to *Kriegslazarett Nr. 7* at Valenciennes as a patient with ear trouble.

CHAPTER TWENTY-THREE

That Fateful Day

Now residing in Rhodesia, is Richthofen's 80th and last victim, 2/Lt. D. G. Lewis; who, in 1938, was invited by the Luftwaffe to visit the reconstituted Richthofen Geschwader.

Following two days of rain, restricting activity, ten claims were made by *J.G.1* on April 6th. Of these, all but one, a Bristol Fighter, were Sopwith Camels. It would appear that five at least were the 130 h.p. Clerget (long stroke) engined Camels of No. 43 Sqn. R.A.F., whose pilots were making special flights southward of their normal area. A patrol from that squadron had left at 2 p.m. and came back with Lieutenant S. H. Lewis missing in C8247 (Clerget 1593/W.D. 30192). During that patrol time both Wolff and Kirschstein made claims for Camels. Then, just after 3 p.m. (G.M.T.), Lieutenants F. Hudson, E. Mather and M. F. Peiler left, flying respectively B2431 (1057/W.D. 30655), C8281 (1265/W.D. 29864) and D6452 (1317/W.D. 29916). None of these returned and correspondingly, Leutnant Weiss, Vizefeldwebel Scholz and Leutnant Just made claims. Finally, from a No. 43 Squadron patrol leaving at 4.45 p.m., Lieutenant T. R. V. Hall in C8248 (1229/W.D. 29828) was shot down, matching a claim made by Leutnant Weiss for his sixteenth victory. Further to these misfortunes, one of their replacement aircraft, signalled for immediately, crashed on the airfield by way of landing. Fortunately the pilot escaped unhurt, but the Camel D1848, was wrecked.

If the regularity of the squadron's patrol losses that day seemed sacrificial, something more akin to a burnt offering happened on the airfield they had used at La Gorgue, a few days later, after a new German attack was launched in the plain of the Lys. The enemy bombardment had severed all telephonic communications and the landing ground was under fire. No. 43 Squadron had already left and No. 208 Squadron were packed ready to leave, should the situation deteriorate. Fog prevented any flying and the smoke from bursting shells, mingling with it, further reduced visibility. When a despatch rider brought news that the enemy had advanced to La Gorgue village, the squadron commander, understandably, gave orders to destroy all equipment that could not be moved. Before the loaded transport vehicles moved off, Camels were collected from the field, the hangars and repair bay and dumped together on the airfield; petrol was swilled over them— and they were set alight! In the blaze, sixteen* Camels at least went up in smoke and flame; one, N6342, was a veteran R.N.A.S. machine that had put in 216 flying hours and in contrast another, D3352, was brand new with only an hour's flying time since leaving the works of Messrs. Clayton and Shuttleworth.

Of the Camels that had been shot down on the 6th, one fell to Richthofen, making his seventy-sixth victory. Once again flying Dr I 127/17 and leading several *Jasta 11* members, he had attacked a flight of low-flying Camels. After only a few shots, his victim, Captain Sidney Philip Smith, in Camel D6491 (110 h.p. Le Rhône No. 54644/ W.D. 48144) was shot down in flames, his body and his aircraft losing their identity in the carnage of the battle below, near Villers-Bretonneux. Possibly Captain Smith, who came from No. 46 Squadron, had joined, or was flying near, a flight of Camels from another squadron, for he had become parted from his own patrol, and was last seen by Lieutenant McConnell of his unit, some forty-five minutes before the time Richthofen gave for his claim.

Richthofen's earlier claim had by then been substantiated, and evidently it had been decided that the three-quarter century mark should warrant special award. That day a telegram, relayed through General von Hoeppner, notified him that he was to receive the Order of the Red Eagle (Third Class) with Crown and Swords. The distinction was in its exclusiveness, for hitherto the decoration had been restricted to royalty, the peerage and generals.

During the afternoon of the 7th, Richthofen again claimed a double victory and although both were confirmed by *KoFl* of 2nd Army and accepted as confirmed victories by the High Command, neither can be satisfactorily accounted for by documentation or witness on the British side. Richthofen, flying in his red Dr I 477/17 at the head of a *Kette* from *Jasta 11*, approached a patrol of S.E.5As over Hangard. By his own account, he fired when still 250 yards distant, which, judged by his usual methods, was at a long range. Nevertheless, the machine suddenly disintegrated and fell scattering wreckage. A British battery commander later expressed an opinion that the S.E. had been struck by a shell from one of his field-guns. Although a rare occur-

---
* The sixteen known to have been burnt were B3773, B3785 B3794, B3853, B3936, B6260, B7189, B7193, B7196, B7201, B7253, D3330, D3335, D3339 D3352 and N6342.

102

rence, such accidents did happen, but that it should happen at the moment Richthofen opened fire, and for once at longer range than usual, is a chance in millions. But who was the victim in this case?

His victim has been given as Captain G. B. Moore, although records show that Captain Moore was not reported missing until the day following. An error in transcription or delay in reporting could have occurred; but confusing the issue further is the fact that his loss, which would fit Richthofen's report as regards time of day, happened to be some forty miles north of the area Richthofen was patrolling! Even supposing that it was a different time and place and that Captain Moore's death was in no way connected with Richthofen, the manner in which he met his death is a mystery. According to records, he left on patrol at 12.52 p.m. G.M.T., flying S.E.5A C1083, in company with eight other S.Es from No. 1 Squadron. He was last seen over Hollebeke at 2,000 feet, when his machine appeared to burst suddenly into flames! There were no enemy aircraft observed in the immediate vicinity! While it would appear that Captain Moore was not Richthofen's victim, there is insufficient evidence to refute earlier statements.

Continuing that same patrol, Richthofen observed some thirty minutes later a *Kette* of three German aircraft pursuing a lone British machine. He would not have intervened, but as he watched, the pursuing fighters were in turn attacked by machines that dived on to the scene. Richthofen then took a hand and getting behind one of the latest arrivals, he fired, but without effect. His adversary twisted and turned as Richthofen followed. Several times he gained a good position and fired before the enemy machine fell and—as Richthofen reported—dashed to the ground and broke to splinters. He claimed a Spad—but the only French type of aircraft lost that day by the R.A.F. was a Nieuport Scout Type 27, B3601 of No. 29 Squadron, and that late in the evening. The only R.A.F. squadron still using Spads was No. 23 and their losses during early April were only B6860 and B6864, both on the 10th of the month.

French Spads might have been patrolling the area, but no French losses were reported and in the absence of a record of Belgian Air Force losses, that possibility cannot be checked. April 7th, exactly a fortnight before he met his death, was Richthofen's 'mystery day'.

Rain and cloud curtailed flying for the next few days. On the 8th no flying at all was possible and preparations for a further move necessitated relief from operations. Although the main sphere of action was to the north where the Battle of the Lys was raging, *J.G.1* were to move to more permanent quarters, their temporary advanced airfields being unsuited for long operations. They moved to Cappy.

Richthofen was plagued with order and counter-order as the move was effected. It had become obvious that the main weight of the attack in the south had been spent and German hopes were now centred on the second phase then raging along the plain of the Lys. Daily Richthofen expected the call to move northward and actually suspended the transfer of equipment to Cappy at one time in anticipation. However, although the order did come—it was only to be countermanded within hours. Again the formation was alerted for a move and again they were stood down.

Claims for victims were made out by the pilots concerned on a German Army Form, to which was appended an endorsement for KoFl of the army concerned to forward, if approved, to the Commanding General of the Air Service. Here is the endorsement by KoFl of the 2nd Army for von Richthofen's 80th victory on 20th April, 1918.

The Commander of *J.G.1* felt frustrated because his unit was not once more at the centre of activity. Certainly the British were being hard pressed. The day *J.G.1* moved to Cappy, Field Marshal Sir Douglas Haig issued a Special Order of the Day to all ranks of the British Army in France and Flanders, bearing words that conveyed well enough how desperate the situation appeared to the British G.H.Q.: '... There is no other course open to us but to fight it out. Every position must be held to the last man; there must be no retirement. With our backs to the wall, believing in the justice of our cause, each one of us must fight on to the end....' Meanwhile Richthofen trudged disconsolately in the Somme mud that formed the surface of the Cappy airfield.

For some reason Cappy depressed Richthofen and possibly most other *J.G.1* members, for the advantages were purely functional. The nearest town, Peronne, was twelve miles away and its shell-shattered aspect was even more depressing than Cappy village. Several days of rain added to a general air of gloom that gave *J.G.1* an atmosphere almost suggestive of the impending disaster to their leader.

Presentiment, however, has no place in war. It is a false diagnosis of fear of the possible, which as service wears on becomes fear of the probable. There is no reason to suggest that Richthofen did not experience fear as did any other man. Skilled as he was, there was an element of chance in every combat and the law of averages is inexorable. During the days that proved to be his last he was kept much to his quarters, writing a treatise on air-fighting, bringing up to date the dicta of Boelcke in the light of recent experiences. It concerned *inter alia*, fighter unit organisation, principles governing the employment of *Jagdstaffeln* and the tactics of air fighting with particular reference to the leader's signalling system.

On April 19th, Richthofen congratulated Loewenhardt upon his appointment to the command of *Jasta 10*, a day of rain before dawn that continued until evening. Although there was rain too on the 20th, the penultimate day of Richthofen's life, twice as many flights were possible, and

Richthofen plays with his dog, Moritz. In the foreground is a wheel chock such as was tied to the dog's tail on the morning that Richthofen took off on his last flight.

on one of them Richthofen scored twice. He was now flying Dr I 425/17; although he may have received it a week or so before, this was his first recorded flight on this triplane. It was an evening flight, made as the weather improved at the close of a showery April day. Once again, when leading a select few from *Jasta 11*, a flight of Camels was sighted before the lines were reached and Richthofen led into an attack. In this he was at first thwarted.

Two flights of six machines each from No. 3 Squadron R.A.F. had set out, but owing to heavy cloud the two flights became separated. It was 'C' Flight which Richthofen had spotted, led by Captain D. Bell, but including as a flight member the Commanding Officer, Major Raymond-Barker. Bell, keeping a good look-out observed the triplanes moving in and immediately brought his flight round to meet them head-on. No sooner had they passed than Richthofen had banked round quickly on to a Camel's tail. It happened to be the Major's machine, which after only a few bullets had struck it, went down burning to fall near a wood.

Another 'C' Flight member, nineteen-year-old Second Lieutenant Lewis, was attacking a triplane finished in a bluish colour scheme, when Richthofen, returning from his first attack, turned towards him. Lewis, by the colour of the red triplane, guessed that his adversary was Richthofen and used every trick and manoeuvre to evade. He almost succeeded and once he thought that his own bullets had struck Richthofen's machine. Diving and banking,

A view of the airfield facilities at Cappy; the flying field and hangars are to the left. After the German retirement, it was used by No. 24 Squadron's S.E.5As.

the minutes seemed like hours, but within three minutes of the Major's demise Lewis was diving earthwards with his seven-gallon gravity tank alight. Richthofen, reporting that the fuselage of the machine burned in the air and the remains dashed to the ground north-east of Villers-Bretonneux, could hardly have doubted that his second victim too, died. Happily it was not so, and his eightieth victim now resides in Salisbury, Rhodesia.

Lewis, by his account, hit the ground at something like 60 m.p.h. Thrown clear, he found that apart from minor burns and superficial cuts and bruises he was not badly injured. His Camel, B7393 (110 h.p. Le Rhône No. 101026/W.D. 10398), was completely wrecked. Only fifty yards away, Major Raymond-Barker's Camel, D6439 (110 h.p. Le Rhône No. 9204/W.D. 31691), was blazing furiously. Staggering to it, Lewis found it impossible to drag his C.O. out. In any case, it was almost certainly too late. His own machine was still burning and as he stood between the two blazing wrecks he saw a flight of S.E.5As come to the rescue of the remaining Camels. In withdrawing, one of the enemy triplanes came low over the two wrecks, the pilot waving. Presumably this was Richthofen, viewing the wreckage of his eightieth—and last—victim. If so, he probably imagined that Lewis was one of the German soldiers who soon arrived on the scene, for the tone of his report suggests that he regarded his two opponents as *finis*.

Came the 21st. A ground mist rose from the low-lying area by the Somme canal and swept across the airfield. The morning air was keen, but a glimmer in the sky gave promise of sunshine later. Spirits that spring morning were ebullient

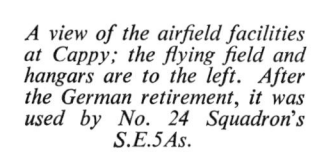

A photograph taken of von Richthofen as he prepared to take-off from Avesnes le Sec in Fokker Dr I 127/17, only a few weeks before he was shot down in Dr I 425/17.

as those pilots detailed for morning duty hung around awaiting the orders that would come as soon as weather conditions were deemed favourable.

Richthofen was there with his pilots. He, too, had good reason to be in high spirits. Already a travel warrant was made out in his name, for in response to an invitation from the father of the late Leutnant Werner Voss, both he and Joachim Wolff were taking leave in two days' time to visit the Voss hunting lodge in the Black Forest. The game this time being woodcock. Laughing and joking with his pilots, he noticed Leutnant Wenzl, a relatively new arrival, taking advantage of the period of waiting by having a quiet nap on a supported stretcher. Playfully he kicked one of the supports away, up-ending Wenzl. The stretcher thus becoming vacant, was repropped by another pilot, who reclined similarly. Again Richthofen in his bantering mood upset the stretcher. Now there were two pilots bent on vengeance, but even in a bout of horse-play junior officers could not very well up-end a Rittmeister—and a *Geschwader* commander at that! A rather negative form of revenge was exacted at the expense of poor Moritz, evidently based on the reversal of the theme—'Love me—love my dog!' For a few minutes later Moritz came nuzzling up to his master, with measured steps as he dragged a wheel-chock, the rope of which was tied to his tail! It was the last time his master was to pat him.

The adjutant, Bodenschatz, had left for the observation post after relaying the news that conditions would permit take-off. From there he saw six machines take off, Richthofen's triplane Dr I 425/17 leading, accompanied by Vizefeldwebel Scholz and his cousin Wolfram, who was making his first offensive patrol. A second group of three *Jasta 11* members comprised Leutnants Weiss, Wenzl and Karjus. The last-named was another recent arrival at Richthofen's instigation. Richthofen had not been satisfied with the calibre of a replacement pilot sent to the *Geschwader* by the 2nd Army *Flugpark*. He flew over to see the park commander and lodge his complaint. Whilst there he saw Leutnant Karjus, who wore a steel claw in place of a left hand lost during earlier service as an observer, and made arrangements for his transfer to *J.G.1*. Karjus was known as *Fliegender Goetz von Berlichingen*, after a German hero-knight of medieval times, who had an iron hook for a left hand.

After take-off, the six machines turned towards their patrol area, directed along a line Marceux–Puchevillers with the object of preventing observation by British reconnaissance machines of the preparations for a new, though limited offensive, in the area of Villers-Bretonneux.

But when the machines returned, individually, having become scattered in a dog-fight, the news was brought by Vizefeldwebel Scholz. Richthofen had been seen going down—on the British side of the lines! There was frantic telephoning to the *Flugmeldedienst* for detail and an informal inquiry was held. The evidence was irrefutable. Their leader was officially missing and a report to that effect was telephoned to 2nd Army H.Q., who forwarded it immediately to Supreme Headquarters.

Awaiting orders for take-off, Cappy, 21.4.18. From the left, Wolfram von Richthofen, Scholz, Karjus, Joachim Wolff, Lischke (administrative officer), von Richthofen, Steinhäuser and Weiss.

105

CHAPTER TWENTY-FOUR *Tribute*

Followed by his military peers, six captains; the funeral cortège of von Richthofen moves slowly off from the airfield at Poulainville.

On the day that Richthofen died, the official communiqué from the German Headquarters gave news of his seventy-ninth and eightieth victories. Whilst congratulations were coming in, G.H.Q., in receipt of the news that Richthofen was missing, were deciding how best the news should be broken to the nation. The loss of a well-known personality could not for long be concealed and, besides, the British, as soon as they had identified their victim, be he alive or dead, would surely broadcast the fact. They did.

Irrespective of Press releases, the next of kin had a right to be told. Thus Major Albrecht, Freiherr von Richthofen, his father, was first of the family to know. There were no tears and no outward signs of anguish. Father and son were both soldiers, Prussian soldiers; it was the duty of an officer to give all, even his life, for Emperor and Country.

So far it was not known if Richthofen had survived and news from neutral sources was anxiously scanned. In the interim a brief Press release gave: 'Rittmeister von Richthofen failed to return from a flying raid over the Somme, April 21st.'

Then came the news from the British side released by G.H.Q., B.E.F., at 9.55 p.m. on Monday, April 22nd. It was relayed by Reuter to neutral sources and by that means reached German newspapers on the 23rd. The communiqué ran: 'After a long spell of stormy weather which greatly hampered aerial work, the 21st inst. brought a change and our aeroplanes were to be seen in the air from dusk to dawn . . . The pilot of one of the hostile machines which was brought down in combat was the well-known German airman and fighter Rittmeister Freiherr von Richthofen, who claimed to have brought down eighty Allied machines. His body has today been buried with full military honours.'

In that last sentence were dashed the hopes of Germany that Richthofen might have escaped with his life. It was a great loss to the German nation, and General von Hoeppner gave much thought to the wording of an official communiqué: 'Rittmeister Freiherr von Richthofen has not returned from a pursuit of the enemy. He has fallen. The German Army has lost its greatly admired pilot and the fighting airmen their beloved leader. He remains the hero of the German peoples for whom he fought and died. His death is a deep wound for his *Geschwader* and for the entire Air Service. The will by which he conquered, and led, that he has handed down, will heal that wound.'

Amongst the many telegrams of condolences that were despatched, went a message from the *Geschwader*, signed by the new commander, Hauptmann Reinhard, to Major Albrecht Freiherr von Richthofen. The telegraphed reply came back:

To Jagdeschwader Nr. 1
    My son still lives as your model.
                            Father Richthofen.

After Richthofen had crashed, his body, when it was realised all life was extinct, had been taken from the aircraft, wrapped in a blanket and conveyed by a squad from No. 3 Squadron A.F.C. to their aerodrome at Poulainville. There, after medical examination, it was prepared for burial and laid in state. Army Form W3314 had already been filled in and since Corps H.Q. was only across the road at Bertangles a burial place and detail were quickly arranged.

In the late afternoon of April 22nd, Richthofen was buried with the military honours appropriate to his rank. His coffin was carried from the hangar shoulder-high by a bearer party of his military peers—six captains from local squadrons. As they approached the cortège, drawn up on the road outside, a firing party, formed from the personnel of No. 3 Squadron, Australian Flying Corps, presented arms while the bearer party moved slowly towards the hearse, a Crossley tender, upon which Richthofen's coffin was then placed; and the various wreaths which had accumulated during the day were positioned by its side. One bore the inscription: 'To our gallant and worthy foe.'

At an order from the senior British officer present, who wore a black mourning armband, the cortège moved off with the firing party leading, marching in two files. Next came the tender and behind it walked the bearer party representing the chief mourners; then an infantry platoon and finally any individuals, not in formed parties, who wished to follow. So went Richthofen to his grave, borne along a sunlit lane, with hedgerows tinted with the verdant shades of April, on such a day as might have raised a spring in the step on a less sombre occasion; but now the lane resounded with the measured tread of the slow march.

The procession halted at the entrance to the poplar-fringed cemetery of the small French village. There, the firing party, a corporal and twelve men under a sergeant, moved into open order to allow the bearer party, now carrying the coffin and led by a chaplain, to move between them, as they stood with their rifles at the present. Richthofen's freshly dug grave was just within the entrance gate, almost in the shade of a hemlock tree. The ceremony around it, simple but impressive, was the Church of England service for military burials. Manfred, an enemy in life, a brother in death, was laid to rest.

The ceremony was watched by many soldiers from nearby units as well as by a number of French civilians. As it came to an end and Richthofen's remains were lowered, the silence around was broken by the orders of the sergeant, calling the firing party to attention. Then in succession came the orders—'Load', 'Present', 'Fire'. Three volleys in all rang out and whilst those around stood rigidly to attention there followed the most plaintive of all bugle-calls—The Last Post. The ceremony was over; the troops re-formed and moved off, this time at the quick march; Manfred Freiherr von Richthofen was dead—and buried.

At the graveside, many officers and men paid their respects individually as they slowly filed past, pausing to salute as they came level with the grave. There was nothing staged in that spontaneous gesture of respect for a fallen foe. Later a cross was erected at the head of the grave. It bore the inscription:

CAVALRY CAPTAIN
MANFRED BARON VON RICHTHOFEN
*Age 22 years, killed in action, aerial combat, near
SAILLY-LE-SEC
SOMME, FRANCE. 21st APRIL, 1918

Traditionally, the cross was made from a broken propeller with three blades lopped, bearing a metal plate at the centre. Later, this cross was replaced by a standard cross of the War Graves Commission.

His death was world news and it was widely reported. On the German side, for example, the next issue of the *Österreichische Flug-Zeitschrift*, was devoted almost entirely to Richthofen. In neutral countries papers such as *Aeroplanet* gave two pages to the news. In Britain it was widely reported, but there was no triumphant acclaim at his downfall, as might well have been expected under wartime conditions. *The Times* commented: 'While probably not as brilliant as Captain Ball, all our airmen concede that Richthofen was a great pilot and a fine fighting man.'

The famous British aeronautical weekly, *The Aeroplane*, gave an unbiased comment: "Richthofen is dead. All airmen will be pleased to hear that he has been put out of action, but there will be no one amongst them who will not regret the death of such a courageous nobleman. Several days ago, a banquet was held in honour of one of our aces. In answering the speech made in his honour, he toasted Richthofen, and there was no one who refused to join. (The occasion was at dinner in No. 56 Squadron's Mess, when Lieutenant

---

* The age given was not correct. It should have been 25.

On a sunny Monday afternoon in April, von Richthofen was borne to his grave at Bertangles. The coffin, carried on a Crossley tender, was preceded by a firing party, slow marching with arms reversed, drawn from the personnel of No. 3 Squadron, Australian Flying Corps.

The bearer party of six captains, led by a chaplain, pass through the firing party who have moved in open order and now stand with arms presented, and enter the cemetery, the gates of which can be seen in this picture. von Richthofen's grave was just within the entrance, almost in the shade of a hemlock tree.

A. P. F. Rhys-Davids, who shot down Werner Voss, raised his glass and proposed the toast of: 'Richthofen, our most worthy enemy.') . . . Anybody would have been proud to have killed Richthofen in action, but every member of the Royal Flying Corps would also have been proud to shake his hand had he fallen into captivity alive.

'His death is bound to have a gravely depressing effect on the German Flying Service for obviously the younger and less brave will argue that if a von Richthofen cannot survive their chances must be small. Equally his death is an encouragement to every young French and British pilot who can no longer imagine that every skilful German pilot that attacks them is von Richthofen himself.

'Manfred von Richthofen is dead. He was a brave man, a clean fighter and an aristocrat. May he rest in peace.'

Not everywhere did this magnanimous tone prevail. Several letters to the British Press, following the publication of pictures of Richthofen's burial, criticised such ceremony on behalf of an enemy airman. It reopened the bitter controversy that the correspondence columns of a certain newspaper conducted over the burial in English churchyards of the crews of Zeppelins that had been brought down on fire over England. The words of a clergyman directed at those who raised the question were equally apt: 'Who art thou to judge another man's servant. To his own master he standeth or falleth.' Such protest, however, was from a very small minority—far removed from the main theatre of operations!

A section of the German Press too, had this same bitterness and failed to see in those pictures of Richthofen's burial service (shown here) the sincerity that was real. Count Reventlow in the *Deutsche Tageszeitung* adopted a particularly ugly tone: 'This homage is nothing but the latest manifestation of the British self-advertisement of sportsmanlike knightliness. . . . For our part we cannot look upon the ceremony shown as sincere. The Allied Press is full of this cant and is beating the big drum of absurd British magnanimity in the accustomed fashion. But they say nothing about how many and how large money prizes were for the one who succeeded in killing von Richthofen. In truth the moneys must have amounted to an enormous sum. This explains why such a bitter controversy raged around the body of the fallen pilot for there was money waiting for the one who inflicted the fatal wound. The very flying officers who bore our hero were all fortunate money-makers.'

This was, of course, nonsense. It is an object-lesson on how wartime propaganda engenders hate.

Bertangles was not, however, von Richthofen's last resting-place. After the war ended it was a policy to re-inter war dead in special large cemeteries, administered by a War Graves Commission. Manfred's body was removed to the large cemetery at Fricourt where some eighteen thousand German dead were buried, the majority unknown by name. There are thousands upon thousands of headstone crosses in France bearing the words: 'Here lies the body of an unknown soldier—known unto God.' Men who were pulverised beyond recognition during those four years of bitter struggle. They lie side by side with hundreds of thousands of others, whose names do appear. It makes not much difference in death. Practically all were once known as husbands, fathers, sons or brothers. Many are still remembered with affection that has not waned over forty years. Thousands who survived were maimed or blinded; some suffer still. There might well be glory in fighting for one's country and a duty to fight for what one believes is right, but let no man be blinded to the cost. The greatest cost is not the astronomical figures that

While the troops stand with heads bared, the firing party of thirteen rifles, 12 men and a corporal, fire three volleys. They are watched by French civilians, troops from nearby units and, as revealed by the military-looking hats still worn, members of the Women's Army Auxiliary Corps (at extreme right).

represent a country's ruined economy, for the right men can plan and build anew. It is the loss of the right men themselves, the cream of the nations, that rotted in foreign fields, to which memorials, headstones and crosses give witness—a silent witness and by some—forgotten.

Manfred was not forgotten. Bolko, his youngest brother, on a grey November day in 1925, trudged along such rows of headstones seeking his brother's grave. It was more than a pilgrimage, he had come to bring Manfred's body home to Germany for reburial. Already a working party had been arranged, to perform the dismal task of transferring Manfred's body to a new zinc-lined coffin in which his body now lies. The intention was to bring the chest back to the Schweidnitz churchyard where lay the father, Albrecht, who had peacefully passed from this life soon after the war. Lothar too, lay there. He had survived the war and entered civil aviation. Faced with engine trouble at the controls of a passenger machine in the vicinity of Hamburg on July 4th, 1922, he had made a desperate attempt to reach Fuhlsbüttel aerodrome, but his machine struck some trees as he came in. Lothar died on his way to hospital. One of the passengers, who escaped, was the German film star, Fern Andra.

However, when it became known by the German authorities that Richthofen's remains were to be brought back to his native Silesia, they respectfully claimed his remains for the nation, to lie in the Invaliden cemetery, where lay those who had been among the most illustrious of the land.

On a goods wagon across France, it had been but one more body that a soldier's family had claimed back from French soil, but after crossing the frontier into Germany it was the return of a dead hero. A family affair became a national matter. Flags hung at half-mast, bells were tolled and respects were paid at each stop as a special train bore the chest to Berlin, which was reached late on November 18th.

After the wreaths had been placed, a photograph was taken of the grave and dropped over the German lines with a message to the effect that von Richthofen had been buried with full military honours.

The lying in state and the cortège escort of Pour le Mérite *holders. These pictures were taken during the reburial ceremonies in November 1925.*

At the unveiling of a reconstructed tombstone to von Richthofen, stands a former leader of his Geschwader—*the German Air Minister—Hermann Göring.*

There the chest was borne to the Gnadenkirche and laid in state. Upon it was placed Richthofen's many decorations together with a Uhlan officer's sword. By it, was the wooden cross taken from the grave at Fricourt.

A state funeral followed on the 20th. Richthofen's chest was borne by eight holders of the *Ordre pour le Mérite* to a horse-drawn gun-carriage. Around it was arranged the many floral tributes, placed by the personnel of the 4th Machine Gun Company of the 9th (Prussian) Infantry Regiment, in whom, since Germany was denied military aircraft under the Treaty of Versailles, were vested the responsibilities for maintaining the traditional interests of the disbanded Air Service. The immediate followers were Richthofen's own mother, together with Bolko, both dressed in black, and behind them came Field Marshal von Hindenburg, President of the German Republic, together with other members of the family and state dignitaries. Behind them came ex-members of *Jagdgeschwader Nr. 1* and *Eskadron Nr. 3, Ulan Regt. Nr. 1*. Passing through a guard of honour provided by the Reichswehr, Richthofen was moved to his last resting-place. It was von Hindenburg himself who threw the first handful of earth into the grave. During October the following year, over the same spot, a large tombstone, erected in the interim, was unveiled with further ceremony. Manfred Freiherr von Richthofen was remembered, as a national hero.

The homage paid to von Richthofen did not end there. Twelve years later, the flat tombstone was replaced by a large memorial. It was unveiled by a former leader of the *Richthofen Geschwader* then a Generalfeldmarschal of the *Luftwaffe* and German Minister of State for Air, Hermann Göring. At the ceremony, one of the red triplanes that had been used by von Richthofen, Dr I 152/17, was exhibited nearby, having been removed temporarily from the *Zeughaus*. A red Albatros biplane, that he had flown was also preserved in the *Zeughaus*, and on the twentieth anniversary of Richthofen's death, a wreath was placed beneath it. Both the aircraft were destroyed by Allied bombing in 1944.

Apart from exhibition in Berlin, a display of a more personal nature was made in a room of his house at Schweidnitz. From the ceiling of this room hung a chandelier made from a rotary engine, taken from the aircraft of one of his victims. The walls were decorated with fabric cut from aircraft that he had shot down.

The name Richthofen was kept alive in other ways. *Deutsche Lufthansa*, the German State airline, named its airliners after famous pilots and a Junkers Ju52/3m bore Richthofen's name. At the Templehof Airport, a new road was named *Richthofen Strasse;* a road in a new Berlin estate, was similarly named, with adjacent roads bearing the names of some of the most famous of his *Geschwader* members. The name lives on.

CHAPTER TWENTY-FIVE

Who killed von Richthofen?

A view of the Somme valley, looking east towards Sailly-le-Sec (top left corner), over which von Richthofen was shot down on April 21st, 1918. This photograph was taken on March 19th, 1918, from the location 'G' on the 'Photo Map' on pages 120-121.

'Who killed von Richthofen?' is now a time-honoured controversy that has never been satisfactorily resolved. Many recent accounts of the manner in which he met his death have undoubtedly been biased by what has previously been published. The two earlier official accounts to be found in 'The War in the Air' Vol. IV H. A. Jones; and 'The Official History of Australia in the War' Vol. V 'The A.I.F. in France, 1918' C. E. W. Bean; represent respectively, the account of the fight from the air, and from the ground. What follows here, is an attempt to recount the fight and fall of von Richthofen in detail, after sifting out all the available evidence and dispelling, it is hoped, a number of 'popular misconceptions' concerning that last flight.

The main point at issue is; was von Richthofen killed by a shot fired by a Captain Brown of No. 209 Squadron R.A.F. in a Sopwith Camel, or did he fall to the fire of an Australian anti-aircraft gunner, posted on the ground?

Because Squadron Commander C. H. Butler was known to be in command of No. 209 Squadron, it has been assumed in several accounts that he led the squadron in the air that day. That was not so. It was in fact not usual for an officer of field rank, the equivalent or above, to fly on routine patrols. On the morning von Richthofen died, the patrolling machines of that squadron were commanded in the air by the man who was credited with shooting Richthofen down, Captain A. R. Brown, D.S.C.

Brown was a Canadian from Toronto, who had studied aviation at the Wright Flying School, Dayton, Ohio. In December 1915, he had sailed for England after being accepted for a commission in the Royal Naval Air Service, but to his great disappointment his appearance at the front was long delayed, for during flying training at Chingford, he crashed and broke a bone in his spine; consequently most of 1916 was spent in hospital. After recovering, he completed his training and joined No. 9 (Naval) Squadron, receiving promotion to flight lieutenant in October 1917. By that time he was already an experienced fighter-pilot.

December 16th saw the arrival of the squadron's first 150 h.p. Bentley-engined Camels, the type in which Brown was to challenge Richthofen, but in less than six weeks, after the squadron had been completely re-equipped, they were taken away! It was policy at that time to rest fighter squadrons in rotation by withdrawing two at a time from the Western Front to Dover or Walmer. No. 9 (Naval) Squadron were ordered to fly to Dover on January 28th, 1918, but since their Bentley Camels were considered superior to the Clerget Camels of a sister-squadron remaining in the fighting area, No. 10 (Naval), the two squadrons exchanged their aircraft.

Recalled to the front in March, No. 9 (Naval) Squadron again commenced to re-equip with Bentley Camels. It was about March 13th that Brown received B7270, the machine in which he was to fight von Richthofen. On the 20th, by which time twelve Camels had been received, the squadron flew back to France. Since, a month later, the majority of the pilots were to be involved in that fight, so fateful for *J.G.1*; their names and aircraft are here recorded as they were booked out from Dover: Squadron Commander C. H. Butler B7273, Flight Commanders F. E. Banbury B7247, O. C. Le Boutillier (an American serving in the R.N.A.S.) D3332, A. R. Brown B7270 and S. T. Edwards B7199; Flight Lieutenants F. J. W. Mellersh B7245 and O. W. Redgate B7250; Flight Sub-Lieutenants A. R. McAfee D3326, W. N. Cumming B7249, M. A. Harker B7272, A. P. Squire D3328 and M. S. Taylor B7200. All the Camels, it may be noted, were Clayton and Shuttleworth-built machines.

Allotted an airfield at Bray Dunes, which next day was shelled as the German offensive opened, the squadron was moved to Teteghem. By that time Brown had already been in action again, bringing down an enemy two-seater whilst acting as escort to a French Caudron.

On April 1st the Royal Air Force had been formed and since both the R.N.A.S. and the R.F.C., which were amalgamated, had each numbered squadrons in numerical sequence, it was necessary to re-designate one of the series.

The R.E.8s of No. 3 Squadron, Australian Flying Corps. It was an attack on two machines of this squadron, by aircraft of von Richthofen's formation, that led to the dog-fight which resulted in Richthofen's death. This picture was taken at Bailleul, before the squadron moved to Poulainville.

Thus, the number 200 was added to all ex-R.N.A.S. Squadrons, No. 9 (Naval) Squadron R.N.A.S. therefore became No. 209 Squadron R.A.F. For a time it was usual to assume army ranks as a temporary administrative expedient and Flight Lieutenant Brown became Captain Brown. By a series of moves, dictated by the battle then raging, the squadron reached Bertangles on April 7th. There the unit had time to reorganise with the advance and rear parties from England and several new members were posted in to bring them up to establishment. One, was a certain Second-Lieutenant W. R. May.

May had commenced flying training in late 1917 and had not completed his air-gunnery course when the German offensive caused training to be cut and pilots rushed to the front. Drafted to France, he was posted from a pilots pool to No. 209 Squadron. However, when he arrived, there was anything but a welcome! Apparently he had got on to a party that included the driver of the tender detailed to transport him to Bertangles! Pilot and driver eventually arrived two days late! Since it was usual for the Pool to signal arrivals to units, there could be no excuse. May was paraded before a much put out Squadron Commander, who refused, under the circumstances, to have him in his unit, ordering his return to the Pool.

Stepping out of the O.C.'s office into the orderly room, who should May see, but an old friend with whom he had been at school in Edmonton, Alberta; 'Roy' Brown, now Captain A. R. Brown, D.S.C. May had no idea that his old school chum was serving as a pilot, and after his reception by the Squadron Commander, he was most relieved to find a friend. Brown knew May intimately as 'Wop', a nickname dating from the time when the very young daughter of a certain Judge Swanson, unable to pronounce May's Christian name, Wilfred, had called him 'Wop'. The name had stuck.

Brown thereupon tried to patch up the matter by seeing his Commanding Officer, who relented to the extent of letting Brown take May into his flight, and transfer another recent arrival to another flight, to make a place. Evidently Brown was held in high esteem—in fact his Confidential Report from the squadron, of which he was, at least officially, unaware, read: 'A very good flight leader and fearless pilot, with good ability to command'. May stayed, and Brown saw to it that he became suitably versed in the tactics of air-fighting.

Came the 21st of April. The morning mist which had delayed *J.G.1* also made No. 209 Squadron late in starting on a routine high patrol at 12,000 feet over the front between Hangard and Albert. The detail, which called for the squadron to be ready for take-off at 8.15 a.m., could not be effected because of the poor visibility and it was over an hour later, at 9.35 a.m., when Brown waved in signal for take-off and led Lieutenants Lomas, Mellersh, MacKenzie and May up into the air. This was the first time May, who was positioned at 'outside-left', had been allowed to take part in an offensive patrol and he had been cautioned by Brown, both as a friend and as his flight commander, not to become embroiled in any fighting that might develop.

At 9.40 a.m., five minutes after Brown's flight had left, the second flight led by Captain Redgate and consisting of Lieutenants Aird, Drake, Edwards and Siddall left the ground, followed at 9.45 a.m. by Captain Le Boutillier leading in Camel B3858, Lieutenants Brock, Foster, Harker and Taylor. The squadron was then flying in extended flight order in three flights of five machines each, along a line which crossed, almost at right-angles, the intending flight path of Richthofen's formation.

At 10.25 a.m., the last flight, Le Boutillier's, were the first to sight enemy aircraft, two Albatros C-type machines over Le Quesnel, flying towards the lines. They dived to the attack, and Lieutenant Taylor, in B3338, the foremost of them sent one of the enemy machines down in flames, whilst the other evidently swiftly made off for the cover of a cloud, for as far as the flight were concerned—it disappeared!

This fight had occurred at almost the southernmost point of the patrol line and Brown's flight, having reached that point and wheeled round to the north-east to return, were witness to that action. Brown himself confirmed Taylor's claim for an Albatros, but since Le Boutillier's flight continued to search for the other elusive Albatros,

112

whilst the other two flights continued on their patrol, visual contact was temporarily lost and that flight was not available in the critical minutes ahead. Meanwhile, two machines had dropped out from Redgate's flight with engine trouble and were forced to return to base. This left Brown with only eight Camels, including his own, immediately at hand, from the fifteen that had set out.

As they flew north-east to recross the River Somme, von Richthofen's formation, having been joined in the air by *Jasta 5*, apparently at full strength, was flying westward along the Somme valley. Its object was to patrol as far as the meeting of the waters of the Somme and the Ancre, over which area the commander of the German 12th Army wished a reconnaissance to be made. The Albatros two-seaters harassed by Le Boutillier's flight, might well have been the very reconnaissance aircraft concerned.

It will be remembered, that when Richthofen had left Cappy, he was flying with his cousin Wolfram and Vizefeldwebel Scholz followed by Karjus, Wenzl and Weiss. This is as recorded in the official diary of the unit. However, from a letter written to Lothar by Joachim Wolff, it is evident that Wolff also set out. In any case, it is generally agreed that Leutnants Wenzl and Weiss, who took off with von Richthofen, joined the *Jasta 5* formation, presumably by pre-arrangement. This would leave von Richthofen flying with his cousin Wolfram, Scholz, Wolff and Karjus, accompanied by *Jasta 5*.

The theoretical patrol lines of the two formations crossed, but, as they were flying at different altitudes on a misty day with low cloud, they might never have sighted each other, had it not been for two R.E.8s from No. 3 Squadron, A.F.C. flying at 7,000 feet on a photographic mission, west of Hamel (Position 'A', Map pages 120-1). These R.Es. were spotted by pilots in the German formation and four triplanes left to attack them. Because of the poor visibility the occupants of the R.E. nearest to them, Lieutenant T. L. Simpson piloting with Lieutenant F. E. Banks observing, were taken by surprise. Banks fired at point-blank range using up some 200 rounds whilst Simpson skilfully manœuvred until they gained the comparative safety of a cloud. Whereupon the triplanes turned their attention to Lieutenants S. G. Garrett and A. V. Barrow, who showed similar resolution and at least one triplane was hit and went down; evidently a *Jasta 5* machine, for there was no *J.G.1* record of this loss. The triplanes then withdrew to return to their main formation.

The German machines were now over the lines and British anti-aircraft guns opened up, the shells bursting with their characteristic white puffs. These drew Brown's attention to the enemy formation and he led in against the triplanes disengaging from the R.Es. At almost the same time, Richthofen had spotted the Camels and his formation turned to meet the attack.

Brown and his men clashed first with the detached triplanes. One of his flight, Lieutenant F. J. W. Mellersh, got in a long burst of fire at a blue-tailed triplane whose pilot was apparently slow in turning. It went down, at first vertically; then flattening out, made back in the direction of Cappy, but finally crashed at Cerisy several miles short. Mellersh had followed it down, but the two other triplanes had in turn followed him, forcing him to spin down to barely fifty feet and then hedge-hop home. They kept up the chase for a considerable distance. After eventually shaking them off, he observed a red triplane crashing and nearby he recognised Captain Brown's aircraft.

The dog-fight which had developed (Position B, Map pages 120-1) followed the usual irregular pattern of twisting, turning and circling as pilots manœuvred for a position in which to bring their guns to bear. Richthofen milled round with the rest, seeking an unwary opponent. First to drop out was a Camel pilot, Lieutenant W. J. Mackenzie, who was hit in the back; but before he left, he mastered his excruciating pain to fire at a triplane that went down, apparently out of control. He was lucky to return and land his Camel, B7245, in one piece, for a burst of fire had gone through the centre of the fuselage and one of the bearers of his 150 h.p. Bentley, No. 509/W.D. 36941, had been shot through.

When May had seen Brown wobble his wings, the signal for attack, and lead down, he had not glimpsed the enemy machines. He remained at 12,000 feet and circled as

von Richthofen's damaged triplane, stripped of its fabric and various accessories by souvenir hunters, exhibited at Poulainville, to where it had been brought by a No. 3 Squadron A.F.C. salvage party. Several of the major components remaining, subsequently ended up in museums.

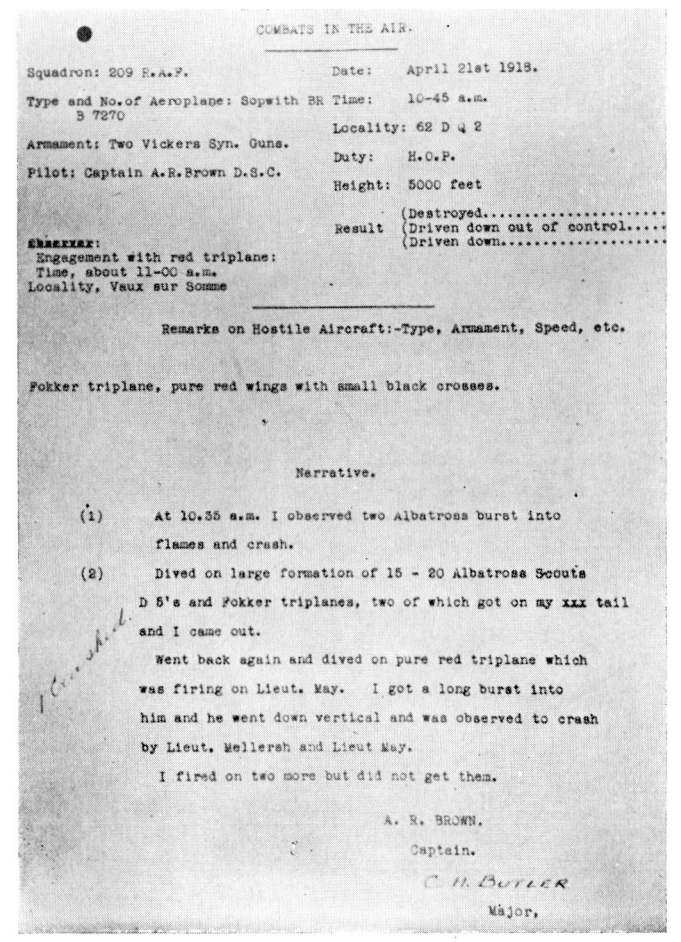

The combat report of Captain A. R. Brown. It will be noted that there is no mention of Richthofen by name. It would appear that Brown himself did not see the 'red triplane' crash. The abbreviation H.O.P. stands for High Offensive Patrol.

instructed. When an enemy machine flew by underneath him, he let it go unmolested, again obeying instructions; but, when a second one appeared, he threw caution to the winds, dived, fired, missed and followed it right into the thick of the fight, where he attacked it again and was credited with shooting it down. There is no record of a triplane being lost at this stage so presumably the machine's fall was checked. As to the identity of this unwary German airman, it was in all probability Wolfram von Richthofen, who, a novice like May, had also been instructed not to become involved in the fighting!

May gave his own impression as follows: 'The fight was at close quarters. Enemy aircraft were coming at me from all sides. I seemed to be missing some of them by inches and there seemed so many that I thought the best thing to do was to go into a tight vertical turn, hold my guns open and spray as many of them as I could. Through lack of experience I held one of my guns open too long; it jammed and then the other. I could not clear them so I spun out of the mess and headed west by the sun for home. After I had levelled out, I looked around, but nobody was following. Feeling pretty good at having extricated myself, the next thing I knew, I was being fired at from behind! All I could do was to try and dodge my attacker, which was a red triplane. Had I known it was Richthofen—I should probably have passed out on the spot!'

Brown had been engaged on the fringe of the fight with two triplanes. He successfully shook these off and flew towards the main fighting. It was then that he saw May drop out—and von Richthofen follow. He dived in swift pursuit.

As he watched, von Richthofen was catching up with May, moving in close and following every evasive turn as he awaited the opportune moment to fire at close range. Brown's dive brought him almost directly over von Richthofen, who apparently did not see him. Brown was in a favourable position to give a burst, but not for sustained fire. It would seem that he fired as he dived west from the direction of Sailly le Sec, but that in flattening out afterwards, he lost sight of the two machines, which were now down to a low altitude. In those fleeting seconds he saw von Richthofen turn round the moment he fired, but whether or not it was the involuntary start of a shot man or one of his continuous backward glances, it is difficult to assess. However, by Brown's account, he had then seemed to slump in his cockpit. When Brown later had confirmation that this machine crashed, there was no doubt in his mind that he had shot it down, and from the wording of his combat report and the indisputable evidence of a crashed triplane, he was rightly credited with the victory.

'Rightly credited' does not necessarily mean that he did indeed shoot the machine down, but that the conditions under which a victory could be credited were fulfilled; a claim, a witness and evidence of the wreckage. The chance shot from the ground, always a possibility, was not considered in view of the combat report.

To the R.A.F. the matter was largely one of statistics. There was the daily communiqué and for April 21st on that aspect it ran:—'The enemy's machines were seen in large numbers but were not aggressive. Eleven machines were brought down in air-fighting and six others were driven down out of control. A hostile observation balloon was also destroyed. Our anti-aircraft fire brought down two other hostile machines. Five of our aircraft are missing.'

von Richthofen's machine was included in the eleven brought down in the air-fighting. There is also the officer's individual record to consider and Captain Brown was credited with a victory that day. True it was, that the British did not publish lists of names with victory scores, as did the French and German Forces. Nevertheless, the close connection between the number of victories scored and such phrases as 'a number', 'several', 'quite a few', 'a large number', 'many' in the citations for awards, leaves little doubt that records were meticulously kept of victories gained and to whom credited. Therefore for statistical purposes and one might almost say officially, Captain A. R. Brown, D.S.C., killed von Richthofen, for he was credited with destroying his machine.

The crux of the matter would now seem to lie in the medical evidence. Did Brown in that time fire the fatal shot? For, from then onwards, until von Richthofen crashed, some 1,600 yards away, all the eye-witnesses on the ground are adamant that there were only two machines concerned, one British being chased by one German; May and von Richthofen. Could von Richthofen have sustained a further mile and a half flight in pursuit, if he had then received the wound that caused his death—a bullet through the chest?

From the accounts of eye witnesses, it would appear that Brown did not again approach near to May until von Richthofen crashed. During this time May was chased at tree-top level. In his own account he said, 'I kept dodging and spinning down until I ran out of sky and had to hedge-hop along the ground. Richthofen was firing continually and the only thing that saved me was my poor flying! I didn't know what I was going to do and I don't suppose Richthofen could figure this out either. . . I started up the Somme Valley at a very low altitude with Richthofen close on my tail. I went around a curve in the river just near Corbie, but Richthofen beat me to it by cutting over a hill and at that point I was a sitting duck, too low down between the banks to turn away. I felt he had me cold and I had to restrain myself from pushing the stick forward and disappearing into the river. I was sure this was the end. Then, as I looked around, I saw Richthofen do a spin and a half, and hit the ground. Looking up I saw one of our machines directly behind. This I joined up with and returned to base'.

The area over which the chase was made was held by the Australian Corps and many of their troops watched the battle overhead. Gunner George Ridgway of the 29th Battery, A.F.A. had a vantage point at a brick stack, where he was engaged in repairing telephone lines, when he heard spent bullets falling around, which drew his attention to a dog-fight. He observed that three machines had broken away from the main fight which was at several thousand feet. When the three machines were down to a few hundred feet he recognised the first as British (May?), the second as German (von Richthofen?) and the third another British machine (Brown?). The first was trying to escape the second whilst the third followed above and at a somewhat greater space interval. This last machine then disappeared from view whilst the other two were observed still flying, one behind the other.

This tends to be confirmed by Lieutenant J. Quinlan of the 55th Battery, A.F.A. who was at an observation post for his battery situated on the southern bank of the Somme. He said in 1929 that von Richthofen was very close to the hunted machine with his machine-guns continuing in action until some 200 or so yards before he crashed. A third plane was noticed, but in his opinion not close enough to engage with von Richthofen. (This would, in any case, appear to be after Brown had got his burst in.) Quinlan went on to say that at the time von Richthofen stopped firing, this third machine would have been about over Corbie church. While it would be most difficult to assess its position from a distance to such degree, it does at least suggest that Brown veered away from the other two towards the south-west and then later turned northward to join up with May.

Certainly, witnesses in Vaux over which May's Camel roared with von Richthofen in close pursuit, saw only those two in the immediate vicinity. Lt.-Col. J. L. Whitham commanding the 52nd Battalion of the A.I.F. had his battalion headquarters in Vaux. He saw but two planes approach, diving in from the east and flattening out over Vaux at less than a hundred feet. It seemed to him that they would crash into a spur at a sharp bend of the Somme, but both rose over it and disappeared beyond. As the almost

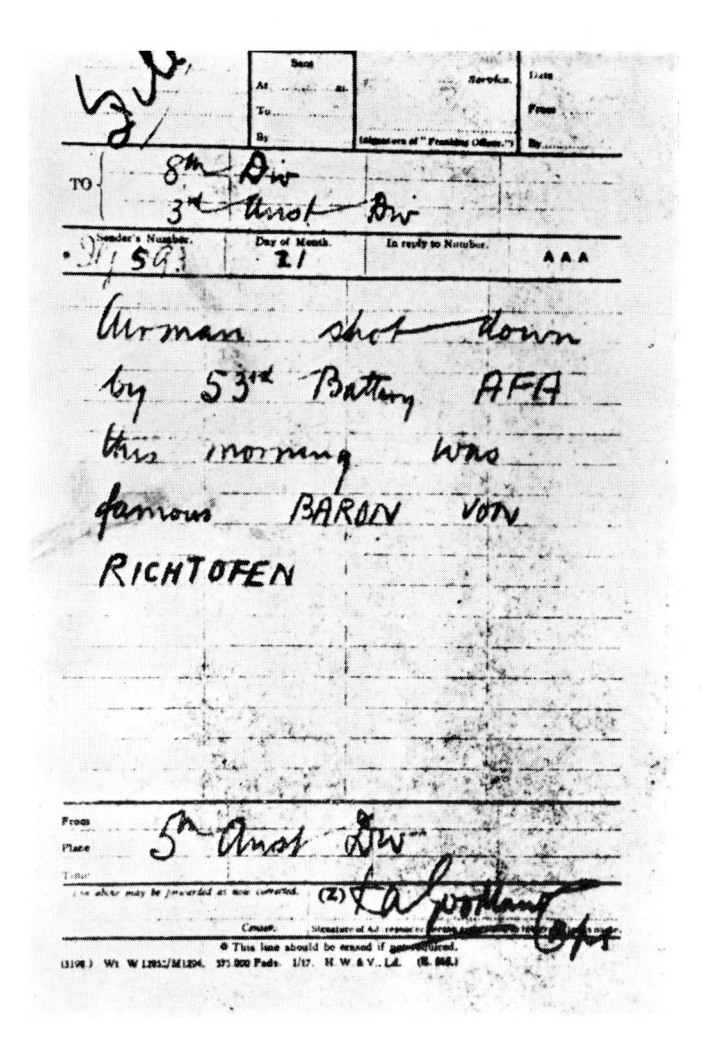

It will be seen from this official message form, that there was little doubt in the minds of the Australians, that it was the 53rd Battery, Australian Field Artillery, that shot down von Richthofen. They did in fact receive congratulations in reply!

deafening noise of their engines died away, firing could be heard.

The chase made quite an impression on the Medical Officer of the 52nd Battalion A.I.F., Captain R. J. Forsyth, A.A.M.C. who noted details in his diary. It was obvious to him that the German machine was the better handled and that 'our boy' was hard pressed. He ran through to the front of his billet as they passed over and he actually feared that May's machine would tip his gate! On, over the village he saw them race, the triplane's guns stuttering at what appeared to be but a thirty feet range.

Other witnesses, such as Corporal J. E. Maclean of the 52nd Battalion A.I.F. scouts, gave similar report as the machines passed over Vaux, where May veered northwards in the approximate direction of his base at Bertangles, but seconds later changed course further north in his efforts to shake off von Richthofen. During that time several guns opened up from the ground. Most of this fire, no doubt, was futile.

It is not without interest to note that years afterwards, in an Australian paper, a rifleman writing anonymously, explained in detail how he had killed von Richthofen! He described the flight of the two machines, his careful aiming,

115

Captain A. R. Brown, D.S.C., who was credited with shooting down von Richthofen. A Canadian, born at Carleton Place late in 1893, he died at Stouffville, Ontario in March 1944.

his pressure on the trigger, his shot—and 'immediately von Richthofen, swerved, wobbled and crashed.' He may well have believed that he had killed von Richthofen, for he described his reactions as he later strode over to view the wreckage. It is not impossible that he, or some other unknown rifleman did actually kill him, but it is most unlikely.

There are other more feasible possibilities. Ground strafing had been a feature of the recent offensive and units had learnt the hard way to post machine-guns for anti-aircraft use against low-flying aircraft. The difficulties in firing from the ground, however, should be appreciated. To fire straight at an approaching aircraft required a steel nerve, for the pilot had only to dive and press his firing buttons to send a hail of bullets at the gun post. The gunner might have a sand-banked emplacement or similar cover but the pilot, although his machine may be disabled, had most of his body sheltered by the engine. From any other position, there was little immediate danger to the ground-gunner from a single-seat machine but the difficulties in assessing an aiming point were considerable.

It was not a simple matter of getting the sights aligned on the aircraft and firing, but of estimating a point in the air ahead of the machine at which to fire, to compensate for the distance moved by the aircraft during the flight of the bullets. With von Richthofen close upon May, it would be necessary at 1,000 yards for a ground-gunner to aim at May to hit von Richthofen! No doubt the Australian gunners were instructed in the art of aiming at moving targets, but the possibilities of obtaining hits were remote. There was, too, the additional hazard that with von Richthofen so close upon May, the wrong machine might be hit!

The two machines, coming from Vaux, crossed the front of Sergeant C. B. Popkin and Gunner R. F. Weston of the 24th Machine-Gun Company, teamed to man one of their unit's Vickers guns mounted for anti-aircraft use (Position C, Map pages 120-1). Popkin, acting as No. 1 on the gun, followed their flight intently and fired as soon as von Richthofen appeared to present a safe target on his own, which allowed only one burst of fire. Both Popkin and Weston averred that their fire took immediate effect and claimed seeing pieces falling from near the engine.

Private G. Sowerbutts of the 44th Battalion also fired, aiming at von Richthofen's engine, just after he had passed over, and was in a position to observe Sgt. Popkin's fire. He remarked that he thought Popkin had got him, as the plane swerved to the right, but it soon straightened out again, continuing in pursuit of May. It then passed over the Bray–Corbie road. One officer, who had had a lateral view from high ground, said that von Richthofen seemed to crouch forward with each burst of fire from his guns.

Reaching the Bray–Corbie road, von Richthofen then came under fire from two Lewis guns of the 53rd Battery, Australian Field Artillery, mounted on posts for anti-aircraft work and fitted with A.A. ring sights. (Position 'D', Map pages 120-1.) They were located on some rising ground, several hundred yards in front of the crest of the pensinsula between the waters of the Somme and the Ancre. The C.O. of the battery, Major L. E. Beavis, had warning of the approach of the aircraft by telephone from a forward observation post. Looking out almost immediately, he spotted the two machines, flying at, he estimated, 150 feet. The Camel was observed to be zig-zagging and the red triplane was trying to keep on its tail. So far the Lewis guns could not be brought to bear for fear of hitting May. But, as May crossed their front, they opened fire. Immediately, reported Major Beavis, the red triplane turned sharply to the north, became somewhat unsteady in flight, turned again north-east and then hit the ground about 400 yards from his men at the Lewis posts, Gunners W. J. Evans and R. Buie under Bombardier J. S. Seccull, the N.C.O. in charge. Finally, Major Beavis observed that there was not another Camel within 2,000 yards.

As von Richthofen turned back, Sergeant Popkin again had a chance to fire. This time the range was longer, but there was then no fear of hitting May. The moment after firing, it seemed to him that the burst had taken effect, for the machine swerved, attempted to bank and make off—but then crashed. Some observers said that the machine rose after its first swerve as if to make height for the flight back— and then swerved and dived to earth.

An officer of the 53rd Battery, Lieutenant J. C. Doyle, describing in 1930 the fall and crash, said the machine staggered, side-slipped into a bank and whilst in the bank swerved in a three-eighths circle towards his lines, and after gliding some hundreds of yards, side-slipped again and crashed into a wurzel heap. (Position E, Map pages 120-1.)

So fell von Richthofen. There are those who say his guns jammed and so he broke off the fight to return to his lines and was then hit; others, that he was hit after deciding to break off and return of his own volition, because it was not usual for him to venture far over the British lines and because the wind for once was in the east, making his return journey the more difficult. Strange that there should be a strong wind on a misty day; yet it was, nevertheless, true, as witness the fortunes of the G.H.Q. Communication Flight R.E.8s that day, which had B6573 overturned in high wind as it was taking off and C4579 crash-landed, possibly due to the pilot misjudging the wind.

If it is not accepted that one of the guns from the ground fired the fatal shot, then it must be that von Richthofen was already suffering a mortal wound as he flew over Vaux and beyond; his strength giving out as he approached the 53rd Battery A.F.A. positions, and eventually he turned, faltered and fell.

But, in spite of the evidence of the observers from the ground, there is a case for Brown having had a *second* opportunity to fire during those last sixty or so seconds of von Richthofen's last flight. May himself, having observed the crash of the red triplane, reported that he then saw a Camel slightly above him. He joined up with this machine to return to Bertangles—it was Brown's machine. Mellersh, as has already been reported, saw von Richthofen crash and noted Brown's machine nearby. It was a sad loss to the Royal Air Force, when Air Vice-Marshal Sir Francis Mellersh was tragically killed in a recent helicopter accident. A short time before he had been interviewed by Major K. S. Brown, our compiler, on this particular aspect. Sir Francis had remembered the events quite clearly and was convinced that it was Brown's machine he saw at the time he observed von Richthofen's machine crash.

One other witness, happily still living, and one it has been possible for Major K. S. Brown to meet, was Captain Le Boutillier.

It will be remembered that this officer led the flight that had become detached. Within a minute or so of the dogfight over Sailly-le-Sec having started, Captain Le Boutillier arrived with his flight and led into the attack. During the fight he observed von Richthofen's machine crash and at a moment or so previous, he had seen three machines, one behind the other, May's, a red triplane—and Brown's.

Two conflicting views are therefore presented, not on the direct issue of who shot von Richthofen, but upon the issue of whether or not Captain Brown was in the vicinity, to have the opportunity to fire *again*, west of Vaux. A number of witnesses, twenty or so, on the ground say he did not, three observers from the air testify that he did. Weight of numbers is not the criterion on this point. The witnesses on the ground were not trained observers of air action, but those three in the air were, and two of them had had considerable experience. Some of the statements of ground witnesses do not bear critical examination. One officer averred that, other than May, the nearest aircraft, when von Richthofen crashed, was a Camel some 2,000 yards away. That is rather a long range at which to identify a machine as a Camel, unless the officer was using field-glasses. In that case it might be difficult to be sure that there were no other aircraft about, since glasses pin-point an object to the exclusion of all else.

After the passage of forty years, it is not possible to arrange an assembly of eye-witnesses, but Major K. S. Brown has tested the possibilities, it would seem, to the absolute degree. In 1953 he centred himself on Amiens for a period, and armed with the military maps of the time, he took up in turn the positions of each of the observers that gave witness for the Australian Official History which, fortunately, quoted map references. Taking into account buildings since erected, he was certain that few of the ground witnesses would have had an uninterrupted view along the flight path it is known that von Richthofen took, or of the air fighting in that area.

The next step was to fly over the area, and this Major Brown actually did, orbitting many times, and putting himself in the position of the three air witnesses, May, Mellersh and Le Boutillier. Finally, and at a speed comparable to Richthofen's triplane, he flew along that much discussed flight path. His impressions were of the great superiority of the vantage point of air observation, even at low altitude, compared with the ground observers positions. Major K. S. Brown is of the opinion that despite the May–von Richthofen chase undoubtedly being the focus of

The Oberursel type engine removed from Richthofen's triplane was built in Frankfürt-am-Main early in 1918. It bore a great similarity to a Le Rhone engine (hence, no doubt, it being labelled as such). The bore and stroke were in fact the same.

most eyes on the ground, the experienced observations of the two air witnesses, which agreed with May's own statement, present a definite case for Captain A. R. Brown having had the opportunity to fire a second time, near to the place where von Richthofen fell. If it were not for this possibility, the case would have rested solely upon whether or not von Richthofen could have sustained a sixty-seven/seventy-three second flight after receiving a fatal wound from Captain Brown's gun. But that factor was not considered at the time.

But what of the evidence in the wreckage? It had fallen just beside the Bray–Corbie road striking a wurzel heap, which brought it to an abrupt stop. The undercarriage was smashed and the petrol tank collapsed, but the wings remained unbroken. Standing orders for the troops in the area, forbade them to expose themselves on or near the road which was under enemy observation, but in their curiosity, these orders were ignored. Troops streamed across to the wreckage, some setting out from Vaux, a mile away to the south, others from the 155th Siege Battery. (Position F, pages 120-1.) Lieutenant D. L. Fraser, one of the first on the scene, undid von Richthofen's safety belt and with the help of some others, lifted him from the cockpit. It was obvious to them that he was dead and his body was laid on the grass. His papers were examined and his identity was then realised. A mad rush for souvenirs then seems to have started and the padre of the 8th Field Artillery Brigade had to prevail upon the troops to surrender personal belongings which they had taken.

Meanwhile the machine was literally hacked to pieces. In this way all evidence of bullet holes was destroyed. The propeller was taken off and was being cut up when an officer succeeding in imposing some control, but stripping of the fabric went on, until the German artillery laid a barrage around the area, making it difficult to approach.

By that time the machine was little more than a framework with engine and guns, most of the instruments having been removed.

Two R.A.F. officers managed to be in on the souvenirs in a rather unusual way. Apparently a young S.E.5A pilot of No. 24 Squadron had performed some rather unnecessary and disturbing evolutions over a battery position the day before and the battery commander had complained to his Wing. The wing commander, Lieutenant Colonel F. V. Holt, D.S.O., ordered the pilot concerned to report to him, and then he accompanied him to the battery concerned to witness his apology. En route they passed the crashed triplane and both set to and collected pieces of red fabric! Visiting No. 24 Squadron on the way back, Colonel Holt distributed pieces of it amongst the pilots.

A salvage party to collect the remains was despatched that evening from No. 3 Squadron A.F.C. under Lieutenant W. J. Warneford the assistant equipment officer. While it was still daylight, Air Mechanic C. C. Collins crept out and recovered von Richthofen's body. After nightfall, when the darkness screened the area from enemy observations, the remains of the aircraft were brought in on a trailer. One of the party, writing as Mr. Boxall-Chapman of Lincoln, in the *News Chronicle* during 1934, revealed that he pocketed two cartridges from the guns and that one had misfired, tending to support the belief that von Richthofen did indeed have a jammed gun.

Von Richthofen's body was placed in a hangar of No. 3 Squadron A.F.C. at Poulainville and prepared for burial. Since by that time, the conflicting claims of the R.A.F. and A.I.F. personnel were appreciated at Headquarters, an informal post-mortem was arranged to discover by surface examination the cause of death. This took place in the afternoon of the 22nd, shortly before burial.

There were found to be superficial injuries to the face, caused by impact with the gun-butts on crashing, but all four medical officers were agreed that the cause of death was a bullet wound through the chest. Colonel T. Sinclair, C.B., R.A.M.C., Consulting Surgeon of the Fourth Army, who probed the wound, reported: 'The bullet appears to have passed obliquely backwards through the chest, striking the spinal column, from which it glanced in a forward direction and issued on the left side of the chest about two inches higher...' Captain G. C. Graham and Lieutenant G. E. Downs, R.A.M.C. officers attached to the R.A.F. in a joint report disagreed

The twin Spandau guns, taken from the wreckage of von Richthofen's triplane are here being examined by three officers of the Australian Flying Corps on the morning of April 22nd, 1918.

Ripping of the fabric from the fuselage side, destroyed the service identity marking of Fokker Dr I 425/17; but on the struts there remained the factory number 2009/18, which has often been quoted since, incorrectly, as its service serial number.

that the backbone was struck. They ventured an opinion that the bullet must have come from a gun on roughly the same level as the German machine and could not have been fired from the ground. However, Colonel G. W. Barber, D.D.M.S., Australian Corps, in a separate examination wrote '... it was just such as would have been inflicted by fire from the ground whilst the machine was banking.'

The point at issue for the examination was—Could the bullet have come from the ground or the air? As the evolutions of the aircraft had not then been studied or witnesses reports co-ordinated, the examination on this aspect was rather futile. We are told that von Richthofen banked, turned and *rose* before he fell; he hunched his body and we know he constantly turned to view behind. His machine was presented in various positions and his body in several varying postures; some of the machine-guns too, were on rising ground. Such a shot might well have come from the ground or the air and there are no logical grounds for disputing either! The point that was missed, was— Could von Richthofen, with such a wound, have continued to pursue May? It was only appreciated in retrospect that most likely Brown's attack took place east of Vaux and the question of whether or not death was instantaneous was not studied. Because the medical officers, through no fault of their own, were not invited to carry out an autopsy on that aspect, it will never be known whether or not, Captain Brown could have shot Richthofen when he *first* fired, for the vital evidence was buried unprobed with von Richthofen.

The 'Photo-Map' overleaf shows at about position 'G' where it is believed Captain Brown *first* fired. Flight paths have been re-constructed from eye-witnesses accounts, but since some witnesses disagree, the point at which he could have closed in for a *second* chance to fire is left for conjecture.

The zig-zagging flights of May and von Richthofen, impossible to draw accurately, would in fact so reduce their forward speeds, that Brown, in spite of his sweep to the south, could well have been close to position 'E' at the time of the crash.

von Richthofen was killed and May lived to fight again. He was to go on to achieve success similar to Brown. Remaining with the squadron until the end of the war, he received promotion to Captain on September 12th, 1918, was decorated with the Distinguished Flying Cross and credited with thirteen confirmed victories and five probables. Later he was to receive an O.B.E. and the Bronze Palm Medal of Freedom for his work before and during the last war. He died in 1952.

Captain Brown, however, was a sick man. For days he had been forcing himself to duty and on April 23rd, the day after von Richthofen's burial, he reported sick, but returned to duty the day following. Next day he was again down sick and was considered by the medical officer to be a critical gastric case. He was packed off to hospital and invalided back to England.

There, he was to receive a bar to his Distinguished Service Cross for his part in that fight of April 21st, 1918. Although von Richthofen was not mentioned by name, there is no doubt that his Fokker Triplane is the one referred to in the citation, which read: 'For conspicuous gallantry and devotion to duty. On the 21st April, 1918, while leading a patrol of six scouts he attacked a formation of twenty hostile scouts. He personally engaged two Fokker triplanes, which he drove off; then, seeing that one of our machines was being attacked and apparently hard pressed, he dived on the hostile scout, firing the while. This scout, a Fokker triplane, nose dived and crashed to the ground. Since the award of the Distinguished Service Cross he has destroyed several other enemy aircraft and has shown great dash and enterprise in attacking enemy troops from low altitudes despite heavy anti-aircraft fire.' Altogether, he was credited with twelve victories.

Lieutenant (Hon. Captain) Arthur Royal Brown, D.S.C. and Bar, was placed on the Retired List of the R.A.F. on April 9th, 1919. If he has been forgotten by name in his old squadron, the deed with which he was credited is remembered yet; for today the crest of No. 209 Squadron Royal Air Force is—'A red eagle—falling'.

THE LAST FLIGHT OF

F

M von R CRASHED HERE
E

D

SGT POPKIN
C

VAUX-Sur-Somme

RIVER SOMME

VAIRE-Sous-Corbie

N

FRONT

CORBIE

HALF-MILE

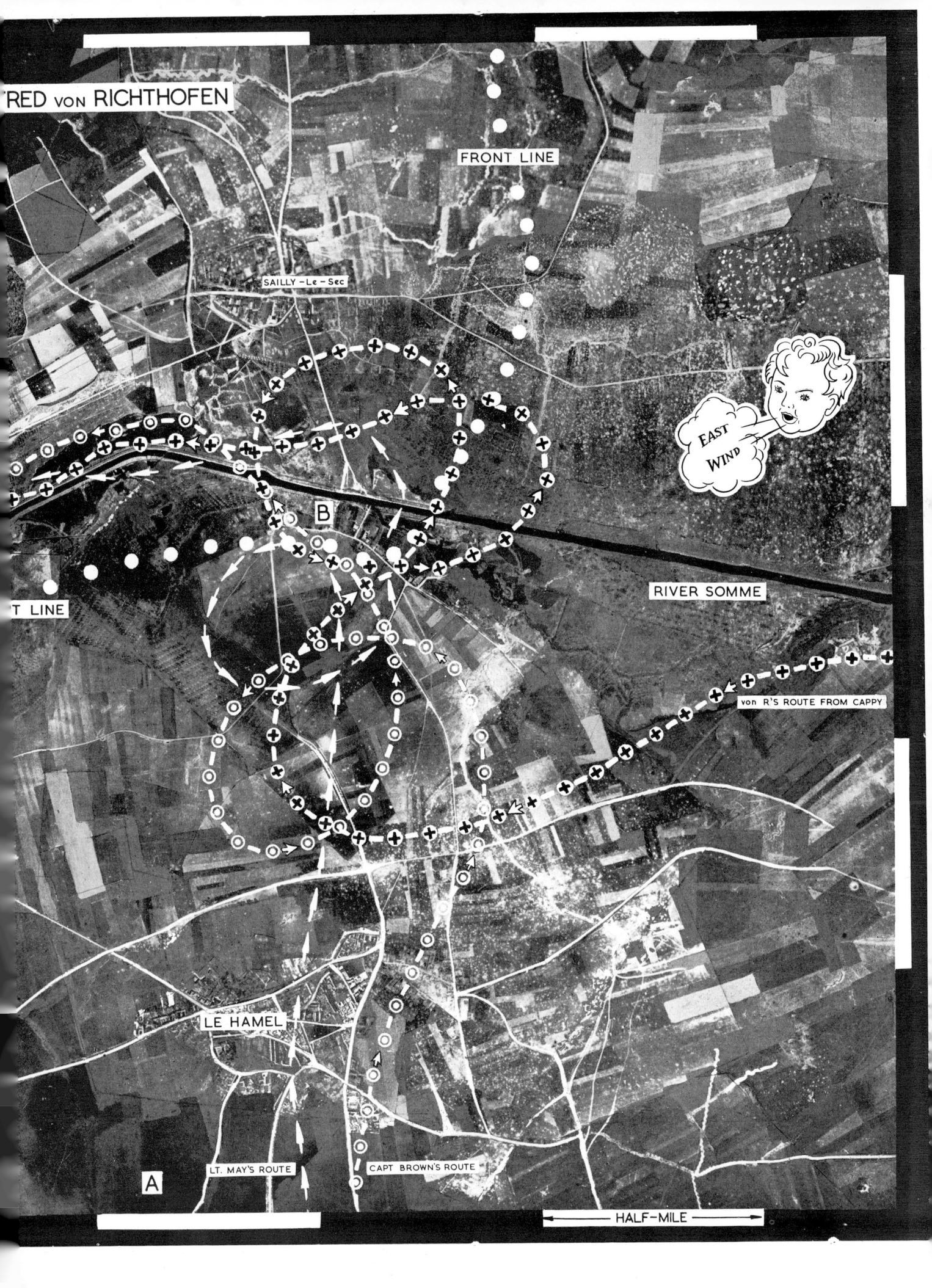

RED von RICHTHOFEN

FRONT LINE

SAILLY-Le-Sec

EAST WIND

B

RIVER SOMME

von R'S ROUTE FROM CAPPY

FT LINE

LE HAMEL

LT. MAY'S ROUTE   CAPT BROWN'S ROUTE

A

HALF-MILE

CHAPTER TWENTY-FIVE—A Final Assessment

By **D. A. RUSSELL**, *M.I.Mech.E.*

In the above official photograph (courtesy the Imperial War Museum), taken about one month before the death of Baron Manfred von Richthofen; is shown a 13-pounder 9 cwt. anti-aircraft gun on a Mark IV motor lorry mounting, in action at Omiecourt. Sergeant-major Franklyn, wearing leather gaiters, is standing nearest the camera. Note the Lewis gun mounted between the front of the lorry and a tree. Who knows that this was not the very gun, operated by Sergeant Franklyn, from which was fired the fatal shot?

Although more arguments and ill-informed opinions have been expressed and, indeed, more nonsense written about the death of Manfred von Richthofen than that of any other fighter pilot of the 1914–18 war, there is no cause to doubt the *sincerity* of the claim made *on behalf of* Captain Roy Brown at the time of Richthofen's death; and the claim *made by* a certain Australian gunner named Robert Buie; which was published in the December 1959 issue of the American magazine *Cavalier*.

However, since the original publication of this book in 1958, evidence of yet *another* claim has come to light, which I personally investigated—that of No. 178101 Battery Quarter Master Sergeant Alfred George Franklyn of the Royal Garrison Artillery. Franklyn was in charge of an anti-aircraft battery attached to the Australian Forces then occupying the area in which von Richthofen crashed: his battery was, in fact, only a few hundred yards from Buie's position.

After learning of Franklyn's claim, and in company with Harleyford's Technical Editor, Mr. E. F. Cheesman, I visited him and asked him to relate *his* version of the events leading to von Richthofen's death.

The six-feet two-inch ex-police sergeant was then employed by the General Steam Navigation Co. Ltd. of London, as their representative dealing with passengers on the sightseeing steamship tours operating from ' the longest pier in the world ' at Southend-on-Sea, Essex, England.

Wearing a naval-type uniform with several 1914–18 war ribbons, he welcomed us at his home and after showing us his British Army documents of service and discharge papers, which we duly authenticated, he told us in his own words how *he* shot down von Richthofen on that fateful 21st April 1918, whilst in charge of anti-aircraft guns on the Bray-Corbie road in the Somme valley.

However, before dealing with Franklyn's claim in detail, it is appropriate to examine more fully, certain aspects of the claim made on behalf of Captain Roy Brown —aspects which have not before received the attention their significance warrants.

Firstly, there is no dispute as to the exact location where von Richthofen crashed, and there is no dispute about the point at which May, followed by Richthofen (who in turn was closely followed by Brown) left the fight, just south of Sailly-le-Sec.

Secondly, Brown only followed Richthofen from just south of Sailly-le-Sec to just *west* of Vaux-Sur-Somme, a distance along the course of the river of approximately three-quarters of a mile. Just *east* of Vaux-Sur-Somme, Brown ceased to follow von Richthofen, and flew due *west* in a wide sweep which took him about a mile north of Corbie, before he turned due north and followed May out of the battle area. The flight routes of these three aircraft are clearly shown on the map on pages 120–121 of this book. This map I ' constructed ' from a large number of ' official ' reconnaissance photographs taken in early 1918—kindly loaned by the Imperial War Museum, London. Many of them had either to be enlarged or reduced to a common scale, after which I pasted them together, and had the routes flown by the three aircraft marked in by Mr. Hepworth.

The work involved in preparing this map alone took over one hundred ' man hours ', and I am satisfied that the flight routes drawn in, based on the corroborated reports of many observers, are as correct as it is humanly possible to make them.

Now here comes the most critical and important point as to whether *Brown* was the one who shot down von Richthofen. The distance flown by von Richthofen before he crashed, *AFTER* Brown ceased to be on his tail, has been very carefully plotted and shown to be not less than *TWO MILES*. I repeat, *carefully* plotted, and this has been possible on account of the known positions of the various ground gunners and other witnesses to the chase of May by von Richthofen along the Somme Valley. As recorded earlier in this book, the authors were able to draw on individual official reports of no less than ten witnesses.

It is known that the maximum speeds of both the Camel and Fokker Triplane were approximately 115 miles per hour. There was a brisk wind blowing from the east which might have increased somewhat the speeds of May's and von Richthofen's aircraft; but it can be authoritatively stated that the *maximum ground* speeds at which these machines would be flying, would not exceed 120 miles per hour. Bearing in mind that May was twisting and turning in evasive action to avoid von Richthofen, the rate of progress over the two miles was almost certainly *less* than this.

Relating this *maximum* possible speed to the known *minimum* distance flown by Richthofen from the time Brown disengaged until von Richthofen crashed, it is easy to calculate that the time taken would not be less than sixty seconds.

Reverting to the report of the Medical Officers who conducted the post mortem examination on von Richthofen, it is clear that the wound was one that would have led to the loss of a large amount of blood; probably amounting to a *haemorrhage* with of course the consequent *blacking-out of all senses within a few seconds*.

We now face two straight-forward questions. Firstly, was it possible for von Richthofen to have remained not only fully conscious, but also in full control of his machine for as long as sixty seconds, which would be the *minimum* time to elapse from the time Brown disengaged until von Richthofen crashed? Secondly, if Brown *did* shoot down von Richthofen, he might well have shot him on leaving the battle area, that is to the south of Sailly-le-Sec. *If that were so*, it would mean that von Richthofen would have flown two and three-quarter miles in the *minimum time* of one minute twenty-two seconds before he crashed. THAT IS JUST NOT POSSIBLE, *BECAUSE OF THE NATURE OF THE WOUND*.

Medical advice I have obtained from various quarters indicates unanimously, that it would be extremely unlikely that von Richthofen could have remained conscious for more than a few seconds, struck as he was with a bullet which passed through his body and which on the way struck the spinal cord, the main connection from the brain to the whole of the body and the muscles controlling it.

One pertinent and telling point which seems to have been ignored in *every* account of the death of von Richthofen so far published, concerns Brown's attack on him during the *early* part of the pursuit of May. Brown clearly states that he fired into the red Triplane which was diving after May. At the *moment of firing* he saw von Richthofen give a *backward* glance either of surprise at the firing or as a routine check to ascertain *whether he himself* was in danger from a stern attack. In looking round, von Richthofen could only have turned his head and shoulders. Being strapped in the narrow confines of the triplane's cockpit he could not possibly have turned so that he *faced* Brown. Since the medical reports agree that the bullet which killed him entered from the front right side, how then could one of Brown's shots have done this when von Richthofen's chest *was never exposed to Brown*, nor was Brown at any time, according to his own reports, firing from any other position than *astern?*

It is my assessment, therefore, ' beyond all reasonable doubt '— by careful mathematical calculations allied to authentic medical opinion—that *had* Captain Brown fired the fatal shot, von Richthofen would have been rendered unconscious and would have crashed within a few seconds from the time the bullet hit him. It therefore follows, *since von Richthofen flew on for* at least a whole minute after Brown ceased to follow him, that Brown *COULD NOT POSSIBLY HAVE FIRED THE FATAL SHOT*.

Although Captain Brown was credited with this victory, it is on record that when interviewed on more than one occasion in later years, this gallant officer, who died in Ontario in March 1944, *never did claim categorically* that it was he who shot down and killed von Richthofen. . . .

We are, therefore, left to consider the *relative merits* of the claims of Buie and Franklyn. In his published claim, Buie gives a clear, and to my mind, honest and fair description of how *he* claims to have shot down von Richthofen's Triplane. But, in addition to him, and indeed to Sergeant Franklyn, it is an undisputed fact that a *number of other men* were firing Lewis guns set up for anti-aircraft purposes. Also, men in the trenches were firing with rifles from a number of points along the route taken by May and von Richthofen. Any *one* of these men could claim that it was *he* who fired the fatal shot. But *no* individual man could *prove* that it was he who did so.

Each man can believe honestly and sincerely that he did it. Each one could go into a witness box at a legally constituted Official Enquiry and swear on oath . . . WHAT? Only that ' to the best of his knowledge and belief '—*he* had fired the fatal shot. But *no man could swear before God that he* fired the fatal shot, and less still could prove that he did.

In Buie's claim a great deal has been made of the message sent by General Rawlinson, Commander-in-Chief of the Australian Expeditionary Force. It is important to my mind to study carefully the wording of this message. It read: ' Please convey to the 53rd Battn., 5th Div., my best thanks and congratulations on having brought down the celebrated German Aviator, von Richthofen.' A second message from the Headquarters of the 5th Australian

An official photograph of the endorsement appended to the British Army Form of B.Q.M.S. Franklyn.

Anti-aircraft Division, which was addressed to Gunner R. Buie, read as follows: 'The attached is a copy of the Commander's telegram of thanks and congratulations received on the occasion of Captain Baron von Richthofen being shot down.' NOWHERE IN EITHER OF THESE TWO MESSAGES IS GUNNER R. BUIE DESIGNATED AS THE INDIVIDUAL WHO SHOT DOWN VON RICHTHOFEN.

General Rawlinson's message was addressed to the 53rd Battn., which consisted of a number of gunners, one of whom was a man Buie referred to as his buddy— '" Snowey" Evans, and who was manning the other gun on my right'. Buie further states that: 'Evans got first clearance and opened up on a range of slightly more than 30 yds.'

How then, can Buie prove that it was *he* who shot Richthofen! Who can prove that it was not 'Snowey' Evans?

Now let us consider the claim of Sergeant Franklyn. He, of course, is as adamant as Buie that it was *he*, Franklyn, who shot down von Richthofen. When I told him of Buie's claim, he laughed without rancour, accepted that Buie made his claim in good faith, but denied that there could be anything in it.

It should be emphasised that Franklyn and his gunners were on this attached duty in the Australian-held sector, *because* of their specific training and experience in anti-aircraft work.

Franklyn joined the Essex County Constabulary in 1913 and except for his war services, he remained in the Police Force until his retirement some years ago. His report of the 'incident' is as follows:

'Baron von Richthofen was brought down by Lewis gun fire on Sunday, 21st April 1918 at 11.03 a.m. about 1,000 yards east of Bonnay. The facts are that I was in charge of two anti-aircraft guns stationed on a sunken road 800 yards east of Bonnay, on the Corbie Road, when Richthofen's Circus as we knew them, were patrolling the line flying at a height of 10,000 to 15,000 ft., and we were engaging them with our two 13/18 lb. A.A. guns.

'Richthofen suddenly left his Circus and dived towards us and at the same time two of our Sopwith Camels which were returning, were on the left of our gun position, being chased by Richthofen.

'We could not fire at Richthofen with our A.A. guns owing to his stunting and low elevation. I immediately rushed to my Lewis machine gun which I had on a tripod and fired at him at very close range about 30 rounds, one round in every four being a "Tracer" bullet, so that the course of the bullet could be observed. I then saw him crash to the ground about 200 yards away from my position.

'The two gun crews of my section all saw what happened and how he was brought down. There were also two Australian Infantry Sergeants standing beside me and one remarked " You have got him, digger ", and I remarked " Yes, he is down all right ". I could not leave myself, so I sent Corporal Bentham to the plane and he came back to me and said that the pilot was dead, and brought back a piece of his plane which I brought home.

'This was reported to my Headquarters, F. Battery A.A. About an hour afterwards a large motor car came to our position from the aerodrome with a high official of the R.A.F. with the pilot of one of the two Camels which were being chased by Richthofen. They asked me what had occurred, and I asked the pilot why he did not engage him, and he said that his machine gun had jammed. After that an R.A.F. tender came up and took the body of Baron von Richthofen away.'

Sergeant Franklyn is supported in his claim by a member of his unit whose report is as follows:

'On 21st April 1918, the 110th Section " F " Anti-Aircraft Battery, Royal Garrison Artillery, was in action by the side of the Bray-Corbie Road. The section consisted of the two 13/18 pounder guns mounted on lorries. We were, at that time, attached to the Australian Division, who were holding a line in front of a ridge of high ground running parallel with the road, and about a quarter of a mile away from the road.

'The ground between our position and the ridge was occupied by Australian Field Batteries.

'Just before mid-day, our attention was attracted by the rattle of machine guns, and there suddenly appeared two Sopwith Camels flying in from the German lines at full speed, and so low that they only just cleared the top of the ridge.

'Immediately behind them, and sitting on their tails was the red plane which events subsequently proved was flown by Baron von Richthofen. He was putting bursts of machine gun fire into both the Camels without however doing any apparent damage.

'We promptly came into action, and with the object of saving the British planes, put up a barrage of shrapnel between them and the Fokker, and at the same time fire was opened on the Baron by our own Lewis gun (manned by Sergeant Franklyn) attached to the Australian Field Batteries. After a short while, the Baron, apparently then realising for the first time the dangerous position he had run into executed an "Immelmann" turn but suddenly went down at a steep angle over the ridge.

    R. H. Barron.
    Late Bombardier.
    No. 296400 " F " Battery A.A.
    Royal Garrison Artillery.'

Whilst still acknowledging 'theoretically' that it was possible for Buie to have shot down von Richthofen, it is pertinent to remark here, that *Franklyn* had passed a course of instruction at an active aervice Army School on antiaircraft gunnery; and further, that he had qualified as a range finder and aircraft spotter. The rank of Quarter-Master Sergeant in charge of a battery of heavy lorry-mounted anti-aircraft guns was no light responsibility, and that Franklyn was fully competent is shown by the certificate issued to him by his Commanding Officer on honourable discharge after the war. 'A very excellent N.C.O. Good organizer. Good command of men.'

We have still to decide whether Buie or Franklyn (provided, of course, that it is accepted it *was* one of *these* two men), fired the fatal shot. In my opinion, it is possible to determine—'beyond any reasonable doubt'—that if, indeed von Richthofen *was* shot down by one of these two men, then it was by Sergeant Franklyn.

This firm opinion of mine depends entirely on the FACT that Franklyn was placed in such a position that *he could have shot down von Richthofen*, whereas in fact Buie (and also 'Snowey' Evans) *were never in the position to have done so*.

Referring to the portion of the map showing the flight paths of both May and von Richthofen from the point where Brown detached east of Vaux-Sur-Somme, to the point where von Richthofen crashed, it will be seen that both Buie and Evans were located to the north west of the flight path of von Richthofen, since von Richthofen was flying in a northerly direction and was thus towards the east of Evans and Buie. How on earth then, could either of these two men have shot von Richthofen with a bullet which entered from the right (east) side of his body and came out at the left (west) side of his body?

On the other hand, Franklyn, was located *due east* of Evans and Buie, and except for about the last few hundred yards of his flight path before he crashed, von Richthofen would for at least *half a mile* be flying to the *west* of Franklyn. Thus, although it cannot be proved, it is perfectly clear that *Franklyn* had a clear approach, and indeed at short range, to have fired the bullet which would have entered von Richthofen's body on the right and passed out on the left.

Whether or not, Sergeant Franklyn fired the fatal shot can never be proved or denied; but I submit that I have now shown conclusively that it was impossible:

    (*a*) For Captain Roy Brown to have fired the shot that killed von Richthofen.

A photograph of ex-B.Q.M.S. Alfred George Franklyn taken in 1959, in the uniform of the General Steam Navigation Co. of London, England.

    (*b*) That it was equally impossible for either Buie, or Evans, or *anybody else firing from the ground to the south, south-west, the west, and the north-west, of von Richthofen to have fired the fatal shot*; because the body of von Richthofen could never possibly have been in the position whereby the fatal bullet could have, as it did, enter at the right side and pass out at the left.

In conclusion, I would like to say that on publication of 'Richthofen and The Flying Circus' I had the honour of visiting Baroness Kunigunde von Richthofen at Wiesbaden. The Baroness kindly autographed a copy of the 'Richthofen' book for me. The date was 9th October 1958. She said that she fully approved of the very considerable efforts of the two authors, and that they had fairly described the life and indeed the quite different characteristics of her two eldest sons, Manfred and Lothar.

[†] Baroness von Richthofen told me that after the end of the 1914–18 war she was visited by a considerable number of Manfred's co-pilots and was also visited by a number of British Officers, both Royal Air Force and Army. She said that it was the unanimous opinion of both German and British Officers that her son had been shot down by fire from the ground. R.I.P.   [†] since died.

(Acknowledgement is herewith made to Fawcett Publications Inc., publishers of 'Cavalier', for permission to reproduce in a slightly edited form, my article published in the January 1961 issue of that magazine.)

CHAPTER TWENTY-SIX

Successors and Successes

Hauptmann Reinhard, successor to von Richthofen, photographed after crashing in his triplane. By the cockpit may be noticed the signal cartridge clip (with one cartridge remaining) an important accessory for a commander.

When at Adlershof in January 1918, Richthofen had flown the prototype Fokker D VII and during the following April, the *Geschwader* received some of the first production models fitted with Mercedes engines. The Fokker D VII did not immediately find favour with Dr I pilots, who were somewhat loath to part with a machine so manœuvrable and with such a good rate of climb. It is said that Anthony Fokker made a number of visits to *Jagdstaffeln* in order to demonstrate and publicise the D VII, and to convince pilots of its superiority.

One pilot who did much to win over confidence in the D VII for *J.G.1* was a very new arrival, Vizefeldwebel Willy Gabriel. According to *Geschwader* records Gabriel did not arrive at *J.G.1* until May 17th, but by his own account, when interviewed in 1958, by Herr Nowarra, he joined on April 15th. Since he transferred direct to *J.G.1* from *Schlachtstaffel Nr. 15*, which at the time was stationed at Cappy, without passing through a *Jastaschule*, he was most likely temporarily attached for a probationary period. Manfred von Richthofen himself had stated to him the conditions on which he would be accepted; that he should realise he was starting anew as a fighter-pilot and there would be no question of resting upon his laurels won with other units. He was further cautioned that if he did not succeed in obtaining a victory within the next four weeks, he was liable to be returned to his unit.

Vizefeldwebel Gabriel was allotted one of the new D VIIs and made his initial flight on the type with Richthofen and several *J.G.1* members watching. They were at first disappointed. After take-off Gabriel did little more than feel the controls and then came in to land—but, he immediately took off again. This time it was in cavalier-fashion; the German slang-word *Kavalierstart* was in fact applied to a take-off with a short run, followed by a steep climb letting the propeller 'draw' the machine—a practice to be later strictly forbidden in the *Luftwaffe*. Gabriel then followed this auspicious start to his second flight by a thirty-minute display of aerobatics. By then it would seem von Richthofen condoned aerobatics, for his reaction was little more than to tell Gabriel that he seemed all right in flight and that he would await his behaviour in a fight. Four days later Richthofen was dead.

Reinhard was now the 'Circus-master'. It would be difficult to fathom the true reasons for Richthofen's own selection of Reinhard as his successor, although by seniority, he was well qualified and in that respect his nomination would be acceptable to the authorities, but something more than that was required by Richthofen. Possibly he had in mind the forty or so young men whose lives were in jeopardy daily. A man who admittedly had less dash than the average, but who nevertheless was fearless and unruffled in any situation and commanded their respect, would prove a more able leader than a dashing hero—and to the best interests of the Fatherland.

Wilhelm Reinhard, born March 18th, 1891 in Düsseldorf, was the son of a factory director who moved later to Frankfurt a.M. where Wilhelm received his education at the Kaiser Friedrich High School. After completing his education in Strassburg, he entered the 14th Regiment of Artillery at Baden as a trainee officer in 1909. Still with the regiment in August 1914 he entrained for Belgium. Early in the war he received his first wound during the fighting around Bixschoote, in Flanders. A leg was shattered and twice amputation was contemplated, but eventually the wound healed satisfactorily. It was in June 1915 that he was accepted for the Air Service and having passed his tests he was piloting at the front by the end of that year. Wounded again, he returned to fly G-type aircraft with *Fl. Abt. (A) 205* during the Battle of Verdun. By that time he was an Oberleutnant. Transferred to the Balkan Theatre in 1916, he had his third long spell in hospital, this time with typhus. Early in 1917 he completed a course in fighter-training at Warsaw, which qualified him for *J.G.1* later in the year. Now, in late April 1918, he was in command of the *Geschwader*.

The loss of von Richthofen undoubtedly had a profound effect on the *Geschwader*, but since he had persisted in continued service at the front, to the realists his fate was inevitable. Guynemer had been the idol of the French people, but he had fallen—and without trace. Ball too, one of the few British airmen whose names had appeared in

*Jasta 10 in July 1918. Left to right—
1. Grassmann; 2. Heldmann; 3. Schaefer;
4. Loewenhardt; 5. Friedrichs; 6. Lehmann, 7. Aue; 8. Schumacher. Möller
is behind Aue, and Schaffen is at far right.*

communiques from the B.E.F., fell. Now Germany's great ace had fallen. von Richthofen had gone, but the *Richthofen Geschwader* remained.

On the day that von Richthofen had died, Wolff had claimed one of the Camels in the engagement, evidently Mackenzie's machine, which fell on the British side of the lines. There was little further activity by *J.G.1* that day or indeed along the front except further to the north in the vicinity of Bailleul, where a patrol from No. 54 Squadron met eleven Fokker triplanes during which two Camel pilots were lost, Lieutenant R. J. Marion in B9315 and Lieutenant C. J. Mason in D6569.

Next day, in spite of dejected spirits, two pilots who had flown on that fateful flight the day before, Wolff and Weiss, set out on patrol and gave battle to another Camel squadron. This time three Camels fell, two to Wolff, his eighth and ninth victories and one to Weiss, his eighteenth.

Lothar, much affected by his brother's loss, swore revenge, reproached himself that he had not been fit enough to fly, disregarded the advice of his doctors and attempted to return to duty. He was frustrated in his desire for revenge and by the bad weather restricting his unit's activity, but when the weather did improve on May 2nd, it proved disastrous for his *Jasta*. Leutnant Hans Weiss was shot down in Fokker Dr I 545/17 and Vizefeldwebel Scholz climbing steeply after take-off from Cappy in his Dr I 591/17, stalled and crashed to his death.

Little could be added to Reinhard's comment upon Weiss as an air-fighter—'As a leader he was outstanding and in the air I yielded to his guidance.' Coming from Hof in Bavaria where he was born in 1892, Weiss had studied engineering at the University of Munich. Volunteering for the Army, he was accepted for a pioneer regiment at Ingolstadt, from which he transferred to the Air Service and took his flying training at the *Bayerische FEA1* at Schleissheim. For over a year he flew C-type aircraft on operations as a Vizefeldwebel. After passing through a *Jastaschule* in October 1917, he became an officer. Scoring twelve victories, including four balloons and a twin-engined bomber, with *Jasta 41*, he had been personally selected by Richthofen, who arranged his arrival at Lechelle on March 27th. It had been Richthofen's intention to appoint him to the command of *Jasta 11*. Now both were dead.

Next day, May 3rd, another *Jasta 11* man was a casualty; Leutnant Just was wounded. The unit was sadly depleted, for apart from the two men killed and one wounded, Steinhäuser was away convalescent and Leutnants Wolff and Wolfram von Richthofen were back in Germany to attend a memorial service to Manfred.

Another *Jasta 11* officer, Leutnant Paul Wenzel had a narrow escape about this time. Having dived into position behind a Camel, he was almost rammed by Hauptmann Reinhard. Jerking the controls to avoid a collision the stress on his aircraft was such that several ribs in an upper wing were broken.

It would seem that about this time, the traditional red finish of the aircraft of the *Geschwader* had given way to various schemes by individual pilots. At first, each pilot had displayed his individual colour on

Hauptmann Reinhard, noted for his sang froid, *appears quite unruffled after crashing in his triplane, which, it may be be noted, had a striped tailplane—red stripes on a white field.*

127

The third and last Commander of the Richthofen Geschwader, *Oberleutnant Hermann Göring.*

the control surfaces and later this was expanded to include the tailplane. Some *Jastas* adopted a *'Jadgstaffel* characteristic', but by May 1918, some *J.G.1* members had become 'extrememists'. Weiss, for example, had been shot down in an all-white triplane! Apart from sheer egotism, the facilitating of recognition in combat, both by their comrades in the air and by their reporting service on the ground, was an obvious advantage of such embellishment. In the case of Leutnant Weiss—Weiss was the German word for white!

By May 10th, *Jasta 11* were again operational and three Camels fell to them, one each to Oberleutnant von Wedel, Leutnant Steinhäuser and Leutnant Wolff. The day was another black one for the Sopwith Camel, for three more fell to *Jasta 6* and yet another to *Jasta 4*. The downing of two D.H.9s and a Bristol Fighter brought the day's score to eleven without loss.

A quieter day, followed by three days of bad weather, gave the *Geschwader* a rest from which they apparently benefited, for on the 15th, thirteen enemy machines were shot down without loss. Kirschstein was the ace of the day, claiming two Bristol Fighters and a Camel. It was one of the most active days in the history of the *Geschwader*, 137 sorties being flown. Udet, about this time, reported back to duty from hospital.

Next day came a reckoning. For the four victories scored, three pilots did not return from patrol; Leutnant Hübner, Leutnant Hans-Joachim Wolff and Sergeant Schmutzler. Not only that, but Cappy was raided by seven British bombers. The aircraft *J.G.1* were encountering at that time were a 'mixed bag'; apart from meeting offensive patrols of Camels and S.Es., French aircraft, particularly Breguets and Spads, were then operating in the area following a re-shuffling of forces after the German offensive. There were too, the D.H.4s and D.H.9s of the Independent Force, flying over the area of the *Geschwader* on their way to bomb Rhineland towns.

Again Cappy was bombed, and considering the depressing influence that the airfield, often waterlogged, had, few members of the *Geschwader* were sorry when a move was ordered to Guise. There they passed from the jurisdiction of the 2nd Army to that of the 7th Army. Before they left on May 20th, a telegram was received from General von Hoeppner, redesignating the unit from *Jagdgeschwader Nr. 1* to *Jagdgeschwader Frhr. v. Richthofen Nr.1*.

Guise was an ancient town whose castle was at that time used as a barracks. Only *Jasta 6* and the *Geschwader* H.Q. was by Guise itself, *Jasta 4* being near Longchamps, *Jasta 10* near Etreux and *Jasta 11* at Lamotte Ferme. The move was in preparation for an offensive directed towards the Chemins-des-Dames and an advance airfield was prepared at Puisieux-Ferme, some three miles north-east of Laon. During the five days available before the offensive opened, the *Geschwader* almost completely re-equipped with the Fokker D VII. Pilots found, that for all the rumours that had circulated, it was an easy machine to fly. It became a saying in the German Air Service that the Fokker D VII made heroes out of green-horns.

Early on May 27th, the *Geschwader* concentrated at Puisieux-Ferme. The attack had already opened with considerable success, after a bombardment by about a thousand guns along a twenty-seven mile front. Complete surprise had been gained, and as an indication of how little the Allies expected attack in that sector, was its manning by five British divisions who had suffered heavily in recent fighting on the Somme and had been moved southward, by arrangement with the French, as a 'rest-cure'! One R.A.F. squadron, No. 52, had been sent down to reconnoitre the area, but in those thickly wooded parts, nothing suspicious was noted. Not without reason had the *Geschwader* flown only locally during the preceding days, lest their presence gave an indication of preparations. The Germans too, had unusual Allies. At night, before the battle, sounds of troops and material being concentrated at railheads and dumps was effectively drowned, in the opinion of an Official Historian, by the croaking of the numerous frogs that rendered a nightly chorus from the River Ailette which ran through No Man's Land!

The *Geschwader* flew eighty-four sorties on the opening day, but only two victories were gained, both by Leutnant von Rautter who claimed a Bristol for his thirteenth and a Breguet for his fourteenth personal victories; the former was most probably a case of mistaken identity for a R.E.8. Few opportunities to score were presented; the opposing aircraft were mostly French and it was noted in the unit record book that they were not so aggressive as the British. However, they did not come through unscathed; on the

An off-duty picture of J.G.1 *personalities. L. to R.: Loewenhardt, Schaefer, Udet (at the wheel), Meyer and Bodenschatz.*

31st, Leutnant von Rautter, who that day had scored his fifteenth victory, fell in battle and Leutnant Rademacher was also posted as missing.

With the initial success of the battle, a move forward was made to a new advance airfield at Beugneux-Cramaille on June 1st. A day on which one victory was gained by Vizefeldwebel Gabriel when a French Spad fell to his guns for his third victory, but on balance, the work was undone by a German machine being presented to the French! A *Geschwader* pilot lost his way and landed on a French aerodrome! It was exactly two years to the day, since a brand new F.E.2d, A5, had left Farnborough at noon on a delivery flight to France and landed intact—on the wrong side of the lines!

June 2nd would have been an auspicious day for the *Geschwader*, but for the loss of Leutnant Heidenreich, reported missing. Reinhard, proving himself worthy of his predecessor, achieved three victories, all Spads; both Udet and Loewenhardt reached their twenty-fifth and the award of the *Pour le Mérite* to the latter was notified by telegram. Loewenhardt and Udet were now in earnest competition, the former drawing ahead by one, next day. The day following neither scored, but that day a Richthofen did—Wolfram achieved his first victory, a Spad two-seater. Another aspirant for leading ace of the *Geschwader* then entered the field—Kirschstein, who, having reached twenty victories two days before, scored three more on June 5th. By the 7th scores were Udet twenty-eight, Loewenhardt twenty-seven and Kirschstein twenty-four. 'Score mania' seemed to have seized the formation and havoc was wrought amongst the French Breguets and Spads, stung into action by the offensive. When, as on June 8th, few aircraft were encountered, Friedrichs made his score up to ten by downing a balloon.

Casualties at the time were remarkably light. Leutnant Otto crashed his aircraft the same day that he shot down a balloon, but escaped with light injuries. Leutnant Janzen was reported missing, but he escaped with his life having been taken prisoner-of-war on the 9th, the day that the *Geschwader* reached their 400th victory since forming just under a year ago. The competition continued. Reinhard, who earlier had, perhaps, lost a little in prestige by a comparatively low score, had been steadily accumulating a sizeable number, reaching a round twenty by June 12th, a day on which he alone scored. Two days later Udet reached thirty and Kirschstein twenty-five; that day Vizefeldwebel Degen was missing. The insatiable quest for victories, caused the number of sorties again to reach 137 on the 15th, but the French were not to be drawn and not one victory resulted. With a further day of little Allied air activity, balloons were again in vogue and a long-standing member of the *Geschwader*, Offizier Stellvertreter Aue claimed one, as well as the promising newcomers Vizefeldwebel Gabriel and Leutnant Friedrichs.

News reached the *Geschwader* of the fall of an old comrade, Leutnant Wüsthoff, who had recently transferred to *J.G.2*. He fell in a fight with 13 S.E.5As of No. 24 Squadron on June 17th landing badly wounded in the French lines. He was taken prisoner and sent to the P.O.W. camp at Chateau Contier, where he suffered much and did not leave it until 1920—and then on crutches.

On June 18th, Reinhard left for Adlershof, to take part in the fighter competition; Kirschstein also attended for a few days. This left Udet and Loewenhardt with a clear field to pursue their hunting. One might have used the phrase 'friendly rivals', but the more one delves into the history of the formation at this time, the more evident it becomes that these two officers treated each other with a certain reserve. Whether or not the nomination of a temporary *Kommandeur* in the absence of Reinhard had any connection with this, it is not known; but for some reason Udet was nominated in temporary command on the 18th and on the 19th this nomination was rescinded in favour of Loewenhardt.

Destined for infamy and to be the butt of cartoonists, Hermann Göring wearing the first of his decorations.

Richthofen's 'will'. He wrote (in effect):—'Should I not return from a flight, Oblt. Reinhard, Jasta 6, is to command the Geschwader—Frhr. v. Richthofen, Rittmeister.'

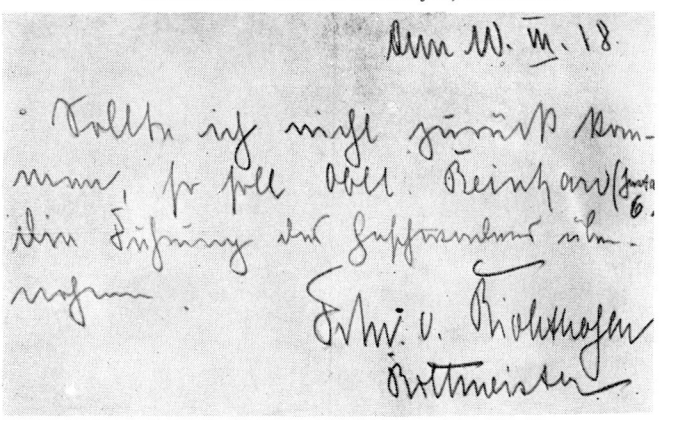

CHAPTER TWENTY-SEVEN *The Geschwader under Göring*

Symbolic of the wastage in aircraft during the German offensive is this scene at the Aircraft Repair Depot, Rang du Flers, July 1918. The significant facts are that 1,032 British aeroplanes were lost during March and April from the beginning of the German offensive, when British strength was 1,232 aircraft. In the foreground of this picture, D.H.9 C1176 is being worked upon, in the background, a burnt S.E.5A fuselage C1902 is being wheeled into a repair bay. On the left an A.W. F.K.8 fuel-tank is being handled.

The *Geschwader* had been passing through one of their most successful periods. Added to that, the B.M.W.-engined version of the Fokker D VII was becoming available and *Jasta 11* were the first to be equipped with it. One of their pilots reported that it climbed to 5,000 metres in just half the time taken by his earlier Mercedes-engined machine.

Mainly French aircraft were being encountered and the competition for the highest score between Loewenhardt and Udet continued. Rain since June 20th had rather limited their activities, but each had added to his number. By the 26th, Udet had thirty-five and Loewenhardt twenty-eight, a day on which a long-standing *J.G.1* pilot was killed, Leutnant Steinhäuser. Early morning on the 28th, the *Geschwader* were out in strength, clashing with a French formation of Spads and at midday there was a further encounter. Without loss, eight single-seater and one two-seater Spads were claimed. That day Kirschstein, away at Adlershof, was notified of his award of the *Pour le Mérite*.

Udet had a narrow escape on the 29th. In combat with a Breguet 14A-2, his plane was badly damaged and he lost control. Jumping out he took to his parachute and came down in an area under bombardment by gas-shells. Only with difficulty did he reach safety, yet that afternoon he was flying again. He had good nerves—then.

However, June, a star month for the 'Circus', ended tragically with the death of Leutnant Hoffmann and the loss of Leutnant Feige. The former was of *Jasta 11* which that day were to have celebrated, following their 300th victory. Their first had been obtained on January 23rd, 1917, when von Richthofen, as their new leader, had scored their first victory. They were now the premier *Jasta*.

July came and the competition continued. On the first day Udet shot down a Spad and a Breguet to make his score thirty-eight. The day following, Loewenhardt, up early with *Jasta 10*, claimed two Nieuports; Udet in the same fight, with *Jasta 4*, claimed a Nieuport for himself. On the third day of the month, Udet reached forty. That day a telegram to the *Geschwader*, set his mind wondering how long Loewenhardt would be in command, for Reinhard was not coming back. He had crashed at Adlershof.

At Adlershof the latest prototype fighter aircraft from several contractors had been lined up for trial by experienced fighter pilots from the front. Upon their reports, the types for production would be decided. An unorthodox aircraft designed by Dornier, the Zepp. (Lindau) D. I., had just been flown by the commander of *Jasta 27*, an Oberleutnant Hermann Göring. As next to fly it, Hauptmann Reinhard was scheduled. He took it up rather steeply to some 3,000 feet, when a strut broke, the top wing collapsed and the machine plummeted to earth. Reinhard was fatally injured. Had the order of flying between the two pilots been changed, the subsequent history of the *Geschwader* might have been considerably altered and who could say what effect it might have had on the course of World War II?

On July 4th, Leutnant Laumann of Loewenhardt's *Jasta 10* was placed at the disposal of the posting authority. Strange indeed that a man who had joined the *Geschwader* with a record of twenty-five victories, should not score a single victory since April. It has been said that his friendship with Udet prejudiced his relations with Loewenhardt, his leader. Certainly it seems that at this time there was a clash of personalities. Perhaps for that reason the new *Kommandeur* was appointed from outside the *Geschwader*; Oberleutnant Hermann Göring was nominated on July 6th and took over on the 14th.

Little had happened during that period; ten days of rain had restricted flying and only two victories had been

130

gained. It may have given Göring a false impression of the organisation or perhaps he arrived with preconceived ideas. Whatever it was, he introduced radical changes. The flying personnel of the *Geschwader* were all called to an address.

The *Geschwader* fell in under the senior officer, Oberleutnant von Wedel, who called them to attention as Göring approached. There followed a small ceremony in which Oberleutnant Bodenschatz, as adjutant, presented the new leader with the so-called *Geschwaderstock*—a cane that had been carried by Richthofen and later Reinhard. Göring then made his introductory speech, and no doubt, the man was a gifted speaker. He expounded his views upon air-fighting and how it should be conducted—and, how *he* would conduct it! The old order was changing and the new, as revealed in that talk by the new leader, was not to the liking of the majority of the pilots.

Hitherto, there had been direction for patrolling and units had been alerted and despatched at the discretion of the leader acting upon notification from the warning posts or by orders from his Army Command; but once the enemy had been sighted, the task in hand had been deemed too obvious for further direction and it became *Freie Jagd*, a free-hunt, or as the British would have put it—a 'free-for-all'.

von Richthofen, tactician that he was, had never enforced regimentation in attack. He often led into action, but he expected his pilots to know the right moment to engage. He had selected them for their courage and trained them to perfection; once the fight was offered, it was up to them. His great asset, largely through experience, was his ability to be aware of what was going on around him in a fight. Reinhard, a man with good perception, if not great ability as a pilot, was not above flying as a member of a patrol and placing one of his pilots in command of the flight. Göring was an organiser and a leader. He had the intention of leading and controlling. *Freie Jagd* was out. In future, Oberleutnant Göring would tell the *Geschwader* where and when to attack.

The day after Göring took over, a promising pilot, Leutnant Fritz Friedrichs was lost. His comrades observed during a patrol at just over 5,000 feet, a trail of white smoke

With the significant monogram on his Fokker D VII, Arthur Laumann, victor of 26 combats, survived to command, for a short time, the Richthofen Geschwader *of the* Luftwaffe.

Leutnant Ernst Udet, who scored 62 victories, was Germany's second highest scoring ace. He survived to hold high office in the Luftwaffe.

coming from the fuselage sides of his Fokker D VII 309/18. Friedrichs turned and went down as if to make back for base, but then came flames. His machine was on fire in the air, due to a technical fault. Parachutes had been issued by that time to many German pilots but the art of packing them had not been mastered. Friedrichs jumped, his 'chute opened straight-away in the slip-stream and caught on the fin, it tore and he crashed to his death.

Friedrichs was born on February 21st, 1895 in Spark, Westphalia. An intention to enter the medical profession was swept aside by the war and in October 1914 he was on the Aisne with Infantry Regiment No. 85. As a lieutenant the following year he served with Infantry Regiment No. 32 in the Serbian campaign. Severely wounded he was considered unfit for further infantry service—so he volunteered for flying! He trained first at *FEA7* in Cologne then at Paderborn and finally in the *Artillerie Fliegerschule* at Juterborg. As a pilot with *Fl. Abt. (A) 264* he received the Iron Cross both First and Second Class. In the first days of 1918 he had passed through *Jastaschule I* at Fanars and within a month had reached *Jagdgeschwader Freiherr von Richthofen*, at his own wish. Now, the *Pour le Mérite*, already on the way to him, was too late.

Whilst Göring had been delivering his speech, nine

The Fokker D VII used by Ernst Udet. On the fuselage side was the letters L O in monogram form, significant of his fiancée.

R.A.F. squadrons (Nos. 27, 32, 43, 49, 54, 73, 80, 97 and 107) had been flying southwards, through rainstorms, to take up positions on the Champagne sector of the front, to reinforce French air units. On the 16th, there came the first clash with the new British units, which suffered the loss of two Camels, both falling to Vizefeldwebel Hemer. Three Spads were also destroyed, which gave Leutnant Bretschneider his sixth victory. Gefreiter Möller his first and Leutnant Loewenhardt his thirty-seventh, all achieved without loss in action, but that day there were serious accidents.

Kirschstein was returning his Dr I to the Army Aircraft Field-Park at Fismes, and as he wished to return to duty quickly, Leutnant Markgraf was ordered to accompany him in the unit's Hannoveranner CL III, to ferry him back. Taking-off on the return journey, Markgraf, apparently an inexperienced pilot, rose too steeply. The machine stalled and crashed, killing both.

Leutnant Bender too, was forced that day to take to his parachute. He made a safe landing. As had Friedrich's, his Fokker D VII, 2063/18, had caught fire in the air. A D VII belonging to *Jasta 45*, stationed in the vicinity, also caught fire and the pilot descended safely by parachute. A court of inquiry convened to investigate the three accidents, which had caused the wildest rumours about sabotage to circulate, came to the conclusion that leaking petrol had been seeping on to the phosphorous ammunition carried, and that this had led to its ignition.

The Allied counter-attack opened on June 18th. With the increase in enemy air activity, Göring had his first chance to lead the *Geschwader* in action. He headed *Jasta 11* in a red Fokker D VII F294/18, with a yellow tail, a machine that had been prepared for Lothar von Richthofen, who that day arrived to resume command of *Jasta 11*.

Shortly after 8 a.m. Oberleutnant Göring sighted an escadrille of French Spads and dived well forward into the attack, before signalling for the *Jasta* to follow. The effect was that Göring claimed an unsuspecting Spad, whilst the rest were at the disadvantage of having to attack machines already warned. Oberleutnant von Wedel and Leutnant Mohnicke both claimed Spads, but it is not known if Mohnicke's claim was confirmed. Göring, soon after his success, signalled the machines to re-formate and led back to base. The machines dropped down over Beugneaux and, approaching their airfield, one by one led in to land, but the last pilot in the formation suddenly opened his engine throttle and climbed. It was Vizefeldwebel Gabriel, who, fuming at Göring's methods, had suddenly decided to go to war on his own account!

Fortune favoured the brave that day. No sooner had Gabriel reached the front, then he spotted another escadrille of Spads and such was his mood, that he made straight for the nearest, closed up behind it—and fired. The Spad exploded in the air. Within seconds he was fighting for his life as the other Spads of the formation made for him, but as three or four attacked at the same time, they hindered each other. Gabriel was able to shoot another down before drawing away. On his way back, musing upon the reception he would receive, he was suddenly aware of whining bullets. Banking round, he saw his challenger, a single Spad that had trailed him from the fight. For four, seemingly long, minutes, they battled. The fight moved over towards Beugneaux, where *J.G.1* members including Göring himself watched the fight. They were down to a few hundred feet when Gabriel's shots finally took effect and the Spad, falling out of control, crashed a short distance from the airfield. Gabriel, sweating, tired but satisfied, landed and went to make his report. Göring met him. Red-faced, quivering with rage, he shouted and raved as Gabriel stood, as was expected of him, rigidly to attention. There was not a pilot whose sympathies were not with Gabriel.

Gabriel's insubordination, such as it was, did not end there that day; he was still incensed by Göring's attitude. Lying on the grass around the airfield with his comrades during an off-duty period that sunny July afternoon, he watched three French Breguets approaching at about 9,000 feet. Already a Fokker D VII from another unit was climbing to meet them, but evidently it had a Mercedes engine. Gabriel, close by his machine, ran to it and took off. Being a *Jasta 11* pilot, he had a B.M.W.-engined Fokker, and was soon rising to the level of the Breguets.

The noise of the machine starting, brought Göring out from his tent. Many eyes were upon him to watch his reaction upon realising that Gabriel was off on his own account—again!

When Gabriel first attacked, the machines were still in view of the airfield. He was unsuccessful. The Frenchmen flew exceedingly well, keeping formation sufficiently close to each other for the observers to give concentrated covering fire, but sufficiently open to allow evasive turns. A steady, controlled formation. Three times Gabriel dived into attack

A typical Fokker D VII, F461, (the 'F' signifying Fokker-built as apart from a sub-contract built model) in factory-finish of clear-doped dyed fabric.

and each time, there was seemingly no effect. Then, as he circled round out of their range contemplating the wisdom of further attack, he noticed the left-hand machine was flying unsteadily. He observed more closely. Both the gunner and pilot had their heads well down. Slowly it dawned upon him that both were dead, his last shots having taken effect. Now it was only a matter of waiting. The propeller was turning more slowly, the machine was dropping; then, lurching, it spun down to earth. Gabriel had achieved a *Geschwader* record—four planes in one day, by the one pilot.

Again Gabriel had to face Göring. There were no congratulations. He was given a direct order never to take-off without signal or order. He had defied his commander and given a practical demonstration of *Freie Jagd*, although, it must be admitted, luck had been very much on his side. There was little Göring could do to punish a senior N.C.O., for it required higher authority that might possibly take a lenient view of a Vizefeldwebel who had disobeyed instructions (not a direct order), and so shot down four enemy machines! There was something he could do—and this he presumably arranged; for a short time afterwards, Gabriel was posted away to an Aircraft Park.

The successful Allied counter-attack forced *J.G.1* to abandon their advanced airfield and move back to two airfields near Monthussart Ferme (*Jastas 4, 10* and *11* to Braisne, *Jasta 6* to Courcelles). They left as French artillery shelled the airfield. It was there on July 25th that Lothar von Richthofen scored his first victory since returning to the front, and its announcement in the newspapers was the first indication to his parents that he was again at the front. It was too, the 500th victory of the *Geschwader* since formation in June the previous year.

On the 26th Göring went on leave and Udet returned from his earlier leave. It was an open secret in the unit that these two men disliked each other. Udet found that Loewenhardt had forty-four victories, four more than he, and in the next few days he increased his lead by a further two. A further move back, to use Puisieur Ferme again, was necessary on the 29th; a day in which Loewenhardt added yet another two to his score. Not until August 1st, did Udet get his chance; then, in succession he claimed that day a Nieuport, a Spad and a Breguet, bringing his score up to forty-three. Lothar also claimed two Spads, bringing his score up to thirty-two.

An all-white Fokker D VII, except for the usual black insignia markings, was sometimes used by Hermann Göring.

The presence of Nieuports in the unit's score-book was due to the appearance of American squadrons on to the Western Front scene. Being as yet inexperienced, in flying the Nieuport 28, that was outclassed by the Fokker D VII; they fell easy prey to experienced German fighters. Installed in a large chateau near Courcelles, that allowed senior staff a room apiece, the spirits of *J.G.1* rose, but soon, August 8th, the tide of battle turned. At 4.20 a.m., the Allies launched their major offensive. Tanks, armoured cars and infantry moved forward screened by a thick ground mist, intensified by smoke bombs. By the end of the day they had advanced seven miles on a broad front. To Ludendorff, that day was 'the black day' of the German Army and even the official communique spoke of it as a catastrophe.

The *Geschwader* were called upon to sweep to the north, but fog delayed their start until after midday and by that time Army Command had directed that no high patrols should be attempted, but that *Jagdstaffeln* should concentrate on protecting artillery and contact patrol aircraft. It was probably that order that led to the formation meeting at a low height, D.H.9 bombers making for the Somme bridges escorted by fighters. The British formation was within sight of the target when it was spotted.

Since it was anticipated that British formations would be met in force, only the most experienced of the fighters from the four *Jastas* had set out, flying in two formations. With skill and determination they attacked, with considerable success. After harrying the bombers on their way back, they landed at a local airfield for refuelling. Whilst so

133

The Göring stance. Of interest is the so-called Geschwaderstock *in his right hand and the harness of the 1918 pattern seat-type parachute.*

grounded, a flight of Bristol Fighters came over and machine-gunned the airfield, but undamaged they rose to fight another flight of escorted bombers. By evening both Loewenhardt and Lothar von Richthofen had scored three victories and Udet two. Thirteen victories for the day.

Wenzel, attempting to cut off the escape of a bomber, became involved in a sharp exchange of fire with its gunner. Eventually he forced the machine to land, to find it was a new British D.H.9A, one of the first to reach the front. He wrongly reported it as a D.H.12.

Early next morning, a flight from the *Geschwader* was up to deal with the early-morning bombing attacks on the Somme bridges that followed closely upon several attacks by night bombers. Encountering a formation of five D.H.9s escorted by four Camels, they destroyed three of the bombers and two of the fighters. Of the two bombers that survived to re-cross the lines, one crashed with a wounded pilot. The cost that day was two pilots wounded, Leutnant Reinhardt and Vizefeldwebel Hemer.

Next day, the 10th, came marching orders for the *Geschwader*; tents were packed and an advance party set out to arrange accommodation and facilities; no mean matter for some 50 officers and 500 men (known strength was 46 officers, 495 non-commissioned officers and men, as on August 31st, 1918). Udet made the first victory that day, bringing his score up to fifty, still three behind Loewenhardt.

For the last two days, only the experienced pilots had been flying in action. It could not last. Sooner or later the newcomers would have to be flung into the battle and Loewenhardt led a detail of new pilots from *Jasta 10* and *Jasta 11*. Around

Oberleutnant Hermann Göring inspects his Fokker DVII 294/18, whilst his mechanics stand respectfully at attention. This aircraft had red wings and the fuselage forward of the cockpit was similarly painted; aft, the fuselage was yellow.

midday a formation of S.E.5As was sighted and Loewenhardt veered away to find his fledglings something easier. Spotting a lone S.E.5A, some 300 feet below he dived at this. Several of his formation followed closely—too closely. The wing of a Fokker D VIII piloted by Leutnant Wentz, rammed into the wings of Loewenhardt's yellow Fokker. Loewenhardt died in the resultant crash.

So Loewenhardt, born April 7th, 1897, the son of a Breslau physician, who had served throughout the war as an officer since September 1914, who had commanded a ski unit during actions in the Carpathian mountains; who had fought in Serbia as an infantryman and as an observer on the Western Front, then as a fighter-pilot in action for over a year gaining fifty-three victories; fell in action, due to a collision. Only a few days earlier he had received promotion to Oberleutnant.

Once more in the area of the German 2nd Army, the *Geschwader* set about making the airfield at Ennemain operational. They slept in tents and had to exist on packed rations, but before they had a chance to settle, marching orders were again received—to Bernes, where they moved on the 12th. A day in which Lothar achieved his fortieth and last victory, by forcing down a Camel. That evening he met his victim, a Captain Summers.

Next day, the 13th, a particularly unlucky day for Lothar, since twice before he had been wounded on the 13th of the month, he received his last wound of the war. During a fight he received a bullet in his right thigh. He cleared from the fight and attempted to jump out, but was too weak. Only with difficulty did he succeed in moving his damaged leg, over which he had lost control, from the rudder bar and guide the machine with his sound leg. Fighting against swooning, he brought his machine down to earth. Removed unconscious to hospital, he remained convalescent until the war was over.

The formation had taken some hard knocks. In between moves they had kept fighting. Leutnants Gussman and von der Wense had not returned and Leutnant Wenzel was slightly wounded. Added to their other recent losses, without replacement, the fighting strength of the *Geschwader* was reduced to that of a *Jasta*.

Last Days of Jagdgeschwader Nr. 1

CHAPTER TWENTY-EIGHT

The S.E.5A had a single gun (Vickers) synchronised to fire through the propeller arc in contrast to the usual German two (Spandaus); but additionally, the S.E.5A had a Lewis gun on a Foster mounting as shown in this photograph.

The tide of battle had turned in the Allies favour. No longer could Germany hope to mass the troops necessary to resume the offensive against the Allies, whose strength grew daily as thousands of American soldiers entered upon the Western Front scene. Hampered by the British blockade at sea, the supply problem of raw materials was acute; aircraft production was affected and lack of fuel was already limiting flying. So far, duty and discipline prevailed and the bitter fighting continued.

To the *Richthofen Geschwader*, on a very active part of the front, fighting was dogged and determined. Göring's leadership, if uninspiring by example—for the man was pompous and selfish—at least proved that he was an able administrator. With the many newly-joined pilots, who had known no other exponent of air-fighting, his tactics could be asserted authoritatively. But when he went on leave, there was a sigh of relief—and a reversion to the old order, at least as far as their limited strength allowed.

Because of losses and the advantages of concentrated formations, the very essence of *Geschwader* organisation, operational patrols were conducted in conjunction with a *Jagdgruppe* under Ritter von Greim and with *J.G.3*. Laumann was recalled from *Jasta 66* to which he had been posted and a long-standing *J.G.1* officer, Leutnant Mohnicke, having fully recovered from his wounds, took over *Jasta 11* in Lothar's place. With Göring away, Udet led the *Geschwader* in his red Fokker D VII 4253/18, marked on the fuselage sides with the name of his affianced—Lo. Until Göring returned, on August 22nd, nine victories were achieved, four by Udet, bringing his score up to fifty-eight.

In war, much can happen in so short a time; Fokker's 'latest' had arrived. The progression had been triplane (Dr I), biplane (D VII) and now there was promised a parasol monoplane (E V). Pilots tended to be conservative in their preference for aircraft types and at the time they had a most satisfactory conventional biplane. When Leutnant Rolff on August 19th was fatally injured at Bernes in one of the first of these new monoplanes, it led to the most ugly rumours of structural failure. Not without some justification, for two or three pilots were to die before the E V, later known as the D VIII, was considered structurally sound.

Apart from the loss of Rolff, Vizefeldwebel Lechner had been wounded on the 16th, Leutnant Freiherr von Barnekow on the 23rd and on the 28th, for the third time, Leutnant Wolff (III) was wounded. It had long been a point of contention with higher authority that a qualified doctor should be established on strength as in earlier days at Courtrai. Perhaps the grim statistics of that August made the point with sufficient force, for on the last day of the month, Dr. Fisser was posted to the formation.

Before the month was out the *Geschwader* had moved again; *Jasta 4* and *10* to Escaufort, near to Busigny where *Jasta 6* and *11* were established together with the *Geschwader* staff. By September 1st, they were once more in position. That day Leutnant Neckel joined to command *Jasta 6*. If ever a man conquered a weak body with an iron will, it was Neckel. Forbidden by his doctor to indulge in exercise at school, it was only after repeated rejection, that he had been accepted for flying training at the Rumpler school in Muncheberg. Completing his training at Gotha, where *FEA3* was established, he served in the East with *Fl. Abt. 25* transferring to *Jasta 12* in September 1917. Receiving promotion to sergeant and then a Lieutenancy, he became leader of *Jasta 19* and at the time of his transfer to *Jasta 6*, he had already scored twenty-four victories.

For the next few weeks, victories came but occasionally; September 7th being the most auspicious day when all four victories claimed, S.E. 5As, were by *Jasta 11* members; two to Wolfram von Richthofen, one to Oberleutnant von Wedel and one to Leutnant Schulte-Frohlinde. Udet returned on the 25th to find the formation yet again in the throes of a move, this time to Metz. Next day he achieved his last two victories, his sixty-first and sixty-second, at the expense of two American D.H.4s; two other D.H.4s fell to *Jasta 4* members, Leutnants Kraut and Gluczewski. It was at that time, that *J.G.2* under Hauptmann Berthold appeared to be the premier *Geschwader;* for, chiefly against inexperienced American units, they made claim to eighty-nine victories in two days. Earlier that month, von Hindenburg had sent congratulations to *J.G.3* under Oberleutnant Loerzer, which had achieved twenty-six victories without loss.

Loerzer was perhaps Göring's greatest friend. Their ways had run together. They had served in the same regiment

135

before the war and had been through some of the early battles together. It was then that Göring had contracted an unfortunate complaint for a young man—arthritis. In hospital at Freiburg he could neither use his hands nor walk properly. Loerzer, learning to fly nearby, had the idea that his friend, although incapacitated in movement, might still do duty as an observer. The two actually took an aircraft without sanction and reported as a ready crew. In *Fl. Abt. 25* they flew together, a curious couple, but they satisfied their commander well enough. Göring had an iron will then; he next learnt to fly. Loerzer had by that time moved on to fighter aircraft with such success that he was soon commanding—*Jasta 26*—and to join him came Göring. Then Göring aspired to leadership, taking over *Jasta 27*—located on the same airfield as Loerzer's *Jasta 26*! Now they were both *Geschwader* commanders.

As commander of a *Jasta*, Göring had been very successful. It was unfortunate for him that in taking over such an élite formation as *J.G.1*, he would be expected to emulate the respected von Richthofen or the well-liked Reinhard. He had at least an authoritative manner and a compelling voice. His great ability was in quickly deciding on a course of action in any situation. His favourite dictum, in fact, was that it was not so important what was done, as long as something was done—and that quickly! Analogous to the English proverb—'He who hesitates is lost'. But now, with his important command of the *Richthofen Geschwader*, he was finding out that no longer was it *the Geschwader*. He strove to exact further effort from his officers and men.

A promising transferee that September was Leutnant Friedrich Noltenius, the son of Professor Hermann Noltenius. Friedrich was a medical student when the outbreak of war altered his career; war-fever enticing him to an artillery unit with which he served on the Eastern Front and in the Serbian campaign. Then for two years he had served on the Western Front, with flying training at *FEA10* Böblingen, coming as a welcome change in 1918. Flying on operations first with *Jasta 24* of *J.G.3*, he scored thirteen victories in as many weeks. He had 'specialised' in balloon-destruction and his first victory with *J.G.1* on October 6th, was a balloon that he sent down in flames.

There came yet a further move for the *Geschwader* on October 9th. By that time they were used to it and the organisation, thanks no doubt to Göring and Bodenschatz the adjutant, was perfect. The vehicles left first and the equipment was being unpacked before the aircraft flew in. They found well-built huts for officers and men and wooden hangars already erected. It was whilst at Marville that the influenza epidemic which had swept through Europe to reach Britain later in the year, overtook a number of the *Geschwader* pilots. However, the day after arrival, before the full effects of the epidemic were felt, the *Jasta* flew sixty-nine *Kriegsflüge*—a comparatively large number in those restrictive times of shortages of experienced pilots and lack of fuel. A particularly brisk action was fought with an American formation. Some thirty Spad 13s from the 1st Pursuit Group, composed of the 94th and 147th Squadrons of the American Expeditionary Force, had set out to destroy balloons on the hill behind Dun-sur-Meuse.

The American machines were spotted by a formation of some ten Fokker D VIIs flown by the more experienced members of the *Geschwader*, irrespective of their *Jasta*. They spotted the American machines, but not, it would seem, before they themselves were observed. Their opposing leader, had they known it, was Captain Edward V. Rickenbacker, the United States leading ace who scored, in all, twenty-six victories. Rickenbacker led round and took the German formation in the rear. Opening fire at the nearest Fokker D VII, he observed it falling in flames before he turned to seek further combat. The pilot, however, taking to his parachute, landed safely in the German lines. It was a Leutnant Kohlbach who had joined *J.G.1* from *Jasta 50* two months before.

The fight went on. Aircraft from another German unit joined in and altogether five of the Spads went down; one of them, piloted by Lieutenant Wilbur W. White who had achieved eight victories, crashed into a Fokker D VII. Apart from Kohlbach, all the *J.G.1* pilots escaped unscathed.

A spell of rainy weather limited flying and for three days in mid-October there was no flying at all. Better weather on the 23rd gave Leutnant Noltenius his chance to 'specialise' further and two balloons fell to him; also, in the course of one of these flights he shot down a Spad. The only other victory of the *Geschwader* that day was a French A.R. falling to Leutnant Neckel. Rain again severely limited flying until the 27th when sixty sorties were made.

The Sopwith Camel, of which well over 5,400 were built, formed the unit equipment of over thirty squadrons on the Western Front. Camel pilots accounted for 1,294 enemy aircraft. B2458 illustrated, was flown by 2nd Lieutenant J. P. Morgan of No. 65 Squadron.

The S.E.5A of which some 5,200 were built, formed the unit equipment of seventeen squadrons on the Western Front. It was with an S.E.5A that Britain's leading ace, Mannock, scored fifty of his seventy-three confirmed victories. The example shown is a Vickers-built model.

That night there was a celebration, following the announcement of the award of the *Pour le Mérite* to Leutnant Arthur Laumann.

The Allied Armies were closing in. American troops in the line opposite Marville were moving forward. By the beginning of November it was obvious that the order to withdraw would shortly be given. As a preliminary, Tellancourt was allotted and heavy stores were transported back to that airfield at a time when the *Geschwader* was beginning to regain a little of its old spirit. The morning of November 3rd had brought little activity, but in the late afternoon when several Allied formations crossed the line, they were met in strength by *J.G.1*. Leutnant Richard Wenzl scored first, getting a Spad to make his score a round ten. Then in succession came seven victories which included the initial scores of Leutnants Geppert and Reinhardt. Their one loss was Leutnant Maushake who was wounded; he had been with the *Geschwader* since it was formed and only a week before he had been appointed to lead *Jasta 4*.

Further fighting was forced on the formation next day, for they were ordered to operate over a broad front whilst *J.G.2* and the independent *Jasta 67* moved back. During the afternoon Leutnants Koepsch and Noltenius harried a formation of D.H.9s causing two to go down out of control; evidently D7355 (Puma 7476/25150) and D7356 (Puma 7426/25100) the only D.H.9s lost that day. Two other aircraft were also claimed by the *Geschwader*. For those last days, it has not been possible to line up German claims with Allied losses. Although American records give detail of their thirty-three D.H.4s lost in action during the war, it would seem that in German claim statements the British D.H.9A with a Liberty engine was being confused with the American-built D.H.4 similarly powered. On the particular day in question, November 4th, the issue is confused by the unexplained loss of four D.H.4s (A7652, F5719, F5727 and F5833) which were missing from a practice flight!

The situation was now desperate. Allied numerical superiority was overwhelming. Only duty kept the *Geschwader* striving grimly to stem the tide. On balance, under the circumstances, they did very well. Petrol was rationed, aircraft spares were difficult to obtain and perhaps even more important for morale, rations were short. Yet they still fought with spirit, bringing five aircraft down. One, which gave Wolfram his eighth victory, was the last aircraft to be brought down by a von Richthofen. The family had destroyed altogether, 128 Allied aircraft. That day the *Geschwader* had its last casualty—Leutnant Kirst was killed.

Next day, at 11.30 a.m. German time, the *Geschwader* fought its last battle in the air against a formation of Spads, achieving a straightforward victory of three without loss, which gave Leutnant Neckel his thirtieth victory and the *Jasta 10* veterans, Leutnants Grassmann and Heldmann, their tenth and fifteenth respectively. Within minutes of landing, however, they were up again in spite of the weather which had turned to rain. They were ordered to fly their aircraft to Tellancourt.

With bitter thoughts on a wet November morning, Göring led the flying personnel in flight, whilst Bodenschatz arranged road transport for the *Geschwader* to converge upon Tellancourt. It was there that they became aware of what was happening in their Fatherland. The German Fleet at Kiel had mutinied, there was street fighting in Berlin and even in some Army units, the troops would no longer obey the officers. The 'officer-class' was accused of using the troops as pawns, of leading from behind, of being a clique that forced their will. To profess to be a staff officer was even dangerous. There were no such signs of unrest in the *Richthofen Geschwader*. The ground staff had had little to complain of their officers. They had seen them take-off to fight and often not return, whilst they remained in comparative safety on the ground, far from the lines. Their respect was borne not so much of Göring's stern discipline, as from what they themselves witnessed.

Three days before the Armistice became effective, Göring summoned the whole *Geschwader* to assemble an hour before midnight. He told them the shattering news, orders had been received to demobilise! As they waited there came order and counter-order. Meanwhile, all around there was confusion and disorder from troops in units who refused to accept any authority other than their own appointed soldier-councils. Some fired off signal-lights and the like, whilst irresponsible elements played with the more dangerous explosives. Once the *Geschwader* had to send a security patrol to protect the local villagers when matters went too far. Transport had to be particularly carefully guarded, for many troops were making their own way home. It had come to that; dissolution of the once proud German Army.

The *Geschwader* still awaited their orders. Now they were impatient lest the advancing enemy troops overran their airfield. They had no wish to fall directly into enemy hands. A decision was made to fly the aircraft to Darm-

Jasta 10 ready to 'scramble'. The four members identified are, left to right: 1 Leutnant Heldmann, 2 Offizier Stellvertreter Aue, 3 Leutnant Grassmann and 4 Unteroffizier Klamt.

stadt, the home of *FEA9*, but rain and mist held them up until the hour of danger passed—the eleventh hour of the eleventh day of the eleventh month, when the Allies, according to their terms of Armistice, halted. The war was over. Orders then reached them to hand over their aircraft to an American receiving unit. This, Göring refused to do and on the 12th he led the formation as it flew to Darmstadt as originally intended. Twenty-seven years later he surrendered himself to the American Army!

At Darmstadt, authority was in the form of soldier-councils, who commenced to impound their aircraft. That was too much for Göring. Striding back to his pilots grouped around the rest of their machines, he ordered them to stand-by for take-off. Then he approached the soldiers who had dared to touch the aircraft of the *Richthofen Geschwader*, which was under his orders. Either the men would release the aircraft or he would attack with the *Geschwader*. The machines were released. Getting in touch with competent authority, Göring received orders to fly to Aschaffenburg, to deliver their aircraft to a French Commission. Göring made it clear, that he would censure no pilot who made a rough landing—in fact, he left no doubt that he would be pleased if they did! The *Richthofen Geschwader* took off on their last flight. Meanwhile the ground-crews, under Bodenschatz, were making their way back by road.

At Aschaffenburg the pilots were demobilised. The evening of their arrival, they were assembled for the last time under Göring. He made a farewell speech reviewing the work of the *Geschwader* and its achievements, recalling its first great leader, Rittmeister Manfred Freiherr von Richthofen. A few, such as Leutnants Koepsch and Heldmann, remembered him well; but to the majority he was just a name, albeit a famous one.

Oberleutnant Göring then summed up the record of the *Geschwader*, consulting a paper that Bodenschatz had prepared from

A group, believed to be of Jasta 11, *basking in the summer sun, awaiting orders. Those identified are 1 Hauptmann Reinhard and 2 Vizefeldwebel Gabriel.*

the formation's record book, during those last days of waiting at Tellancourt. The *Geschwader* had gained 644 victories in the air, since Oberleutnant Dostler had commenced the scoring with a balloon he had shot down just north of Ypres on July 5th, 1917, until the last three victories, with hardly a minute between them, on November 6th, 1918. During that time fifty-six pilots and six ground crew men had been killed and fifty-two pilots and seven ground crew men wounded. After reviving many memories, Herr Göring sat down.

So ended the *Geschwader Frhr. von Richthofen Nr. 1*. Their aircraft, mostly in the red finish significant of the *Geschwader*, were delivered grudgingly and not a little damaged to the French who catalogued, stored and later destroyed them. Since the Armistice terms had stipulated the surrender of specific numbers of aircraft and amounts of certain armaments in good condition, the damaging of their aircraft proved of little avail, for sound machines were demanded in lieu, to count against the numbers stipulated in the terms. In point of fact, the full number of aircraft demanded was never surrendered, and ex-*J.G.1* members among other Air Service personnel entered into various intrigues to deny the Allies their due. Others bowed to the inevitable and departed quietly to their homes. They had fought well and had obeyed their orders to the letter—even their last order, to lay down their arms.

The air-fighters of that war have been often described as Knights of the Air. If that term can in any way be considered applicable, then perhaps the personnel of the *Richthofen Geschwader* may be considered of the highest order, for, although other individuals may be thought greater, only in the *Richthofen Geschwader* were so many men of mettle brought together to serve. Only the cause was not worthy of them.

Survival and Revival

CHAPTER TWENTY-NINE

Oberstleutnant Laumann, late of J.G.1 in 1918, reviews the men of his command, I Group of the newly-formed Jagdgeschwader Richthofen Nr. 2 at Döberitz-Elsgrund in 1935. The aircraft in the background are Arado Ar 65s.

The German G.H.Q. had notified the Kaiser and the Chancellor towards the end of September 1918 that if a military collapse was to be avoided, an Armistice must be arranged. By early November revolution had broken out in a number of towns, the Fleet had mutinied, Ludendorff had resigned and the Kaiser had fled to neutral Holland. Negotiations to conclude hostilities at noon (Central European Time) on November 11th, 1918, came in time to avoid a complete military collapse, and allowed the German Army the satisfaction of averring that they were not beaten in the Field. *J.G.1* among other Air Service units felt that they had not suffered defeat in the air. Certainly it was true that whilst troops at home and along the lines of communication rebelled, those at the front, in the main, stood firm and remained loyal to their officers. If needs be, many would have fought to the bitter end.

A silver candlestick, presented to the re-constituted Richthofen Geschwader, from the surviving members of the original formation. It bears their inscribed names around the base. In larger letters can be seen 'Göring' and beneath it 'Jasta 11 V. Wedel'.

After the war, the conditions of the Armistice, for which Germany had sued, were finally set out in the Treaty of Versailles. Among other things, Germans were deprived of the right to have or produce military aircraft. The Treaty was, however, something of a compromise, for there was little unity of purpose among the Allies. Clemenceau, Premier of war-ravaged France, wished to exact the maximum, indeed the impossible of reparations. Lloyd George, the British Prime Minister, required a solution based on history—the restoration of the balance of power in Europe. Woodrow Wilson, the President of the United States, had the most commendable ideal, but the least practical to effect in view of America's subsequent isolationist policy that persisted until the Second World War.

The threat of Communism to Germany in 1919 was narrowly averted and the German nation, saddled with war reparations, struggled through the early postwar years, dispirited and humiliated. In November 1925, when von Richthofen's body was brought home to rest in Germany the whole nation had been moved; memories were revived of Germany's military greatness, that contrasted with the seemingly dismal future. When a hope for the future did come, by a leader who won easy appeal by his militant theme, it was vested in a man destined to drag the nation to degradation—Adolf Hitler.

By that time much had happened. von Richthofen's re-burial ceremony had been the first time since the war that there had been a full-scale military parade in Berlin. As homage to a soldier fallen in battle, it was not an occasion upon which countries who had been party to Versailles could wag a warning finger. They might have sensed with apprehension the resurgent pride in German arms, but they did not discern the more subtle activities of certain elements, who cleverly bided their time.

Already several German aircraft firms, banned from producing aircraft in their own country, had set up factories in Sweden, Denmark, Switzerland and Russia. When, by the Paris Air Agreement of 1926, Germany was permitted the construction of stipulated civil sporting and touring types of aircraft, there was already the nucleus of an aircraft industry to serve the nation which had become remarkably air-minded. The progression to faster and more powerful

During 1938 the Richthofen Geschwader was re-equipped with the Messerschmitt Me 109, the contemporary of the Spitfire and Hurricane. Here, aircraft of the Geschwader, distinguished by their badge of a red 'R' on a white shield, are being maintained on a Czechoslovakian airfield.

sporting types of aircraft and to three-engined airliners, eventually constituted a potential Air Force, and in March 1935, the existence of the *Luftwaffe* was formally announced.

Göring had figured predominantly in its formation. He had been elected to the Reichstag in 1928 and the following year he had pressed for an Air Force. When Hitler came to power in 1933 he saw in Göring—a man whom he had first met at Munich in 1922—a figure of promise. He had the prestige of his military service, faith in Germany's future and he was a brilliant speaker. Very soon he was holding four governmental posts, of which the most important was Special Commissioner for Aviation. He was also Game Warden of all Germany!

To foster *esprit de corps* in the recently announced, if not newly constituted *Luftwaffe*, the traditions of World War I were adopted at the instigation of Göring. By a special order, signed by Hitler on March 14th, 1935, *Jagdgeschwader Richthofen Nr. 2* was formed. The unit was organised into two groups, one with Arado Ar 65s at Döberitz-Elsgrund and the other with Heinkel He 51s at Jüterborg-Damm. Their first commander, was, appropriately enough, Oberstleutnant Arthur Laumann, late of the original *Richthofen Geschwader*.

Appropriately the aircraft were given red cowlings, the colour significant of the original *Geschwader*. The Heinkel He 51s, under Major Meyer commanding *Gruppe II* at Jüterborg-Damm, bore at first German civil registration letters, examples being D-IDIE, D-IJAY and D-IQEE. This was significant of the deception that had been practised, for the D-IAAA to D-IZZZ allocation had been allotted for touring aircraft! Later, the swastika appeared on the fin and then the Latin cross insignia on the fuselage sides.

There were openings for many ex-1914-18 war pilots and with Göring at the helm, ex-members of *J.G.1* were particularly welcome. Some who survived the war, however, did not survive the peace. Kurt Wüsthoff had returned to Germany in 1920, bitter over the scant medical attention he had received in French captivity. For a further two years he was under treatment in Dresden until he was fit to take up business. After becoming an agent for an Austrian car factory he once more took to the air, this time as a publicity pilot. During a flying display to raise funds for a memorial to Immelmann, he crashed in his Udet U 12 'Flamingo' after twice-looping. It was believed that his nerve, as a result of his suffering, had failed. He died of his injuries five days later on July 23rd, 1926.

Friedrich Noltenius, the 'balloon-specialist' of *J.G.1*, had returned to his medical studies, and later he emigrated to the Argentine where he wrote several books of a philosophical nature. Returning to Germany in 1933, he set up a practice in Berlin, but was also co-opted for duty at the Air Medical Research Institute. Engaged on aero-medical research, he was killed in an aircraft crash at Adlershof on March 12th, 1936.

A sad fate overtook Dr. Ernst, Freiherr von Althaus. He had left *J.G.1* shortly after its formation at von Richthofen's request. His sight was failing and there was little point in becoming an instructor in the *Jastaschule* to which he was transferred, so he returned to the infantry as a company-commander. Taken prisoner by the Americans, he was released in September 1919, when he became interpreter to an Allied Commission. Studying law, he was well

Werner Mölders, leading German ace of the Second World War, meets von Doering, who held temporary command of the Richthofen Geschwader *after Richthofen was wounded in July 1917.*

140

on the way to a successful career when, in 1930, he became completely blind.

However, many were fit and well and probably the most important recruit was Udet. He had led the life of a playboy, roving to South America, flying in displays, exhibitions and races. He had flown over African jungles for film companies as well as over Arctic wastes. He was remembered as being, next to von Richthofen, Germany's highest scoring ace.

Udet might well have been a good pilot and a popular figure, but his suitability for high office and in a technical capacity, is open to question. It was in February 1936 that he was appointed Inspector of Fighters and Dive Bombers, and in the following June he was appointed to the highest technical office of the German Air Ministry, being responsible for the direction of both production and design. His chief failing was in regarding his position as that of chief test pilot to the *Luftwaffe*, a role that no doubt he could have filled most satisfactorily. He often flew himself. Handling characteristics he was most competent to advise, but in his office, there were more embracing issues to resolve. Manœuvrability is but a facet in technical evaluation. Serviceability and applicability were issues sadly out of his depth.

Perhaps his greatest failing was that he loathed making decisions. Of a genial nature he allowed himself to be led. Benefiting from his wider experience in the First World War, he clashed with Feldmarschall Milch on the issue of creating a large aircraft repair organisation. He was talked out of a project which events subsequently proved necessary. Many of the failings of the *Luftwaffe* were beyond his control, and there is no doubt that Göring, to preserve his own prestige in Hitler's eyes, sought often to make Udet a scapegoat.

In the fall of 1936, the commander of *J.G.2* had been succeeded by Oberst von Massow. Under him the unit re-equipped the following year with the first production batch of the famous Messerschmitt Me 109s, known as the Bf 109B-1, which followed closely upon a small pre-produc-

A photograph of Göring taken by the U.S. Army at Kitzbuhel, shortly after his capture. He had insisted upon having a bath and a change of uniform before posing. He had been held by S.S. troops at Berchtesgaden, under orders from Hitler to execute him, and his capture was, at the time, almost a relief.

tion batch used for service trials. With their Messerschmitts, *J.G.2* (*Richthofen*) were sent to Czechoslovakia under the military moves that provoked the Munich crisis in the summer of 1938.

Transferred to the West shortly before the invasion of the Low Countries, the unit was placed under von Bülow, younger brother of Walter von Bülow who had commanded *Jasta Boelcke* in January 1918. During the Battle of Britain, *J.G.2* were one of eight (*J.G.2, 3, 26, 27, 51, 52, 53* and *76*) *Geschwader* ranged against Britain. Stationed in France and the Low Countries, *J.G.2* were interchangeable for operational control between two of the German air fleets, *Luftflotten 2* and *3*.

They suffered heavy losses and during September 1940 they were well below establishment as shown by the aircraft strength return of their *Staffeln: I/J.G.2* and *II/J.G.2* at Beaumont-le-Roger 42 (51) and *III/J.G.2* at Le Havre 19 (30). The authorised establishment strength given in brackets shows that they were a third under strength. On a typical day for which statistics are available, September 15th, when some 200 bombers operated against London and thirty or so against Portland and Southampton, *J.G.2* were actively engaged protecting the bombers and claimed five Spitfires for a recorded loss of four of their Me 109s.

Early in October their Commanding Officer was killed and a famous German ace of World War II took over. Major Helmuth Wick, who was accredited with achieving forty-two victories at that early stage of the war. He

Two men, Göring and Udet, who had served together in the Richthofen Geschwader of World War I, rose in World War II; the one to command an Air Force and the other to direct its technical services. They were both fated to die by their own hands. Here they are shown together in 1941.

The man who defied Göring. Vizefeldwebel Gabriel of 1918 as Hauptmann Gabriel in the Luftwaffe *at Jüterbog, 1943. Original members of the* Richthofen Geschwader *had the privilege of wearing a special red band around the right arm, as shown here. This band bore the words* Jagdgeschwader Frhr. v. Richthofen Nr. 1.

continued to add to his score, but he did not long survive. His fifty-sixth victory, claimed over Bournemouth was his last before falling in combat.

When, in the summer of 1941, Germany launched the attack upon Russia, *J.G.2* (*Richthofen*) and *J.G.26* were the only two fighter formations left in the West. They were deliberately baited by the R.A.F. in an effort to relieve pressure on the Russians, by flying fighter sweeps of up to 300 fighters. The R.A.F. code name for these operations was 'Circus'! The very same word that had been used to describe the *Richthofen Geschwader* of 1917-18. Such operations succeeded in reducing the operational strength of *J.G.2* and *26*, normally at about 200 aircraft, to something like 140 by August 1941. Several experienced fighters were, as a result recalled from the Eastern Front. One, Major Walter Oesau, took over command of *J.G.2*.

Oesau, a pupil of the most famous of German aces of the Second World War, Werner Mölders, was perhaps the most outstanding of *J.G.2* commanders. He had been born at Meldorf in Schleswig-Holstein in 1915. His first victory was achieved on July 15th, 1938 when under Mölders' command, he shot down a Russian Rata (I-16) over Cueras in the Spanish Civil War. During the Battle of Britain he led a *Gruppe* in Mölders *J.G.51*, steadily increasing his score during that period. A transfer to the Russian Front in 1941, gave him great opportunity for fast scoring and on one day he claimed seven Soviet aircraft. His appointment to the command of *J.G.2* appears to have been stage-managed very well by the *Luftwaffe*—at a time when he had exactly eighty victories!

By that time the *Luftwaffe* was beginning to appreciate the measure of British resistance and their attrition on the Eastern Front. The German industry could not match up to the requirements of the *Luftwaffe* and if a scapegoat was required, it could be laid at the door of the Director General of Equipment. Udet, who could face enemy fire, could not stand criticism. He thrived on popularity and the world seemed a bleak place when people spoke in harsh terms. He had always been sensitive, and now his nerve was failing. The responsibilities of high office were more wearing to him than the risks of test-flying. He could no longer face his task; Göring his professed friend he did not trust—he never had. To be removed from office by his Führer he dare not contemplate. He did not have to, for in June 1941 he made the most important decision of his life; raising his revolver, he pointed it towards his head—and fired.

With Udet a dead hero, almost cynically it can be imagined, a new formation was named by Göring the *Geschwader Udet*. The German public were not to know the truth. However, in the bitter fighting that followed with the intensifying of Allied attacks, the German *Geschwader* were apt to lose their identity in the hurried re-formations that were carried out. In those last days there was little time for the members of *J.G.2* to mark a red 'R' on their aircraft. Perhaps, in any case, it was only too significant that history was repeating itself to the full. It was, but this time there was no Armistice, the terms being simply—Unconditional surrender.

By that time Göring was an impossible figure to command an Air Force. In fact, towards the end, on April 26th, 1945, Feldmarschall von Greim took over as Commander-in-Chief. Two months later he had committed suicide. Göring, knowing that at last he had lost favour with his Führer and knowing full well how that could end, gave himself up to an advancing American army unit. Little remained of the Göring that had once commanded the most famous of all fighting formations. He died by poison administered by his own hand. In that way he cheated his executioner on October 16th, 1946, a few hours before his death sentence by the Nuremberg Court was to have been carried out.

A determined looking man, Major Oesau was the last commander of the Jagdgeschwader Richthofen Nr. 2, *who led in the bitter fighting that preceded the German collapse in April/May 1945. Now that the German Air Force has been reconstituted within the framework of N.A.T.O., it might well be that an ex-member of the* Richthofen Geschwader Nr. 2 *will be chosen to lead yet a third* Richthofen Geschwader?

What Now Remains

CHAPTER THIRTY

In much the same way that every municipal museum professes to have Oliver Cromwell's sword, so it would seem that some relic of von Richthofen's famous red triplane is considered an essential item of display by all museums with a military collection. Some may be of doubtful origin, but those mentioned here in State Museums are no doubt genuine.

As an airframe, the triplane in which Richthofen died, Fokker Dr I 425/17, Constructor's No. 2009/18, was not preserved. It was in such poor condition due to damage in the crash and to the ravages of souvenir-hunters, that it was scrapped. Repair would not have been justified at a time when there was a backlog of work at repair depots on operational machines. The question of technical evaluation of the wreckage did not arise as a Fokker Dr I had earlier been brought down intact. That was in fact Stapenhorst's machine (Dr I 144/17, Constructor's No. 1858, Completed 20.10.17). The circumstances by which it fell into British hands are described on page 91. For evaluation trials it was given the Ministry of Munitions identity G.125, and for a time its red finish with black-and-white dicing in a band around the fuselage aft of the cockpit, remained. Thus finished and in a flyable condition it was exhibited at the Agricultural Hall in London during 1918, but eventually it ended up on a scrap-heap. Since rumour at the time gave this machine as Richthofen's, some parts taken from it may have been erroneously represented as from the more famous red triplane. It would now be almost impossible to discriminate between such relics.

The largest single piece of von Richthofen's aeroplane preserved, was the engine, which now stands in the Imperial War Museum. There has been much controversy over its type and origin. Unfortunately the engine number-plate appears to have been 'lifted' by a souvenir-hunter, but there is important evidence from *The Times* war correspondent, who, after examining the wreckage, reported the triplane as No. 2009 and the engine as a Le Rhone type built in Frankfurt in March 1918. Evidently a number-plate was then attached. That evidence should dispel any belief that the engine was built under licence by Thulin in Sweden. The head-offices of Motorenfabrik Oberursel A.G. were in

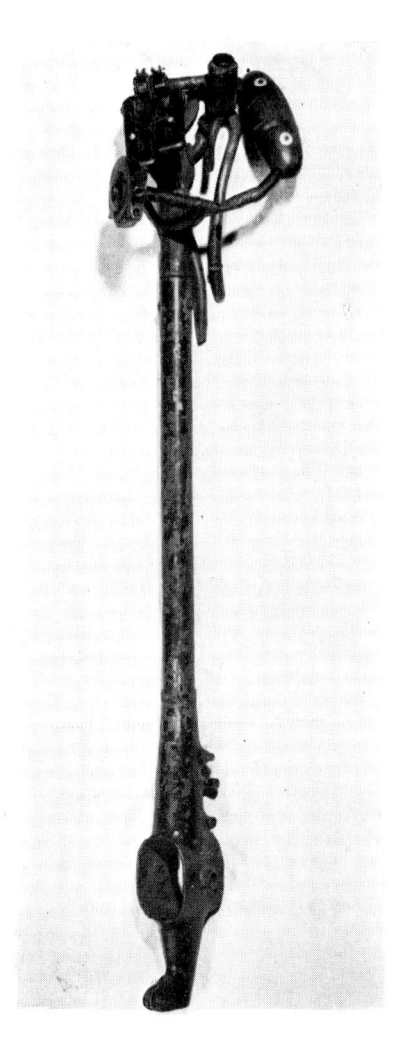

These three items, relics of von Richthofen's triplane, are held by the Australian War Memorial. They are: top, the compass; left, the control column and bottom, a piece of wood from the propeller. Another item, held in Australia, is the foresight and backsight of the Lewis gun used by Gunner Robert Buie.

143

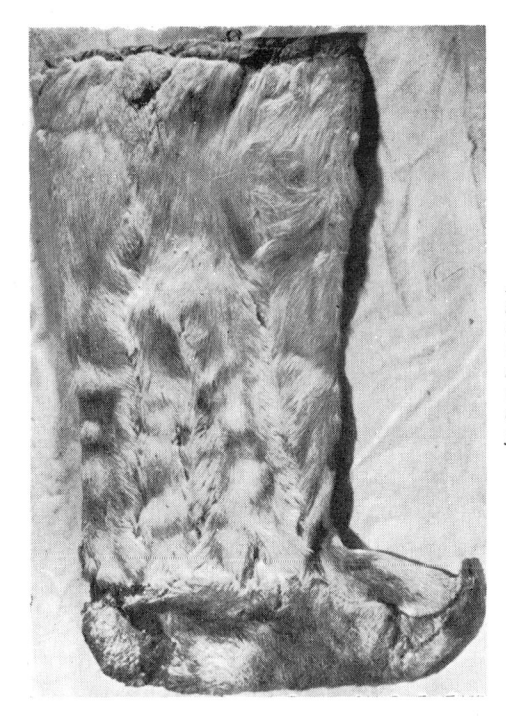

Whether or not Australian gunners shot Richthofen down, Australian troops were on the spot to collect souvenirs. Here is one of von Richthofen's flying boots, now in Australia.

Frankfurt and the engine details are consistent with the 110 h.p. Oberursel UR II type. There is no mystery in *The Times* reporting it, and the Imperial War Museum labelling it, as a Le Rhone type, for they were basically correct. The Oberursel company had held a Gnome Rhone licence since before the war, and the Oberursel UR II was very similar to the 110 h.p. Le Rhone; in fact the bore and stroke were identical.

Considered a great prize among the souvenir-hunters was the national insignia markings on the fabric covering of enemy aircraft. From Richthofen's triplane, two of the six have survived for permanent preservation; appropriately one is held in Australia and the other in Canada. The Australian one bore a legend inconsistent with any report upon von Richthofen's downfall, yet the fabric would appear to be genuine enough; for it was Captain E. C. Adams who wrote the legend, and that officer was responsible for placing a guard over von Richthofen's body shortly after the crash. At that time, the conflicting claims and rumours were no doubt responsible for his legend, which ran: 'German aeroplane brought down by Lieutenant Barrow, A.F.C., near line (J19B) 11 a.m. 21/4/18. The pilot was killed. The pilot of this 'plane was the famous German airman Capt. Baron von Richthofen who is said to have brought down seventy-nine Allied 'planes. The fabric bearing the cross I cut from the left lower wing: E. C. Adams, Captain.'

The cross held in Canada bears the signatures of No. 209 Squadron members. It would appear to have been taken from the fuselage side. No doubt many individuals had cuttings of the fabric at one time, but how many still exist cannot now, of course, be ascertained. One piece is held by our compiler, Major Brown, autographed by Captain A. R. Brown. It was presented to him by the widow of the late Air Vice-Marshal Sir Francis Mellersh, K.B.E., A.F.C. The colour of this piece of fabric was, in fact, considered when preparing the dust-cover colour for this book.

Obviously the Australian War Memorial at Canberra preserves its relics of the epic fight for the part thought to have been played by Australian ground gunners, and the Royal Canadian Military Institute at Toronto is concerned in representing a Canadian's participation in the proceedings, viz. that of Captain A. R. Brown. Part of the wording on the display card for the pilot's seat held in Canada, runs as follows: 'This case contains the seat of the Fokker Triplane of Baron Manfred von Richthofen, regarded as the most distinguished of the German airmen in the Great War, having eighty-two planes to his credit. He was shot through the heart by Captain Roy Brown, D.S.C. and Bar, Royal Air Force, of Carleton Place, Ontario, in an air engagement over the Somme Valley, April 21, 1918. When the German triplane reached the earth a claim was made by the crew of a machine-gun, and also by an anti-aircraft battery, that they had fired the shot which ended the career of Baron von Richthofen. Captain Roy Brown having been given this trophy and memento, has kindly deposited it in this Museum.'

The Australian War Memorial, in displaying the sights of Gunner Buie's Lewis gun, guardedly refer to this as 'a gun brought to bear'. It is, however, thought that this caution is not so much taken because there is any doubt that the bullet came from the ground—but rather doubt as to whose gun, Buie's, Popkin's or Sowerbutts! The Imperial War Museum remains strictly neutral in this controversy,

This piece of fabric from von Richthofen's triplane, Dr I 425/17, bearing the signatures of No. 209 Squadron personnel, shows evidence of having the Greek Cross painted over the earlier Cross Patée. The walking stick was carved from a piece of a propeller blade.

and cautiously the engine is labelled as from the triplane 'shot down' on April 21st, 1918.

Those relics are all that now remain. Much was lost during the war. What happened to the two Spandau guns taken from the triplane remains a mystery to this day. The destruction of the Zeughaus during an Allied raid on Berlin, destroyed relics which included complete aircraft that had been flown by von Richthofen, also irreplaceable photographs and records.

The Richthofen-room which constituted at first a private and later a public museum at Schweidnitz, was ransacked by the Soviets in late 1944, and the fate of the relics and records which included the sixty victory-cups is not known. Fleeing before a victorious Soviet Army, the Baroness Kunigunde von Richthofen had time only to gather hurriedly her personal belongings and the most treasured of her gallant son's mementos. The rest had to be left. She found sanctuary in the West and now lives in Wiesbaden.

But more important than—what now remains, is, *who* now remains? Quite a number of ex-*J.G.1* members are living, and their affiliation to an 'Old Eagles' club led to an easy tracing. The club had started up between the wars, when a 'Richthofen Dinner' was held in Berlin each year on April 21st. It was open to attendance by all who had flown or worked with Richthofen in *J.G.1* and invariably Hermann Göring headed the table. Richthofen was solemnly toasted, but apart from that it was a convival occasion.

During World War II the ceremony lapsed, as many members were serving in the *Luftwaffe*. After the war their meeting was banned by the Allies, who, after the Potsdam Conference, made proclamation as follows: 'The complete disarmament and demilitarisation of Germany.... To these ends: All German land, naval and air forces with all their organisations, staffs and institutions which serve to keep alive the military tradition of Germany shall be completely and finally abolished in such a manner as permanently to prevent the revival or re-organisation of German militarism.' Yet, but six years later, the United States Government made proposals that Germany, within the N.A.T.O. framework, might provide ten divisions with their

Fair shares! This piece of fabric is held by the Australian War Memorial in Canberra and that opposite by the Royal Canadian Military Institute in Toronto.

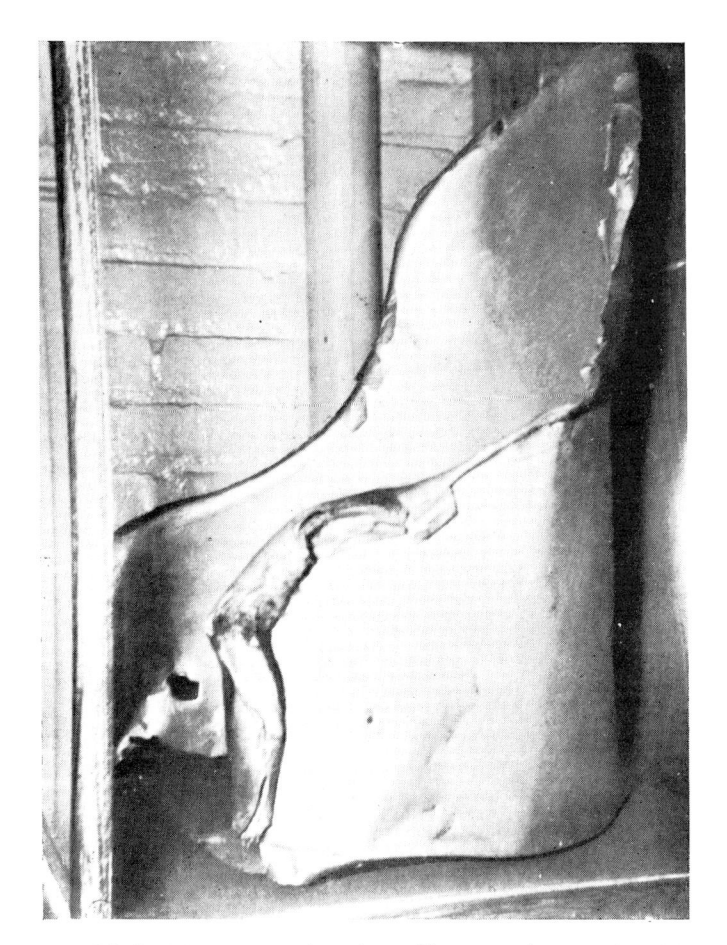

Of aluminium construction, plywood bottom and at one time covered red doped canvas—the seat from Richthofen's triplane.

own air support. Thus had events overtaken policies. There could now be little objection to an association of 'Old Eagles'!

They still meet or keep in touch, and those checked during 1959, just before this edition went to press, were as follows: Wilhelm Allmenröder (who did not actually serve in *J.G.1*, but in *Jasta 11* with von Richthofen, shortly before his brother Karl was killed); Gustav Bellen; Carl Bodenschatz; Dr. von Conta; von Doering; Hans Eissfeldt; O. L. Förster; Viktor von Fabrice; Willi Gabriel; C. Galetschky; Alfred Gerstenberg; Heinz Graf von Gluszewski-Kwilicki; Justus Grassman; Gisbert-Wilhelm Groos; Walter Grosch; Alois Heldmann; Franz Hemer; Rudolf Klamt; Friedrich August Freiherr von Köckeritz; Egon Koepsch; Kurt Küppers; Arthur Laumann; Hans-Carl von Linsingen; Walter Lehmann; Kurt Lischke; Friedrich Wilhelm Lübbert; Heinrich Maushake; Alfred Niemz Werner Nöldecke; Hans-Georg von der Osten, Heinz Otto; Leopold von Raffey; Karl Riehm; Oskar Rousselle; Otto Rödiger; Geog Simon; Kurt Schibilsky; Karl August von Schoenebeck (who took an English wife and who is still an active pilot and an international aircraft sales representative); Professor Julius Schulte-Frohlinde; Hans Suck; Alfred Wenz and Paul Wenzel.

And what of the future? It is well within the bounds of possibility that a fighter formation in the re-established German Air Force will be named after von Richthofen—and this time equipped, perhaps, with British aircraft! What would Manfred, Freiherr von Richthofen have thought?

APPENDIX ONE

Family Lineage

The Baroness von Richthofen, being presented with a model of her son's famous red triplane, by Major Kimbrough S. Brown. U.S.A.F. Photo taken April 1956.

The motif for the Richthofen family was written by the Ambassador, Emil Freiherr von Richthofen:

Reicht auch der Stammbaum nicht ins graue Altertum
Ist's dennoch ein gar altes wackres Geschlecht
Cristallhell, ungetrübt blieb seines Namens Ruhm,
Hoch hielt es stets die Wahrheit, Ehre und das Recht
Treu seiner Väter Brauch, fromm tapfer, brav und schlicht
Hat Gottes gnäd'ge Huld vor Schaden es bewahrt
O, wank auch fürder nicht vom Pfad der Christenpflicht
Führ Deinen Namen stolz nach echter Ritterart
Es blühe machtig dies Geschlecht, der Ehre Bild
Nie fall'ein Schatten auf sein edles Wappenschild.

As the motif points out, the Richthofen family was not of the ancient German nobility. Their origin, as far as can be traced, was in the town of Bernau, then a town of greater importance than Berlin, which lay to the south. In Bernau, between the years 1543 to 1555, lived a certain Sebastian Schmidt, a native of Coblenz. As a pupil of the great German religious reformer, Martin Luther, he had become a deacon and following the custom with men of learning at that time, he latinised his name, calling himself Faber. The wife he took, Barbara Below, was the daughter of a Berlin councillor. These two were the founders of the family, but it is doubtful if their offspring, Samuel, born 1545, would have risen to the nobility, had it not been for the friendship of Sebastian with Paulas Schultze (or Schultheiss)—the name in either case meaning town mayor.

Paulas was born in Bernau on June 16th, 1521, and rose to become a high official of the Kurfürst of Brandenburg and Archbishop of Magdeburg. A trusted counsellor at the court of his king, he was entrusted with several missions to the court of Emperor Ferdinand I. His reward from a grateful sovereign was a coat of arms, showing him according to his latinised name, Praetorius—a praetor, being a chief magistrate. There remains his epitaph—*Vir prudens et orator gravissimus*—A prudent man and outstanding orator.

Praetorius had no male heirs. Before his death at the age of forty-four he adopted the son of Samuel and Barbara, who took the name of Samuel Praetorius and succeeded to the escutcheon and fortune. Samuel moved to Frankfurt, there to become a judge and later mayor, in which office he died in 1605. His son, Tobias, by marrying a lady of noble birth and using some of the family fortune to be among the first to purchase land in Silesia, greatly enhanced the prestige of his offspring, a son Johann, who, three years before his death, became by decree of Emperor Leopold I, Ritter Johann Praetorius with the surname von Richthofen. From Johann descended the Richthofen family that settled in Silesia, taking residences in Jauer, Striegau, Liegnitz and Schweidnitz. Remaining true to the German-Austrian Empire, they were regarded as good Prussians by Frederick the Great, who, after his conquest of Silesia against Maria Theresa, granted the knighthood of Ritter Praetorius, a barony, thereby becoming Freiherr von Richthofen.

The Richthofens were typical Prussian landowners and several male descendants served as officers, but some achieved fame in other spheres. The learned Karl Freiherr von Richthofen specialised in jurisprudence at the University of Berlin, and Ferdinand (1833-1905) is remembered

Manfred Freiherr von Richthofen's widowed mother with his youngest brother. A picture taken in Berlin at Christmas, 1954 of the Baroness Kunigunde von Richthofen with her only surviving son, Karl Bolko, Freiherr von Richthofen, who, although trained for a military career, became a successful businessman.

146

A family group at Schweidnitz. The two famous be-medalled brothers with their parents, brother Bolko and sister Ilse. Photo taken at a family gathering in 1917.

Translation—(It should be appreciated that the initial letter sequence, rhyme and metre are lost in the translating).

Although the family tree goes not back into grey antiquity
It is nevertheless the name of an old and gallant family.
Like a crystal, clear and unclouded has remained its glorious name.
And ever has it kept truth, honour and right,
According to the custom of its ancestors; pious, brave, simple and true.
God's gracious favour has protected it from harm;
Pray that in future they will ever follow the path of Christian duty.
Show the name proudly in the manner of a true knight,
That this name may become as a symbol of honour
And never a shadow fall upon its noble escutcheon.

as an explorer who penetrated to the remote regions of China and later became Professor of Geography, first at Leipzig and later at Berlin. During the years 1867-68, he resided in California and produced a work in English, *Natural System of Volcanic Rocks*, published in San Francisco. Oswald von Richthofen was a State-Secretary for Foreign Affairs under Kaiser Wilhelm II and four Richthofens, Karl, Ernst, Hartmann and Praetorius, were members of the Reichstag.

The Richthofen to reach highest rank in German military service was Wolfram who had served in the *Richthofen Geschwader*. After the war he had studied engineering, but upon learning of the intention to re-create an Air Service, he set all else aside to become a *Luftwaffe* officer. His rapid promotion to high rank was due, no doubt, to the prestige of his name and the fact that when war came, he already had operational experience. As Chief of Staff to Generalmajor Sperrle who commanded the Condor Legion in Spain, and later as Commander of the Legion, he soon became an expert in the use of aircraft in a close support role.

During the last War he commanded *Fliegerkorps VIII*, first in the Polish campaign of 1939 and then switching over to the West, where, in the spring of 1940, he saw his aircraft, in concert with the German Army, achieve in four weeks what the Kaiser's Army had failed to achieve in four years. Onward to the Balkans and Russia until in 1943, promotion to the command of *Luftflotte 2* (Mediterranean Area) separated him from his *Korps*. As a Generalfeldmarschall he was placed on the retired list in November 1944 at the age of 48. He died a year later from a tumour on the brain.

Perhaps one of the most interesting members of the family was Frieda von Richthofen, daughter of Friedrich Freiherr von Richthofen. It was whilst that branch of the family visited England in 1912, that D. H. Lawrence met Frieda and followed her back to Germany.

Lawrence may well have had apprehensions of his own in taking a daughter from a noble German family, who was several years his senior, and who had already experienced an unhappy marriage. Enamoured as Lawrence undoubtedly was, Frieda's apparent inability to exist without servants exasperated him—yet, the match was successful, for intellectually they were well suited.

Lawrence was a gifted writer and a poet, noted for his 'artisan power of expression'. Among his many other works, several may have been influenced by the von Richthofens. But if other Richthofens provided background, there is little doubt that a von Richthofen—Frieda—was the inspiration, to one of the most famous of the modern English poets.

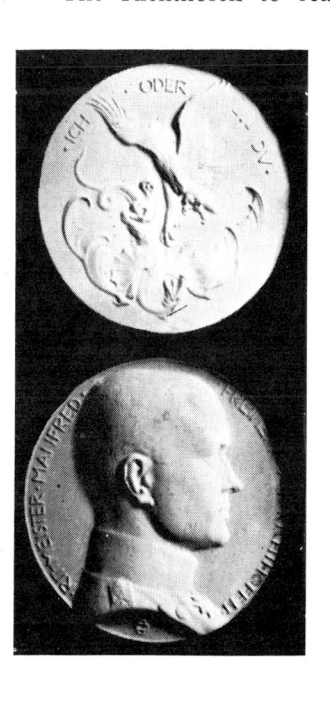

A medallion struck in honour of Manfred Freiherr von Richthofen, is one of the treasured possessions that his mother managed to bring away from Schweidnitz, before the Soviet troops arrived. Housed in a special case, to show obverse and reverse sides, they hang today in the Baroness's sitting room.

147

APPENDIX TWO

Jagdgeschwader Nr. 1

THE PERSONNEL OF JAGDGESCHWADER Nr. 1

A nominal roll with details of all known pilots and/or officers on the staff of *Jagdgeschwader Nr. 1*
from inception on June 24th, 1917 to disbandment on November 11th, 1918

Rank and Name	Jasta	Victory Score	Date of Joining	Remarks
Lt. Hans Adam	6	21	24. 6.17	Staffelführer 30.8.17. Killed 15.11.17
Lt. Adomeit	10	—	3. 8.18	From *Jastaschule I*. To *Jasta 62*, 21.9.18
Oblt. Ernst Frhr. v. Althaus	10	9	24. 6.17	From *Jasta 14*, 6.7.17. Staffelführer. To *Jastaschule II* as instructor 30.7.17
Lt. Alvensleben	4	—	24. 6.17	To *Jasta 21*, 27.11.17
Lt. Anders	4	—	24. 6.17	Posted, date not known
Offz. Stellv. Paul Aue	10	10	?	Wounded 19.9.17
Vfw. Bachmann	6	2	?	Missing 21.10.17
Lt. Bahlmann	4	1	26.10.18	From *Jastaschule II*. Victory 5.11.18
Lt. Bahr	11	—	27.11.17	Killed 6.3.18 in Fokker Dr I 106/17
Lt. Raven Frhr. v. Barnekow	11	11	15. 8.18	From *Jastaschule I*. Slightly wounded 23.8.18
Vfw. Barth	10	1	22. 7.17	Killed 30.1.18 in Alb. D V 4565/17
Lt. Gustav Bellen	10	1	11. 8.17	Victory (Balloon) 21.9.17. Left October 1917
Lt. Bender	10	—	?	Transferred to *Jasta 4*, 30.5.18
Uffz. Beschow	6	—	23. 9.17	Wounded 10.3.18. To Park 2, 20.4.18
Uffz. Biewers	10	—	24. 4.18	To Park 7, 12.7.18
Lt. Block	6	—	20. 9.18	From *Jastaschule I*
Fl. Blümener	6	—	21. 7.18	Killed 8.9.18
Lt. Bockelmann	11	3	24. 6.17	Severely wounded 3.9.17
Oblt. v. Boddin	11	—	24. 6.17	Admin. Officer, also a pilot. To *Jasta 59*
Oblt. Carl Bodenschatz	—	—	2. 7.17	Joined from *Jasta 2*, as *J.G.I.* Adjutant
Lt. Böhren	10	—	11. 9.18	From *Jastaschule I*. Missing 18.10.18
Oblt. Oskar Frhr. v. Boenigk	4	26	24. 6.17	To *Jasta 21* during October 1917
Lt. Bohlein	10	1	?	Killed 16.3.18
Lt. Bouillon	4	—	?	To Park 4, 29.11.17
Lt. Otto Brauneck	11	9	24. 6.17	Shot down by No. 70 Sqn. R.F.C. 26.7.17
Lt. Otto v. Breiten-Landenberg	6	6	?	Severely wounded 26.4.18
Lt. Moritz Bretschneider-Bodener	6	6	19. 4.18	Shot down in flames 18.7.18
Uffz. Brettel	10	2	24. 6.17	Wounded 15.8.17
Lt. Brocke	6	—	17. 5.18	Posted-out 30.7.18
Vfw. Burggaller	10	—	10. 9.17	From *Jastaschule I*. To Park 2, 1.4.18
Vfw. Clausnitzer	4	3	24. 6.17	Taken prisoner-of-war 16.7.17
Lt. v. Conta	11	—	?	Posted out 29.4.18 and rejoined 21.5.18. To Hospital 29.7.18. Posted 11.9.18 for observer's duties
Lt. Czermak	6	1	24. 6.17	Date of victory 28.7.17
Vfw. Degen	6	—	17. 5.18	Missing 14.6.18
Lt. Karl Deilmann	6	6	24. 6.17	Last victory (F.E.) 17.8.17
Vfw. Delang	10	—	?	To Park 2, 10.4.18
Lt. Demandt	10	—	?	Missing 30.11.17
Uffz. Derflinger	10	—	26. 8.18	Transferred to *Jasta 4*, 9.9.18. To Park C, 30.9.18
Oblt. Kurt B. v. Doering	4	11	24. 6.17	Staffelführer. To *Jagdgruppe 4*, May 1918
Lt. v. Dorrien	11	—	2. 7.18	Wounded 25.7.18. To FEA5 10.10.18
Oblt. Eduard Dostler	6	26	24. 6.18	Staffelführer. Missing 21.8.17
Lt. Heinz Dreckmann	4	11	29. 8.17	Killed 30.7.18
Uffz. Eiserbeck	11	—	?	Missing 12.4.18
Lt. Esser	11	—	24. 6.17	To Park 17, 13.6.18 as Technical Officer
Lt. Feige	10	—	30. 5.18	Missing 30.6.18
Lt. Festler	11	—	26. 7.18	Killed 11.8.18
Lt. Ulrich Fischer	4	—	?	To *Flugpark 2*, 27.4.18. Returned 26.8.18. Missing from *Jasta 6*, 29.10.18

148

Rank and Name	Jasta	Victory Score	Date of Joining	Remarks
Fl. Flassbeck	4	—	26.10.18	From *Jastaschule II*.
Lt. Otto L. Förster	11	4	21. 5.18	Admin. Officer. To *Jastaschule I*, 4.9.18
Lt. Fritz Friedrichs	10	21	11. 1.18	Killed 15.7.18 in Fokker D VII 309/18
Vfw. Willi Gabriel	11	11	15. 4.18	From *Schlachtstaffel 15*, To Park 2, 22.8.18
Lt. Carl Galetschky	6	2	18. 8.17	Date of last victory 7.10.17. Left January 1918
Lt. Geppert	4	1	1.10.18	From *Jastaschule II*. Victory 3.11.18
Lt. Alfred Gerstenberg	11	—	31. 8.17	Wounded 20.10.17. Finally left in October 1918
Lt. Gilles	10	—	22.10.18	From *Jastaschule II*
Lt. Heinz, Graf. v. Gluczewski	4	3	?. 1.18	Remained with formation until disbandment
Oblt. Hermann Göring	—	22	6. 7.18	From *Jasta 27*. *J.G.1*. Commander
Lt. Justus Grassmann	10	10	26. 6.17	Last victory (Spad) 6.11.18
Lt. Graul	4	—	4. 8.17	From Park 4
Lt. Gisbert-Wilhelm Groos	11	6	24. 6.17	To *Jastaschule II*, 16.9.18. Wounded 14.9.17. Returned 10.7.18
Oblt. Walter Grosch	4	6	14. 8.18	Wounded 24.8.18. Posted 12.9.18
Lt. Siegfried Gussmann	11	5	?	Posted out and rejoined 22.8.18
Uffz. Hardel	10	—	24. 8.17	Wounded 20.10.17
Oblt. Hartmann	6	—	18. 5.18	No further details available
Lt. v. Hartmann	4	—	27.11.17	Presumed posted out, date not known
Vfw. Hecht	10	—	?	Missing 27.12.17
Lt. Heidenreich	6	—	17. 5.18	Missing 2.6.18
Lt. Held	4	—	22.10.18	From *Jastaschule II*
Vfw. Alois Heldmann	10	15	24. 6.17	Promoted Lt. Last victory (Spad) 6.11.18
Vfw. Franz Hemer	6	18	10. 9.17	Wounded 9.8.18. Promoted Lt. 20.9.18
Uffz. Hennig	10	—	11. 9.18	From *Jastaschule I*
Gefr. Henschler	10	—	?	Promoted Uffz. 2.8.18. To *Jasta 66*, 25.8.18
Lt. Hertz	4	1	7. 9.17	Victory (Nieuport) achieved 17.9.17
Lt. Hildebrandt	4	1	28. 8.18	From *Jastaschule I*. Victory 3.11.18
Lt. Hirschfeld	4	—	?	To *Jasta 81*, 28.8.18
Lt. Hoffmann	11	—	30. 5.18	Killed 30.6.18
Lt. Graf. v. Hohenau	11	—	26. 6.18	Wounded 25.7.18. Died 26.7.18
Lt. Hübner (I)	4	3	24. 6.17	Killed 14.8.17 in fight with No. 1 Sqn. R.F.C.
Lt. Hübner (II)	4	1	30. 3.18	Missing 16.5.18
Sgt. Jagla	11	—	11. 5.18	To Park 7 as C pilot 29.7.18
Lt. Johann Janzen	6	13	24. 6.17	*Staffelführer* 3.5.18. Captured 9.6.18
Lt. Jessen	4	2	30. 5.18	Last victory (Spad) 4.8.18
Lt. Joschkowitz	4	1	18. 9.17	From *Jastaschule*. To Park 2, 1.4.18
Lt. Erich Just	11	6	18. 9.17	Wounded 1.3.18 and 3.5.18
Lt. Karjus	11	—	30. 3.18	To Park 2. 29.5.18
Lt. Keseling	10	—	?	Missing 24.3.18
Lt. Hans Kirschstein	6	27	13. 3.18	Killed in aircraft accident 16.7.18
Lt. Kirst	10	—	12.10.18	Killed 5.11.18. (Last *J.G.1*. casualty)
Uffz. Rudolf Klamt	10	—	12. 8.18	Remained with formation until disbandment
Lt. Hans Klein	4	22	26. 4.18	*Staffelführer Jasta 10*, 27.9.17. Wounded 19.2.18
Lt. Koch	6	—	4. 8.17	From Park 4
Lt. Freiher Friedrich v. Köckeritz	11	3	30. 7.18	From *Jastaschule I*. Remained until disbandment
Lt. Egon Koepsch	4	9	2.10.17	Transferred to *Jasta 11*, 20.10.18
Lt. Wilhelm Kohlbach	10	5	17. 8.18	From *Jasta 50*
Lt. Kortüm	10	—	?	To Park 19, 14.4.18
Lt. Kraut	4	1	3. 8.18	From *Jastaschule I*. Victory 26.9.18
Lt. Krayer	10	—	29. 7.18	Transferred to *Jasta 6*, 31.7.18. To *Jasta 45*, 13.9.18
Vfw. Fritz Krebs	6	6	24.6.18	Shot down in flames 16.7.17
Lt. Krefft	11	—	24. 6.17	*J.G.1*. Technical Officer
Lt. Krüger (I)	4	1	24. 6.17	Died from wounds received 17.7.17
Lt. Krüger (II)	4	—	24. 4.18	To Park 2, 11.5.18
Lt. Kühn	10	3	?	To Park 2, 3.5.18
Vfw. Küllmer	6	1	24. 6.17	Victory achieved 28.7.18. No further record
Lt. Kurt Küppers	6	5	24. 6.17	Posted to Command of *Jasta 48*, January 1918

Rank and Name	Jasta	Victory Score	Date of Joining	Remarks
Lt. Arthur Laumann	10	26	24. 4.18	*Staffelführer* 14.8.18
Vfw. Lautenschlager	11	1	24. 6.17	Shot down by German aircraft 29.10.17
Vfw. Lechner	6	—	14. 8.18	To hospital 16.8.18. Posted 30.8.18
Lt. Walter Lehmann	10	—	17. 6.18	Missing 1.8.18. Taken prisoner-of-war
Lt. Hans-Carl v. Linsingen	11	—	27.11.17	Wounded in Pfalz D III D4223/17 24.1.18
Oblt. Kurt Lischke	6	—	9. 7.17	Admin. Officer. To Park 2, 6.5.18
Lt. Erich Loewenhardt	10	53	24. 6.17	*Staffelführer* 19.4.18. Promoted Oblt. Killed 10.8.18
Lt. Friedrich-Wilhelm Lübbert	11	—	?	Wounded in combat with S.E.5A 17.2.18
Lt. Maletsky	10	—	29. 7.18	From a *Jastaschule*
Lt. Markgraf	6	—	11. 7.18	Killed in aircraft with Kirschstein 16.7.18
Vfw. Marquardt	4	—	24. 6.17	Posted to *Jasta 26*, date not known
Uffz. Martens	11	—	6. 8.18	To *Jasta 64*, 10.10.18
Lt. Matthies	4	—	?	To Park 2, 11.5.18
Lt. Matzdorf	6	2	30. 5.18	To *Jastaschule II* 19.9.18
Lt. Heinrich Maushake	4	7	20.11.17	Wounded 3.11.18
Lt. Meise	10	—	11.10.18	From *Jastaschule II*
Lt. Karl Meyer	11	4	24. 6.17	Transferred to *Jasta 4*, 1.2.17. To *Jastaschule II* 19.9.18
Lt. Eberhardt Mohnicke	11	9	24. 6.17	Wounded 1.3.18 in Dr I 155/17. Posted 8.9.18
Gefr. Möller	10	1	10. 7.18	Missing 18.7.18
Oblt. Müller	11	1	15. 7.17	Fatally injured in accident 27.10.17
Lt. Ulrich Neckel	6	30	1. 9.18	*Staffelführer* until disbandment
Lt. Alfred Niederhoff	11	7	24. 6.17	Killed 28.7.17 in combat with No. 56 Sqn. R.F.C.
Vfw. Alfred Niemz	11	4	30. 9.18	Last victory (D.H.9) 4.11.18
Vfw. Niess	6	—	23. 9.17	No further details available
Fl. Nitsche	10	—	30. 3.18	To Park 7 as C pilot 10.7.18
Lt. Werner Nöldecke	6	1	17. 6.18	Wounded 22.7.18
Lt. Friedrich Noltenius	6	20	21. 9.18	Transferred to *Jasta 11*, 20.10.18
Lt. Ohlrau	10	1	24. 6.17	Victory (Sopwith) 17.8.17
Lt. Hans-Georg v. d. Osten	11	5	11. 8.17	Transferred to *Jasta 11*. Wounded 28.3.18
Lt. Heinz Otto	10	—	6. 5.18	Wounded 6.6.18. Posted out 16.6.18
Lt. Pastor	11	—	24. 9.17	Killed 31.10.17 in Fok Dr I 121/17
Vfw. Patermann	4	2	24. 6.17	Killed 12.7.17
Lt. v. Puttkamer	4	—	30. 5.18	To Park 7 as C pilot 11.7.18
Lt. v. Raczek	11	—	18. 8.18	From *Jastaschule II*
Lt. Rademacher	10	—	14. 5.18	Missing 31.5.18
Vfw. Leopold v. Raffey	6	—	24. 6.17	Promoted Lt. 17.4.18. Posted out 30.8.18
Lt. Viktor Rautter	4	15	24. 6.17	Killed 31.5.18. Was also known as v. Pressentin
Uffz. Reimers	6	2	21. 7.18	Missing 4.9.18
Oblt. Wilhelm Reinhard	11	20	24. 6.17	*Staffelführer Jasta 6*. Promoted Hptm. *Geschwader Kommandeur* 23.4.18. Fatally injured in accident 3.7.18
Lt. Reinhardt	4	1	22. 7.18	Wounded 9.8.18. Victory 3.10.18
Fl. Rhode	4	—	18. 8.18	From *Jastaschule II*
Rittm. Manfred Frhr. v. Richthofen	—	80	24. 6.17	*Geschwaderkommandeur*. Wounded 6.7.17. Killed 21.4.18
Lt. Lothar Frhr. v. Richthofen	11	40	25. 9.17	Brother of Manfred Frhr. von Richthofen. *Staffelführer*. Promoted Oblt. Wounded 13.3.17, 13.3.18 and 13.8.18
Lt. Wolfram v. Richthofen	11	8	4. 4.18	Cousin of Manfred Frhr. von Richthofen
Lt. Karl Riehm	—	—	4.10.18	Technical Officer, *Geschwader* staff
Fl. Riensberg	10	—	?	Wounded 8.11.17. Killed 18.1.18
Lt. Dr. Rieth	6	1	11.10.18	Victory (Spad) 29.10.18
Lt. Otto Rödiger	6	—	28.10.18	From *Jastaschule II*
Lt. Rolff	6	3	30. 6.18	Fatally injured 19.8.18 in Fokker D VIII
Lt. Römer	10	—	21. 9.17	Killed 2.10.17 in Pfalz D III
Lt. Oskar Rousselle	4	—	24. 6.17	Wounded 10.8.17
Vfw. Rudenberg	10	—	9. 9.17	No further details available
Lt. Hugo Schaefer	10	—	28. 6.18	Technical Officer of *Jasta 10*
Vfw. Schaffen	10	—	10. 7.18	To Park 4, 20.8.18
Oblt. Scheffer	11	—	13. 7.17	No further details available
Lt. Kurt Schibilsky	10	—	15. 8.18	From *Jastaschule II*. Captured 4.10.18

Rank and Name	Jasta	Victory Score	Date of Joining	Remarks
Lt. Schiemann	6	2	?	Last victory achieved on 29.10.18
Lt. Schliewen	6	—	15. 8.18	From *Jastaschule I*
Lt. Schmidt	6	—	9. 9.18	From *FEA6*
Sgt. Schmutzler	4	—	?	Died of wounds received 10.5.18
Lt. Karl-August v. Schoenebeck	11	2	7. 7.17	From *Fl. Abt. (A) 203* 7.7.17. To *Jasta 33*, February 1918
Vfw. Edgar Scholz	11	7	?	Killed taking off from Cappy 2.5.18
Lt. Schröder	10	—	6. 5.18	To *Fl. Abt. (A) 206* 7.6.18
Fw.Lt. Schubert	6	3	24. 6.17	*J.G.1.* staff 6.9.18. Promoted Lt. 1.10.18
Lt. Julius Schulte-Frohlinde	11	4	28. 8.18	Last victory (D.H.9) 4.11.18
Lt. Schulze	4	—	?	Fatally injured 30.11.17
Sgt. Friedrich Schumacher	10	5	?	Wounded 24.7.18. Posted out 21.8.18
Lt. v. Schweinitz	11	—	27.11.17	Fatally injured 27.12.17 in Alb. D Va D5313/17
Lt. Siemelkamp	4	1	—	To Park 2, 10.4.18
Lt. Sienz	10	—	14.10.18	From *Jastaschule II*
Lt. Georg Simon	11	—	24. 6.17	Left *Geschwader* 4.7.17
Lt. Skauradzun	4	—	?	Wounded 8.3.18 in Pfalz D III D4042/17
Lt. Skowronski	6	—	24. 4.18	To Park 3, 1.7.18
Lt. Eberhardt Stapenhörst	11	4	30. 6.17	Taken prisoner of war 13.1.18
Lt. Werner Steinhaüser	11	10	?	Wounded 17.3.18. Killed 26.6.18
Lt. K. Stock	6	—	13. 7.17	From *Jasta 22*
Lt. Walter Stock	6	3	24. 6.17	Last victory achieved 10.8.17
Lt. Stoy	10	—	31. 3.18	Wounded 2.5.18. Posted 16.6.18
Uffz. Strecker	10	—	29. 7.18	To hospital 4.8.18. Posted out 30.8.18
Vfw. Stumpf	6	1	4. 8.17	From Park 4. Wounded 30.9.17
Lt. Hans Suck	4	—	14.10.18	From *Jastaschule II*
Lt. Tüxen	6	2	24. 6.17	Flying accident 11.11.17
Lt. Ernst Udet	11	62	18. 3.18	To hospital 3.4.18. *Staffelführer Jasta 4*, 21.5.18
Lt. Werner Voss	10	48	30. 7.17	*Staffelführer* 30.7.17. Killed 23.9.17
Vfw. Wawzin	10	1	1. 9.17	No further detail known
Oblt. Erich Rüdiger v. Wedel	11	13	23. 4.18	*Staffelführer* 8.9.18. Last victory 5.11.18
Oblt. Weigand	10	3	11. 7.17	Wounded 14.9.17. Killed 25.9.17
Lt. Hans Weiss	11	16	?	Transferred to *Jasta 11*, 1.4.18. Killed 2.5.18
Lt. v. d. Wense	6	—	6. 8.18	From *Jastaschule I*. Killed 11.8.18
Lt. Wentz	11	—	26. 7.18	Killed 10.8.18 in collision with Loewenhardt
Lt. Alfred Wenz	11	—	5.18	Was with *Jasta 11* until November 1918
Lt. Paul Wenzel	6	10	?	Wounded 11.8.18. Posted out 30.8.18
Lt. Richard Wenzl	11	12	27. 3.18	Transferred to *Jasta 4*, 20.10.18
Uffz. Werkmeister	10	—	23. 9.17	Killed 25.9.17 in combat with No. 56 Sqn. R.F.C.
Lt. Wilde	4	1	?	Victory (Sopwith Triplane) 5.10.17
Lt. v. Winterfeld	4	2	24. 4.18	To hospital 29.7.18. Killed 5.9.18
Lt. Kurt Wolff	11	33	24. 6.17	*Staffelführer*. Killed 15.9.17
Lt. Joachim Wolff	11	10	6. 7.17	Wounded 23.11.17. Killed 16.5.18
Lt. Wolff (III)	6	—	?	Wounded 27.8.18. Posted out 20.9.18
Vfw. Kurt Wüsthoff	4	27	?	Promoted Lt. To *J.G.1.* staff 16.3.18. P.o.w. 17.6.18
Oblt. Zander	11	—	29. 9.18	Attached for special duty
Lt. Zwitzers	4	—	23.10.17	No further detail known

N.B.—Rank is given as on joining *J.G.1*. Victory score is the total number of victories achieved throughout war service. Where personnel were already serving in *Jagdstaffeln 4, 6, 10* or *11* on 24.6.17 (the date on which *Jagdgeschwader Nr. 1* officially formed) the date of joining is given as that date. As far as possible the date and reason for leaving *J.G.1.* has been given in the remarks column; where this information cannot be traced, the date of last victory, where known, is given to assist placing the time of service in *J.G.1.* New arrivals late in 1918 were mostly serving at the time of disbandment, and therefore in the remarks column the unit from which they came is given; this information when known is also given when other details cannot be traced. Where date of wounding is given as the last entry it may be presumed that it was sufficiently severe to necessitate being struck off the *Geschwader* strength. Also known to have served in the *Geschwader*, but of whom no details of their service can be traced are Hans Eissfeldt and Viktor von Fabrice.

APPENDIX THREE

Medals and Motors

Manfred von Richthofen's medals. Mounted separately, bottom left round to bottom right: Bulgarian Order of Military Valour; Hungarian Order of the Holy Crown; Iron Cross 1st class; Imperial Germans Pilot's Badge; Order of the Royal House of Oldenburg; Pour le Mérite; Pilot's Badge (German Navy); Turkish Star of Gallipoli; Turkish Imtjaz Medal; Turkish Liakat Medal.

Captain A. R. Brown's medals. The D.S.C. and bar (see page 119 for citation), British War Medal (1914-1920) and the Victory Medal.

Row of medals with ribbons, left to right: Iron Cross 2nd class; Order of the House of Hohenzollern; Saint Henry's Military Order—Saxony; Order of the House of Ernestine—Saxony; Griffon Cross; Hessen Phillips Order; Saxe-Coburg-Gotha Duke Carl Edward Medal; Lippe-Schaumburg Cross for Faithful Services; Hanseatic Cross—Lübeck; Hanseatic Cross—Bremen; Hanseatic Cross—Hamburg; Austrian Imperial Order of the Iron Crown; Austrian Military Service Cross.

Top left and right: The Argus and Benz engines. Each 4-cylinder and of 100 h.p. They powered the Albatros B II, B IIa and C I aircraft. Bottom left:

The 14-cylinder 160 h.p. Obersursel which powered some Fokker E III; E IV and D III aircraft.
Bottom right: The 6-cylinder 185 h.p. B.M.W. which powered some of the Fokker D VII aircraft.

Victory Log

APPENDIX FOUR

On the following six pages are given an illustrated victory log of the claims of Manfred, Freiherr von Richthofen. They are set out with captions giving information in the following order: First line: The official German claim number, the aircraft type, unit and service to which the aircraft belonged, the date and the location of the wreckage. Second line: The rank and name of the occupants of the aircraft where known, with a note upon their fate. It will be noticed that the first two victories do not bear claim numbers. Richthofen averred that these victories were achieved, but they did not receive confirmation by the German military authorities.

There has been much controversy concerning the victory score of Richthofen and even now, after years of research, this matter cannot be fully resolved. Perhaps it never will be. However, recent research has brought much new information to light and has settled most of the outstanding controversies. Major Brown would have it represented that he does not accept Claim No. 5 as an accredited victory, but by accepting No. 6A, he is agreed upon the generally accepted total of eighty confirmed victories. Herr Nowarra was concerned about the evidence from German sources conflicting with British documents, but these points have in the main been resolved, by accepting that Richthofen himself wrongly identified several of the aircraft types he claimed.

The Editor must confess to a mistake of his own in another work, where A2607 was given as the D.H.2 in which Major Hawker, V.C. (Claim No. 11), was shot down. In this he was misled by a report in the *Österreichische Flug-Zeitschrift* to that effect. Subsequent research has shown that D.H.2 A2607 was lost the day previous to Major Hawker's D.H.2 No. 5964 fitted with a Gnome Monosoupape engine No. 6138B540 and armed with Lewis gun No. 14563; the gun Richthofen took as a trophy.

In representing aircraft types, the correct designation B.E.2c, B.E.2d or B.E.2e cannot in every case be confirmed even where the serial number has been ascertained. For example, in the production batch of B.Es by Wolseley Motors Ltd., serialled A3149-3168, there were both B.E.2c and B.E.2e variants.

Richthofen's easy victory over Second Lieutenant C. G. Gilbert (Claim No. 31) may be further explained by the fact that he had crashed in D.H.2 No. 7849 on March 17th, 1917, eight days before he was shot down, suggesting that not only was he suffering from a recent severe shaking, but that also he was new to the Nieuport type aircraft.

When Richthofen led *Jasta 11* to their devastating attack upon a flight of R.E.8s of No. 59 Squadron R.F.C., destroying all six; it is doubtful, in the resulting mêlée, if any one of the R.E.8s could be positively identified as Richthofen's victim. It has been generally assumed that Captain Stuart and Lieutenant Wood in R.E.8 A3190 were his victims (Claim No. 41), but they might well have been the occupants in any one of the other five R.E.8s (A3199, A3206, A3216, A3225 or A4191).

The occupants of the Boulton & Paul-built F.E.2b 7020 (Claim No. 46) had miraculous escapes. This aircraft was salvaged by the R.F.C. It was extensively damaged, having turned over three times on landing and the engine was badly damaged by machine-gun fire. The radiator had been shot through in several places.

Claims Nos. 54, 55, 73, 78 are open to question on the various aspects of aircraft type, unit or service, and the fate of the personnel involved and the points in question are dealt with in the text.

New evidence suggests that Victory No. 24 was claimed in error and that B.E.2d 5785 of No. 2 Squadron with Lt. J. B. E. Crosbee and Sgt. Prance (wounded) was concerned.

Photographs purporting to show the wreckage of aircraft Richthofen shot down have not been included in this work; the reason being that their authenticity cannot be checked. They are suspect as wartime propaganda pictures and in fact, the captions to German Press photos for his thirteenth and fortieth victims, were actually different views of the same crashed R.E.8!

A Bristol Fighter comes to grief; on this occasion fortunately without loss of life, and on the British side of the lines.

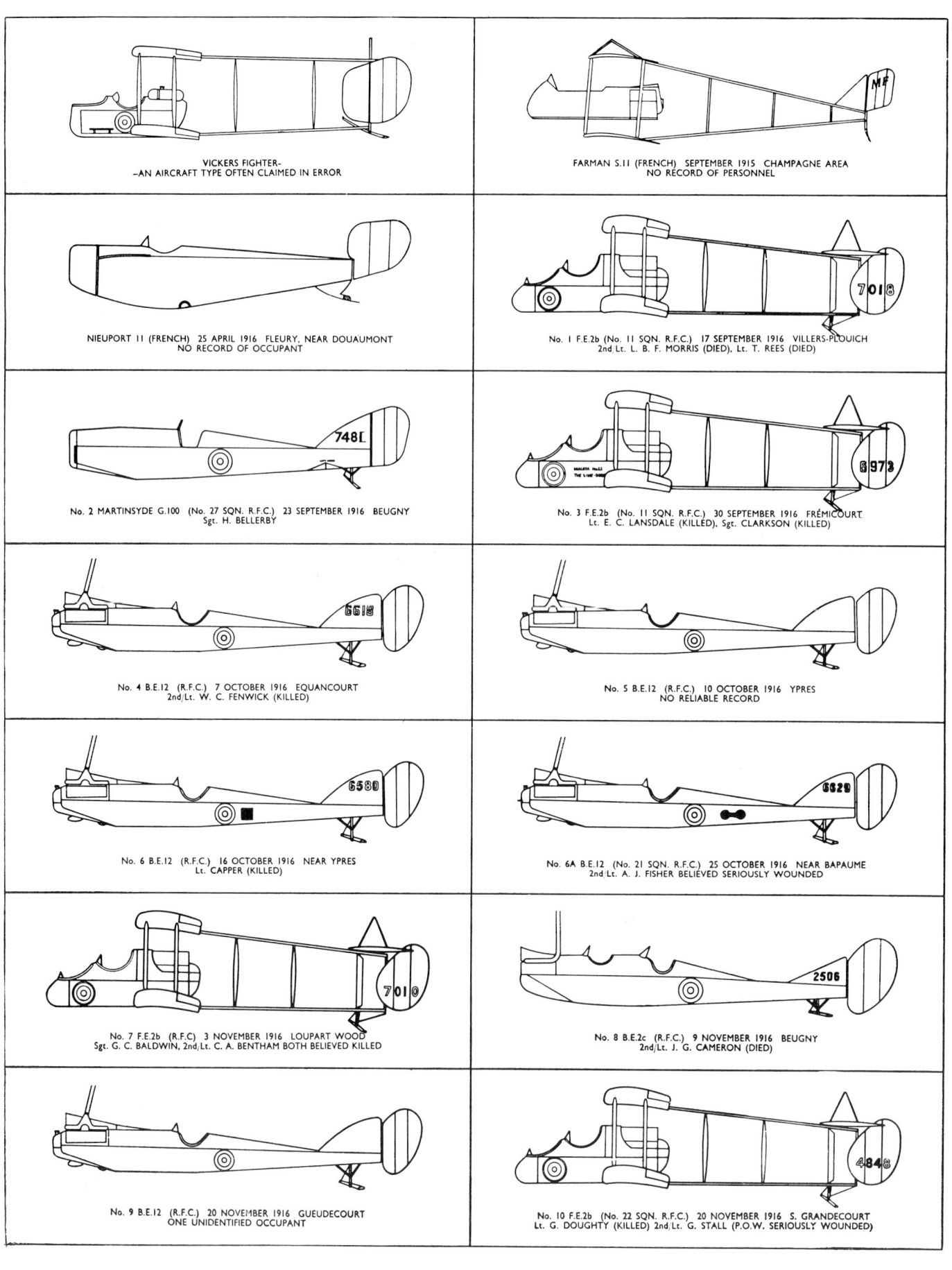

VICKERS FIGHTER-
-AN AIRCRAFT TYPE OFTEN CLAIMED IN ERROR

FARMAN S.11 (FRENCH) SEPTEMBER 1915 CHAMPAGNE AREA
NO RECORD OF PERSONNEL

NIEUPORT 11 (FRENCH) 25 APRIL 1916 FLEURY, NEAR DOUAUMONT
NO RECORD OF OCCUPANT

No. 1 F.E.2b (No. 11 SQN. R.F.C.) 17 SEPTEMBER 1916 VILLERS-PLOUICH
2nd/Lt. L. B. F. MORRIS (DIED), Lt. T. REES (DIED)

No. 2 MARTINSYDE G.100 (No. 27 SQN. R.F.C.) 23 SEPTEMBER 1916 BEUGNY
Sgt. H. BELLERBY

No. 3 F.E.2b (No. 11 SQN. R.F.C.) 30 SEPTEMBER 1916 FRÉMICOURT
Lt. E. C. LANSDALE (KILLED), Sgt. CLARKSON (KILLED)

No. 4 B.E.12 (R.F.C.) 7 OCTOBER 1916 EQUANCOURT
2nd/Lt. W. C. FENWICK (KILLED)

No. 5 B.E.12 (R.F.C.) 10 OCTOBER 1916 YPRES
NO RELIABLE RECORD

No. 6 B.E.12 (R.F.C.) 16 OCTOBER 1916 NEAR YPRES
Lt. CAPPER (KILLED)

No. 6A B.E.12 (No. 21 SQN. R.F.C.) 25 OCTOBER 1916 NEAR BAPAUME
2nd/Lt. A. J. FISHER BELIEVED SERIOUSLY WOUNDED

No. 7 F.E.2b (R.F.C.) 3 NOVEMBER 1916 LOUPART WOOD
Sgt. G. C. BALDWIN, 2nd/Lt. C. A. BENTHAM BOTH BELIEVED KILLED

No. 8 B.E.2c (R.F.C.) 9 NOVEMBER 1916 BEUGNY
2nd/Lt. J. G. CAMERON (DIED)

No. 9 B.E.12 (R.F.C.) 20 NOVEMBER 1916 GUEUDECOURT
ONE UNIDENTIFIED OCCUPANT

No. 10 F.E.2b (No. 22 SQN. R.F.C.) 20 NOVEMBER 1916 S. GRANDECOURT
Lt. G. DOUGHTY (KILLED) 2nd/Lt. G. STALL (P.O.W. SERIOUSLY WOUNDED)

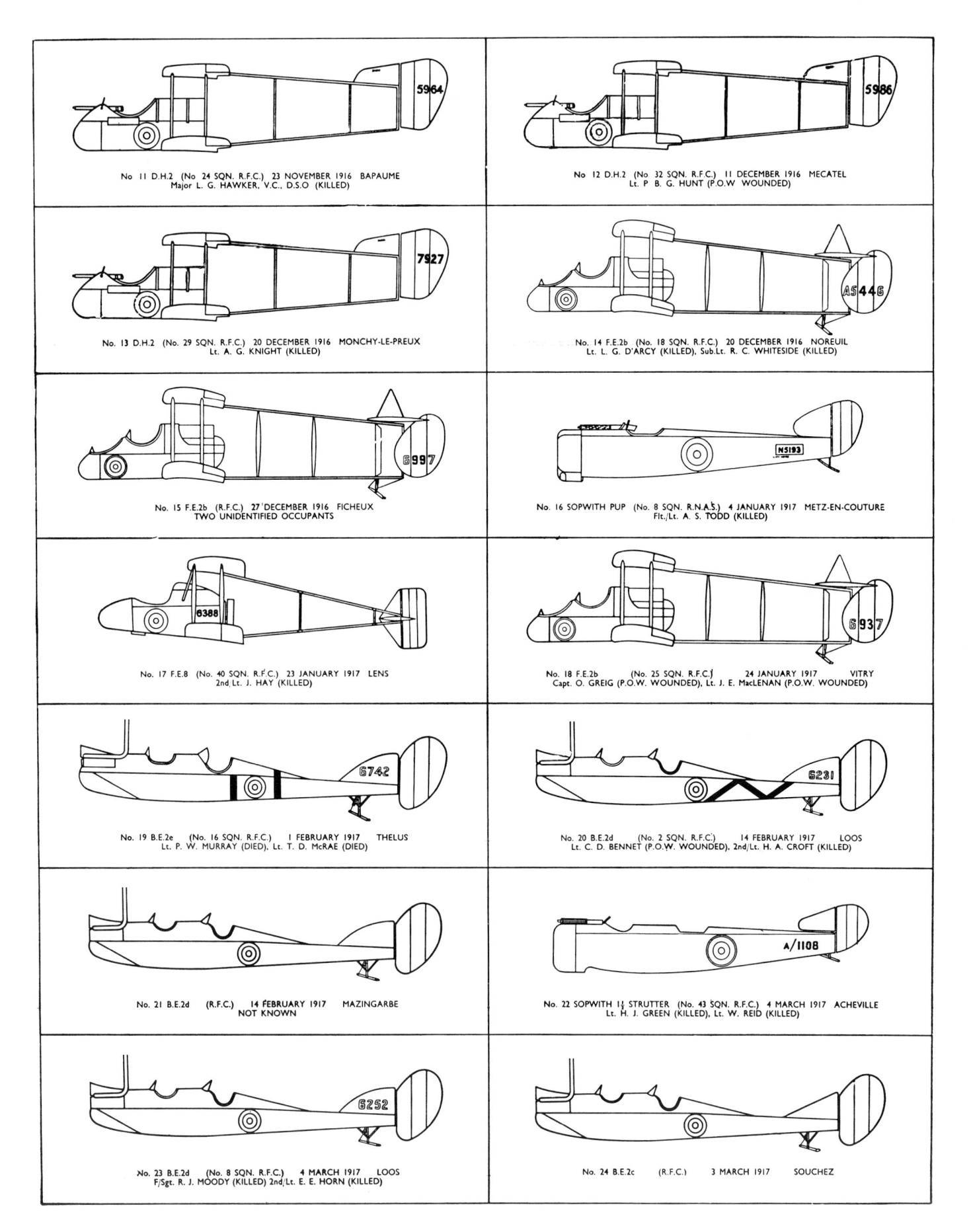

No. 11 D.H.2 (No 24 SQN. R.F.C.) 23 NOVEMBER 1916 BAPAUME Major L. G. HAWKER, V.C., D.S.O (KILLED)	No. 12 D.H.2 (No 32 SQN. R.F.C.) 11 DECEMBER 1916 MECATEL Lt. P B. G. HUNT (P.O.W WOUNDED)
No. 13 D.H.2 (No. 29 SQN. R.F.C.) 20 DECEMBER 1916 MONCHY-LE-PREUX Lt. A. G. KNIGHT (KILLED)	No. 14 F.E.2b (No. 18 SQN. R.F.C.) 20 DECEMBER 1916 NOREUIL Lt. L. G. D'ARCY (KILLED), Sub.Lt. R. C. WHITESIDE (KILLED)
No. 15 F.E.2b (R.F.C.) 27 DECEMBER 1916 FICHEUX TWO UNIDENTIFIED OCCUPANTS	No. 16 SOPWITH PUP (No. 8 SQN. R.N.A.S.) 4 JANUARY 1917 METZ-EN-COUTURE Flt./Lt. A. S. TODD (KILLED)
No. 17 F.E.8 (No. 40 SQN. R.F.C.) 23 JANUARY 1917 LENS 2nd/Lt. J. HAY (KILLED)	No. 18 F.E.2b (No. 25 SQN. R.F.C.) 24 JANUARY 1917 VITRY Capt. O. GREIG (P.O.W. WOUNDED), Lt. J. E. MacLENAN (P.O.W. WOUNDED)
No. 19 B.E.2e (No. 16 SQN. R.F.C.) 1 FEBRUARY 1917 THELUS Lt. P. W. MURRAY (DIED), Lt. T. D. McRAE (DIED)	No. 20 B.E.2d (No. 2 SQN. R.F.C.) 14 FEBRUARY 1917 LOOS Lt. C. D. BENNET (P.O.W. WOUNDED), 2nd/Lt. H. A. CROFT (KILLED)
No. 21 B.E.2d (R.F.C.) 14 FEBRUARY 1917 MAZINGARBE NOT KNOWN	No. 22 SOPWITH 1½ STRUTTER (No. 43 SQN. R.F.C.) 4 MARCH 1917 ACHEVILLE Lt. H. J. GREEN (KILLED), Lt. W. REID (KILLED)
No. 23 B.E.2d (No. 8 SQN. R.F.C.) 4 MARCH 1917 LOOS F/Sgt. R. J. MOODY (KILLED) 2nd/Lt. E. E. HORN (KILLED)	No. 24 B.E.2c (R.F.C.) 3 MARCH 1917 SOUCHEZ

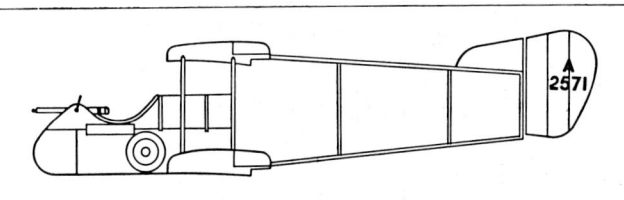

No. 25 D.H.2 (No. 29 SQN. R.F.C.) 9 MARCH 1917 BAILLEUL
Lt. A. W PEARSON, M.C. (KILLED)

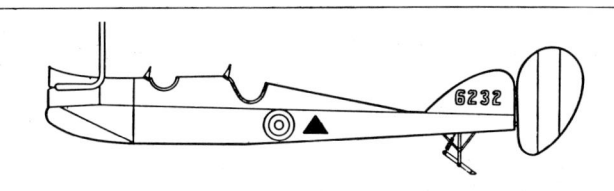

No. 26 B.E.2d (No. 2 SQN. R.F.C.) 11 MARCH 1917 VIMY
2nd/Lt. J. SMITH (KILLED), Lt. E. BYRNE (KILLED)

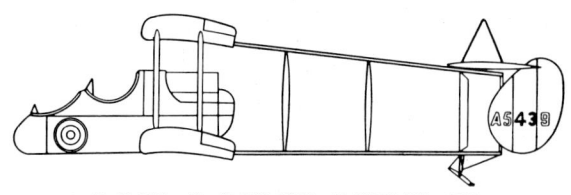

No. 27 F.E.2b (No. 25 SQN. R.F.C.) 17 MARCH 1917 OPPY
Lt. A. E. BOULTBEE (KILLED) Air Mech F KING (KILLED)

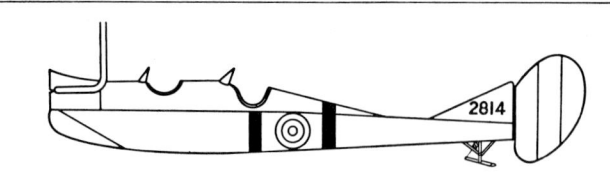

No. 28 B.E.2c (No. 16 SQN. R.F.C.) 17 MARCH 1917 VIMY
2nd/Lt. G. M. WATT (KILLED), Sgt. F. A. HOWLETT (KILLED)

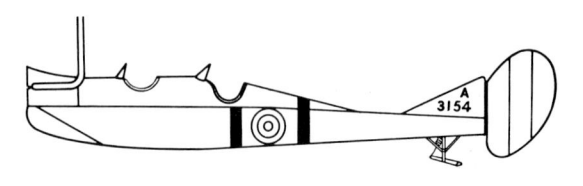

No. 29 B.E.2c (No. 16 SQN. R.F.C.) 21 MARCH 1917 LA NEUVILLE
Sgt. S. H. QUICKE (KILLED), 2nd/Lt. W. J. LIDSEY (KILLED)

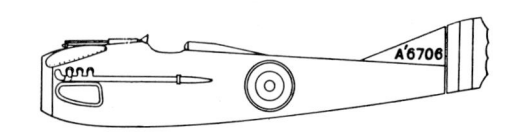

No. 30 SPAD S.7 (R.F.C.) 24 MARCH 1917 GIVENCHY
Lt. R. P. BAKER (P.O.W. WOUNDED)

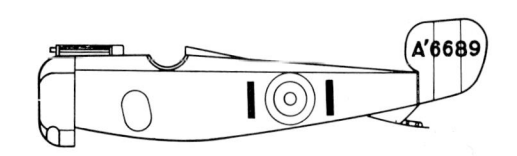

No. 31 NIEUPORT 17 (No. 29 SQN. R.F.C.) 25 MARCH 1917 TILLOY
2nd/Lt. C. G. GILBERT (P.O.W.)

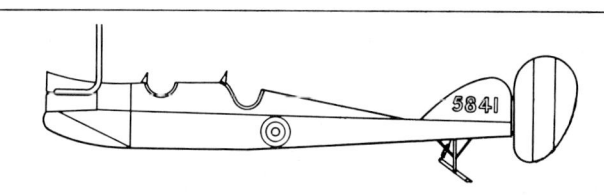

No. 32 B.E.2d (R.F.C.) 2 APRIL 1917 FARBUS
Lt. J. C. POWELL (KILLED), Air/Mech. P. BONNER (KILLED)

No. 33 SOPWITH 1½ STRUTTER (No. 43 SQN. R.F.C.) 2 APRIL 1917 GIVENCHY
2nd Lt. P. WARREN (P.O.W.), Sgt. R. DUNN (KILLED)

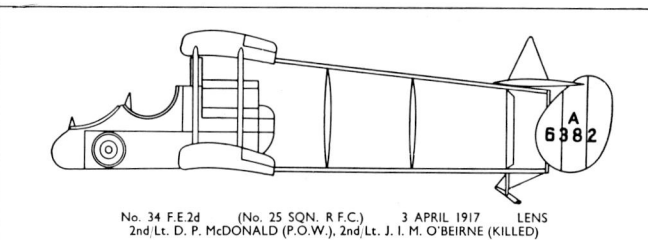

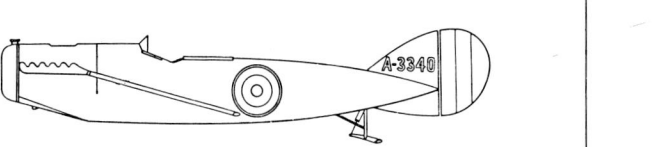

No. 34 F.E.2d (No. 25 SQN. R.F.C.) 3 APRIL 1917 LENS
2nd/Lt. D. P. McDONALD (P.O.W.), 2nd/Lt. J. I. M. O'BEIRNE (KILLED)

No. 35 BRISTOL F2A (No. 48 SQN. R.F.C.) 5 APRIL 1917 LEMBRAS
Lt. A. M. LECKLER (P.O.W. WOUNDED), Lt. H. D. K. GEORGE (DIED)

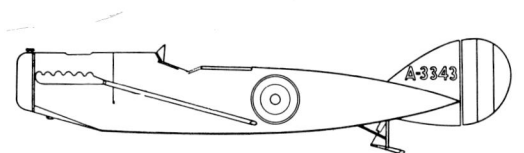

No. 36 BRISTOL F2A (No. 48 SQN. R.F.C.) 5 APRIL 1917 QUINCY
Lt. A. T. ADAMS (P.O.W WOUNDED), Lt. D. J. STEWART (P.O.W.)

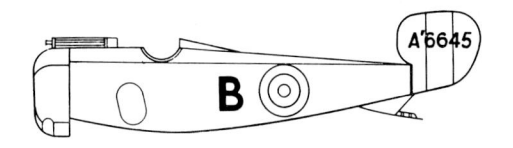

No. 37 NIEUPORT 17 (No. 60 SQN. R.F.C.) 7 APRIL 1917 MERCATEL
2nd Lt. G. O. SMART (KILLED)

No. 38 SOPWITH 1½ STRUTTER (No. 43 SQN. R.F.C.) 8 APRIL 1917 FARBUS
Lt. J. S. HEAGERTY (P.O.W. WOUNDED), Lt. L. H. CANTLE (KILLED)

No. 39 B.E.2e (No. 16 SQN. R.F.C.)   8 APRIL 1917   VIMY
2nd Lt. K. I. MACKENSIE (KILLED), 2nd Lt. G. EVERINGHAM (KILLED)

No. 40 B.E.2c   (R.F.C.)   11 APRIL 1917   WILLERVAL
Lt. E. C. E. DERWIN (WOUNDED), Gnr. H. PIERSON (WOUNDED)

No. 41 R.E.8 (No. 59 SQN. R.F.C.)   13 APRIL 1917   VITRY
Capt. J. STUART (KILLED), Lt. M. H. WOOD (KILLED)

No. 42 F.E.2b (No. 25 SQN. R.F.C.)   13 APRIL 1917   MONCHY
TWO UNIDENTIFIED OCCUPANTS

No. 43 F.E.2b (No. 25 SQN. R.F.C.)   13 APRIL 1917   HENIN
2nd Lt. A. H. BATES (KILLED), Sgt. W. A. BARNES (KILLED)

No. 44 NIEUPORT 17 (No. 60 SQN. R.F.C.)   14 APRIL 1917   BOIS BERNARD
Lt. W. O. RUSSELL (P.O.W.)

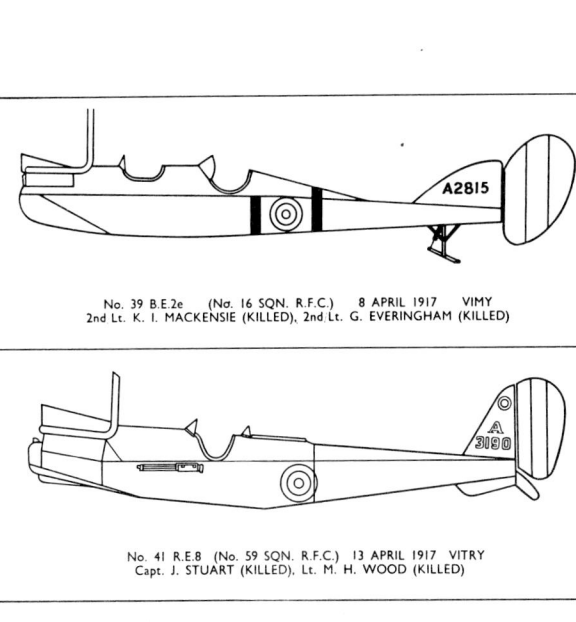

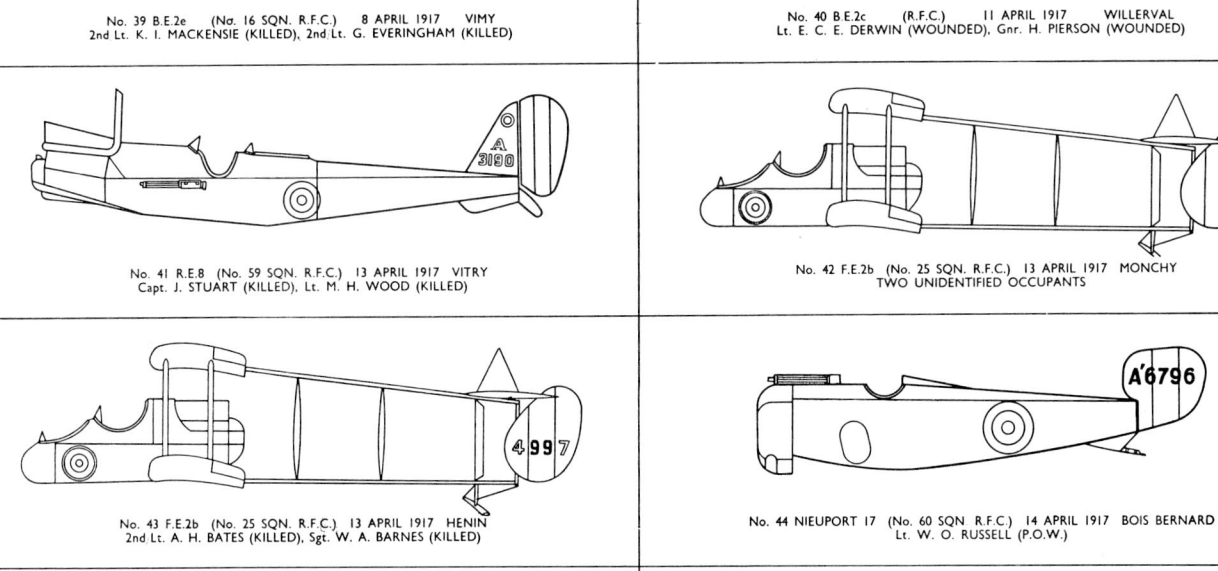

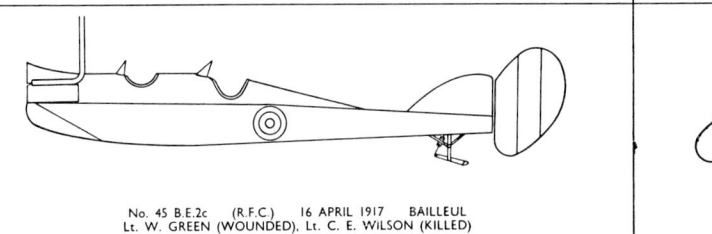

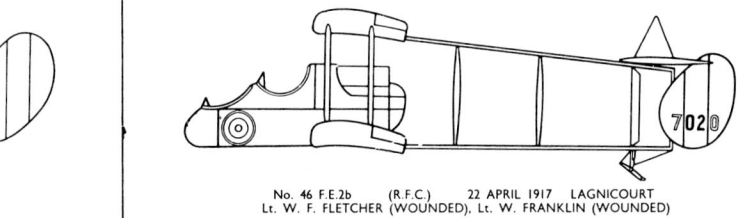

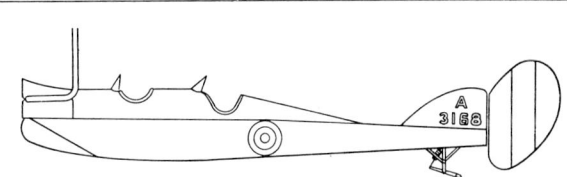

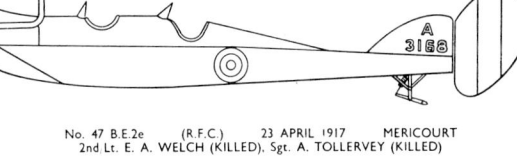

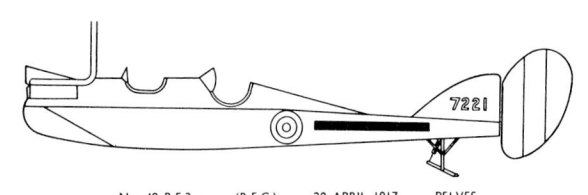

No. 45 B.E.2c   (R.F.C.)   16 APRIL 1917   BAILLEUL
Lt. W. GREEN (WOUNDED), Lt. C. E. WILSON (KILLED)

No. 46 F.E.2b   (R.F.C.)   22 APRIL 1917   LAGNICOURT
Lt. W. F. FLETCHER (WOUNDED), Lt. W. FRANKLIN (WOUNDED)

No. 47 B.E.2e   (R.F.C.)   23 APRIL 1917   MERICOURT
2nd Lt. E. A. WELCH (KILLED), Sgt. A. TOLLERVEY (KILLED)

No. 48 B.E.2c   (R.F.C.)   28 APRIL 1917   PELVES
Lt. R. W. FOLLIT (KILLED), 2nd Lt. F. J. KIRKHAM (P.O.W. WOUNDED)

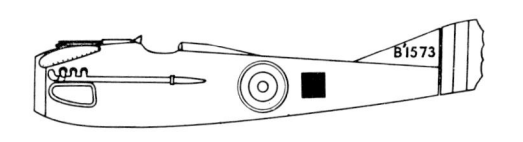

No. 49 SPAD S.7 (No. 19 SQN R.F.C.)   29 APRIL 1917   LECLUSE
Lt. R. APPLIN (KILLED)

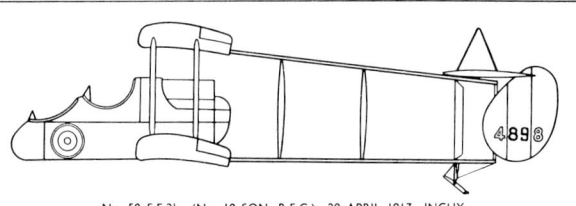

No. 50 F.E.2b (No. 18 SQN. R.F.C.)   29 APRIL 1917   INCHY
Sgt. G. STEAD (KILLED), Cpl. A. BEEBEE (KILLED)

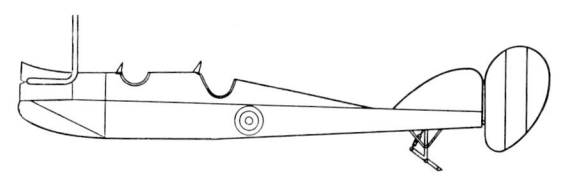

No. 51 B.E.2d   (R.F.C.)   29 APRIL 1917   ROEUX
TWO UNIDENTIFIED OCCUPANTS

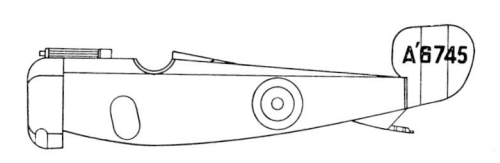

No. 52 NIEUPORT 17 (No. 40 SQN. R.F.C.)   29 APRIL 1917   BILLY-MONTIGNY
Capt. F. L. BARWELL (KILLED)

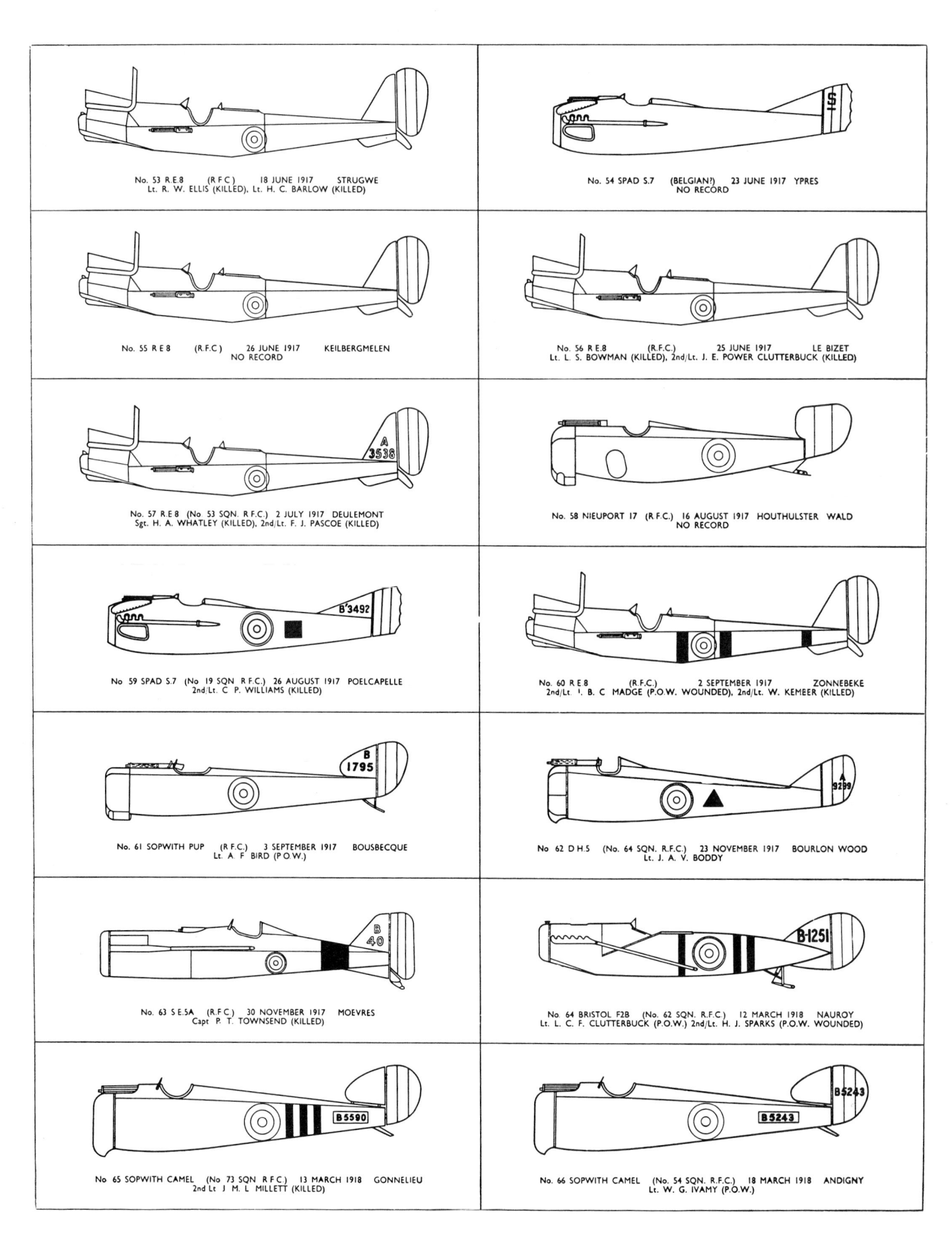

No. 53 R.E.8   (R F C)   18 JUNE 1917   STRUGWE
Lt. R. W. ELLIS (KILLED), Lt. H. C. BARLOW (KILLED)

No. 54 SPAD S.7   (BELGIAN?)   23 JUNE 1917   YPRES
NO RECORD

No. 55 R E 8   (R.F.C)   26 JUNE 1917   KEILBERGMELEN
NO RECORD

No. 56 R E.8   (R.F.C.)   25 JUNE 1917   LE BIZET
Lt. L. S. BOWMAN (KILLED), 2nd/Lt. J. E. POWER CLUTTERBUCK (KILLED)

No. 57 R.E.8   (No. 53 SQN. R.F.C.)   2 JULY 1917   DEULEMONT
Sgt. H. A. WHATLEY (KILLED), 2nd/Lt. F. J. PASCOE (KILLED)

No. 58 NIEUPORT 17   (R.F.C.)   16 AUGUST 1917   HOUTHULSTER WALD
NO RECORD

No 59 SPAD S.7   (No 19 SQN R.F.C.)   26 AUGUST 1917   POELCAPELLE
2nd/Lt. C. P. WILLIAMS (KILLED)

No. 60 R E 8   (R.F.C.)   2 SEPTEMBER 1917   ZONNEBEKE
2nd/Lt. B. C MADGE (P.O.W. WOUNDED), 2nd/Lt. W. KEMEER (KILLED)

No. 61 SOPWITH PUP   (R.F.C.)   3 SEPTEMBER 1917   BOUSBECQUE
Lt. A. F. BIRD (P.O.W.)

No 62 D H.5   (No. 64 SQN. R.F.C.)   23 NOVEMBER 1917   BOURLON WOOD
Lt. J. A. V. BODDY

No. 63 S E.5A   (R.F.C.)   30 NOVEMBER 1917   MOEVRES
Capt P. T. TOWNSEND (KILLED)

No. 64 BRISTOL F2B   (No. 62 SQN. R.F.C.)   12 MARCH 1918   NAUROY
Lt. L. C. F. CLUTTERBUCK (P.O.W.) 2nd/Lt. H. J. SPARKS (P.O.W. WOUNDED)

No 65 SOPWITH CAMEL   (No 73 SQN R F C.)   13 MARCH 1918   GONNELIEU
2nd Lt J M. L MILLETT (KILLED)

No. 66 SOPWITH CAMEL   (No. 54 SQN. R.F.C.)   18 MARCH 1918   ANDIGNY
Lt. W. G. IVAMY (P.O.W.)

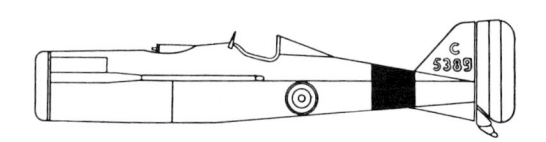

No. 67 S.E.5A (No. 56 SQN. R.F.C.) 24 MARCH 1918 COMBLES
2nd/Lt. W. PORTER (KILLED)

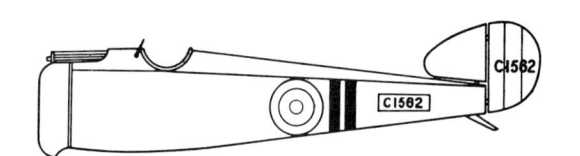

No. 68 SOPWITH CAMEL (No. 3 SQN. R.F.C.) 25 MARCH 1918 CONTALMAISON
2nd/Lt. D. CAMERON (KILLED)

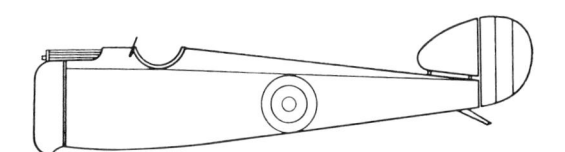

No. 69 SOPWITH CAMEL (R.F.C.) 26 MARCH 1918 CONTALMAISON
2nd/Lt. W. KNOX (KILLED)

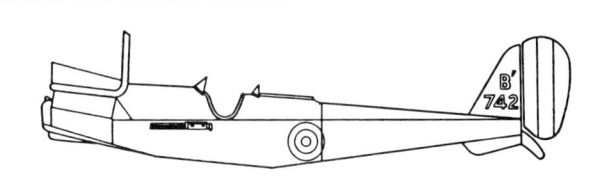

No. 70 R.E.8 (No. 15 SQN. R.F.C.) 26 MARCH 1918 ALBERT
2nd/Lt. V. J. READING (KILLED), 2nd/Lt. M. LEGGAT (KILLED)

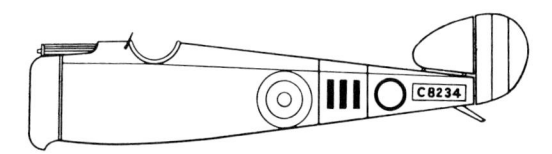

No. 71 SOPWITH CAMEL (No. 70 SQN. R.F.C.) 27 MARCH 1918 AVELUY
Lt. H. W. RANSOM (KILLED)

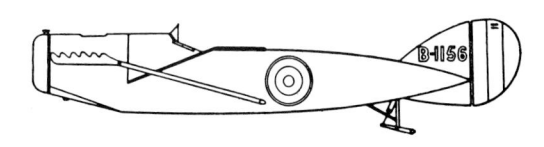

No. 72 BRISTOL F2B (No. 20 SQN. R.F.C.) 27 MARCH 1918 FOUCAUCOURT
Capt. K. R. KIRKHAM (P.O.W.), Capt. J. H. HEDLEY (P.O.W.)

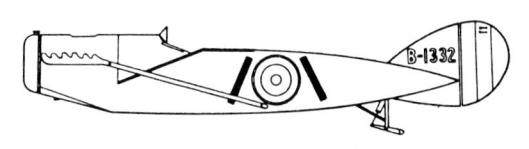

No. 73 BRISTOL F2B (No. 11 SQN. R.F.C.) 27 MARCH 1918 CHUIGNOLLES
Capt. H. R. CHILD (KILLED)

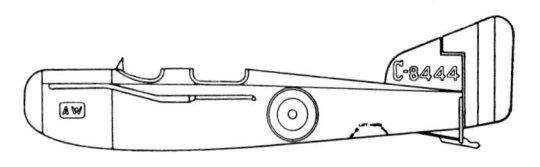

No. 74 A.W.F.K.8 (No. 82 SQN. R.F.C.) 28 MARCH 1918 MERICOURT
2nd/Lt. J. B. TAYLOR (KILLED), 2nd/Lt. E. BETLEY (KILLED)

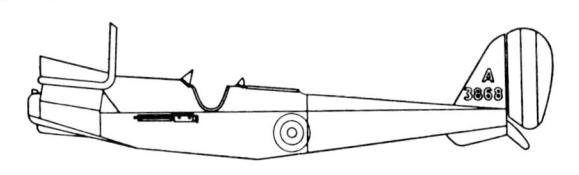

No. 75 R.E.8 (No. 52 SQN. R.A.F.) 2 APRIL 1918 MOREUIL
2nd/Lt. E. D. JONES (KILLED), 2nd/Lt. R. F. NEWTON (KILLED)

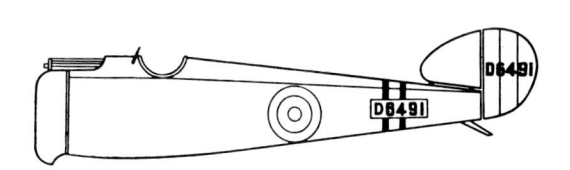

No. 76 SOPWITH CAMEL (No. 46 SQN. R.A.F.) 6 APRIL 1918 VILLERS-BRETONNEUX
Capt. S. P. SMITH (KILLED)

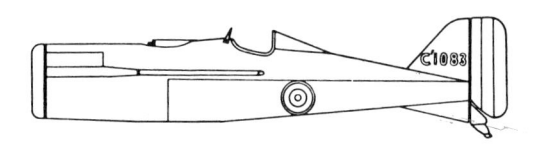

No. 77 S.E.5A (No. 1 SQN. R.A.F.) 7 APRIL 1918 HANGARD
Capt. G. B. MOORE (KILLED)

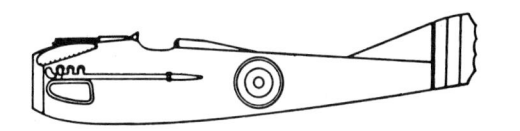

No. 78 SPAD S.7 (R.A.F.) 7 APRIL 1918 VILLERS-BRETONNEUX
NO RECORD

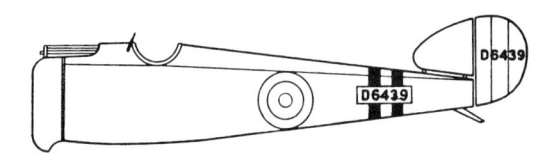

No. 79 SOPWITH CAMEL (No. 3 SQN. R.A.F.) 20 APRIL 1918 BOIS-DE-HAMEL
Major R. RAYMOND-BARKER, M.C. (KILLED)

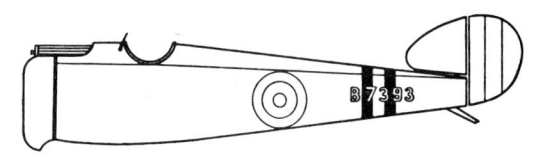

No. 80 SOPWITH CAMEL (No. 3 SQN. R.A.F.) 20 APRIL 1918 VILLERS-BRETONNEUX
2nd Lt. D. G. LEWIS (P.O.W. WOUNDED)

ALBATROS C I GENERAL

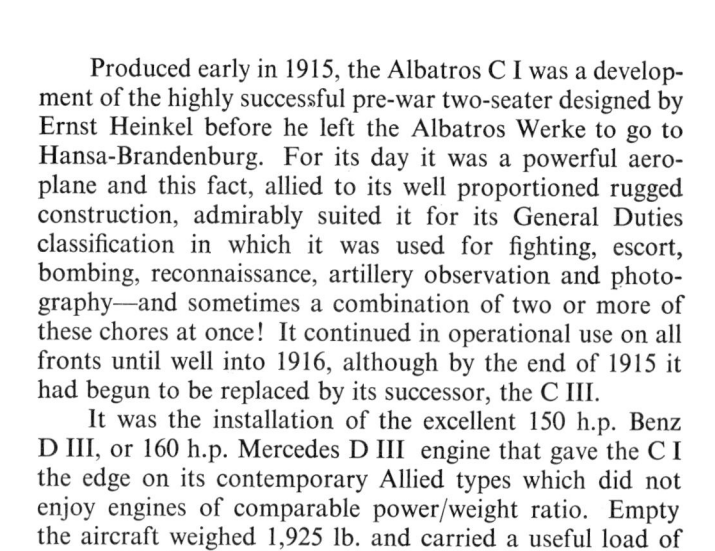

Produced early in 1915, the Albatros C I was a development of the highly successful pre-war two-seater designed by Ernst Heinkel before he left the Albatros Werke to go to Hansa-Brandenburg. For its day it was a powerful aeroplane and this fact, allied to its well proportioned rugged construction, admirably suited it for its General Duties classification in which it was used for fighting, escort, bombing, reconnaissance, artillery observation and photography—and sometimes a combination of two or more of these chores at once! It continued in operational use on all fronts until well into 1916, although by the end of 1915 it had begun to be replaced by its successor, the C III.

It was the installation of the excellent 150 h.p. Benz D III, or 160 h.p. Mercedes D III engine that gave the C I the edge on its contemporary Allied types which did not enjoy engines of comparable power/weight ratio. Empty the aircraft weighed 1,925 lb. and carried a useful load of some 639 lb. Performance figures with the 160 h.p. Mercedes were as follows: maximum speed, $82\frac{1}{2}$ m.p.h. and climb, 3,280 ft. in $9\frac{3}{4}$ mins., 6,560 ft. in 25 mins., 9,840 ft. in $58\frac{1}{2}$ mins. with a ceiling of approximately 10,000 ft. Tankage of 150 litres gave an endurance of about two hours.

Armament consisted of a free moving Parabellum machine gun, on a rotating ring mount in the rear cockpit. Storage space for a small bomb load was provided in cylindrical containers fixed on the C/G between the two cockpits. No forward firing armament was provided at this juncture, as no synchronising gear had yet been devised.

Although quite orthodox in appearance the Albatros C I did have one or two unique features. The wings, however, were a fairly normal two-bay structure built up on two wooden main spars, the forward spar being in very close proximity to the leading-edge and the rear spar at mid-chord. This resulted in an extremely flexible trailing-edge which added considerably to lateral stability. Ribs were of spruce ply and the whole wing structure fabric covered; the trailing-edge was of wire which resulted in the distinctive scalloped appearance associated with so many German aircraft. Ailerons were of steel tube construction, of inverse taper, and operated via cables through the lower wing. The centre-section cut-out was of vee-shape with slightly curved sides and extended forward to the rear spar. Both interplane, and centre-section trestle struts, were of streamlined steel tube and braced with stranded cable. Stagger and sweep were both nil, dihedral was in the nature of 4 deg. and incidence 4.8 deg.

One of the unique features of this machine was the plywood covered fuselage. Built on a foundation of six longerons (two ash and four spruce) and sturdy ply formers, no internal wire bracing was needed and an extremely rugged structure resulted. Apart from a slightly rounded decking aft of the rear cockpit the fuselage was quite

C I's; with Ia, distinguished by centre-section radiator, at top and bottom of column. All are 160 h.p. Mercedes version except penultimate photo which has 150 h.p. Benz (push-rods identify). The variety in exhaust manifolds is of interest.

PURPOSE TWO-SEATER

'slab sided' and tapered to a vertical knife-edge at the rear. The extremely angular tail surfaces were of considerable area and made for great stability. All the fixed surfaces were of triangular profile while the outline of the control surfaces was approximately trapezoidal. The fabric covered empennage was completely constructed of steel tube and of 'flat plate' section. Pilot's controls consisted of a normal rudder-bar and a wheel type control column for aileron and elevator control. Throttle was conveniently situated to the left hand and in the event of any failure in the linkage to the engine, the motor automatically went to full throttle and did not stop as was the arrangement on Allied types. Instruments fitted included revolution counter, altimeter, fuel pressure gauges, fuel pressure pump, magneto switches, temperature gauge, etc. Air speed indicators were not usually fitted in the cockpit of any German aircraft; but when carried they were of the anemometer type, and clamped to a strut easily visible to the pilot. A compass was usually slung in the apex of the centre-section trestle or in the lower wing root.

There was nothing exceptional about the undercarriage which was of normal steel tube vee-type, the axle being sprung with elastic cord. The ash tail skid was likewise sprung with this cord.

On the earlier C Is the exhaust was ejected from the cylinders into a tapering expansion chamber on the starboard side and from thence was ducted away aft in a long exhaust pipe extending to the rear cockpit. Later machines had the more familiar collector manifold exhausting over the top wing from a single, near vertical, 'chimney' pipe. Radiators of the Hazlet type were mounted on the fuselage sides. These were built up in sections which had the advantage that by adding, or taking away a section a different size engine or varying climatic conditions could be suited.

Due to the period of usage the majority of Albatros C Is were of natural linen fabric—doped and varnished—finish with cross patée in the usual locations.

Apart from the later C III, the C I was probably the most extensively built Albatros C type. It equipped, either partially or completely, practically all operational flying units during 1915. It undoubtedly served as one of Manfred von Richthofen's mounts when he was flying on the Russian front. It also served on the Austro-Hungarian front and this model was usually fitted with the Austrian 150 h.p. Rapp engine. Latterly the side radiators were dispensed with and a centre-section radiator, similar to that of the C III, was fitted, when the aircraft was known as the C Ia. Subcontractors of the C I or Ia were L. F. G. Roland and Mercur Flugzeugwerke.

B. F. W. Flugzeug, Munich, also produced a version of the Ia powered with a 180 h.p. Argus As III engine.

More C Ia's. Centre, shows an aircraft still flying in 1936 with current registration; seen at bottom is L.F.G. built machine. Top is same aircraft as shown opposite. 2nd and 4th are C I's, with Mercedes and Benz engines respectively.

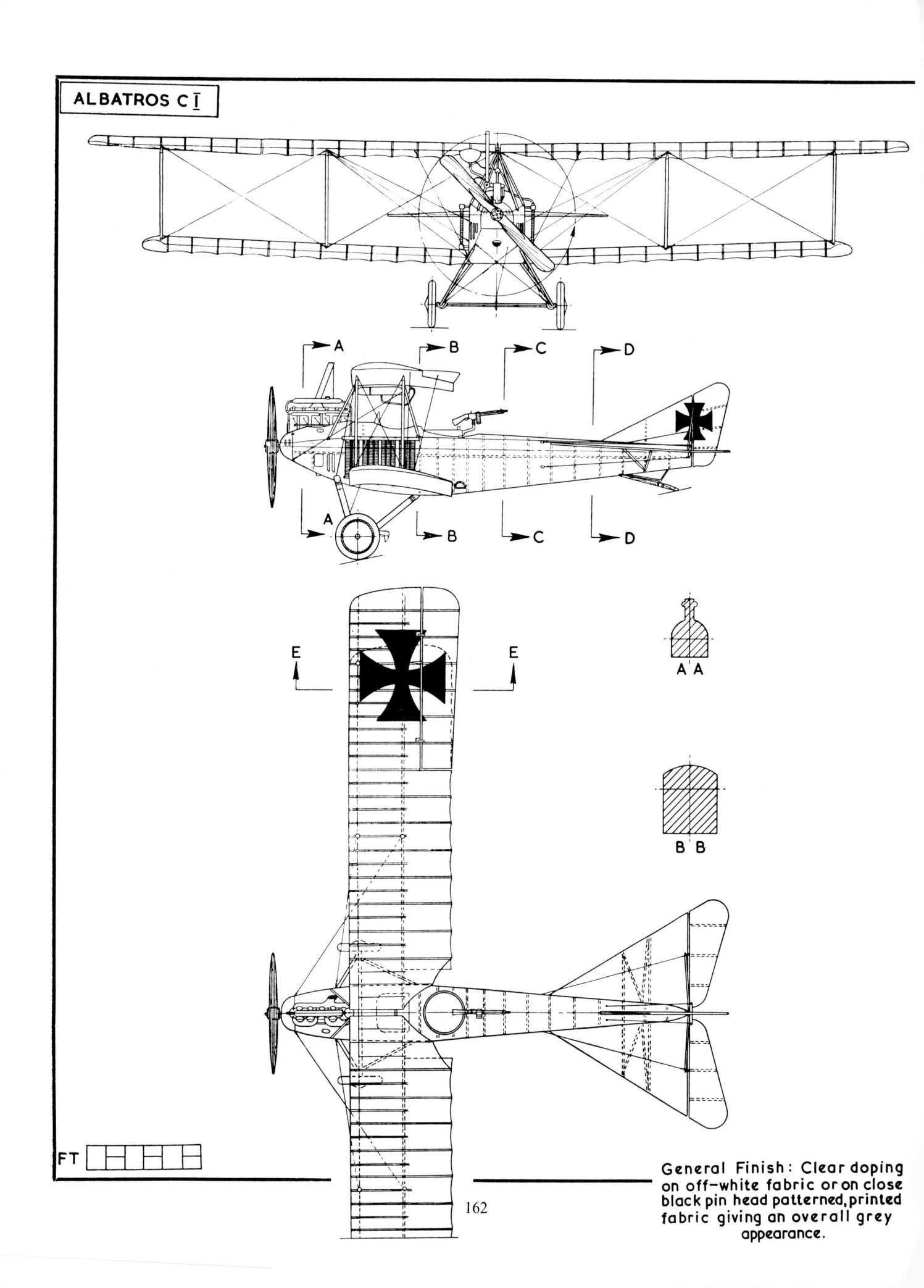

ALBATROS C I

General Finish: Clear doping on off-white fabric or on close black pin head patterned, printed fabric giving an overall grey appearance.

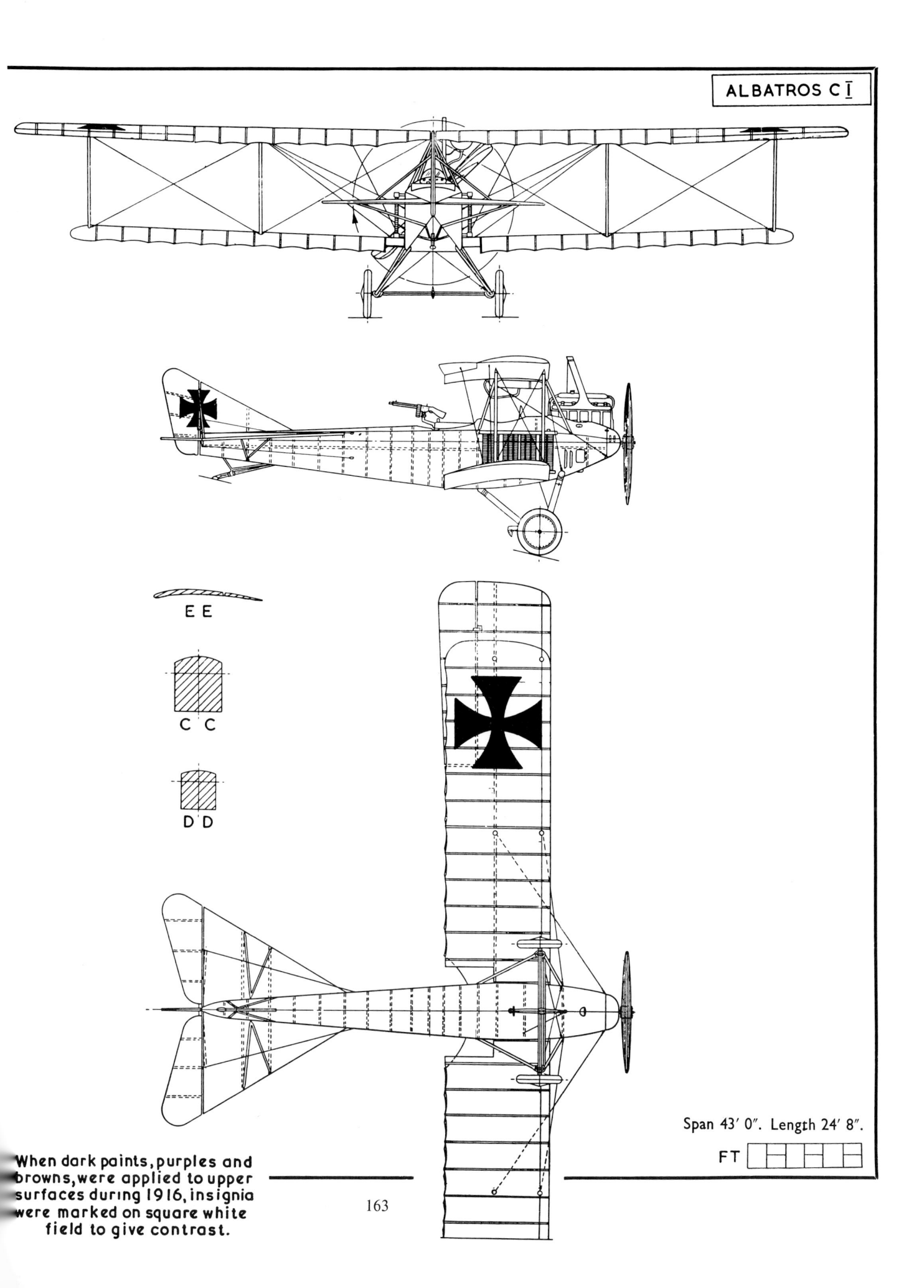

ALBATROS C I

E E

C C

D D

Span 43' 0". Length 24' 8".

When dark paints, purples and browns, were applied to upper surfaces during 1916, insignia were marked on square white field to give contrast.

ALBATROS C III GENERAL

The Albatros C III was built by a number of firms under licence. Examples of these are shown on these two pages.
Top. A captured C III in Italian hands. Second left and bottom photographs show standard models of the C III built by the parent company, and having the 160 h.p. Mercedes engine. The photograph in between them is of the Hansa-built version and shows the main difference to be in the exhaust layout.

A product of Thelen and Schubert, the Albatros design team, the C III was, in fact, the second of the orthodox tractor biplane two-seaters in this company's line of 'C' class products. The C II, incidentally, was a somewhat unique experiment into the realms of 'pusher' aircraft, being a two-seater somewhat on the lines of the British F.E. pattern.

The C III was intended for reconnaissance, photography, bombing and artillery-observation duties and became a widely used type for these chores during the period of its operational use from late 1915 to early 1917.

Introduction of the Albatros C V plus competition from other makers' designs, such as Rumpler, brought its career on the Western Front to an end resulting in retirement to do valuable work in other theatres of war—Italy and the Middle East—and on training duties in Germany. In postwar years some examples remained in use in the Polish Air Force. The Albatros C III was of conventional design being a two-bay tractor biplane with pilot and observer/gunner. The engine was normally a 160 h.p. Mercedes D III but in some models this was replaced by a 150 h.p. Benz III engine. The weight empty was 1,928 lb. and loaded 3,044 lb. and in this condition the maximum speed was about 85 m.p.h. The climb was as follows: 9 minutes to 3,280 ft.; 22 mins. to 6,560 ft.; 40 mins. to 9,840 ft.; and the service ceiling was 12,000 ft. The normal tankage of 57 gallons gave an endurance of $4-4\frac{1}{4}$ hours.

Armament was initially limited to one free Parabellum machine-gun mounted on the standard gun ring of the rear cockpit but in the later models this was augmented by a synchronised Spandau gun situated on the cowling to starboard of the engine and fired by the pilot. A small bomb load could be carried and storage for these was provided in cylindrical chutes in the rear cockpit.

The Albatros C III in general appearance followed the usual German two-seater layout, having no really outstanding characteristics. The wings, of which the top one had slight overhang, were constructed of wooden spars and ribs covered with canvas. There were two spars with alternate ribs extending to the trailing-edge or the rear spar which was situated approximately at the half-chord position. Ailerons, which were not of constant chord, were fitted to the top wing only and were cable-operated. A semi-circular cut-out was situated in the trailing edge of the top wing above the gunner's cockpit.

The interplane struts were of streamlined steel tube as were those of the trestle type centre-section. Dihedral was 2 deg. but there was neither stagger nor sweepback.

The fuselage was a strong, three-ply covered box-like construction which had no wire bracing, as was common practice in other designs of the time, and only the curved top coaming of the rear fuselage showed any attempt to

PURPOSE TWO-SEATER

Top. Another photograph of a standard C III built by the parent company. Note the absence of tips to the propeller blades! The second photograph shows the model built by L.V.G. with a new fin and rudder design.
In photographs 3 and 4 are seen the C III versions built by the Linke-Hofmann and D.F.W. companies respectively. In the case of the latter another change in the fin and rudder layout is evident.

relieve the slab-sided appearance as a whole. The fuselage terminated in a horizontal knife-edge, coincident with the hinge-line of the separate elevators. The tail unit shows a neat and unbalanced rudder with triangular fin and a lower and, in area, much smaller fin below the fuselage. A tail plane of deep chord and considerable area was used. The pilot's cockpit was equipped with stick and wheel type elevator and aileron controls with the usual rudder-bar and below the seat was situated the main fuel tank. Instruments included compass—usually inset in the lower wing adjacent to the pilot's cockpit, fuel pressure and temperature gauges, tachometer, altimeter and magneto switches. Fittings for W.T. and photographic equipment, when required to be carried, were included in the rear cockpit.

The undercarriage was of the customary two-wheel type, the legs being of streamlined steel tubing and the axle being 'bound in' with rubber cords at either end. Attached to the axle in some models was a claw brake, situated in the centre and operated by cable from a lever in the cockpit. The tail-skid was of metal-shod wood pivoted at the apex of four short steel struts.

The engine was enclosed by metal cowlings in an efficient if not highly streamlined manner which left the greater part of the cylinders exposed. Although the exhaust stack was generally of the type illustrated in the G.A. of this aircraft certain variations in the arrangement of the six exhaust pipes proper may be noted in photos of some licence-built C III aircraft, and in the case of the Benz engined model the whole exhaust assembly was on the port side of the engine and consisted of a comparatively large chamber extending the length of the cylinders with the 'horn' at the forward end. The radiator was rectangular in front elevation and a parallelogram in section with a prominent feed pipe looping forwards and downwards towards the leading cylinder. In characteristic German fashion the radiator was mounted against the leading edge, and in the centre of, the top wing, being supported on the front centre-section struts by two brackets.

Since the Albatros C III was in use at the time which spanned the introduction of camouflage on German aircraft examples of both the plain varnish finish of the earlier types and the dark colourings of the later aircraft may be encountered. The camouflage colouring usually took the form of a combination of dark green and purple on the side and top surfaces while the underside of wings and belly was painted in a light tint, often a pale blue.

The cross patée appeared on the top and bottom wing-tips and both sides of rudder and fuselage. Except in the case of all white aircraft this cross, which was in black, was outlined in white or appeared on a square white panel.

Exact production figures for the C III are not available, but it was undoubtedly built in considerable numbers not only by Albatros Werke but also under licence by Linke-Hofmann (who built the Benz engined version), D.F.W., constructors of a trainer version with dual control, Siemens-Schuckert and Hanseatische Flugzeugwerke ('Hansa') who alone are said to have produced about 150 of the type.

ALBATROS C III

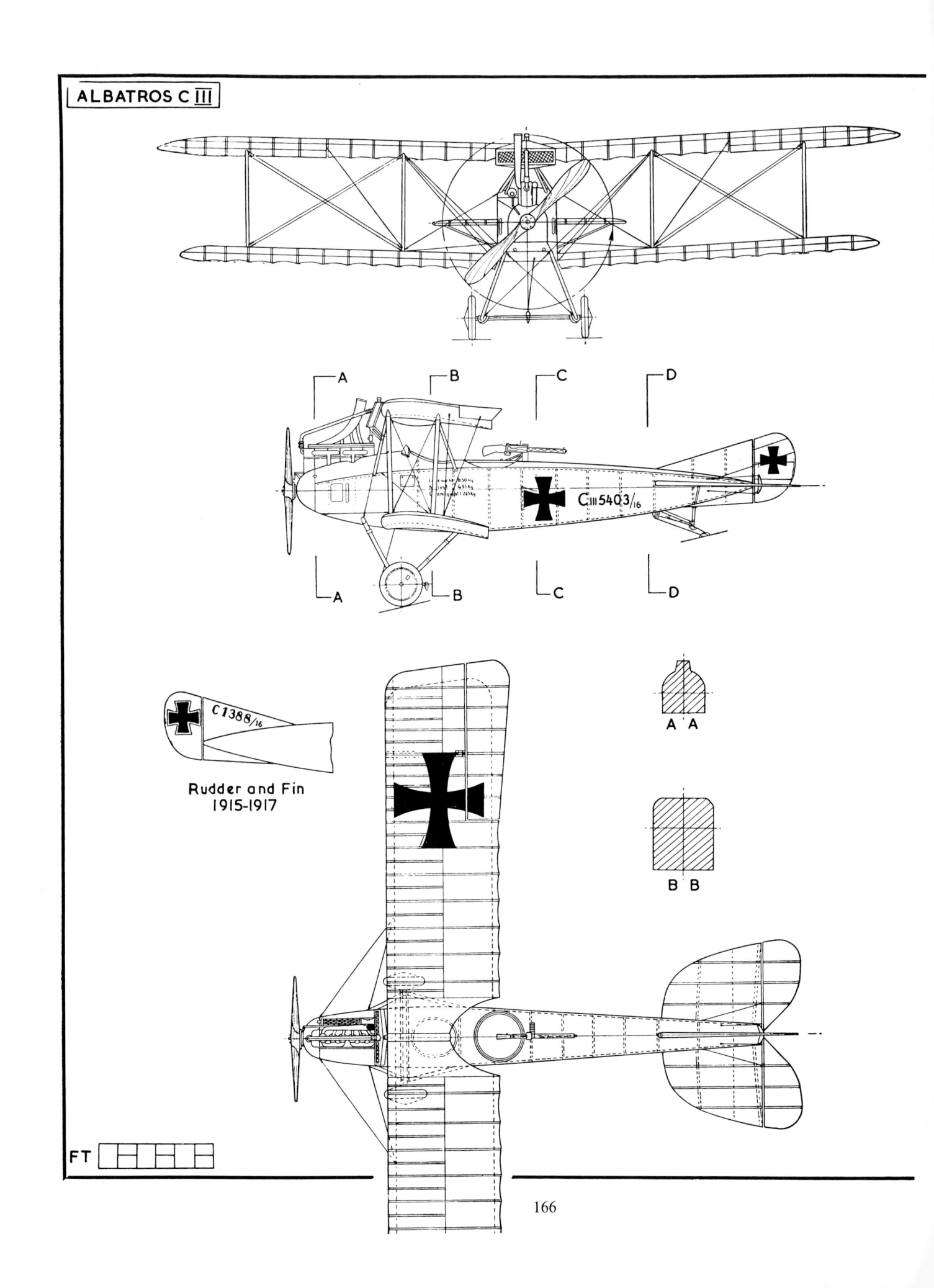

Rudder and Fin
1915-1917

FT

166

ALBATROS C III

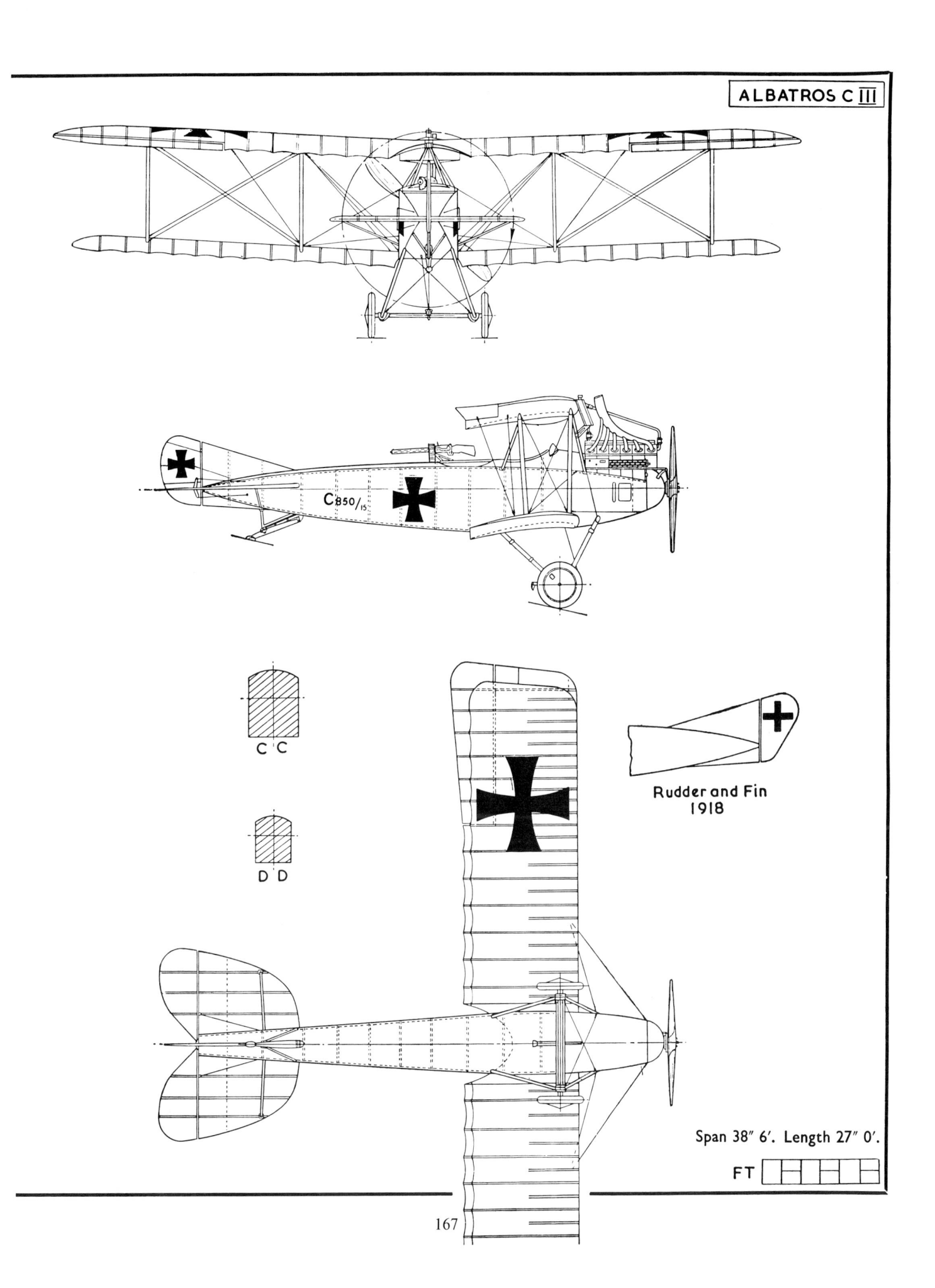

Rudder and Fin 1918

Span 38" 6'. Length 27" 0'.

ALBATROS D II

Pilots of Albatros D IIs preparing for a take-off. In this case the unit is Jagdstaffel 9.

In August of 1916 the Albatros company produced a biplane scout known in the company as the L 15 and officially designated the D I. With the 160 h.p. Mercedes engine it soon became an obvious choice for the *Jagdstaffeln* then being formed into organised fighting units, and together with its successor the D II and the Halberstadt scouts, formed the equipment of these units when they commenced their large-scale operations against the British and French squadrons and which were to reach their climax in the infamous 'Bloody April' of 1917.

After the success of the intitial model, the D I, production was settled on the D II (L 17) which differed chiefly in a change of centre section strut arrangement. The D II, equipped with the 160 h.p. Mercedes, weighed 1,485 lb. empty and carried a load of 300 lb. at a maximum speed of 110 m.p.h. It climbed to 3,280 feet in 3 minutes, 6,560 feet in $5\frac{1}{2}$ minutes, 9,840 feet in $9\frac{1}{2}$ minutes and the ceiling was in the region of 17,000 feet.

The armament was the standard twin synchronised Spandau machine-guns.

The wings of the D II were of orthodox appearance and construction; they consisted of a one-piece top plane with two rectangular-sectioned wooden spars and ribs spaced $16\frac{1}{4}$ inches apart. False ribs in the upper leading edges gave added strength. The ailerons, of which there were two, were hinged on auxiliary spars and fitted on the top wing only. These were operated by cables and cranks inset in the wing. A semi-circular cut-out in the trailing edge improved the view forwards and upwards. The lower wing was in two parts and fixed by quick-release pins, within the wings, to abutments on each side of the fuselage. Internally and externally the wings were wire-braced and fabric covered.

The interplane and centre-section struts were of streamlined steel tubing, the former consisting of one pair of parallel struts on each side while those of the centre-section were in the form of an 'N', to become familiar on the later Albatros types. This latter strut system was a change from the original trestle type centre-section used on the D I and was the chief visible difference between the two types. Incidentally, the trestle system was popular amongst German aircraft designers of the time and consisted of two inverted V's joined by a cross-piece running fore and aft between their apices and to which the top wing was attached along its centre-line. In the case of the D I, a slot in each end of this horizontal member of the cabane permitted an adjustment of stagger to be made from 0 to 12 cm. Eyebolts, protruding below the main spars and into the slots, were locked by means of a bolt passing through one of five holes in each side of the slot, the selected hole giving the desired amount of stagger. In the fuselages of the D I and D II is seen the high degree of streamlining obtained by the Albatros designers in their scout aircraft. This was the result of the semi-monocoque type of construction employed and in view of the importance of, and interest in, the introduction of this type of fuselage a somewhat more detailed description of its constructional features is given. Six longerons were used, three to each side, those in the centre being of a rectangular section and of spruce. The top and bottom longerons were also of spruce and, except at their junction with the formers, of 'L' section. Beyond the cockpit, however, ash was the

In this late model of the Albatros D II captured by the French, it will be noted that the radiator is inset in the top wing.

168

SINGLE-SEAT SCOUT

The earlier model D II with the radiators situated below the centre-section struts.

material used. Whereas the top and middle longerons were situated one above the other those on the bottom were rather closer together. Ribs, or formers, ⅗ in. thick and ¾ in. deep, and reinforced in the vicinity of the longerons, were spaced approximately two feet apart. The engine bearers were carried on four three-ply formers in the section forward of the cockpit. The overall three-ply covering of the fuselage was then tacked and screwed over the framework thus formed. No internal bracing by wires or struts was necessary in this strong yet simple structure. In section the fuselage ranged from circular at the nose to a horizontal knife-edge at the tail, with rounded top and bottom and flat sides in the centre portion. The smooth lines were augmented at the nose by the addition of a large spinner over the propeller boss.

In the tail unit the upper and lower fins were of three-ply covering over a wooden framework, the lower one being formed by the supports of the tail-skid. The unbraced tailplane, which had a wooden frame, was, like the steel tube framed elevator and rudder, fabric covered. These last two controls were balanced.

The Mercedes engine was cowled in the usual neat manner of Albatros scouts with the exhaust pipe above and to starboard of the fuselage. In the D I and the earlier models of the D II the radiator system consisted of two box-like structures of the honeycomb type which protruded from each side of the fuselage above the lower wing. On the later models, however, a radiator was installed, inset, in the top wing. Unconfirmed reports designate this aircraft as the D IIA when thus equipped. The undercarriage was of normal V type, having the rear struts braced by cables, the axle being sprung with interlaced rubber cord. An interesting feature of the undercarriage struts was the method of attachment to the fuselage. This was done by means of sockets into which the legs fitted and by tightening one screw in each socket the legs could then be locked in position.

In addition to the usual instruments the cockpit had a rather unique control column of steel tube with the double grip handle at its top and inside of which were the two triggers connected to the guns by Bowden cables. The interesting feature incorporated in this control was the device by means of which the pilot could lock the stick against fore and aft movement, thus leaving both hands free, the aileron control being operated by his knees!

The colour schemes of the Albatros D I and earlier D II were influenced by the camouflage system being introduced into use by the Germans in 1916. This consisted of large irregular areas of green, mauve and/or brown on the upper and vertical surfaces with light blue or similar tints below. Prior to service use—or if no camouflage was applied—the plywood fuselage was left in its normal varnish finish resulting in a yellowish or straw appearance. The national marking of the period was the cross patée and this was applied to the top and bottom wing tips, fuselage and rudder sides. It was in black on a white square background or outlined in white. The serial number, and sometimes the abbreviation of the parent company's name, was usually painted on both sides of the rear fuselage or fin in either black or white. Personal and unit insignia were to be seen on the D II on occasions (see illustration) but not with any frequency.

The prototype Albatros D II, seen here without machine-guns, displays little, if any difference from the production model seen above.

169

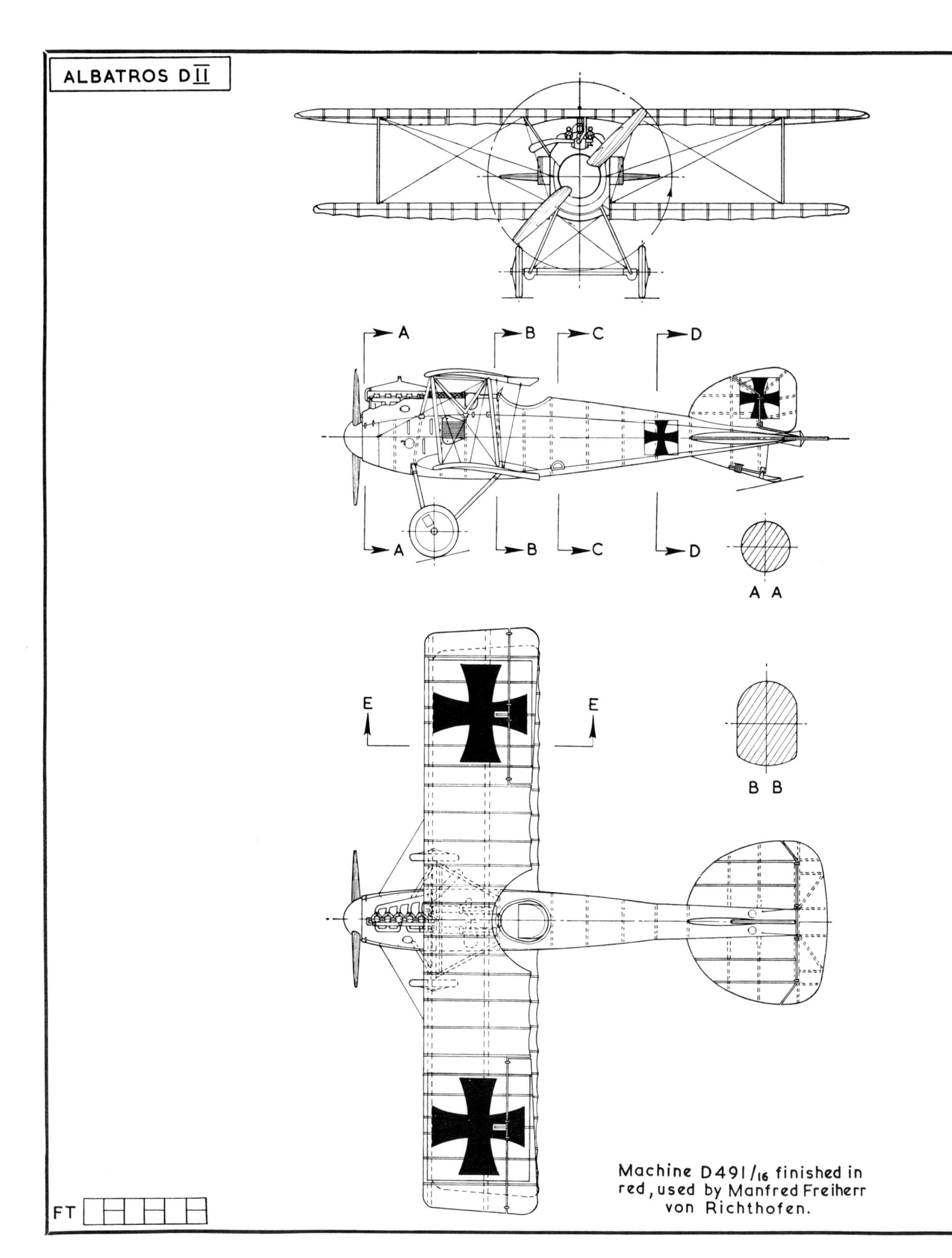

ALBATROS D II

Machine D491/16 finished in red, used by Manfred Freiherr von Richthofen.

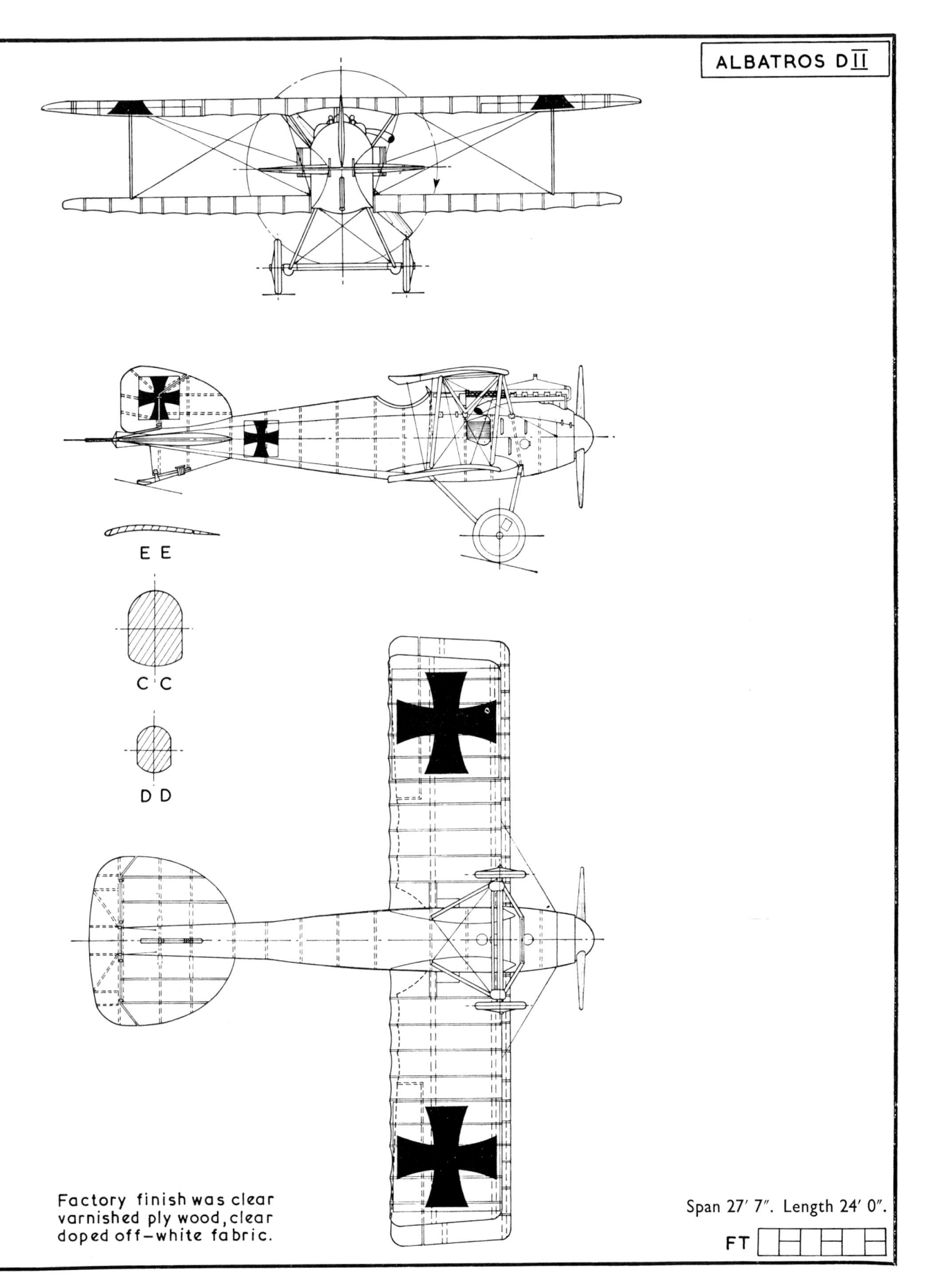

ALBATROS D II

E E

C C

D D

Factory finish was clear varnished plywood, clear doped off-white fabric.

Span 27' 7". Length 24' 0".

FT

ALBATROS D III

Left: This D III was used late in the war and probably for familiarization purposes. Note the absence of guns and the strengthening struts on the lower wing leading edge. At bottom left, is a captured D III in Allied colours and on the right one is seen in its more natural surroundings—a German aerodrome.

With the success assured of the Albatros D I and D II, in the *Staffeln*, by the end of 1916, Thelen, the Albatros company designer, produced a new model, the L 20, which was accepted for service use when it was given the type designation D III. It was very similar in many respects to the two earlier scouts from the same company but had one important difference. This was the introduction of a new wing layout with the 'V' type interplane struts in place of the more commonly used parallel type. Coming into service at the end of 1916, the D III eventually became the principal scout type in use and continued to hold this position until about mid-summer of 1917. It enabled its pilots to gain superiority for the German scout *Staffeln* and at the same time build up considerable individual scores. The D III played an important part in the history of scout flying as it operated at a time when formations of large numbers of aircraft were, for the first time, being used in combat. By the end of the summer of 1917 it had been replaced in France by the Albatros D V and Va types in front-line service, but continued in action on the Italian and Middle East fronts for some time after this period. The famous 160 h.p. Mercedes was the engine chosen for the D III and this was installed in a well-streamlined nose after the manner of the D II, with the exhaust carried away by a single pipe down the starboard side. With this power unit the maximum speed was 105 m.p.h. It climbed to 3,280 feet in $3\frac{1}{2}$ minutes; 6,560 feet in $7\frac{1}{4}$ minutes; 9,840 feet in 12 minutes; and 13,120 feet in $18\frac{3}{4}$ minutes. The weight loaded was 1,949 lb. and empty 1,454 lb. With twenty-two gallons of fuel the endurance was two hours. The armament consisted of the standard twin synchronised Spandau machine-guns in the cowling ahead of the cockpit. The wings of the D III showed a radical change from that of the D II, being of the sesquiplane type which for some years past had been the chief characteristic of the Nieuport products. The top plane retained the two spars of the earlier D I and D II but only one was used in the narrow chord lower wing. Another feature introduced in the D III wings was the considerable sweep-back on all four wing-tips in place of the more square-cut shape used hitherto. The construction of the wings was of spruce spars and plywood ribs with a covering of fabric and the usual wire trailing-edge. Ailerons were fitted in the top wing only and were cable-operated and of unequal chord. They were of a light steel tube framework covered with fabric. A fairly large semi-circular cut-out above the cockpit gave improved vision forward and upwards. Inset and positioned about the centre line of the top wing, was the radiator. The interplane struts—for the first time in what was to become the familiar 'V' shape—and those of the centre section, which were splayed outwards were of streamlined steel tubing.

The construction of the D III fuselage closely followed that of the D II being of a semi-monocoque type. The

172

S/SEAT SCOUT

Right: The high degree of streamlining of the D III is apparent in this photo.
Bottom, left: Shows the version built by the Austrian branch of the Albatros company, O.A.W. The spinner has been eliminated without destroying streamlined effect. Bottom right: A rare photograph of a D III in flight.

framework, over which a complete covering of three-ply was tacked and screwed, consisted of formers at approximately two-foot intervals and six longerons, mainly of spruce but of ash in the nose section. The positions of these longerons resulted in fuselage cross-sections varying from circular in the nose to slab-sided with curved top and bottom at the mid-way position and a horizontal knife edge in the extreme tail. The vertical fin was built as part of the fuselage and had a three-ply covering over its wooden frame while the covering-in of the tail-skid supports with the same material completed the lower fin.

Fabric covering was used in all the tail components but the framework of the tailplane was of wood in place of the steel tube used in the one-piece elevator and the rudder with straight trailing edge, both of which were balanced and cable-operated. Streamlined steel tube in the standard 'V' pattern formed the undercarriage with the axle sprung by rubber cord at the extremities. The cockpit had the following instruments: altimeter, air-pressure gauge, tachometer, compass, and throttle in addition to the usual rudder bar and a control column of the type used in the D II complete with double gun triggers and the unique elevator locking system.

The ultimate results of the practice of painting-up scout aircraft in the many varied styles became apparent about the time of the introduction of the Albatros D III into general use. On leaving the factory, the standard lozenge-patterned fabric of indigo, blue, green and violet was used on the wings and tail plane surfaces, the fuselage being left in the natural varnished wood tint of straw. These colours were invariably over-painted by the unit and the pilot to whom the aircraft was allotted and it appeared in almost any combination of colours and designs. The only uniformity was found in certain *Staffeln*, such as the four led by von Richthofen, when a basic background colour was adhered to and individual pilots added distinctive markings of their own. The military designation letter, serial number and year of building appeared in either black or white lettering on both sides of the fin or rear fuselage. The national markings used on the D III were almost invariably the white outlined black cross patée, though instances of the cross without the outlining also occurred. Also, an exception in the type of cross may have been marked on D III's which had been retained in use for some non-operational purpose up to and beyond the spring of 1918. In addition to the standard model built in Germany, a version of the Albatros D III was built in Austria by the Osterreischische Flugzeugfabrik A.G. (Oeffag.) at their Wiener Neustadt works. They constructed three models having successively the 185, 200 and 225 h.p. Austro-Daimler engines in place of the Mercedes. Although in all other respects similar to the standard D III, these products had a more fully cowled engine, the cylinders being completely enclosed and six short stub exhaust pipes taking the place of the long exhaust of the original type. The performance with these more powerful engines was considerably improved, the maximum speed being increased to 106 m.p.h.

173

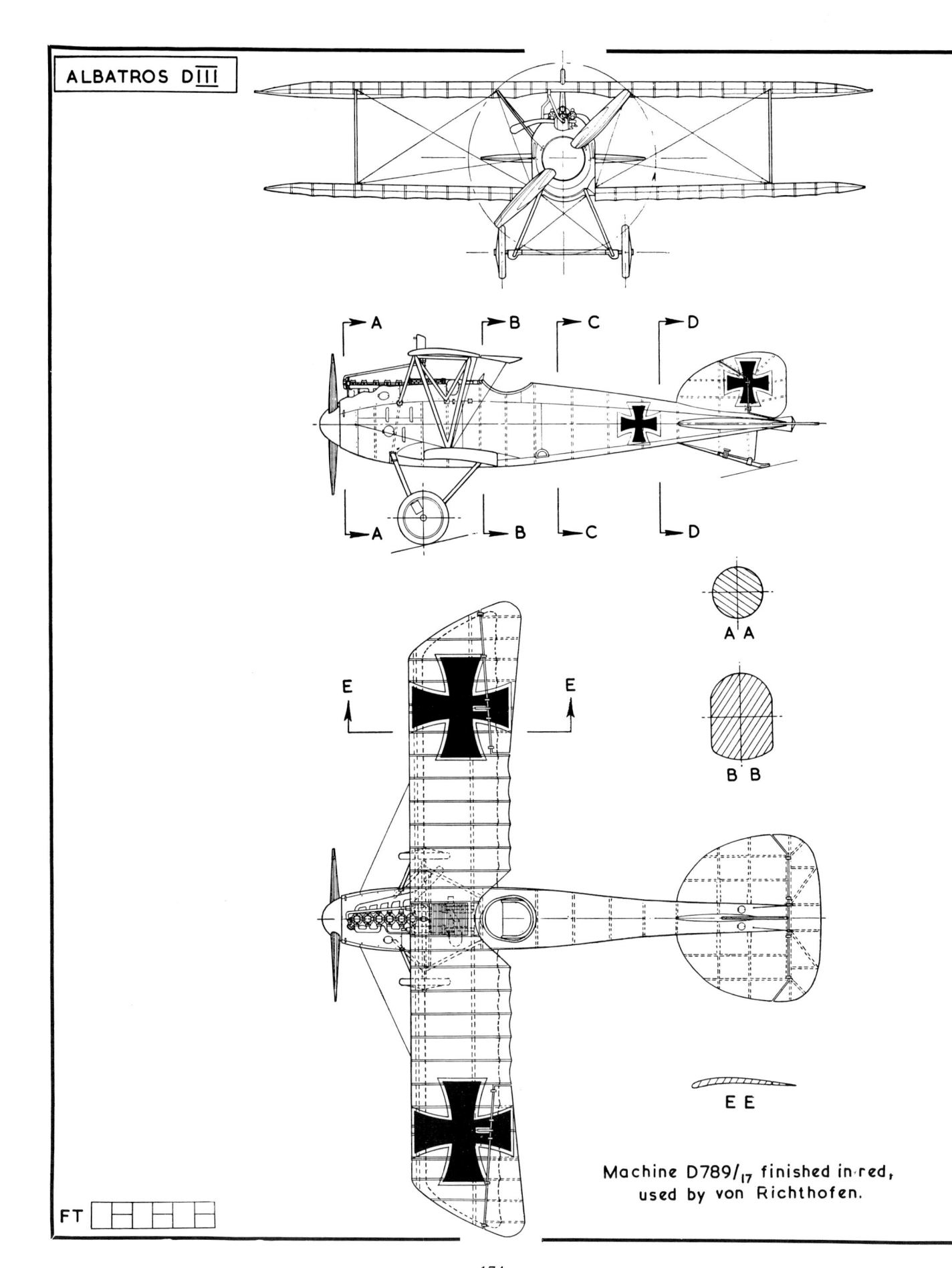

ALBATROS D III

Machine D789/17 finished in red, used by von Richthofen.

FT

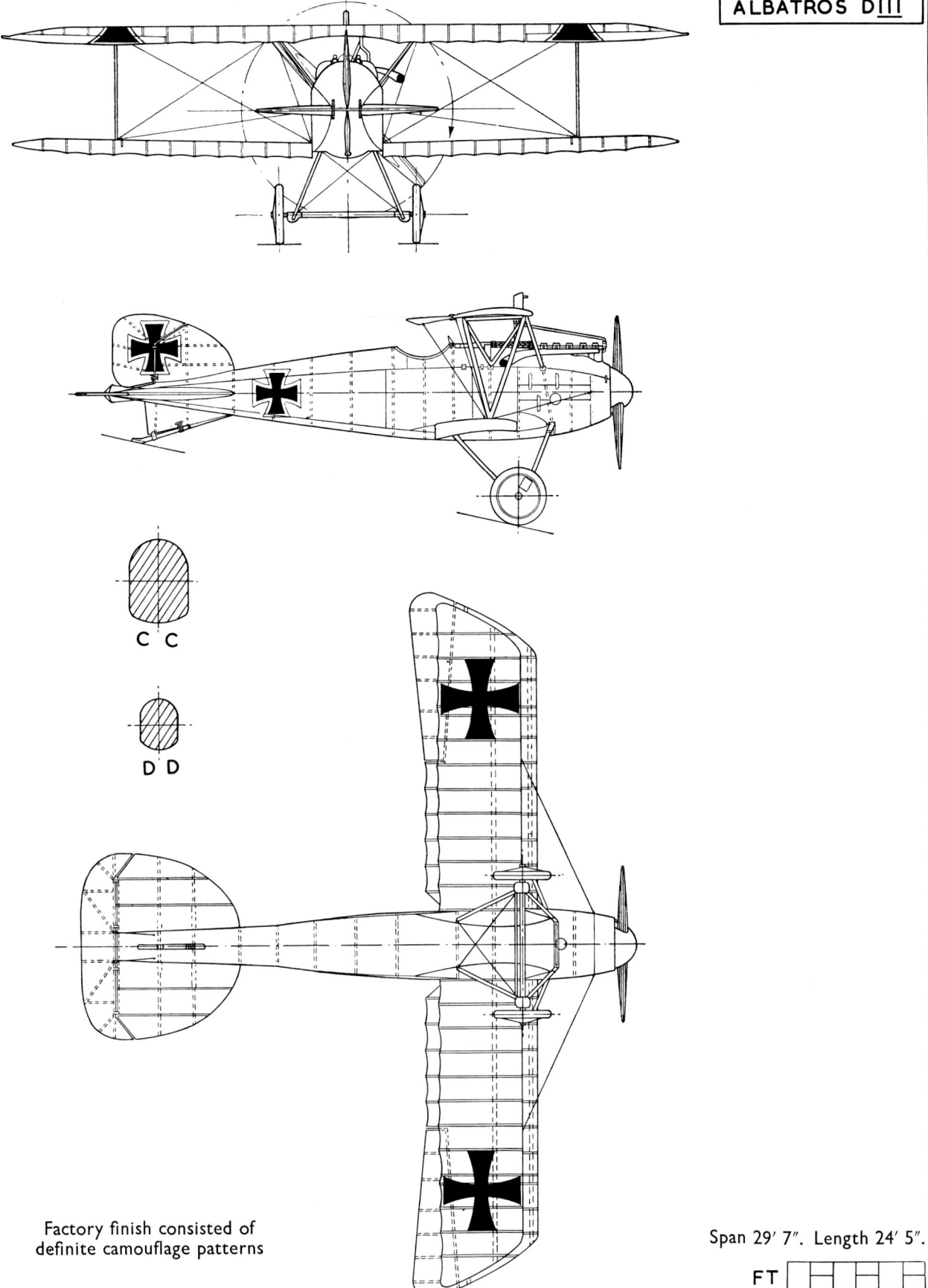

ALBATROS DIII

C C

D D

Factory finish consisted of definite camouflage patterns

Span 29' 7". Length 24' 5".

FT

ALBATROS DV/DV

Top to bottom; a captured D Va in British hands. Note the auxiliary strut on the lower wing leading edge, rounded rudder and faired axle. The second and third photos depict what is thought to be the prototype D V. At the bottom is seen a D Va built by Ostdeutsche Albatros Werke (O.A.W.) fitted with a high headrest.

In early 1917 the Albatros design team of Thelen and Schubert produced the D V scout which followed closely the layout of their previous very successful D III. In the Albatros company designation this aircraft was known as the L 30. This was applied also to the D Va due to appear in June of the same year. These two models were destined to replace the D III, then coming to the end of its service career, and to become the backbone of the German scout squadrons throughout 1917 and well into 1918. At one time both models were in use simultaneously and in some cases were to be found operating together in the same units. In this period they constituted the bulk of the scout types and were flown not only on the Western Front but also in Italy, with the Austrians, and in small numbers in the Middle East. The D V lower wing unfortunately was prone to twist about the single spar in combat manœuvres and this resulted in many cases of structural failure—one source puts the fatalities as high as twenty-three in three months—necessitating the strengthening of the lower wing by, initially, extra rigging wires and, latterly, the addition of small auxiliary struts which ran from the leading edge to the lower part of the 'V' interplane struts. This strut will be seen on photos of the modified D V and the earlier D Va models. Redesigning at this point in the later D Vas eliminated the need for the strut and the weakness appears to have been overcome as a result.

The standard engine installed in the D V/Vas was the 180 h.p. Mercedes—a 160 h.p. Mercedes with raised compression ratio—but subsequent engines tried were the 220 h.p. Mercedes and the 200 h.p. Benz. The latter was intended for high altitude operation and one set of unauthenticated performance figures quote the climb of a D Va thus equipped as being 10,000 feet in less than twelve minutes! With the 180 h.p. Mercedes the maximum speed was about 130 m.p.h. at low altitude and 100 m.p.h. at 10,000 feet. At a normally loaded weight of 2,050 lb. (1,460 lb. empty), the ceiling was 20,000 feet and the climb: 2 mins. to 2,000 feet, 4 mins. to 3,280 feet and 21 mins. to 13,000 feet. The endurance was about two hours. Conforming to the standard armament practice of the time, twin synchronised Spandau machine-guns were fitted in both models.

The upper wing of the D V/Va was in one piece and of spruce spars and plywood ribs, the covering being of fabric except for a plywood strip in the top surface, extending the full wing span and back as far as the main spar. A wire trailing edge gave the familiar scalloped effect on the top and lower wings. The unequal chord ailerons, on the top wing only, were of light steel tubing and fabric covering. Set in the top wing and to starboard of the centre-line was a Treves and Braun radiator. The single spar lower wing was generally of similar construction and until modified carried extra bracing to the top wing overhang prior to the introduction of the small strut mentioned previously. Some reports state that the designation D Va dates from the time of this extra bracing.

In the tail unit, ply covered wooden frames formed the upper and lower fins which were built as part of the fuselage,

'SEAT SCOUT

Right: Another view of the prototype D V, and below are three photos of D Vas. The first shows one under test by the French authorities. While the clear lines of the type are seen to advantage in the head-on view. At the bottom is another example of a captured D Va in British hands.

while the one piece elevator was of fabric covered steel tube as was the rudder.

The fuselage of both the D V and Va differed from that of the D III by virtue of their oval cross-section in place of the flat sided type in the earlier aircraft. The structure was of plywood panels in formers and longerons with no internal bracing, resulting in the excellent streamlined effect being obtained, characteristic of these aircraft. The engine, almost entirely enclosed in the nose section, was further covered by the use of a spinner of considerable diameter which completed the neat installation. The undercarriage of streamlined steel tubing, had an auxiliary 'wing' fairing the axle, and this is reputed to have provided sufficient lift to counteract the whole weight of this unit.

The similarity of the D V and Va has given rise to some difficulty in their identification and the following points should be noted in this connection. The trailing edge of the rudder in the former type was straight, as in the D III, while that of the D Va was rounded. The lower fin on both was taken back to the horizontal knife-edge of the fuselage whereas in the D III its vertical trailing edge was approximately below the rudder hinge-line. A headrest of normal dimensions was fitted on the D V, but on the rare occasions that one was used in the D Va, it was of an easily removable type and noteworthy for the height it rose above the cockpit. This particular type of headrest was introduced as a result of the pilot's seat being raised nine inches in the D V and Va as compared to the D III and the elevated gun sighting arrangements of the Va. Another feature, though not readily noted, was the difference in gap measurement, the Va being $1\frac{1}{2}$ inches less than the D V.

The decoration of the D V/Va types included all the usual personal and unit markings which, by the great variety of bizarre background designs, ensured the reputation of these types as being possibly the most—literally—colourful scouts used by either side during the entire war.

Basically the wings, elevators and rudder were covered with the lozenge patterned fabric of such colours as green, mauve, pink and blue, while the varnishing of the plywood areas resulted in a yellowish tint on these areas. The cross patée was almost invariably outlined by a narrow white margin and the serial number, on the fin, appeared in either black or white.

The D V/Va—last of the Albatros scouts to see active service—were flown by practically all the German aces at some time in their careers and in considerable numbers by *Jagdstaffeln* generally. The operational life of these types was about eighteen months in which time perhaps they became the best known of the scouts opposing the Allies.

After the War, the American Receiving Commission arranged for twelve D Vs and ten D Vas to be shipped to America.

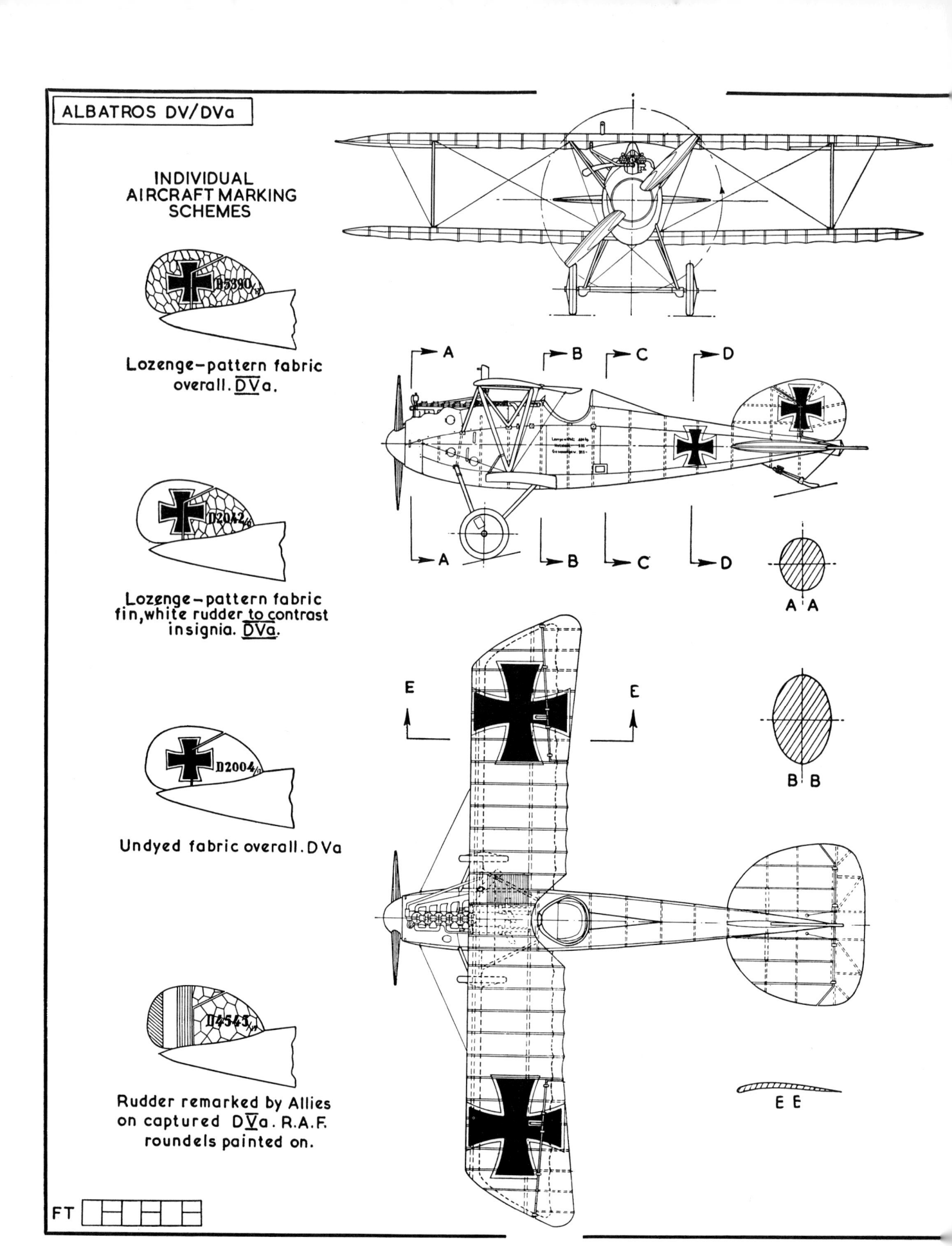

ALBATROS DV/DVa

INDIVIDUAL AIRCRAFT MARKING SCHEMES

Lozenge-pattern fabric overall. DVa.

Lozenge-pattern fabric fin, white rudder to contrast insignia. DVa.

Undyed fabric overall. DVa

Rudder remarked by Allies on captured DVa. R.A.F. roundels painted on.

FT

ALBATROS DV/DVa

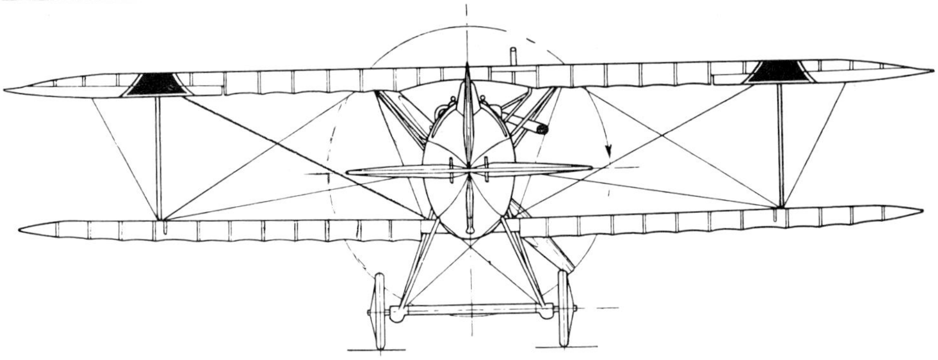

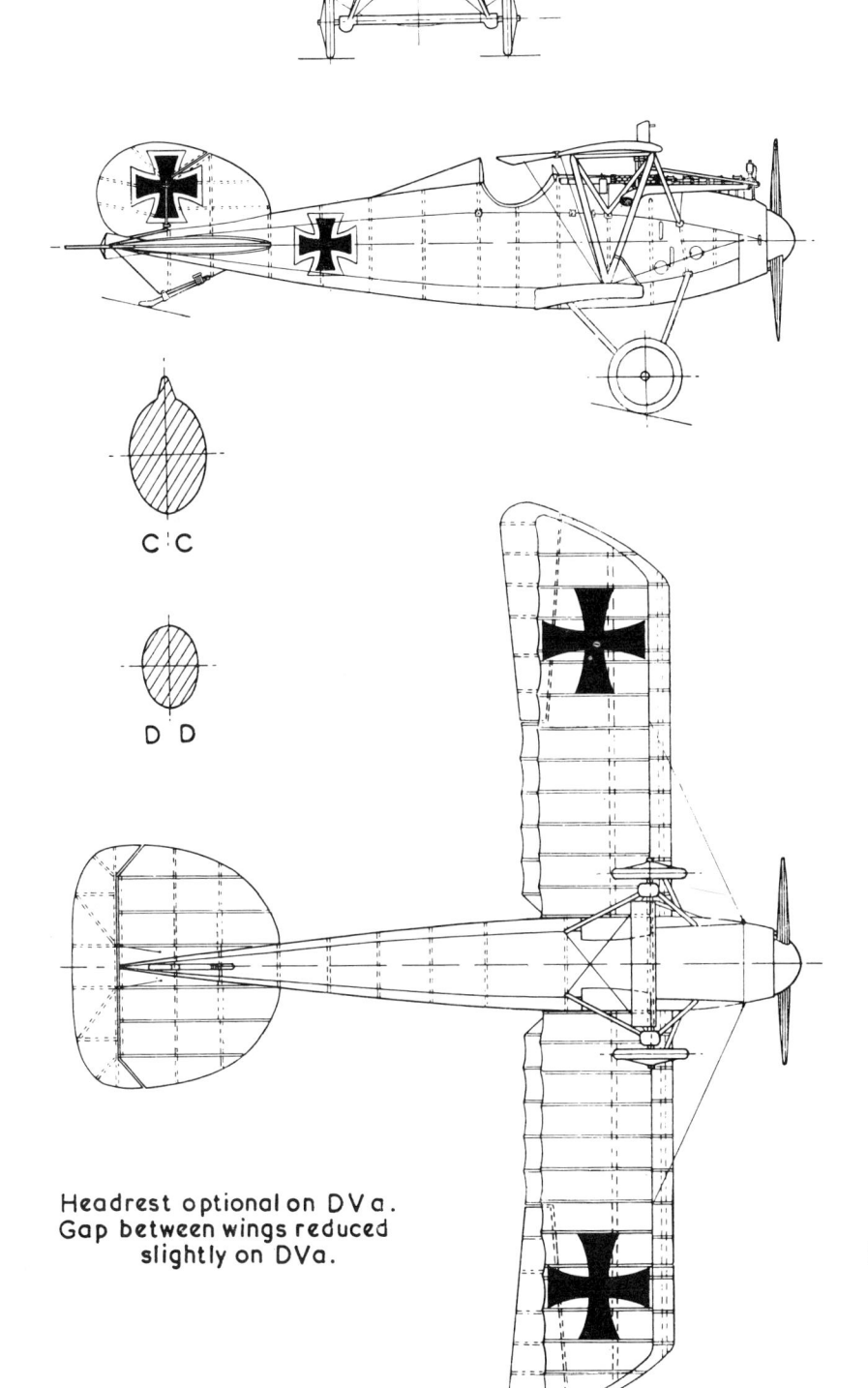

INDIVIDUAL AIRCRAFT MARKING SCHEMES

Red finish overall used by Manfred Freiherr von Richthofen D$\overline{V}$

As above D$\overline{V}$

Used by Leutnant Adam commanding Jagdstaffel Nr.6. D$\overline{V}$a

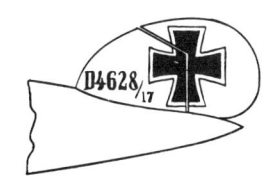

Used by Leutnant Gussmann of Jagdstaffel Nr.II. D$\overline{V}$a

Headrest optional on DVa. Gap between wings reduced slightly on DVa.

Span 29' 7". Length 24' 5".

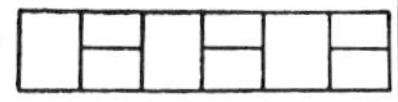

FOKKER D III

In this photo is seen an ex-operational Fokker D III which was exhibited in Germany demonstrating the type flown by Oswald Boelcke. This was an early type having wing-warping controls.

By the latter part of 1915 it was becoming obvious to the Fokker company that further development of their very successful line of monoplane fighters was not feasible and a changed layout was investigated. This resulted in the designing of a two-bay biplane type, the Fokker D I, which appeared early in 1916, and two subsequent models, to be known as D II and D III. Basically they were of similar appearance but differed in dimensions and the type of engine fitted. Kreutzer, the Fokker designer at that time, seems to have brought out the D II prior to the D I, according to the dates available for their introduction into service for it may be noted that the factory designations of M.18z and M.17z applied to the D I and D II respectively. The D II had the 100 h.p. Oberursel rotary engine whereas the stationary 120 h.p. Mercedes powered the D I. Both were built in some numbers—about twenty-five of the D I type were constructed—and both saw active service. At different times they had warp-wing control or ailerons, but their period of operation was inevitably limited due to their moderate performance and poor firepower, having only one machine-gun. The D I was the first stationary engined biplane scout to be used by Germany, but Boelcke's report that it was too stable, doubtless led to the curtailment of its construction and further use. Consequently they very soon compared unfavourably with contemporary German scouts such as the Albatros and Halberstadt types and even in the final form of this design, the D III (M.19) with the 160 h.p. Oberursel engine, the performance was insufficient to prolong its use. This power plant proved to be something of a liability, indeed, combining loss of performance at height with unreliability, and the D III, of which more were built than of the D I and D II, was unable to justify its use on front-line service relegated to other fronts or to training schools.

The two row 160 h.p. Oberursel rotary engine may be clearly seen in this D III also the Spandau machine-gun.

In a training role it was used until late 1918. As its period of service in France was mainly prior to the formation of the *Jagdstaffeln* the D III did not wholly equip any unit but like all scout types up to this time was to be found attached to what were primarily reconnaissance formations, and performed protective duties for the other aircraft doing this work. Nevertheless a number of famous pilots flew the type early in their careers, amongst the most noted being Manfred von Richthofen, and Oswald Boelcke who flew the D III while awaiting the re-equipment of his *Jagdstaffel 2* with Albatros D Is and D IIs. Other aces known to have flown the type were Ernst Udet, who survived the war with over sixty victories and Otto Kissenberth, who destroyed nineteen Allied aircraft.

The 160 h.p. Oberursel III engine which powered the Fokker D III was a twin-row, fourteen-cylinder rotary which had also been installed in the last of the monoplane types, the E IV, in late 1915. At this early date criticism had been levelled at it and apparently little or no improvement was made in its defects by the time of its use in the D III. With this engine the maximum speed was approximately 100 m.p.h. The climb figures were: 3 minutes to 3,280 feet; 7 minutes to 6,560 feet; 12 minutes to 9,840 feet and 30 minutes to 15,500 feet which was also the ceiling. The weight loaded was 1,560 lb. and empty 995 lb. Fuel for 1½ hours flight was carried.

The armament was normally twin Spandau machine-

S/SEAT SCOUT

In this photograph taken at Johannisthal the raised centre section in the top wing is apparent as also are the cooling holes in the cowling and the absence of ailerons. The varied headgear of the bystanders may also be noted!

guns but it is reported that in the interest of improved performance only one gun was fitted on occasions.

The wings were of the two-bay layout and of the same dimensions throughout. They were fabric covered with two wooden spars and ribs of the same material. From the leading-edge and between each main rib were three false ribs. Wings were internally and externally wire-braced. To improve the forward and upward view for the pilot there was a cut-out in the top wing trailing edge which like that of the lower wing was of stiff wire, hence the 'feathered' appearance. The depth of the fuselage and the quite small gap between the upper and lower wings necessitated the raising of the entire centre-section to enable installation and facilitate use of the machine-guns. Examples of the D III were fitted with or without cable-operated and balanced ailerons. These two versions were known in the company designation system as the M.19K or M.19F respectively but no change of military designation was made upon the introduction of ailerons which took place in the later production models and both versions were known as the D III. The aileron modification was probably not generally available at the period when the type was in front-line service but it appeared later on aircraft at schools and on foreign service. The operation of the wing-warping system in this aircraft was carried out by four cables from the control column which were connected with the top and bottom extremities of the four rear main struts—two of these cables being led to the base of the struts by way of the cabane. The centre-section struts of steel tube were in 'N' form and vertical in both front and side elevation. Although there was considerable positive stagger on the wings neither dihedral nor sweep-back was incorporated. The fuselage was of wire-braced welded steel tube and its cross-sections from the circular engine cowling rearwards became hexagonal and finally a horizontal knife-edge at the tail. From the cockpit, metal panelling on both sides of the fuselage swept forwards and downwards in arcs to the lower wing and mid-chord position, thus streamlining the rounded nose into the hexagonal section of the fuselage. The 160 h.p. Oberursel was semi-enclosed in a deep chord cowling—more inclined to the French pattern than German and had uncommon features in the additional cooling holes in its face, and the bracing provided across the diameter of the cowling for a front engine bearing, necessitated by the weight of this engine.

The tail unit, also of welded steel tubing of a lighter gauge, and fabric covered, was of the design used in the monoplanes and earlier 'D' types. A balanced but unbraced rudder of 'comma' shape, which protruded well below the fuselage, was cable-operated, as were the elevators which were balanced and moved about a common tubular spar.

The undercarriage, of orthodox design, had wire braced V's which consisted of streamlined steel tube with wooden fairings similar to the main interplane struts. Rubber cord bound the axle to the apices of these V's in the usual manner. A steel-shod wooden tail-skid was mounted in the apex of an inverted pyramid of steel struts.

The instruments carried in the cockpit consisted of altimeter, fuel pressure gauge, compass and fuel flow indicator, while on the two-handled control column, were the firing buttons and a 'blip' switch. A steel tube rudder bar with stirrups completed the controls.

Fokker D IIIs on active service were to be seen in both the plain varnish finish of uncoloured linen fabric or the early form of camouflage being introduced from the end of 1915. In this the wings, fuselage and tail were painted green and brown with the under surfaces of the wings a light blue. The cowling and adjacent plates seem to have been invariably left in the natural metal finish. The cross patée in black was painted on the tips of the top and bottom wings, the fuselage sides and the rudder, and was only outlined in white or painted on a white panel when the camouflage system was applied. The abbreviation of the maker's name, serial number and year of construction usually appeared low down on the fuselage sides below the cockpit.

Just over 300 aircraft of the D I to III types were built, by far the majority being D II and D IIIs. Although originally quite a successful design, the early 'D' class Fokker scouts were not capable of being further developed sufficiently to compete with the Halberstadt and especially the Albatros products which gained the approval of the authorities and resulted in the short operational life of the D III.

FOKKER D III

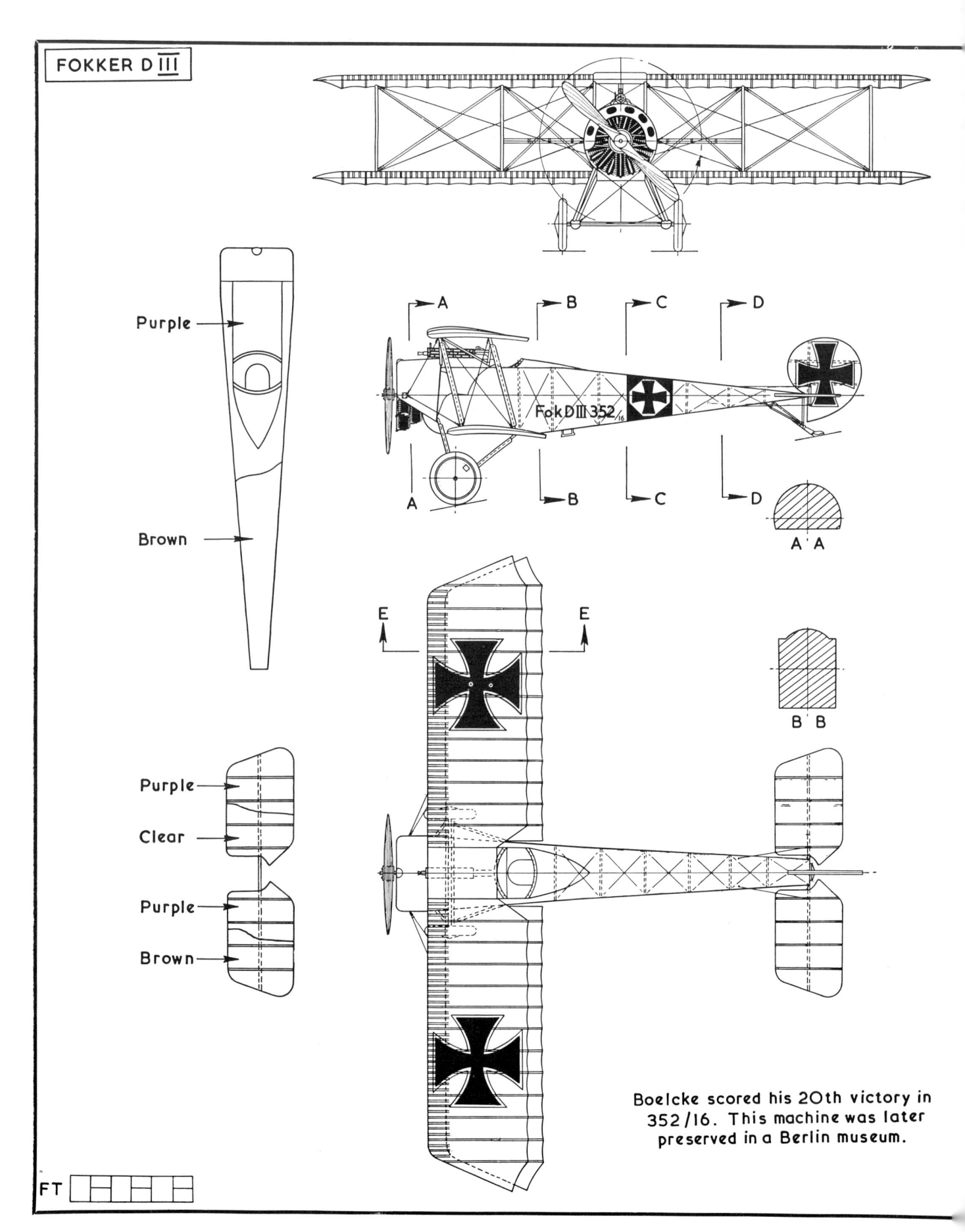

Purple
Brown

Purple
Clear
Purple
Brown

FT

Boelcke scored his 20th victory in 352/16. This machine was later preserved in a Berlin museum.

182

FOKKER D III

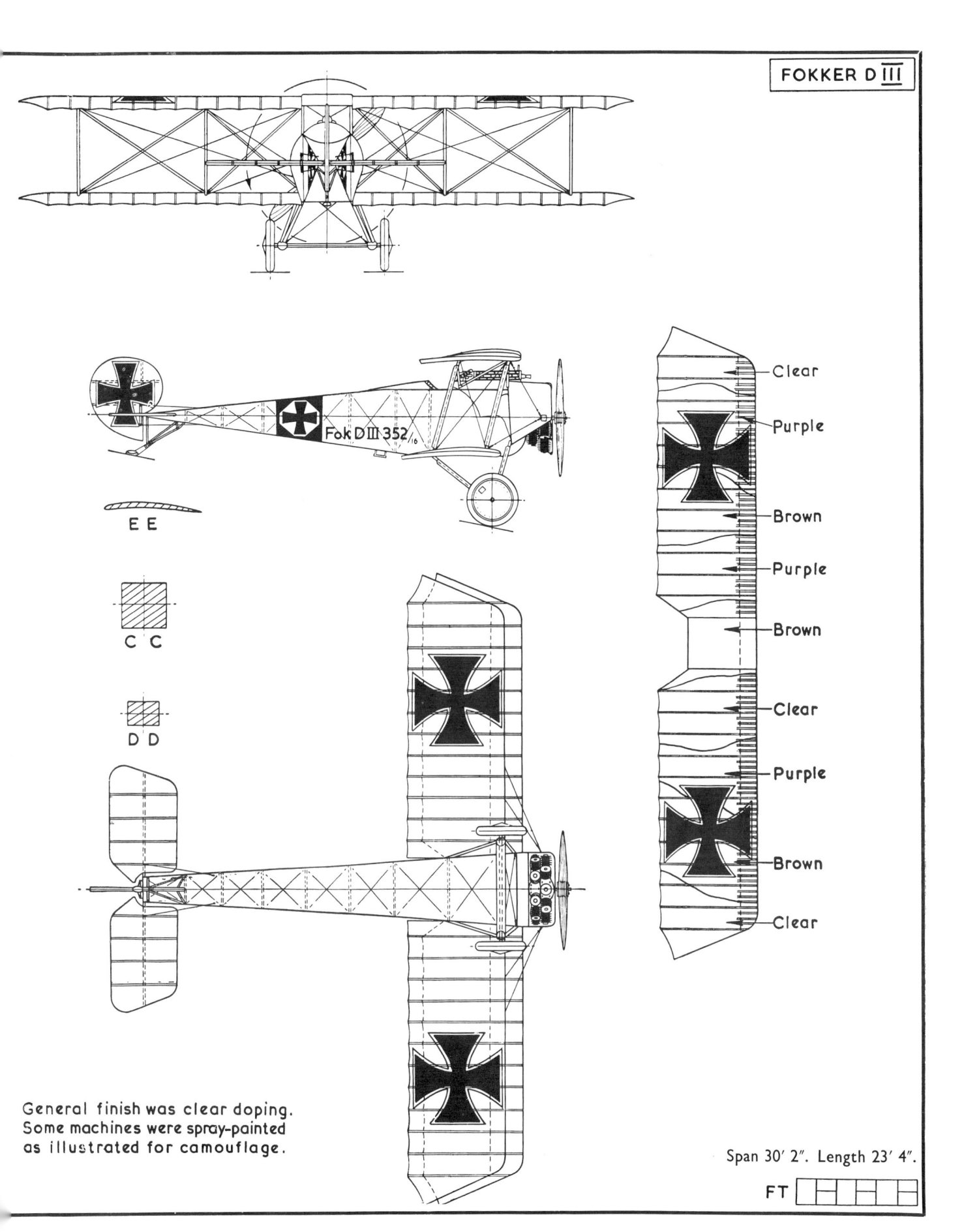

Clear
Purple
Brown
Purple
Brown
Clear
Purple
Brown
Clear

E E

C C

D D

General finish was clear doping. Some machines were spray-painted as illustrated for camouflage.

Span 30' 2". Length 23' 4".

FT

FOKKER D VII

A standard Fokker D VII with 170 h.p. Mercedes engine. This actual aircraft was taken to the U.S.A. for investigation by the U.S.A.S. authorities. Hence the marking P.108 on the rudder.

The Fokker D VII probably represents the peak of achievement in German fighter aircraft used operationally in World War I. Although some of the designs of 1918, which appeared too late for use on the Front, had superior performances in certain respects, the D VII certainly compared favourably with them in all-round ability and was much superior to its contemporaries during its period of service from May to November 1918, a fact confirmed by its large scale construction and widespread use.

Developed from the Fokker-designated V II, originally, it was the second of the trio of famous fighters to be designed by Reinhold Platz and won the first open competition held at Johannisthal, Berlin, in January 1918 for the purpose of selecting the best fighter in which production might become almost standardised. Its success was due to the complete approval it won from the number of famous 'aces' who test flew it in their capacity as a panel of judges. Their decision was wholly in favour of the D VII and large orders were at once given for its construction not only by the parent firm but also by their great rivals Albatros Werke the Austrian branch of this company (O.A.W.), and A.E.G. all of which were to build the type under licence. Some idea of the numbers produced may be gained from the fact that Fokker alone built over 330 aircraft of the type.

The standard engines fitted to the D VII were, the famous Mercedes D IIIa of 170 h.p. (basic rating, 160 h.p.) and the 185 h.p. B.M.W. which appeared late in 1918 and was fitted chiefly to Fokker factory-built models, under the designation D VII F.

The empty and loaded weights, with the Mercedes engine, were 1,540 and 1,936 lb. respectively and with 20 gallons of fuel and 4 of oil its endurance was about $1\frac{3}{4}$ hours. Maximum speed at low altitude was 120 m.p.h., 110 m.p.h.

Seen at right is the later version of the D VII fitted with the 185 h.p. B.M.W. engine.

at 10,000 ft. and the landing speed approximately 60 m.p.h. The climb under the above conditions was as follows, 4 mins. to 3,280 ft., 12 mins. to 9,840 ft., $31\frac{1}{2}$ mins. to 16,405 ft., and the service ceiling of 18,000 ft. was reached in 44 minutes. With the B.M.W. engine the performance figures were somewhat better throughout. The armament consisted of the standard twin synchronised Spandau guns situated in the cowling ahead and within reach of the pilot.

The usual Fokker cantilever wooden wings were used with two separate spars—unlike the single compound one of the Dr I. The leading edges were again of plywood with the ribs of the same material while the balanced, unequal chord, aileons (on the top wing only) were of welded steel tube with wire trailing edges, similar to the wing proper which had a slight 'cut-out' ahead of the cockpit. The lower wing was of similar construction and in one piece which necessitated a recess on the lower longerons to house the centre section of this wing flush with the belly at this point. A metal sheet covered the whole of this 'inset' in a neat and streamlined manner. Normal fabric covering was employed throughout the wings.

The interplane 'N' struts and the pyramidal and somewhat involved centre-section strutting were of streamlined steel tubing.

The fuselage was of wire braced, welded steel tube throughout in the manner of the Dr I. The top-decking, aft of the cockpit, had a fabric covered plywood section similar to the Triplane, the remainder of the fuselage being

S/S SCOUT

Another view of the 185 h.p. B.M.W.-engined D VII carrying the 'F' serial letter which denotes its manufacture by Fokker. This photo shows to good advantage the standard patterned fabric.

merely fabric covered. Metal cowlings covered the engine from the nose radiator back to the cockpit on the fuselage top and to the lower wing leading edge on the sides and the belly. These latter plates had cooling louvres and inspection panels incorporated.

The tail unit of balanced elevators, fin, balanced rudder and strut braced tail plane was of welded steel tubing with fabric covering throughout.

The exhaust system was either of the external type running horizontally aft and terminating at the rear of the engine on its starboard side or one of individual pipes, which converged into one main exhaust within the cowling and was led out through a hole in the starboard side.

The undercarriage struts were of streamlined steel tube and the axle—anchored and sprung by rubber chords at each end—was enclosed in the familiar Fokker aerofoil covering as was the Dr I. The tail-skid, too, had the characteristics of the Triplane being of ash with a steel shoe.

The cockpit was equipped with the usual stick type elevator and aileron control at the top of which was a grip which incorporated the firing buttons and an auxiliary throttle lever. A simple stirrup type rudder bar of steel tubing, the main throttle, on the port side of the cockpit, magneto and fuel tank switches plus a hand pump completed the controls. The instruments provided were an altimeter, a tachometer, compass and fuel gauges.

The colouring of the D VII was dictated by the standard hexagonal patterned fabric used by the constructors. These hexagons were elongated in shape, being approximately 12 in. long by 6 in. wide and were of various colours. Commonly used tints were blues, browns, greens, pinks and violet. The lower surfaces followed the same pattern but were of a lighter shade. The engine cowling was generally of dark green overall or a combination of several colours similar to those in the printed fabric of the wings and fuselage. The rudder was usually painted all white, providing a contrasting background for the black cross carried on both sides.

The crosses forming the national marking seems to have invariably been of the Greek type in one of its varieties. When used on the wings and fuselage of normal camouflage pattern, these crosses were outlined in white if not painted in a square white panel or an all white background. The serial number, constructors name and military designation were painted on the fuselage in black or white either fore or aft of the cross, in the former case the cross being situated somewhat nearer the tail than the usual position—half-way between the cockpit and sternpost.

As with all the late German fighter aircraft, the D VII was very much decorated by its pilots either in pursuance of a unit system, such as in *Jagdgeschwader Nr. 1* or to their individual wishes. These many and varied markings were applied to both fuselage and the horizontal tail surfaces and took such forms as interwoven initials of the pilot or personal badges and coloured stripes respectively. Short, humorous sentences were not unknown, even, and Ernst Udet carried the German equivalent of 'Not this time!' across his elevators, but the ultimate in this direction (and optimism!) must surely have been the aircraft carrying the plea 'Don't shoot, dear friends!' across the fuselage—in English!

Like the Fokker Triplane and the Albatros fighters the D VII was flown by a great many of the famous German pilots who utilised its excellent flying qualities to the best advantage in running up their scores.

Licence-built by O.A.W., this D VII was surrendered to the 1st Aero Sqdn.; U.S.A.S. at Trier Airfield after the Armistice.

185

FOKKER D VII

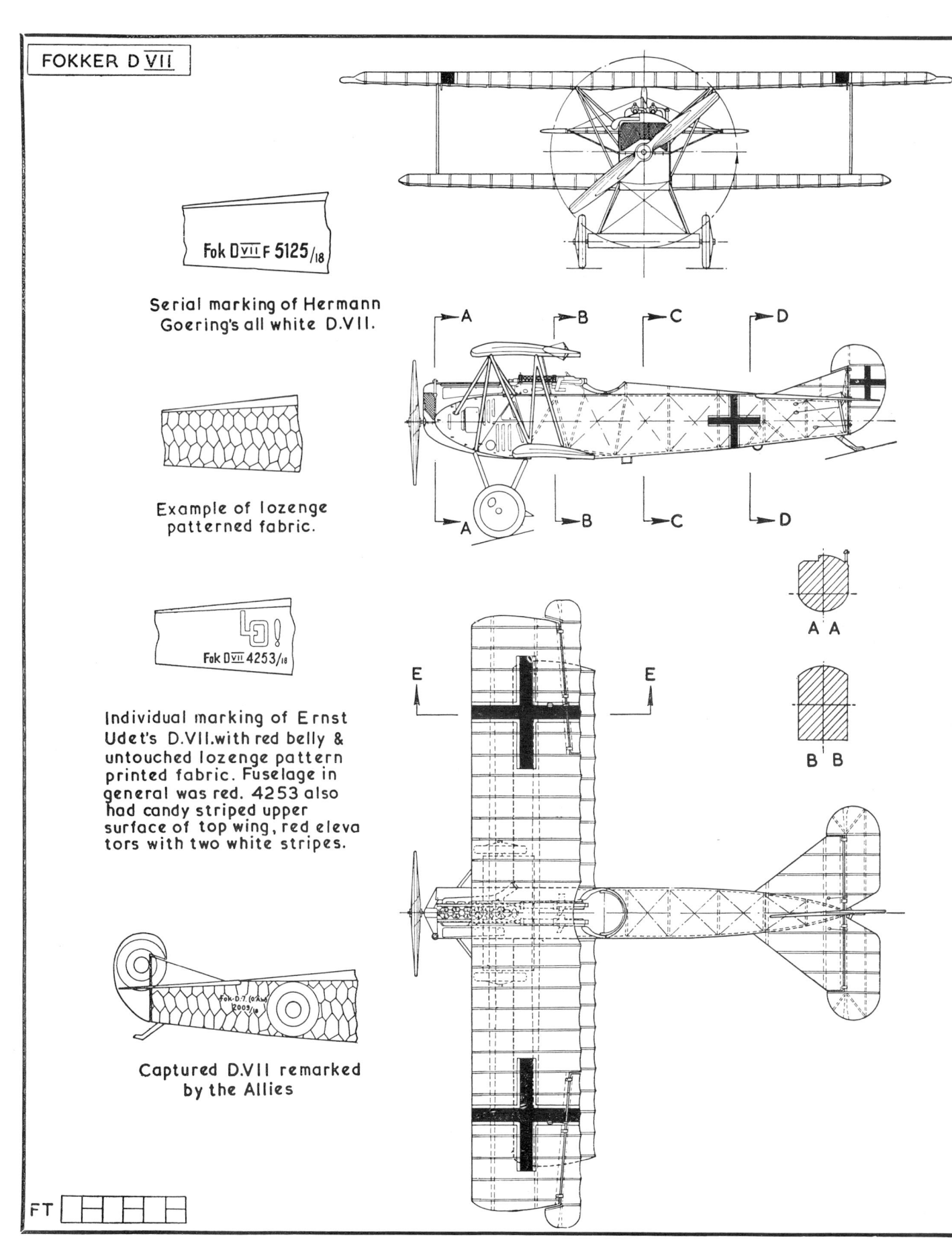

Serial marking of Hermann Goering's all white D.VII.

Example of lozenge patterned fabric.

Individual marking of Ernst Udet's D.VII. with red belly & untouched lozenge pattern printed fabric. Fuselage in general was red. 4253 also had candy striped upper surface of top wing, red elevators with two white stripes.

Captured D.VII remarked by the Allies

FT

FOKKER D VII

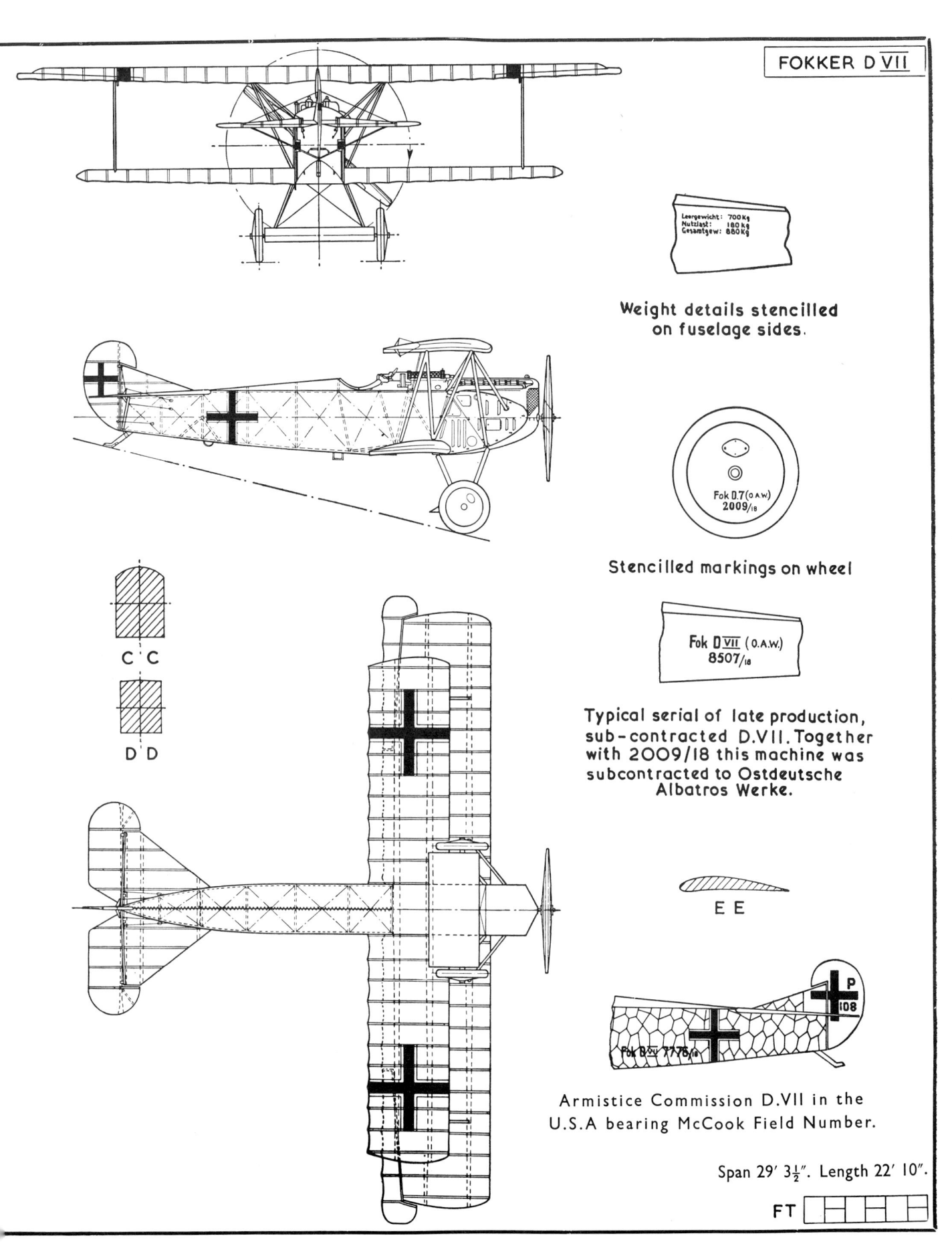

Weight details stencilled on fuselage sides.

Stencilled markings on wheel

Fok D VII (O.A.W.) 8507/18

Typical serial of late production, sub-contracted D.VII. Together with 2009/18 this machine was subcontracted to Ostdeutsche Albatros Werke.

Armistice Commission D.VII in the U.S.A bearing McCook Field Number.

Span 29' 3½". Length 22' 10".

FOKKER E V/D VIII

FOK E V 138/18. An early production model of the monoplane when known as the E V.

Although the Fokker D VIII was not available for use in any numbers before the signing of the Armistice it has been included in this series to show the type of scout with which it is almost certain the *Staffeln* of the German Air Service would have been equipped on a very large scale at the end of 1918 and onwards had hostilities not ceased when they did.

In the same way as the D VII had won the scout competition of January 1918 so the E V (Eindecker V) as this parasol monoplane was originally known, proved successful in the second series of tests held in April of that year at Johannisthal. Once again Platz was responsible for the design, taking as the basis a Fokker monoplane type known as the V 26, which was already very similar to the final aircraft, but requiring some changes in the design including the incorporation of balanced elevators, a larger rudder—reshaped from the original 'comma' type—the addition of a triangular fin, modified centre section and inset ailerons.

The selection of the E V as the winner by the scout pilots concerned in the examination of the various aircraft at Johannisthal was unanimous, and Fokker was virtually awarded a contract for its construction provided the E V passed the military loading tests to be carried out at Adlershof. To conform to the official requirements, intended for braced wings, the rear spar was strengthened and six aircraft of the type were dispatched to various *Staffeln*. At the front the results were almost catastrophic for the future of the E V. Whereas the front spar reacted under load in a normal manner, the modified rear one remained rigid and the resulting torsion caused wing failure in three of these first six aircraft, when subjected to the stresses of combat flying. At about this time approximately fifty to sixty E V's were ready for issue but these were grounded while enquiries proceeded into the cause of the failures.

It appears that the Fokker staff eventually found the cause by closely observing the progressive results of sandbag loading tests and their findings vindicated their original design, which was then reverted to, the E V once again being put into production. The introduction of the designation D VIII was most probably made at this time although a definite date for this change is not known with any certainty. By the time production was once more in full swing it was autumn of 1918 and the type could not be put into widespread use prior to the coming of peace.

Staffel records indicate that the D VIII in small numbers—often only one or two aircraft—was on their strength in late 1918 but so far it has not been possible to trace a *Staffel* wholly equipped with the D VIII and although Rudolf Stark of *Jasta 35* speaks of *Jasta 23, 32* and *34* flying the type this is almost certainly reference to the small numbers spread thinly amongst the units. It is significant, also, that no Allied pilots reported *units* of these aircraft at any time, merely that they were encountered in *Staffeln* of mixed types.

The engine of the D VIII was the 140 h.p. Oberursel, a nine-cylinder rotary which gave a maximum speed, low down, of about 124 m.p.h. The landing speed was approximately 55 m.p.h. At a loaded weight of 1,334 lb., the empty weight being 893 lb., the climb figures obtained were: 2 minutes to 3,280 feet, $4\frac{1}{2}$ minutes to 6,560 feet; $7\frac{1}{2}$ minutes to 9,840 feet and $10\frac{3}{4}$ minutes to 13,120 feet with a service ceiling of 20,000 feet. The fuel carried was sufficient for $1\frac{1}{2}$ hours flight and the armament comprised the standard twin synchronised Spandau machine-guns. In the construction of the wing the usual Fokker cantilever system with two tapering box spars was used. These were of spruce and birch and whereas the rear spar was straight throughout its length, the front spar was swept back towards the wing-tips from each side of the centre section struts. An unusual feature was the overall covering of the wing and the cable-operated ailerons with 1·3 mm. three-ply sheeting. The centre section struts were of streamlined steel tubing and were of exactly the same type and dimensions as those of the Fokker D VI biplane.

The fuselage had the usual diagonal wire bracing of the bays as in the Dr I and D VII types and was a welded steel tube box girder, the tubing used being progressively reduced in diameter from 22 mm. at the nose to 18 mm. at the tail. The method of streamlining the circular engine cowling (of aluminium) into the square-sectioned fuselage was obtained by a wooden rib extending from the firewall to the cockpit on each side of the fuselage and situated on the thrust line, with normal fabric covering or a fabric covered three-ply fillet of triangular shape as used on the Dr I. The rest of the fuselage was fabric covered as were the welded steel tube rudder, fin and tail plane, the latter being strut braced.

SINGLE-SEAT SCOUT

FOK D VIII 697/18. Shown here is the D VIII as it became known in its final orm.

The influence of the D VII appeared again in the shape of the fin and rudder. The tail-skid of steel shod wood was pivoted in the fuselage bottom, forward of the sternpost and sprung at the top end within the fuselage by rubber cords. Streamlined tubing formed the undercarriage legs and the familiar auxiliary lifting surface fairing enclosed the axle and the coil spring shock-absorbers, to complete the customary Fokker practice in this component.

The stick and rudder bar controls were also of standard type and the instrumentation included tachometer, compass, fuel pressure gauge and ammeter. The layout of the cockpit, however, seems to have left something to be desired and one examining pilot reported as 'very inconvenient' the throttle being on the port side of the fuselage while the air adjustment control was on the left hand side of the double-handed control stick! In addition to this the close proximity of the machine-guns to the front of the cockpit and the potential danger to the pilot in the event of a crash was criticised, though in this respect the D VIII was certainly no worse than most scouts of the time. Reports on the handling qualities of the D VIII seem to be generally favourable. It was very manoeuvrable with a rapid take-off and good climb. The controls were sensitive and though it was tail-heavy it was not tiring to fly. The landing speed was considered to be low and there was a tendency to swing to the right during take-off and landing. The only adverse comment of the D VIII may be said to be the inclination to drop the right wing when making the approach for landing.

At the time of the introduction of the D VIII, or the 'Flying Razor Blade' as it became known, printed lozenge pattern fabric was in general use. This was composed of variously coloured hexagons—usually greens, mauve, browns and pink—and all aircraft of this type seem to have been covered with this material. The usual colouring was therefore in these combinations over wings and fuselage but the rudder was in most cases all white with the black Greek cross. The crosses on the fuselage and above and below the wings were something of an innovation being full depth between top and bottom longerons and full cord respectively. They were outlined by narrow white borders. The serial number, constructor's name and year of building appeared on both sides of the fuselage low down, and approximately below the cockpit. This lettering was in black or white.

The D VIII is not known as a much decorated aircraft—probably because of its limited use on operations—but occasional photographs depict it carrying a personal or unit insignia. Nor can it claim to have been a high scorer though this certainly was no reflection on its capabilities. No evidence is available to prove that any of the famous German aces flew this type long enough to gain any large number of victories in it and thus regain some of the prestige it had to some extent, lost in the unfortunate early days of its career.

A quite different, but unauthenticated story regarding the operational use of the Fokker monoplane is as follows: the initial issue of six aircraft, probably E Vs, was made to *Jasta 23* in June 1918 to augment and replace the Fokker D VII, they were then flying. In two weeks this unit suffered three fatal crashes due to wing failure and the type was grounded. After investigation and subsequent modifications *Jasta 1, 11,* and *23* commenced re-equipping with what was, presumably, now known as the D VIII, and this was completed by September 24th. This front-line service was not destined to be of long duration, being limited to about one week, as the start of the break-up of organised fighter operations in early November caused the withdrawal of the *Jasta* flying the D VIII.

The clean entry, and streamlined qualities of the D VIII are well shown in this head-on view.

FOKKER D VIII

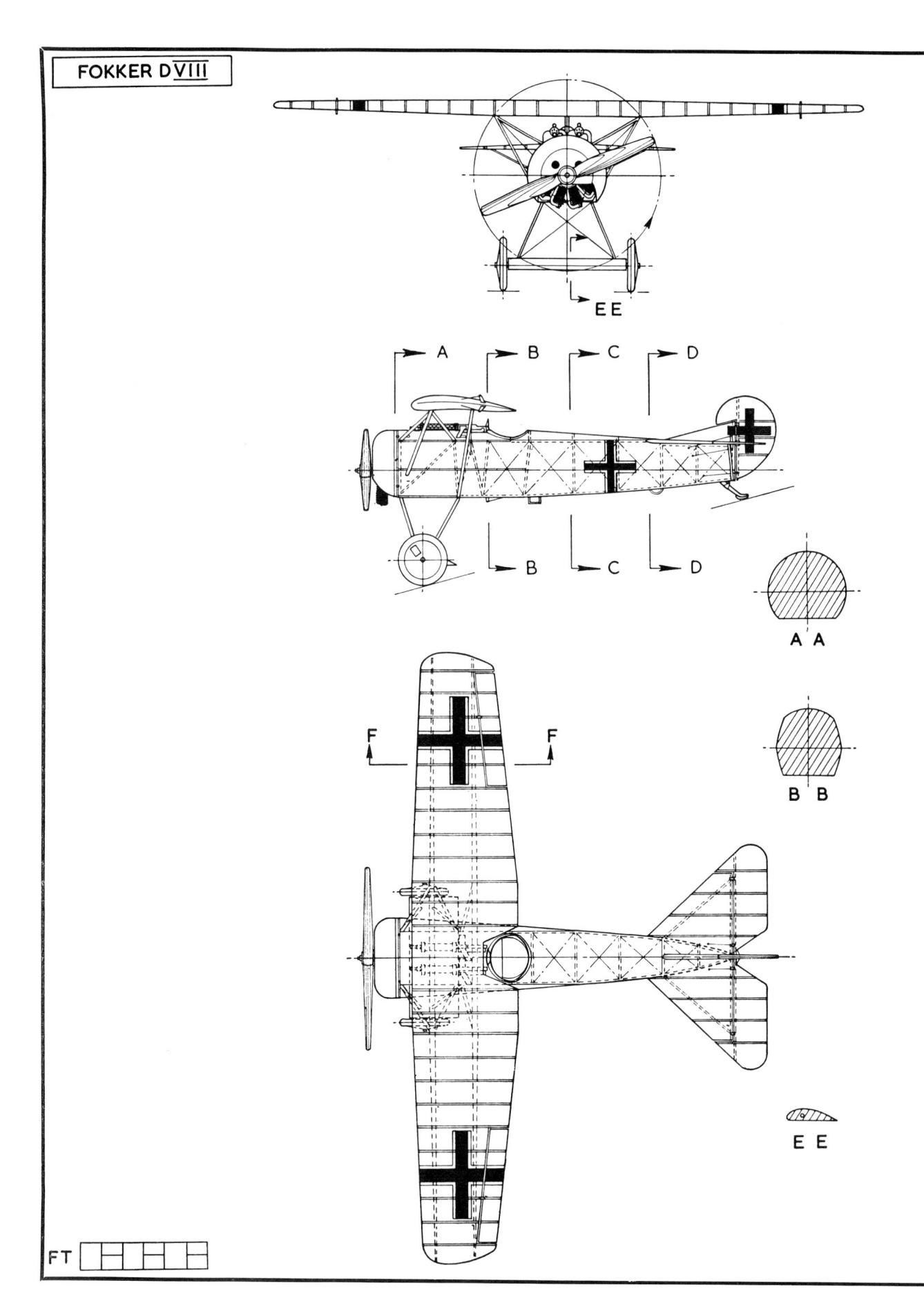

FOKKER D VIII

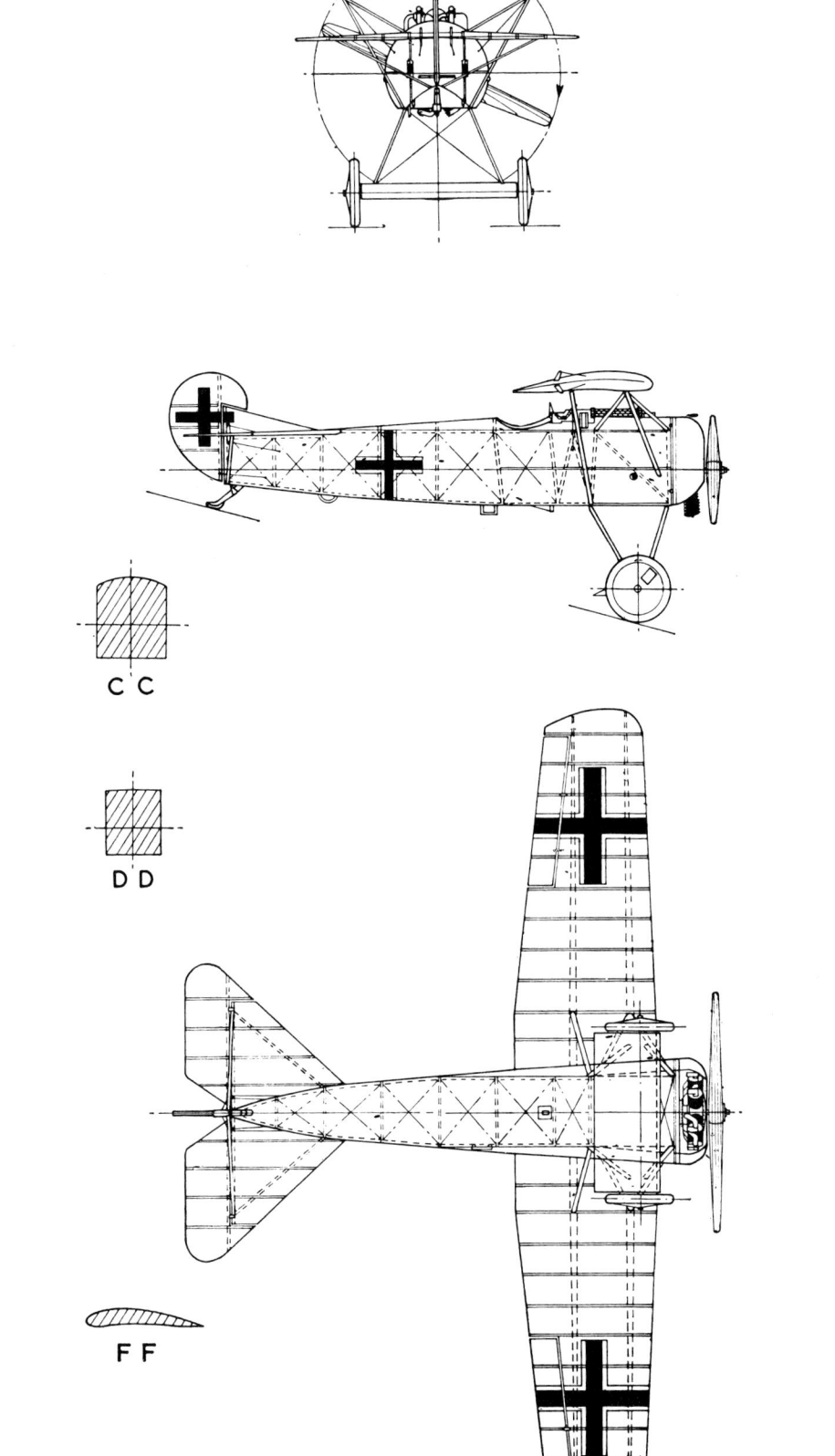

Span 27' 6". Length 19' 6".

THE FOKKER Dr I

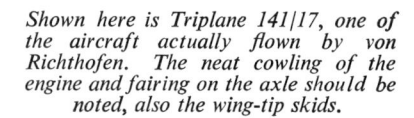

Shown here is Triplane 141/17, one of the aircraft actually flown by von Richthofen. The neat cowling of the engine and fairing on the axle should be noted, also the wing-tip skids.

In August and September of 1917 a new type of German scout aircraft of unorthodox design—for the German Air Force at least—was noted by Allied pilots operating on the Western Front. This was soon found to be from the Fokker stable and was, in fact, the work of their very successful but, even now, unknown designer Reinhold Platz and not, as is generally believed, of Anthony Fokker himself.

This newcomer was allotted the official designation Dr I (i.e. Dreidecker I) indicative of its triplane wing layout and was to prove itself to be one of the most famous of all the German fighters of the 1914–18 War. With the great advantage of having the patronage of Manfred von Richthofen himself, its fame was virtually assured from the outset and the combination of his association, its somewhat unorthodox design and to a lesser extent the garish colourings common to almost all triplanes has perpetuated its memory rather more than those of certain other (and in some cases, more efficient) types such as the Fokker D VII.

The operational life span of the Dr I was approximately one year from the time when it began to re-equip certain of the Albatros DV/Va and Pfalz type units until it was in turn replaced by the Fokker D VII. At one time, early in its career, the triplane came under some suspicion by the authorities as a result of instances of wing failure, but this trouble seems to have been eliminated though reports suggest that prolonged diving was not possible on this type. In this connection it is interesting to note that the investigation carried out by our own Technical Department, of the Department of Aircraft Production, on a captured Dr I, Serial 144/17, speaks almost scathingly of the design and construction methods employed, though these views may have been prejudiced to some extent, in the interests of propaganda.

The Dr I was developed from an interesting triplane model of about similar size and construction and known in the Fokker factory as the V-4. This had no interplane struts which were later incorporated in the production version in order to eliminate vibration of the wings and not, as the fable would have us believe, to satisfy the doubts of the military authorities who, it was claimed, could not reconcile an absence of struts with safety!

The most generally used engine is quoted as being the 110 h.p. Oberursel rotary but it is most likely that many of the engines employed were Le Rhones of the same horsepower which were built under licence in Sweden by the Thulin factory and exported to Germany where their frequent use, due to their superiority over the Oberursel type, gave rise to the erroneous story on the Allied side that these were captured engines.

In the experimental field the following engines were installed, the 145 h.p. Oberursel UR III, 160 h.p. Goebel III and the 160 h.p. Siemens Halske III, the last named having a four-bladed propeller. None of these projects were proceeded with, however. The fuel carried was 16 gallons of petrol which permitted flight for approximately 2 hours at 10,000 feet. At a loaded weight of 1,259 lb. (empty 829 lb.) the maximum speed was 115 m.p.h. low down and 80 m.p.h. at 18,000 feet. Landing speed was about 30 m.p.h. The climb figures were $1\frac{3}{4}$ mins. to 3,280 ft.; $3\frac{3}{4}$ mins. to 6,560 ft.; $6\frac{1}{2}$ mins. to 9,840 ft.; 10 mins. to 13,120 ft.; 14 mins. to 16,400 ft., and the ceiling between 18–20,000 ft. The armament consisted of two synchronised Spandau machine-guns to port and starboard in the top cowling with the gun buttons on the control column.

The cantilever construction of the three wings eliminated all internal and external bracing wires. Each wing had one wooden box spar of full span and of considerable depth. The ribs were of ply and the leading edges on all three wings were covered with the same material as far back as the spars, elsewhere the covering was of fabric throughout. Cable operated ailerons were fitted to the top wing only and were of the balanced type, constructed of welded steel tubing and inboard were terminated irregularly where they formed the outboard extremities of the top wing cut-out in the trailing edge. Trailing edges were formed by stiff wire which gave the scalloped effect to so many aircraft of this period.

The inverted 'V' centre section struts were of streamlined steel tubing and attached to the top wing spar from the upper port and starboard frame tubing of the fuselage.

The centre wing had two quarter circle cut-outs adjacent to the fuselage to improve the forward and downward vision, but the lower wing was of constant chord throughout. At the tips of this wing, in the later models,

192

SINGLE-SEAT SCOUT

Another view of 141/17. Pilots did not always use the same aircraft, and amongst others, von Richthofen flew 102/17, 107/17, 114/17, 127/17, 152/17, 425/17 in which he was killed, and 477/17.

were two ash skids rigidly mounted on the underside. The one piece 'I' struts were of considerable depth but only about half an inch thick.

The fuselage framework, which tapered to a vertical sternpost, was constructed of $\frac{5}{8}$, $\frac{11}{16}$ and $\frac{3}{4}$ inch steel tubing welded at the joints and braced in the individual bays by wires running diagonally from small quadrants of tube welded into the corner of the bays. The covering of the fuselage was for the most part of fabric but in order to merge the circular engine cowling into the square cross-section of the fuselage a triangular shaped ply fillet was fitted on each side immediately behind the engine cowling. These extended rearwards to a point just behind the cockpit. A similar method provided the curved top decking from the cockpit to about halfway to the sternpost.

The triangular shaped tailplane, which was braced from below by two struts, the balanced elevators and typical Fokker rudder of comma outline were all of welded steel tubing with fabric covering. The rudder was balanced.

The undercarriage, the legs of which were of streamlined steel tubing, had its axle enclosed in an elaborate fairing built round it which might be regarded as an auxiliary lifting surface. The usual rubber cording served to absorb the landing impact by limiting the vertical movement of the axle. A steel shod ash tail-skid was provided with shock absorber cords and a limiting cable at its top end within the fuselage and a pivoting point at the bottom of a vertical strut which was situated slightly forward of the sternpost.

The Le Rhone or Oberursel engine was normally housed in a cowling of rather more covered frontal area than on Allied engine installations of the rotary type. It was partly cut away in a bottom segment of about 90 deg. and had two large diameter holes in the face above and at either side of the propeller shaft hole. Examples of the open fronted type, similar to the British and French designs, may occasionally be seen.

The usual instruments including tachometer, compass, fuel pressure gauge and ammeter were installed in the cockpit and the seat, which was of welded steel tube with leather covering was adjustable. The control column had a double-handed grip and this incorporated an auxiliary throttle lever, and engine cut-out switch, two buttons by which selective firing of the guns could be controlled and an inverted lever which fired both guns simultaneously.

The colourings and markings of the Dr Is in operational use varied too widely to permit anything like reasonable coverage to be made here, but it may be said that some uniformity was maintained in *Jasta 11* by the overall use of red on planes and fuselage plus individual markings, usually in white. In the case of von Richthofen himself his Fokker Dr. Is 152/17 and 425/17 were all-red, but his 102/17 had a white rudder.

The cross patée, and later the Latin cross, in black was carried on the top and bottom wing tips and on the sides of the fuselage and rudder. These crosses were invariably on a background of a square white panel or outlined with a narrow white margin.

Inspection of photos of some Dr Is shows a vertical streaky effect on the sides of the fuselage and top surfaces, this being the original finish of grey/green and brown with the under surface of light blue provided by the factory before the hexagonal pattern camouflage was introduced. In certain instances the serial painted in black on the fuselage side, below and just aft of the cockpit, appears as 'FOK F I'. This was the Fokker company's own designation for the type before the introduction of the subsequent and more usual 'FOK Dr I'.

As far as is known the number of Fokker triplanes constructed was in the region of 600 with a maximum of 170 in use at one time, this being in mid-1918. The Dr I was the mount of many of the most famous of the German aces for in addition to the von Richthofen brothers such well-known aces as Voss, Wolff, Gontermann, von Tutschek and Udet flew the type. Designed as it was for manœuvrability and climbing ability the Dr I could best be likened to its contemporary, in the Allied side, the Sopwith Camel, as a dog-fighting aircraft. In view of the fact that the Dr I never comprised the equipment of the majority of *Jagdstaffeln*, its prominence in the history of German fighter activities of World War I can chiefly be attributed to its association with von Richthofen and his Circus and its successful work in their hands.

Although a variety of German types found their way to the other theatres of war no confirmation can be obtained that any examples of the Fokker triplane ever operated elsewhere than on the Western Front.

FOKKER Dr I

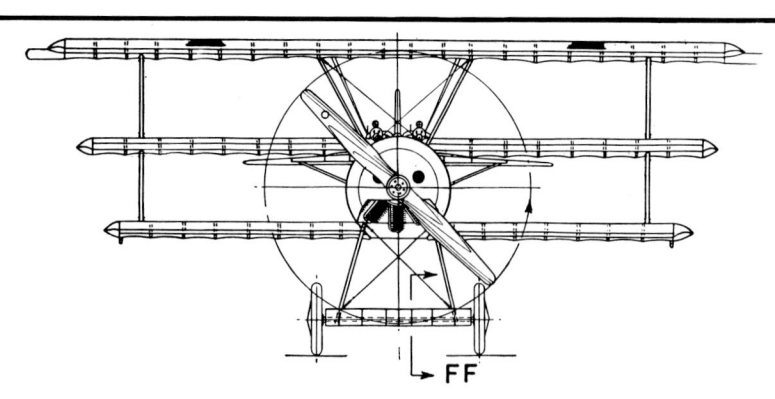

FUSELAGE MARKINGS

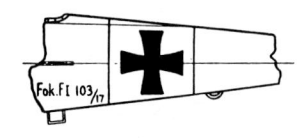

Werner Voss's silver blue machine

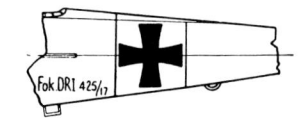

von Richthofen's scarlet machine

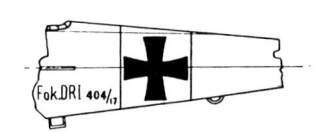

von Tutschek's pale green machine

Wing skid optional fitting

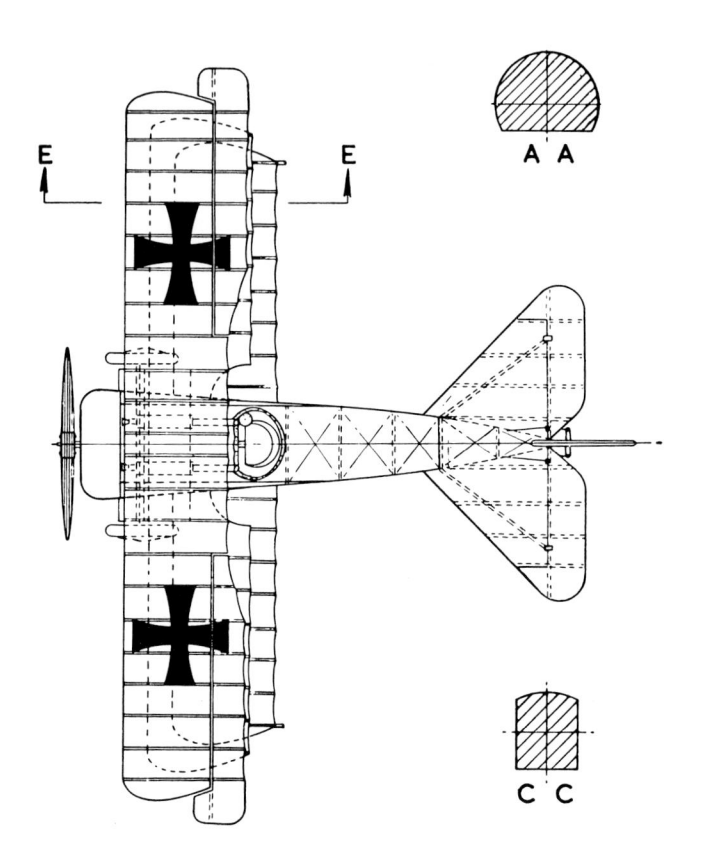

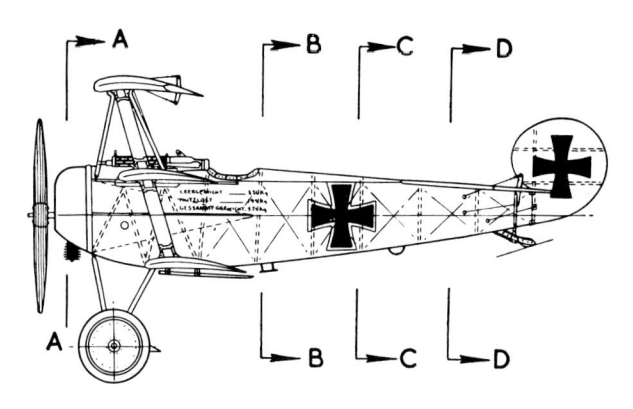

TRIPLANES FLOWN BY VON RICHTHOFEN

Fok. FI 102/17 (Wolff killed in this)
Fok. DRI 114/17 (crashed on 30.10.17.)

FOKKER Dr I

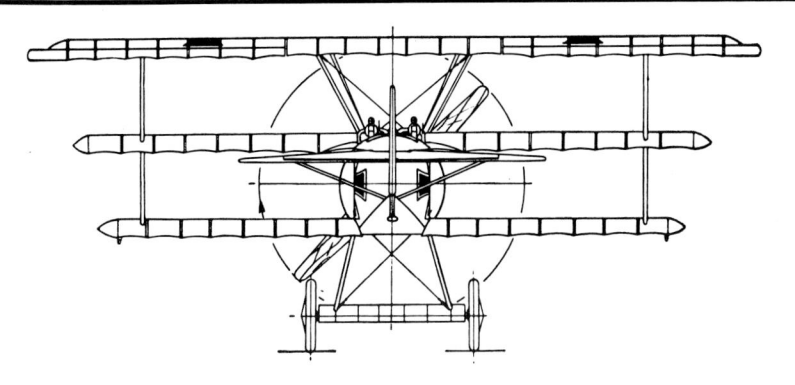

INSIGNIA

Alternatives 1917

1918   1917

1918   1918

Special Individual Markings
used by Werner Voss
on engine cowl
of Fok. F I 103/17

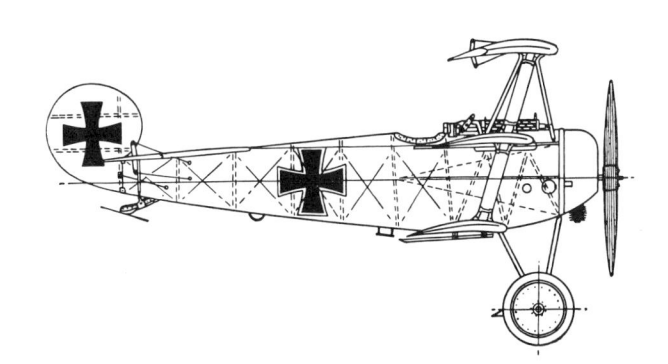

Fok. DRI 152/17 (all red, was in a Berlin museum)
Fok. DRI 425/17 (all red, von Richthofen killed in this machine)

Span 23' 7". Length 19' 0".
FT

FOKKER E I to E IV

The Fokker E II, second in the line of these famous monoplanes, and specifically designed as a military aircraft in mid-1915. Up to this time the Fokker monoplanes had been modified pre-war designs. Primarily intended for scouting (reconnaissance) duties, not all E IIs carried a machine-gun.

Forerunner of the Fokker E I–IV series of monoplanes was the aircraft on which Anthony Fokker used to give aerobatic demonstrations before the war, the M 5. The E I (M 14) was the first machine to be fitted with a successful interrupter gear which enabled the gun to be fired through the air-screw disc. Fokker had evolved the gear after the capture of the Frenchman Roland Garros, who had used a fixed automatic rifle without any synchronising gear, merely fitting steel wedges to his airscrew to deflect any bullets that might have hit it—the Dutchman immediately saw that an interrupter gear was what was wanted.

When the gun gear had been successfully tested, the first Fokker E Is were taken over by Max Immelmann and Oswald Boelcke. The E I had originally been designed simply as an unarmed scout monoplane, the carrying of a fixed machine-gun had never been envisaged, nevertheless the machine was immediately successful, largely because it had little in the way of opposition and Allied machines quickly became known, unhappily, as 'Fokker Fodder'.

Successors to the E I were the E II and E III types which were almost identical except that the latter had the more powerful nine-cylinder Oberursel rotary of 100 h.p.; the E II being fitted with the seven-cylinder Oberursel of 80 h.p. These two types were produced in greater numbers than any other Fokker monoplanes and first became operational during the summer of 1915. Both aircraft spanned 31 ft. 2¾ in. and were 23 ft. 7½ in. in length. Gross weight of the E II was 1,233 lb. The E III grossed 1,344 lb. Maximum speed of each was 82 m.p.h. and 90 m.p.h. respectively.

Composite construction was used in the E I–IV series of monoplanes. The wings were wood, the remainder steel tube and each varied slightly in detail and dimension. The wings were of constant chord with angularly raked tips, there were no ailerons, wing warping being used for lateral control. Twin spars of 'I' section formed the foundation of the structure, light wooden members comprised the leading and trailing edges. The ribs, of poplar, were of very thin section to facilitate warping; compression members were of steel tube, and braced with standard wire cable. The actual wing cables numbered sixteen—four above and four below to each panel—the forward cables attached to the forward spar were rigid rigging bracing; those fixed to the rear spar operated the warp control from cranks under the fuselage, the upper cables running over a pulley wheel at the apex of the tubular fuselage pylon. The wings were easily dismantled for transportation by road, when they were packed flat against the fuselage sides That aircraft should be easily transportable from place to place towed behind a vehicle, was part of the specification at that time.

The fuselage was a welded steel tube, slab-sided structure which tapered to a horizontal knife-edge at the rear and through the rear tube the elevator spar passed. The fuselage frame was cross braced both longitudinally and transversely with stranded steel cable. The circular section aluminium cowl housing the 80 h.p. Oberursel engine (100 h.p. in E III) was cut away at the bottom—resulting in a horseshoe profile—to prevent the accumulation of unburnt fuel and lessen fire risk. The rounded section of the cowl was continued in a curved metal panel on the top surface of the fuselage as far aft as the cockpit

The Fokker E III, seen here, was the same basic design as the E II but had the more powerful engine. Both carried the Fokker company designation, M 14.

SINGLE-SEAT SCOUT

This photo depicts Anthony Fokker seated in an M5L, the forerunner of the line of Fokker monoplane scouts. Although similar to the later models such differences as the position of the wing, the very high pylon, and the more numerous rigging/warping wires due to a greater span, should be noted.

where it terminated in leather padding. The machine-gun was mounted on top of this decking, slightly off-set to starboard. The flat fuselage sides were also metal panelled back to the cockpit and 'elephant ear' fairings attached to the trailing edge of the cowl extended—and tapered—rearwards as far as the wing, under which the exhaust gases were deflected. Behind the engine was mounted a small divided fuel tank, part of which held the pure castor oil lubricant, the remainder serving as an auxiliary gravity tank. The main, cylindrical, fuel tank was fixed just behind the pilot's bucket seat.

Cockpit fittings were rudimentary and attached direct to the airframe. On the left were altimeter and fuel switch from main to auxiliary; to the right: fuel pressure gauge, fuel flow indicator with cut-off valve, fuel pump switch (engine or manual) and throttle valve. In the centre between the instruments was the map holder board, necessitated by the 'scouting recce' duties which were undertaken. The tubular control column was fitted with a two-handled grip top with the gun trigger and 'blip switch' in the centre. The rudder bar was a plain steel tube fitted with stirrups.

The tail assembly boasted no fixed surfaces, the balanced rudder was of the famous Fokker comma profile and the balanced elevators were trapezoidal in outline; construction was of light-gauge steel tube. The complete airframe, with the exception of the metal panels forward, was covered with linen fabric.

The undercarriage chassis was a somewhat complicated mass of steel tubes, which in addition to supporting the wheels, formed the anchorage for the underside wing bracing cables. The shock absorbers, of elastic cord, were inside the fuselage at the top of the main vertical strut which travelled in the slot formed between two closely spaced vertical fuselage members. The ash tail-skid was mounted on a light quadrupod to which was also hinged the lower extremity of the rudder.

It was not until the end of 1915 that camouflage began to be introduced and the majority of E types were finished in plain natural linen fabric, doped and varnished, which resulted in a creamy shade that soon darkened and dirtied with weathering and usage. Patée crosses appeared both underneath and on top of the wings, on the fuselage sides and on the rudder. Although the background colour was light the crosses were often painted on a white square.

Mention must be made of the E IV (M 15) which was a somewhat bigger (span 32 ft. 9¾ in.) and heavier (gross weight 1,595 lb.) aeroplane than the E II and E III, and was powered with the fourteen-cylinder, two-row, Oberursel rotary of 160 h.p. This machine was one of the first to have twin machine-guns as standard equipment, but few were built due to the vagaries of the power plant and the superior performance of the contemporary D class fighters, which were being produced by Halberstadt and Albatros. A special model with three guns was built for Immelmann but it was not successful and he reverted to his E III in which he was eventually killed.

Finally, it was on the Fokker monoplane that Max Immelmann evolved the famous manœuvre—a sharp climb followed by a vertical turn and a dive in the reverse direction—which became immortalised as the Immelmann Turn.

An E II comes to grief in landing. In this view the cables operating the wing warping system are clearly seen.

FOKKER E III

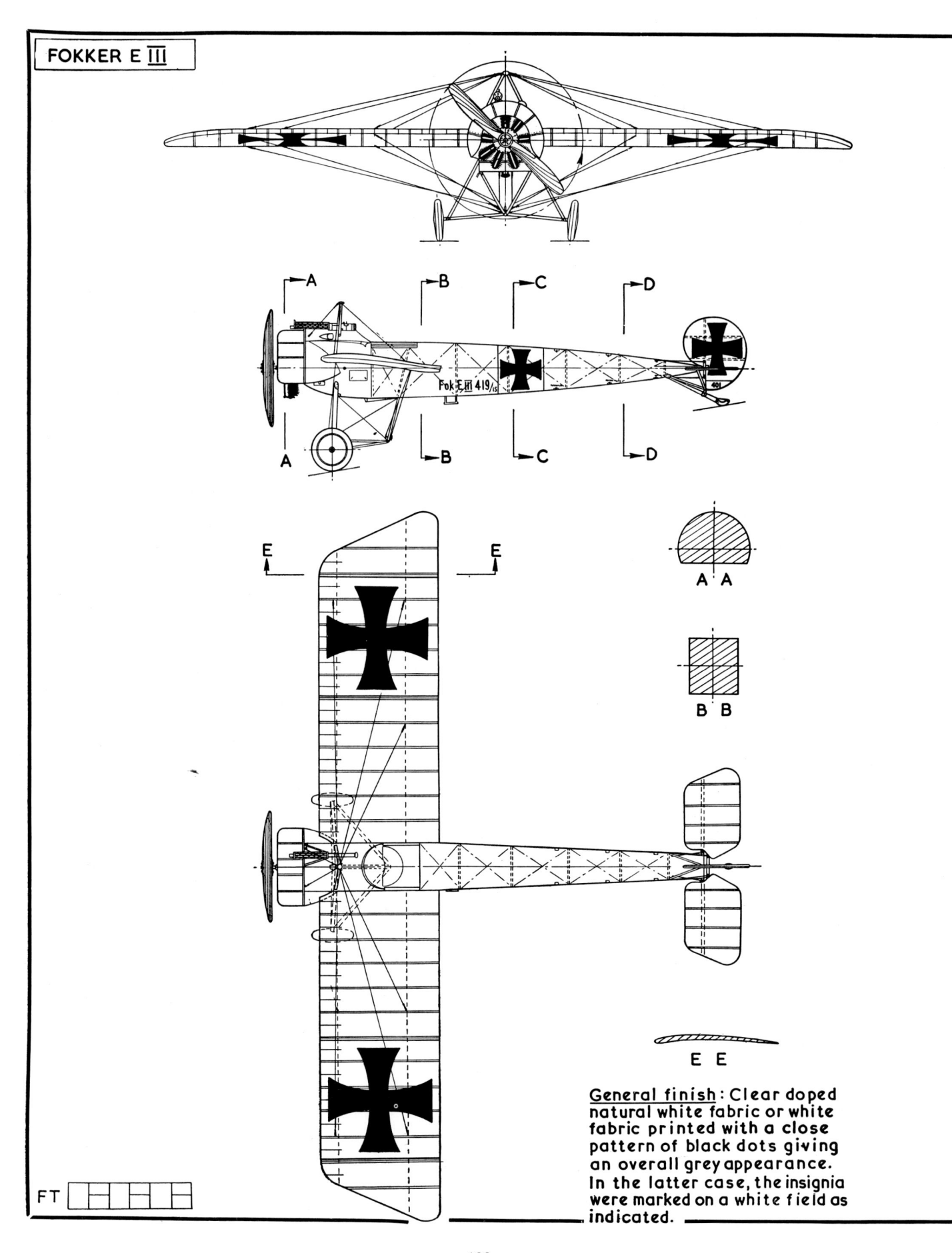

General finish: Clear doped natural white fabric or white fabric printed with a close pattern of black dots giving an overall grey appearance. In the latter case, the insignia were marked on a white field as indicated.

FOKKER E III

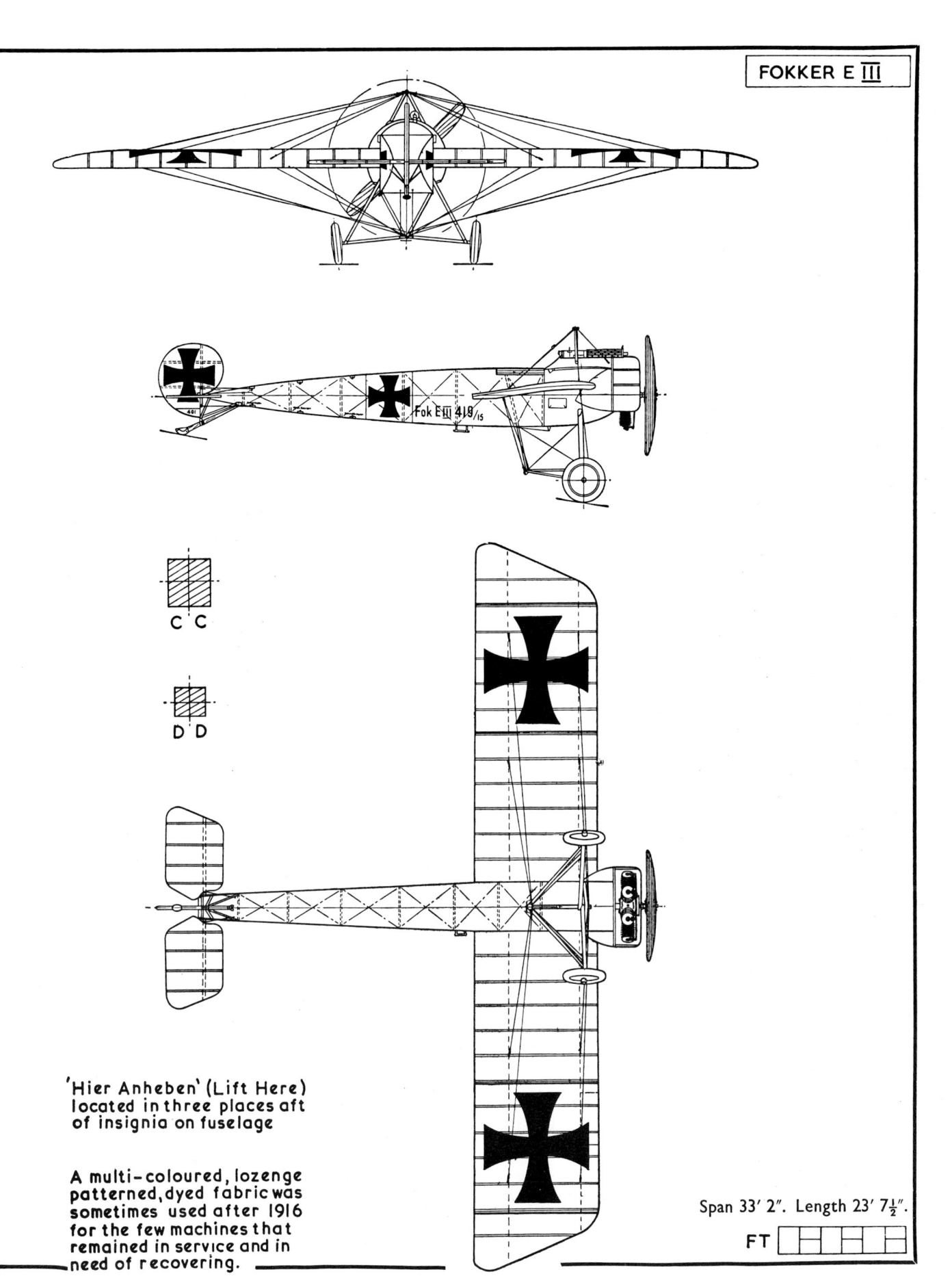

'Hier Anheben' (Lift Here) located in three places aft of insignia on fuselage

A multi-coloured, lozenge patterned, dyed fabric was sometimes used after 1916 for the few machines that remained in service and in need of recovering.

Span 33' 2". Length 23' 7½".

HALBERSTADT D II AND D III

Halberstadt D II with 120 h.p. Mercedes fitted with long exhaust pipe, later dispensed with. Vulnerability of empennage may be noted.

Before the war the Halberstadter Flugzeugwerke, G.m.b.H. at Hartz had been known as the Deutsche Bristol Werke having manufactured Bristol Coanda type monoplanes. However, with the outbreak of hostilities early A type monoplanes were built, also B type biplanes for training purposes. In 1915 a neat two-bay single-seat scout biplane appeared; the Halberstadt D I, powered with an Argus engine and with radiators mounted on the fuselage sides. Later in the year the aircraft was modified to use a car-type radiator mounted on the nose in front of the engine; this was known as the D Ia. In 1916 the radiator system was again altered, this time to one of aerofoil section mounted in the starboard centre-section, also the more reliable 100/120 h.p. Mercedes engine was installed and this machine was designated D II, the basic airframe having been little altered throughout. In this form the aeroplane went into production and began to be issued to the *Kampfstaffeln*, to supplement the Fokker D types. It should be remembered that very little attempt was made to standardise the equipment of units and at this period of the war often a quite heterogeneous collection of aircraft had to be maintained. Still further improvement was aimed at by the introduction of balanced ailerons and the fitting of the 120 h.p. Argus motor, this then became the D III: further points which distinguished it from the D II were the vertical instead of pylon centre-section struts, and a semi-circular instead of angular cut-out. However, the type was now rapidly becoming eclipsed by the new Albatros scouts which had the advantage of more powerful engine and twin machine-gun installation.

Although specimens were captured, comprehensive performance figures do not seem to have been recorded. The following unconfirmed data would appear somewhat optimistic: Climb to 3,280 feet in 4 minutes, to 9,840 feet in 15 minutes. Maximum speed was 90/95 m.p.h. and duration 1½ to 2 hours. Weight empty was 1,145 lb. and loaded 1,608 lb. A single machine-gun, synchronised to fire through the airscrew disc, was fixed to the starboard side of the engine. (See illustration below).

The wing structure was of two-bay format, quite heavily staggered; the upper wing was of slightly greater span than the lower and both were of equal chord and almost rectangular tip shape. The upper wing was mounted quite close to the fuselage, and with the generous centre-section cut-out and stagger a fairly good degree of vision was afforded the pilot. In construction the wings were quite orthodox with twin spruce spars of 'I' section and built-up ribs. A light wooden trailing-edge member was also fitted which resulted in a straight outline and not the scalloped effect which characterised so many German aeroplanes. D II ailerons were of parallel chord and operated by a crank lever working in a slot in much the same manner as on the Albatros machines; on the D III a considerable horn balance portion was added to the tips. Interplane struts were of streamlined steel tube and attached to the spars with hinged fittings, so that for transportation the wings could be collapsed to lie one on top of the other.

Basically the fuselage was a wooden braced box-girder which tapered to a horizontal knife-edge; the longerons being of square section, hollow and bound with fabric. The extreme rear bay, through which the rudder and elevator cables were fed, was covered with 1 mm. three-ply. The same material was used for the decking forward of the cockpit, except for the panels immediately adjacent to the engine and at the extreme nose, which were of metal. Aft of the cockpit was a curved turtle deck of light stringers and formers which peculiarly terminated flush with the

An uncamouflaged D II of Kampfstaffel 2, 1916, shows location of machine-gun on starboard side of Mercedes engine fitted with 'chimney' exhaust.

SINGLE-SEAT SCOUT

A Halberstadt D II reputedly flown by Oswald Boelcke. Full serial, lost in reproduction, was D605/16. Note also the identity numerals 42.

fuselage midway between cockpit and tail. The control stick was very similar to that of contemporary Fokkers, i.e. a straight steel tube with a two-handled grip top, the lower end projecting through the bottom of the fuselage for the connection of the lower elevator cables. A plain straightforward steel tube constituted the rudder-bar, with small end plates attached to prevent the pilot's feet from slipping off. Flight and engine control instruments consisted of altimeter, tachometer, clock, fuel quantity and pressure gauges, magneto switches, etc., although precise details are not available.

Streamline steel tube was used for the undercarriage chassis, which was of normal 'V' type. The wheels were mounted on a steel tube axle which was anchored by elastic shock cord wound round the apices of the V's. The tail-skid was of ash shod with steel, mounted externally on a light steel tube tripod.

The 120 h.p. Mercedes engine in the D II (120 h.p. Argus in the D III) was neatly installed; metal side panels closely hugged the cylinder block and little more than the camshaft (or valve springs in the case of the Argus motor) was exposed. The nose was completed with a rounded metal pressing through which the airscrew shaft protruded. The typical German exhaust manifold ejected horizontally.

Halberstadt D IIs were in use during the transition period to camouflaged aircraft and were seen in both the creamy primrose shade of clear doped linen fabric (when new) and in the current camouflage shades. These consisted at first of large irregular patches of dark green and reddish-brown on the upper and vertical surfaces; underneath either the natural linen finish was left or a coat of pale sky blue applied. After a short period a purple-mauve shade was substituted for that of the red-brown. Patée crosses, either on a square white background, or latterly narrowly outlined with white, were painted in the usual locations.

The Halberstadt D II, together with the Fokker D III, formed the equipment of Oswald Boelcke's *Staffel* during 1916 and doubtless was the foundation of the many other *Jagdstaffeln* that were in the process of being formed that year. *Jagdstaffel 2* was to be commanded by Boelcke (Hauptmann Zander was appointed to *Jasta 1*) and when Richthofen joined the unit at Lagnicourt on September 1st, the new Albatros D IIs were still awaiting delivery and did not arrive until the 16th. All the aircraft available —for practice only—in the meantime, were two Fokker D IIIs, an Albatros D I and a Halberstadt which Boehme had managed to scrounge. Doubtless Richthofen flew the Halberstadt during the period but it cannot be confirmed that he used it successfully.

According to contemporary reports the Halberstadt was prone to spinning and the combination of a heavy in-line engine with no fixed tail surfaces would indicate a tendency to spiral instability. However, it is obvious with such tail surfaces the D II was a sensitive aeroplane that demanded constant vigilance from its pilot, but doubtless this same factor contributed to its manœuvrability in combat.

Although by no means brilliant aircraft, these Halberstadts provided a useful 'stop-gap' until the Albatroses became available in sufficient numbers.

D II rear view depicts a further exhaust variation, also shows two-bay wing structure with wash-out on all four wing-tips.

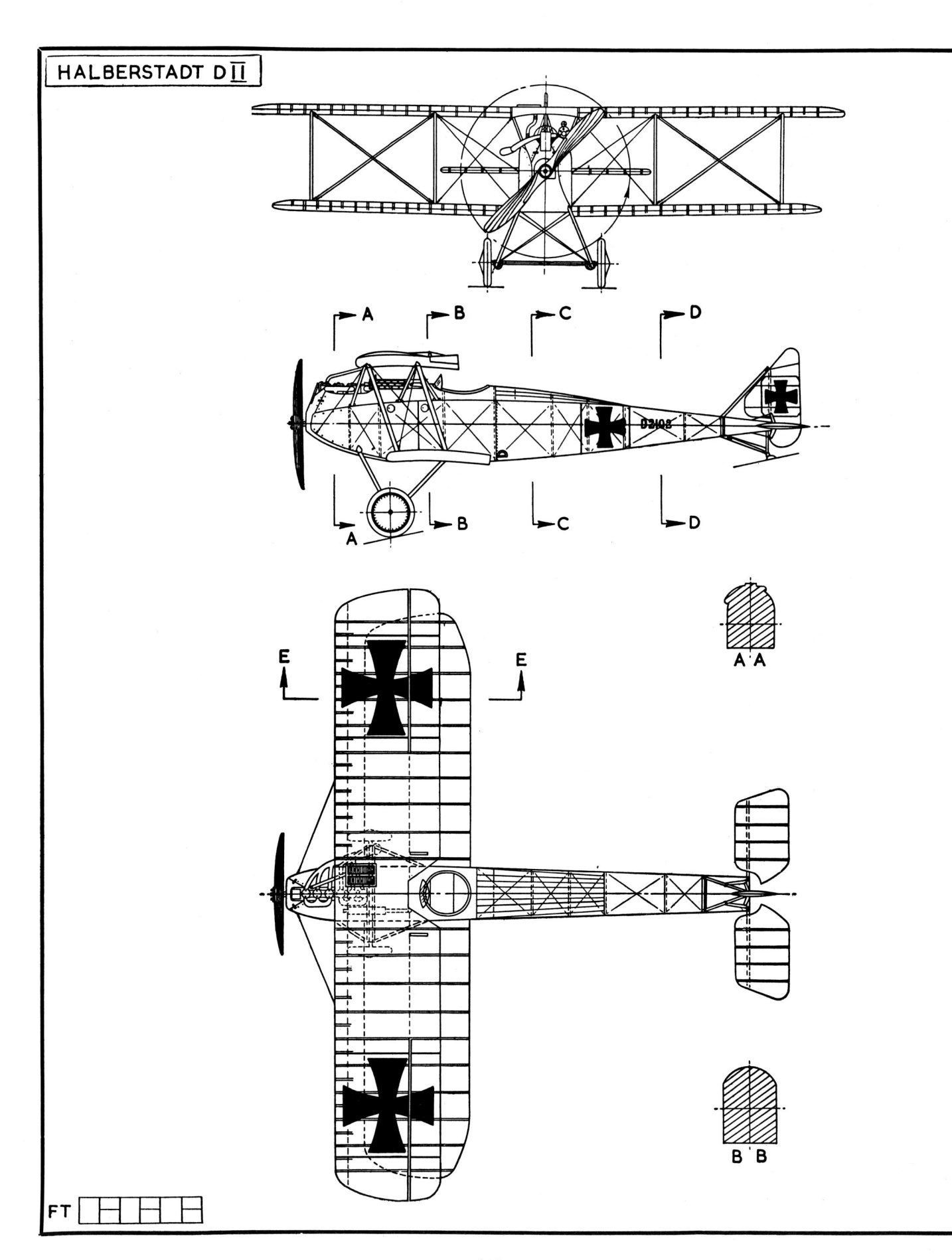

HALBERSTADT D II

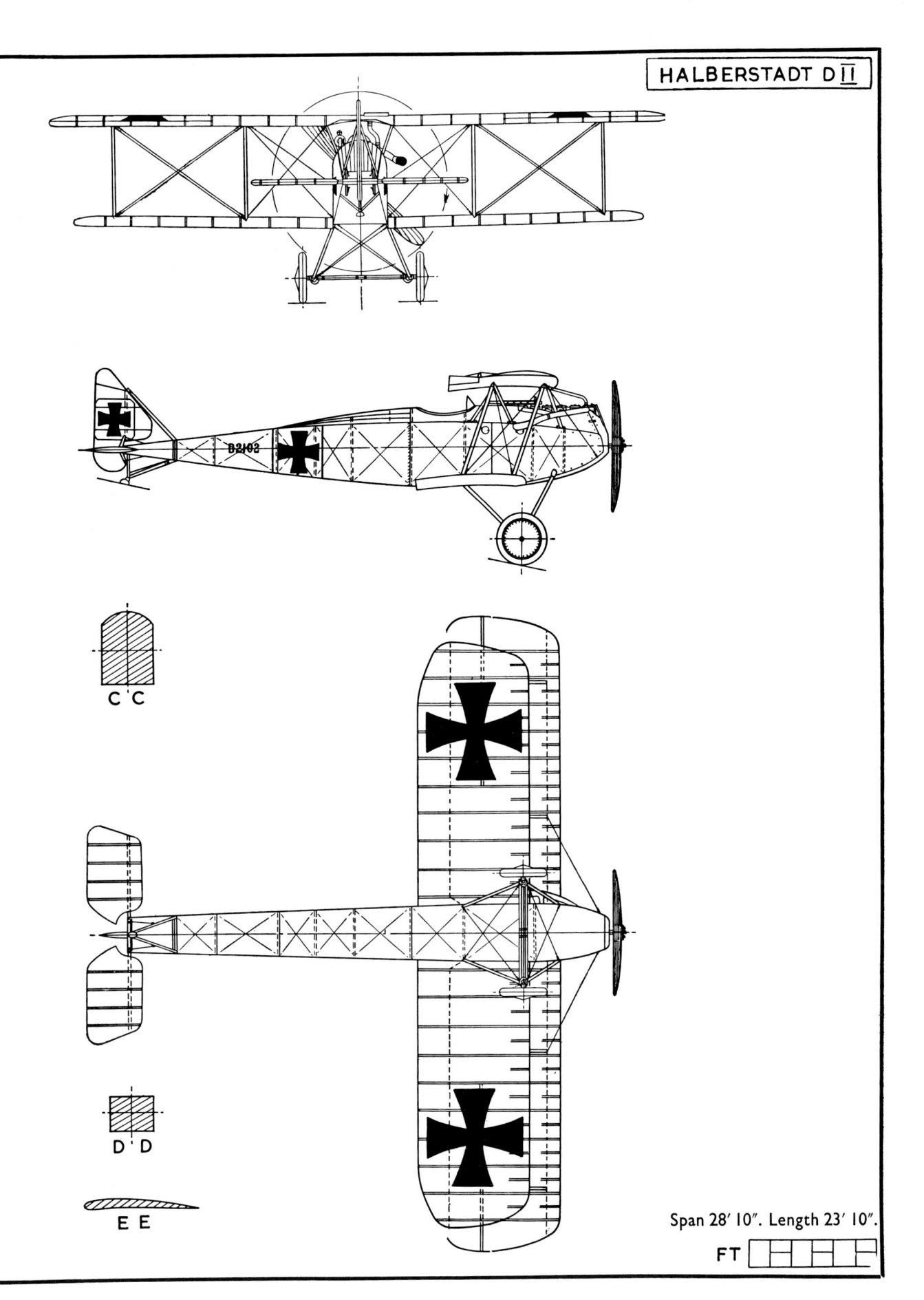

HALBERSTADT D II

Span 28' 10". Length 23' 10".

PFALZ D III SINGLE

Manfred von Richthofen about to test the rotary-engined Pfalz Dr I triplane developed from the D VII, descendant of the D III.

The Pfalz Flugzeugwerke at Speyer on Rhine was formed under the auspices of the two Eversbusch brothers who acted as chief engineer and chief test pilot. The firm was founded largely to provide aircraft for the southern German states, in particular Bavaria. The earliest products were virtually copies of the French Morane parasol monoplane; later a series of E type monoplanes, similar in appearance to the Fokker *eindeckers*, were produced. With the advent of the D-type single-seat biplanes Pfalz built under licence L.F.G. Roland D Is and D IIs and then, in 1917, produced their own design in this classification—the D III. This machine has been frequently likened to its contemporary Albatros types, and although it did bear a superficial resemblance, close examination shows it to be considerably dissimilar in both profile and detail design.

Powered with a 160 h.p. Mercedes D III engine (the D IIIa had the more powerful 180 h.p. motor) a captured specimen attained 102·5 m.p.h. at 10,000 feet, to which height it climbed in 17 minutes 30 seconds; 91·5 m.p.h. was achieved at 15,000 feet, to which height it took 41 minutes 40 seconds. Service ceiling was 17,000 feet; 21½ gallons of petrol and 4 gallons of oil gave an endurance of approximately 2 hours. Empty weight was 1,580 lb. and loaded 1,861 lb.

Armament fitted consisted of the classic twin, fixed, forward-firing machine guns. On the earliest production models the guns were mounted inside the fuselage with just the muzzles protruding; later they were mounted directly on top of the fuselage to facilitate servicing.

The angularly raked wings,

D III side view shows monocoque fuselage profile to advantage. Aluminium finish may be noted, also unusual 'hockey-stick' tail-skid.

of unequal span and chord, were built up on two hollow box-spars of spruce with three-ply facing on the flanges. Ribs were of ply-wood flanged with spruce; false ribs, spaced between, were little more than ash strips. The starboard side of the centre-section contained the radiator, which conformed to the aerofoil section; in the corresponding port side of the centre-section was located the gravity petrol tank. Ailerons of parallel chord with a small balance portion at the tip were also of wooden construction and operated by cables feeding through the lower wing and connecting to the crank lever. The small centre-section cut-out encroached into the trailing edge no more that a foot. Interplane struts were of wood of approximate 'V' form and slightly splayed. The centre-section struts, likewise of wood, were rather unusual in that they were of an inverted 'U' shape of considerably flattened outline. Only 2 degrees of dihedral was rigged on the lower wings, the roots of which were carefully faired into the fuselage. The top wing was flat and the whole wing structure was covered with linen fabric.

The fuselage was a streamlined monocoque based on the construction method of the Rolands that Pfalz had earlier built; the basic frame of formers and longerons was 'wound' with strips of 1 mm. plywood in a diagonal direction, this shell was then overlaid with another layer of strips wound in the opposite direction. The whole was then covered with fabric, doped and varnished, which resulted in an extremely strong structure. The fin—built integral with the fuselage—and tailplane were of wood and covered with a plywood skin, the latter was of inverted aerofoil section to assist dive recovery. Rudder and one-piece elevator were fabric covered and the former was fabricated from steel tube.

Neatly installed in the nose was the 160 h.p. Mercedes D III engine with much of the cylinder block protruding

SEAT SCOUT

Designer Eversbusch (Right) and test pilot Baierlein (Left) pose in front of a Pfalz D III.

but closely encowled with removable metal panels to facilitate accessibility. A neat little spinner completed the nose entry. A variety of exhaust manifold shapes were fitted but invariably ejected horizontally through a single short pipe of varying curvature. The manifold of the D IIIa was more standardised—of saxophone shape with the bell adjacent to the front cylinder.

Pilot's controls were orthodox although the control stick differed slightly from normal. Instead of the spade-grip top it was fitted with inverted 'cow-horn' handles, the left hand one incorporating an auxiliary twist-grip throttle for combat use. The triggers were located in the centre convenient to depression by either thumb. The rudder-bar was fitted with pivoted foot pedals equipped with adjustable leather straps. No actual instrument panel was fitted; the various instruments which constituted mainly: rev. counter, altimeter, fuel pressure and quantity gauges, magneto switches, fuel pressure hand pumps and petrol cocks, were fastened direct to various parts of the airframe convenient to the pilot's hand or vision.

The undercarriage was a normal 'V' type steel tube structure with the axle and dual spreader bars enclosed in a streamline fairing, the wheels were sprung with elastic shock cord. The hockey-stick shape tail-skid was hinged at the extreme fuselage end, the 'handle' lying horizontally along the underside and sprung at the forward end with elastic cord.

It would appear that almost the whole production line of Pfalz D IIIs was finished completely with aluminium dope and patée crosses positioned above and below the wings and on both sides of the fuselage and rudder. The later D IIIa's were covered with the standard lozenge-printed camouflage fabric although the fuselages were still silver doped. Patée crosses were carried until April 1918 when the straight sided Greek crosses—more often seen on the D IIIas—were introduced. When received by *Jagdstaffeln* the aircraft were invariably decorated with some form of unit identity marking—usually a distinctive nose or tail colour—and some form of individual identity device was also applied. Rudolf Stark in his book *Wings of War* mentions having his Pfalz D III painted with a lilac-coloured spinner and a band aft of the cockpit.

During the summer of 1917 *Staffeln* began to have their Albatros D IIIs and Roland D IIs replaced or supplemented by the Pfalz D III and Albatros D V/Va. Many of the less famous units, in particular the Bavarian formations, were often composed of a mixture of Albatros, Pfaz and Roland types which could not have made for ease of maintenance.

The Pfalz was easily distinguished from the Albatros by its more angular raked wing-tips, its angular tailplane and its fin and rudder reminiscent of the L.V.G. C types. The Pfalz D IIIa differed little visually from its predecessor, the lower wing-tips were more rounded and the tailplane was nearer semi-circular in plan form having been increased in area from approximately 12 to 16 square feet.

Although Manfred von Richthofen is not thought to have flown the D III operationally, the machine undoubtedly partially equipped some of the *Staffeln* that made up the famous *Jagdgeschwader Nr. 1*.

A front view shows nose entry neatness, engine fairing and altogether the clean appearance. Note wash-out in lower wing-tips.

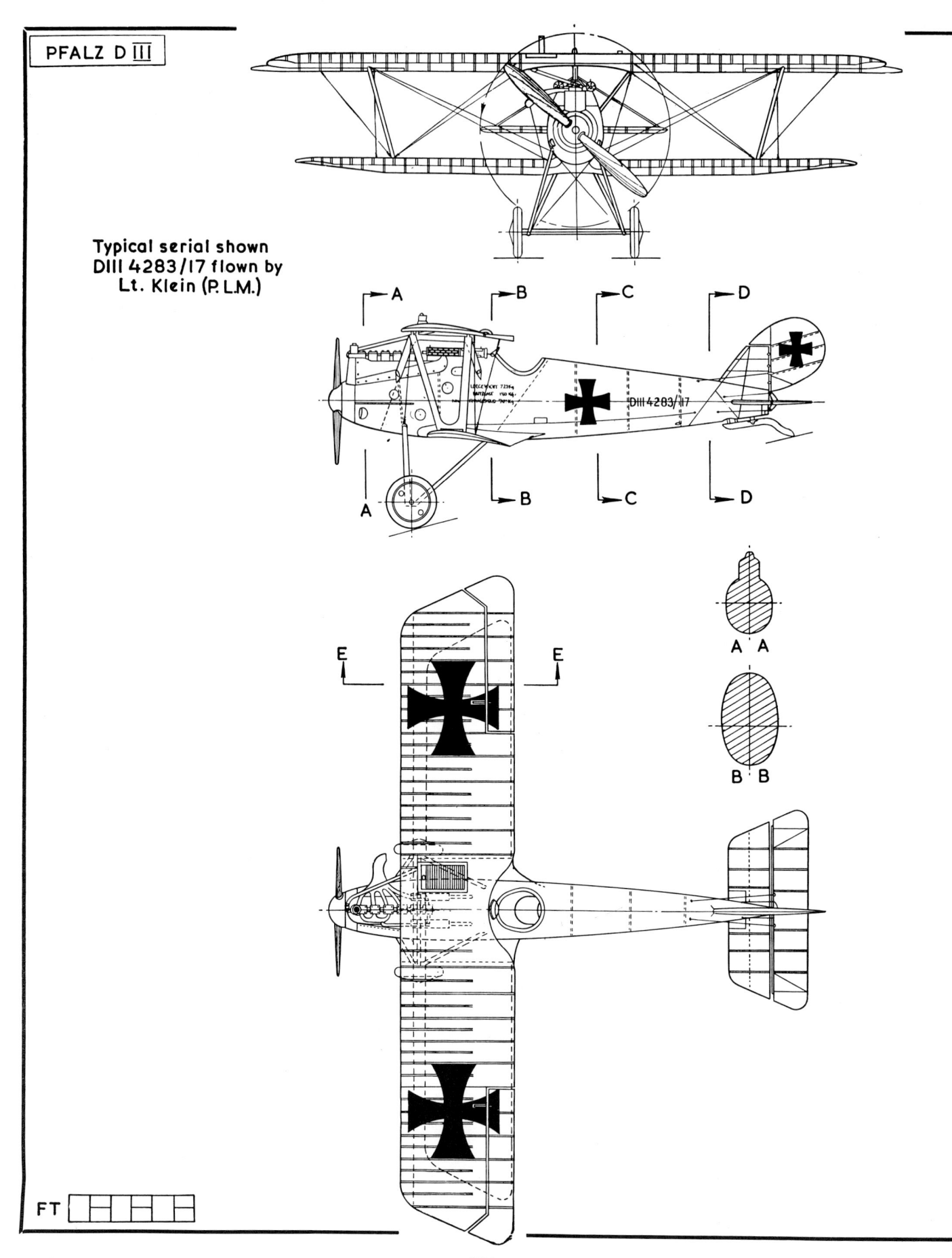

PFALZ D III

Typical serial shown
DIII 4283/17 flown by
Lt. Klein (P.L.M.)

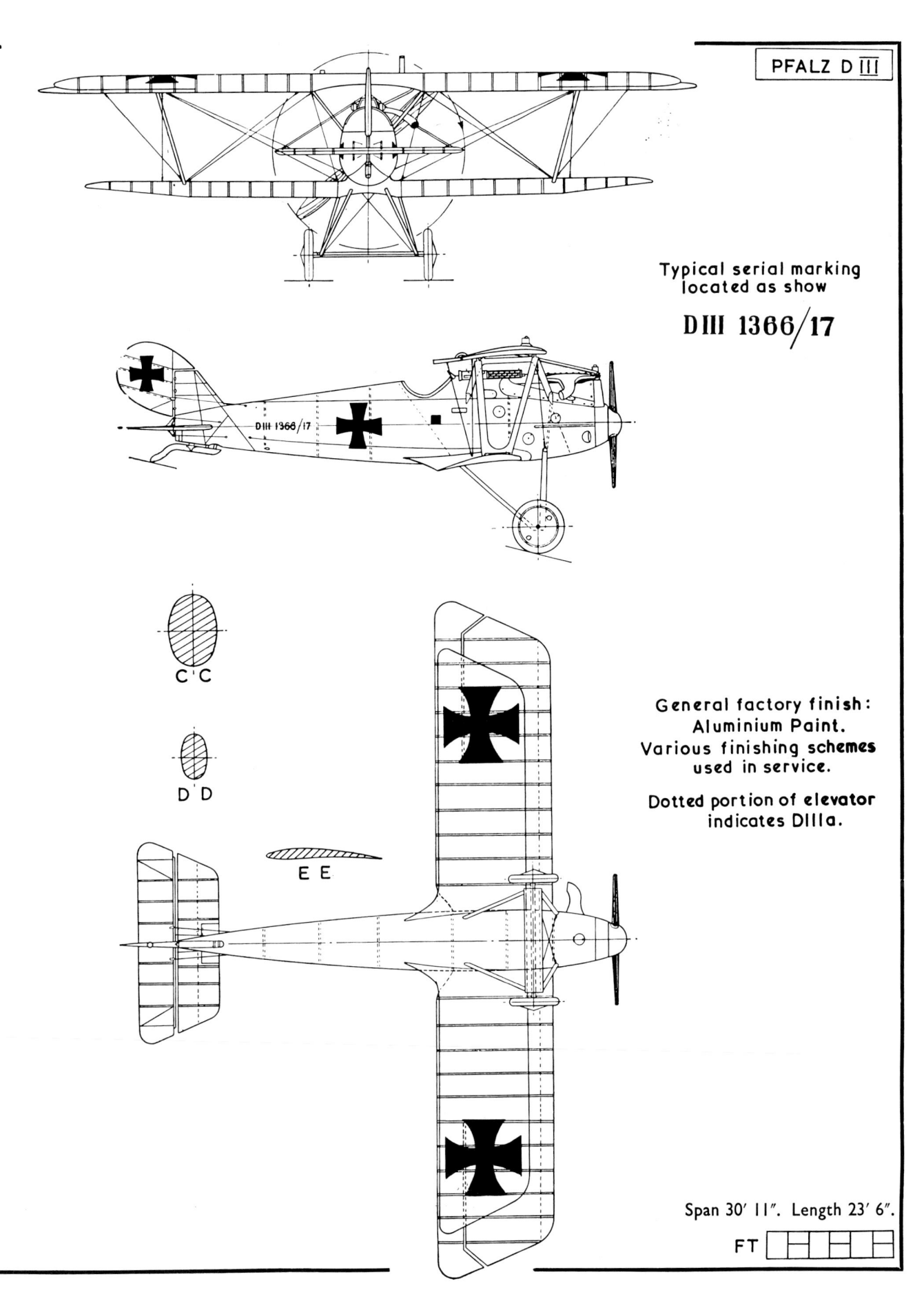

PFALZ D III

Typical serial marking located as show

DIII 1366/17

General factory finish: Aluminium Paint. Various finishing schemes used in service.

Dotted portion of elevator indicates DIIIa.

Span 30' 11". Length 23' 6".

APPENDIX SIX

Glossary

TRANSLATION OF GERMAN TERMS

Note: Lit.=Literally Spec.=Specifically

Armee Flugpark: Lit: 'Army Aviation Park'. Spec: a replacement depot from which replacement aircrews were drawn to fill vacancies in tactical aviation units.

B.A.M. (Brieftauben-Abteilung-Metz): See *B.A.O.* Generally similar in function as *B.A.O.*, except *B.A.M.* largely concentrated on inland targets. Later *Bogohl II.*

B.A.O. (Brieftauben-Abteilung-Ostende): Lit: 'Mail-Pigeon-Section-Ostende'. Spec: a discreet organisation developed for early anti-submarine patrol work and coastal patrol and bombing. Later *Bogohl I.*

Chef des Feldflugwesens: Lit: 'Chief of Field Aviation'. Spec: an early German Air Service staff position on the General Headquarters Staff. At the time of creation, this position was authorised at one Major.

Der Tag: Lit: 'The Day'. Spec: a German term applied to the starting date of any major offensive.

Feldflieger-Abteilung: Lit: 'Field flying section'. Spec: the early German Air Service Field Aviation unit designation generally for photography and reconnaissance.

Feldlazarett: Lit: 'Field Hospital'. Spec: a military hospital located close to combat areas to receive battle casualties.

Flieger-Ersatz-Abteilung (F.E.A.): Lit: 'Aviator Replacement Section'. Spec: the early German Air Service flying training unit for all pilots.

Flug-Abwehr: Lit: 'Flight defence'. Spec: a term for anti-aircraft defence.

Flugmeldedienst: Lit: 'Flight Reporting Service'. Spec: an early warning system whereby German ground observers reported the infiltration of enemy aircraft to fighter units by direct telephone through a control centre.

Flugwachen: Lit: 'Flight Watches'. Spec: the individual series of ground observer posts performing the *Flugmeldedienst* function.

Flugzeugmeisterei: Lit: 'Aircraft Master Office'. Spec: the term applied to the German Directorate of Aircraft Production.

Freiherr: Lit: 'Free man'. Spec: the older German word for Baron.

Führer: The German word for 'leader'. (Also can mean 'driver', but only when applied to the operator of a vehicle.)

Grosskampfflugzeug: Lit: 'Large Battle Aeroplane'. Spec: the term applied to any of several 1915 twin-engined aircraft.

Haus Orden von Hohenzollern mit Schwerten: Lit: 'The Order of the House of Hohenzollern with Swords'.

Inspektion der Fliegertruppen: Lit: 'Inspector of Aviator Troops'. Spec: the controlling agency over the several 'Aviator Battalions'.

Inspektion der Luftschiffertruppen: Lit: 'Inspector of Airship (and balloon) Troops'. Spec: the controlling agency over the several 'Airship Battalions'.

Jagdgeschwader (J.G.): Lit: a 'Group of Hunting Echelons'. Spec: a grouping of three or four *Jasta* into a single composite unit under a Group Commander (*Geschwader Kommandeur*) to achieve more effective deployment of fighter forces, either singly or in semi or full group formation.

Jagdgruppe: A temporary grouping under a single commander of an indefinite number of *Jasta* for mass deployment; generally during, or in advance of, major offensives.

Jagdstaffel (Jasta): Lit: a 'Hunting Echelon'. Spec: the 1916 German Air Service equivalent to a British Fighter Squadron, but smaller in size, numerically designated from No. 1 upwards.

Jager Bataillon: Lit: a 'Hunter Battalion'. Spec: a combat unit of riflemen in battalion strength. Similar in many respects to the infantry unit, but an earlier German predecessor to infantry. Sometimes mounted on horseback.

Jastaschule: Lit: 'Hunting Echelon School'. Spec: the term applied to the German Air Service schools for fighter pilots.

Kampf-Einsitzerstaffel: Lit: 'Fighting-single-seater-echelon'. Spec: the first specially appointed fighting air units intended for air combat and tactical reconnaissance.

Kampfgeschwader: Lit: 'Battle Group'. Spec: the first numerically designated bombing units of the German Air Service created from the earlier *B.A.O.* and *B.A.M.* units. Later *Bogohl: Bombengeshwader der Obersten Heeresleitung.*

Kette: Lit: 'Chain'. Spec: the subdivision of a *Jasta*, consisting of three to six aircraft. Also an element of the flight formation when the entire *Jasta* was airborne.

Kommandeur der Flieger (Kofl.): Lit: 'Commander of Aviation'. Spec: the officer (and office) of each German Army exercising tactical control of assigned aviation units. (Replaced *Stabsoffizier der Flieger.*)

Kommandierender General der Luftstreitkräfte (Kogenluft): Commanding General of the Air Forces. Created late in 1916 upon realising partial autonomy of the Air Service. (Formerly *Chef des Feldflugwesens.*)

Kriegsflug: Lit: 'War Flight'. Spec: the German equivalent of 'Sortie' meaning a single combat flight.

Kriegslazarett: Lit: 'War Hospital'. Spec: a general hospital, staffed and equipped to handle more serious cases than a *Feldlazarett.*

Leibkürassier: Lit: 'Life-Cuirassier'. Spec: a mounted home guard military unit which still wore the 'Cuirass', or metal breastplate.

Luft Einschiess (munition): Lit: 'Air Ranging'. Spec: a ballistics term applied to special ammunition which exploded at a predetermined time after leaving the muzzle of the gun. Only applied to air ammunition.

Luftschutzoffizier: Lit: 'Air Protection Officer'. Spec: an officer at the *Flugmeldestation* who received the reports of enemy aircraft infiltration, and telephoned them to fighter units within his sector for intercept action.

Luftwaffe: Lit: 'Air Weapon'. Spec: the term for the German Air Force, in World War II as opposed to the term *Luftstreitkräfte* used in World War I.

Ordre pour le Mérite (P.L.M.): The highest German award for conspicuous service and gallantry. The German equivalent of the Victoria Cross or Congressional Medal of Honour. Awarded, however, under lesser conditions of qualification than the V.C. or C.M.H.

Schutzstaffel: Lit: 'Protection Echelon'. Spec: a *Staffel* designated and equipped for the purpose of escorting *Fliegerabteilung* and providing protection from enemy fighters. Escort squadron.

Stabsoffizier der Flieger (StoFl.): Lit. 'Staff Officer of Aviation'. Spec: an officer generally of Captain's rank assigned to each German Army as the staff aviation officer.

Staffelführer: Lit: 'Echelon Leader'. Spec: 'Squadron Leader'.

Spandau: The type designation given the most popular German air machine-gun. Actually a Maxim 7·92 mm. gun manufactured at the arsenal at Spandau.

Taube: Lit: 'Dove'. Spec: the term assigned to any of several early German monoplanes whose wings resembled those of birds.

von: The German word for 'of'. When used as a surname prefix denotes the former status of nobility.

TYPE DESIGNATIONS OF GERMAN AIRCRAFT

A. Two-place, single engine, unarmed monoplanes, such as the 'Taube' machines and early Fokkers. Used mostly for scouting, although a Taube dropped the first bomb on Paris in 1915.

B. Two-place, single engine, unarmed biplanes, such as Albatros B I, B II, L.V.G. B I, etc. Mostly used for reconnaissance, early photography and training. Some B types produced throughout entire war as training or school machines and the B designation later became accepted for basic training aircraft.

C. Two-place, single engine, armed biplanes, such as Albatros C I, C III, Aviatik C II, L.F.G. C II, etc. Used for reconnaissance, photography and artillery spotting. Initially armed with a single flexible Parabellum machine-gun in rear cockpit. Later a single fixed Maxim (Spandau) synchronised machine-gun was also standard installation for operation from front cockpit.

CL. Essentially redesigned and re-developed C types, made initially lighter and more manœuvrable with the idea of employment as two-place fighters. Best known types were Halbertadt CL II and Hannoveranner CL IIIa. Armed with two forward firing guns, and a single flexible gun at rear cockpit.

CLS. Largely same as CL. Used only by Halberstädter Flugzeugwerke to designate a specifically designed aircraft (CLS I) for ground support employment.

D. Single-place, single engine, armed biplanes (Doppeldecker), such as Albatros D I, D II, D III, Fokker D V, D VII, Pfalz D III, D XII, etc., armed usually with two fixed synchronised Maxim (Spandau) machine-guns. The early Halberstadt D models carried only a single synchronised weapon.

DJ. Single-place, armed, single engine, ground support and anti-tank fighter fitted with armour plate around engine and cockpit area. Only example was A.E.G. DJ I.

Dr. Single-place, single engine, armed triplanes (Dreidecker), such as Fokker Dr I, Pfalz Dr I, etc. Used and equipped the same as D types.

E. Single-place (occasionally two-place), single engine, armed monoplanes (*Eindecker*), such as Fokker E I, E II, E III, E IV, Pfalz E I, E II, etc. In actual use, the Fokker E II was a two-place unarmed (except for instructional purposes) trainer, initially employed for scouting and interception, followed exclusively by interceptor employment. The Fokker E IV was equipped with three synchronised guns.

FI. Fokker factory designation for first Fokker Triplanes produced. There were three, F I 101/17, F I 102/17 and F I 103/17. Standard German Army type designation (Dr I) and numbering followed after F I 103/17.

G., Multi-place, armed, twin-engined biplanes (*Grossflugzeug*), such as A.E.G. G III, Gotha G IV, etc. Used initially for coastal patrol-bombing and later exclusively for medium and long range day and night bombing.

GL. Essentially the same as G types, except lightened in weight in an effort to provide a faster bomber which could possibly out-run fighters. Two examples were the Gotha GL VII and GL VIII.

J. Two-place, single engine, armed biplanes, fitted with armour plate in engine and cockpit area, such as Junkers J I, J II and Albatros J I and J II, etc. Used exclusively for ground support, trench strafing, and related low altitude work.

K. Early 1915 designation for twin-engine, armed multiplace biplanes, conceived as Battleplanes (*Kampfflugzeug*) before the theory of bombing was put to practical use. One example, the A.E.G. K I evolved into the A.E.G. G I.

N. Essentially certain C types modified and designed for limited night bombing. The Sablatnig N I was one example of this designation.

R. Multi-place, multi-engine, armed 'Giant' (*Riesenflugzeug*) biplanes for long range, heavy bombing, such as Linke-Hofmann R II, Zeppelin-Staaken R IV, Siemens-Schuckert R II, etc. Linke-Hofmann R II had four engines coupled to a single propeller in nose of fuselage!

APPROXIMATE RANK EQUIVALENTS

Fl. (Flieger)	Enlisted Pilot.*
Geft. (Gefreiter)	Lance-Corporal.
Uffz. (Unteroffizier)	Corporal
Vfw. (Vizefeldwebel)	Sergeant-Major.
Fw. Lt. (Feldwebel Leutnant)	Warrant Officer.
Offz Stellv. (Offizier Stellvertreter)	Acting Officer.*
Lt. (Leutnant)	2nd Lieutenant.
Oblt. (Oberleutnant)	1st Lieutenant.
Hpt. (Hauptmann)	Captain.
Rittm. (Rittmeister)	Captain (of Cavalry).*
Maj. (Major)	Major.
Oberst.	Colonel.

* No comparable equivalent in British Army.

Personnel

INDEX

	Pages
ADAM, Lt. H.	70, 75, 78-81, 85, 144, 175
Adams, Lt. A. T.	152
Adomeit, Lt.	144
Aird, Lt.	112
Allmenröder, Lt. K.	37-9, 41, 46, 56, 59, 64, 66, 78
Allmenröder, Lt. W.	37, 59, 141
Althaus, Oblt. Frhr. v.	24, 38, 66, 74, 136, 144
Alvensleben, Lt.	144
Anders, Lt.	69, 144
Andra, Fern	109
Andrews, Capt. J. O.	35
Anslinger, Lt. L.	79
Applin, Lt. R.	54, 153
Arnim, Lt. v.	28
Aue, Offz. Stellv. P.	93, 123, 125, 134, 144
Aver, Lt.	90
BACHMANN, Vfw.	85, 144
Bahlmann, Lt.	144
Bahr, Lt.	93, 144
Baierlein, Herr	90, 201
Baker, Lt. R. P.	152
Baldamus, Lt. H.	38, 78
Baldwin, Sgt. G. C.	150
Ball, Capt. A.	54, 58-9
Banbury, Capt. F. E.	111
Banks, Lt. F. E.	113
Barlow, Lt. H. C.	154
Barlow, Lt. L.	82
Barnekow, Lt. Frhr. v.	131, 144
Barnes, Sgt. W. A.	153
Barrow, Lt. A. V.	113
Barth, Vfw.	90, 92, 144
Barwell, Capt. F. L.	153
Bates, 2/Lt. A. H.	153
Beauchamp, Capt. de	66
Beauvricourt, Comte	23
Beavis, Maj. L. E.	116
Beebee, Cpl. A.	153
Bell, Capt. D.	104
Bellen, Lt. G.	144
Bellerby, Sgt. H.	150
Below, Barbara	142
Below, Samuel	142
Bender, Lt.	93, 128, 144
Bennet, Lt. C. D.	151
Bentham, 2/Lt. G. A.	150
Bernert, Lt. O.	78
Berr, Oblt. H.	38, 78
Berthold, Oblt. R.	38, 41, 78, 131
Beschow, Uffz.	93, 144
Bethge, Lt. Hans	78
Betley, 2/Lt. E.	155
Biewers, Uffz.	144
Bird, Lt. A. F.	80, 154
Bishop, Lt.-Col. W. A.	54
Block, Lt.	144
Blume (horse)	12
Blümener, A.	144
Bockelmann, Lt.	38, 144
Boddin, Oblt. v.	71, 144
Boddy, Lt. J. A. V.	87, 149, 154
Bodenschatz, Oblt.	66, 80, 98, 105, 124, 127, 134, 144
Boehme, Lt.	28-31, 90, 195
Boelcke, Hpt. O.	22-32, 38, 176, 176-8, 195-7
Boelcke, Lt. W.	23
Boenigk, Oblt. Frhr. v.	70, 74, 80, 81
Boenisch, Lt.	38
Bohlein, Lt.	93, 144
Böhren, Lt.	144

	Pages
Bongartz, Lt. H.	79
Bonner, A/M P.	152
Bouillon, Lt.	144
Boultbee, Lt. A. E.	43, 152
Bowman, Lt. G. H.	70
Bowman, Lt. L. S.	154
Boxall-Chapman, Mr.	118
Brandis, von	28
Brauneck, Lt. O.	67, 74, 144
Breiten-Landenberg, Lt. v.	93, 144
Bretschneider, Bodemer, Lt.	128, 144
Brettel, Uffz.	75, 144
Brock, Lt.	112
Brocke, Lt.	144, 152
Brown, Capt. A. R.	111-9, 140, 148
Buckler, Offz. Stellv.	79
Buddecke, Hpt. H. J.	38, 69, 79
Buie, Gnr. R.	116, 140, 139
Bülow, Lt. W. v.	78
Burggaller, Vfw.	93, 144
Butler, Maj. C. H.	111, 114
Byrne, Lt. E.	152
CAMERON, 2/Lt. D.	115
Cameron, 2/Lt. J. G.	150
Cantle, Lt. L. H.	152
Capper, Lt.	150
Carganico, Hpt.	27, 38
Chaworth-Musters, Lt.	59
Child, Capt. H. R.	99, 155
Clarkson, Sgt.	150
Clausnitzer, Vfw.	68, 70, 144
Claye, Capt. H.	95
Clutterbuck, Lt. L.	94, 154
Collins, A/M C. C.	118
Conta, Lt. v.	93, 144
Croft, 2/Lt. H. A.	151
Crowe, Capt. C. M.	59
Cumming, Lt. W. N.	111
Cunnell, Capt. D. C.	67
Czermak, Lt.	144
Czernin, Count	91
D'ARCY, Lt. L. G.	151
Degen, Vfw.	125, 144
Deilmann, Lt.	144
Delang, Vfw.	93, 144
Demandt, Lt.	90, 144
Derflinger, Uffz.	144
Derwin, Lt. E. C. E.	153
Dietlin, Lt. A.	79
Doering, Oblt. v.	66, 68, 71, 81, 136, 144
Dorrien, Lt. v.	144
Dossenbach, Lt. A.	38, 78
Dostler, Oblt. E.	41, 66, 68, 71, 75, 78, 79, 134, 144
Doughty, Lt. G.	150
Downs, Lt. G. E.	118
Doyle, Lt. J. C.	116
Drake, Lt.	112
Dreckmann, Lt. H.	93, 144
Dunn, Sgt. R.	152
EDWARDS, Capt. S. T.	111-2
Eiserbeck, Uffz.	144
Ellis, Lt. R. W.	154
Eschwege, Lt. v.	79
Esser, Lt.	38, 71, 93, 144
Evans, Gnr. W. J.	116
Everbusch, Alfred	90, 200
Everbusch, Ernst	90, 200
Everingham, 2/Lt. G.	153

	Pages
FAHLBUSCH, Lt.	38
Feige, Lt.	126, 144
Fenwick, 2/Lt. W. C.	150
Ferdinand I, Emperor	142
Festler, Lt.	144
Festner, Vfw.	38, 46, 61, 64, 79
Fischer, Lt. U.	145
Fisher, 2/Lt. A. J.	150
Fisser, Dr.	131
Flassbeck, Fl.	145
Fletcher, Lt. W. F.	153
Fokker, A. H. G.	73, 82, 100, 122, 192-3
Follit, Lt. R. W.	153
Förster, Lt. O. L.	145
Forsyth, Capt. R. J.	115
Foster, Lt. R. M.	112
Frankl, Lt. W.	38, 78
Franklin, Lt. W.	153
Fraser, Lt. D. L.	118
Friedrich, Prince Eitel	19
Friedrichs, Lt. F.	93, 97, 99, 123, 125, 127, 145
GABRIEL, Vfw. W.	122, 125, 128-9, 134, 138, 145
Galetschky, Lt.	145
Garrett, Lt. S. G.	113
Garros, Roland	192
George, Lt. H. D. K.	152
Geppert, Lt.	133, 145
Gerlich, Oblt.	38
Gerstenberg, Lt.	27, 85, 145
Gilbert, C. G.	149, 152
Gilles, Lt.	145
Gluczewski, Lt. Graf v.	71, 93, 131, 145
Gontermann, Lt. H.	78
Göring, Hermann	110, 124-34, 145, 182
Göttsch, Lt. W.	78
Gough, Gen. Sir H.	97
Graham, Capt. G. C.	118
Grassmann, Lt. J.	93, 123, 133, 134, 145
Graul, Lt.	74, 145
Green, Lt. H. J.	151
Green, Lt. W.	153
Greig, Capt. O.	40, 151
Greim, Ritter von	131, 138
Griggs, Lt. A.	87
Groos, Lt. G.	80, 81, 141, 145
Grosch, Oblt.	145
Guenther, Lt.	28
Gussmann, Lt.	71, 87, 93, 96, 98, 130, 145, 175
Guynemer, Lt. G.	38, 123
HABER, Lt.	38
Haehnelt, Hpt.	24, 79
Hall, 2/Lt. C. S.	48
Hall, Lt. T. R. V.	102
Hamilton, Lt. W. N.	54-5
Hammond, Lt. A. W.	99, 100
Hardel, Uffz.	85, 145
Harker, Lt. M. A.	111-2
Hartmann, Oblt.	145
Hartmann, Lt. v.	145
Harvey-Kelly, Maj. H. D.	54-5
Hawker, Maj. L. G.	34-5, 149, 151
Hay, 2/Lt. J.	151
Hazell, Lt. T. F.	78
Heagerty, Lt. J. S.	152
Hecht, Vfw.	90, 145
Hedley, Capt. J. H.	155
Heindenreich, Lt.	125, 145
Held, Lt.	145

	Pages
Heldmann, Lt. A.	93, 123, 134, 134, 145
Hemer, Vfw. F.	93, 101, 128, 130, 145
Hennig, Uffz.	145
Henschler, Gefr.	145
Hertz, Lt.	145
Hildebrandt, Lt.	145
Hinch, Lt.	38
Hindenburg, Field Marshal v.	61, 110
Hintman, Lt.	38
Hirschfeld, Lt.	145
Hoeppner, Gen. v.	60, 95, 106
Hoffmann, Lt.	126, 145
Hoffmann, Hpt. M.	90
Hohenau, Lt. Graf. v.	145
Höhndorf, Lt. W.	38, 78
Hoidge, Lt. R. T. C.	59, 72
Holck, Count	19, 20, 26
Holt, Lt.-Col. F. V.	118
Horn, 2/Lt. E. E.	151
Howe, Sgt. Hans	38
Howlett, Sgt. F. A.	152
Hübner, Lt.	124, 145
Hübner, Lt. A.	70, 78, 145
Hudson, Lt. F.	102
Hughes, Capt. G. F.	95
Hunt, Lt. P. B. G.	151
IMELMANN, Lt. H.	33
Immelmann, Lt. M.	24, 32, 38, 78, 193
Ivamy, Lt. W. G.	96, 154
JAGLA, Sgt.	145
Janzen, Lt. J.	93, 125, 145
Jessen, Lt.	145
Johnson, G/C J. E.	11
Jones, 2/Lt. E. D.	155
Joschkowitz, Lt.	145
Just, Lt. E.	66, 90, 93, 98, 102, 123, 145
KARJUS, Lt.	105, 145
Kastner, Hpt.	23
Kember, 2/Lt. W.	154
Kennedy, Capt.	95
Keseling, Lt.	145
King, A/M F.	43, 152
Kirkham, 2/Lt. F. J.	153
Kirkham, 2/Lt. K. R.	155
Kirmaier, Lt. S.	32
Kirschstein, Lt. H.	95, 99-102, 124-8, 145
Kirst, Lt.	133, 145
Kissenberth, Lt.	176
Klamt, Uffz. R.	134, 145
Klein, Lt. Hans	69-71, 79, 87, 90-3, 145, 202
Knaggs, Lt. K. J.	59
Knight, Lt. A. G.	151
Knowles, Capt. M. B.	48
Knox, 2/Lt. W.	155
Koch, Lt.	74, 145
Köckeritz, Lt. v.	141, 145
Koepsch, Lt. E.	90, 93, 134, 145
Kohlbach, Lt. W.	132, 145
Kohze, Oblt.	96
Koolhoven, Frederik	100
Kortüm, Lt.	145
Kospoth, Count	12
Kraut, Lt.	131, 145
Krayer, Lt.	145
Krebs, Vfw.	68, 70, 145
Krefft, Lt.	38, 46, 61, 71, 75, 81, 90, 93, 145
Krüger, Lt. R.	68, 145

210

Krüger, Lt. 145	Müller, Lt. 78, 85	Richthofen, Karl Frhr. v. 142-3	Stead, Sgt. G. 153
Kühn, Lt. 66, 92-3, 145	Mulzer, Lt. Ritter v. 38, 79	Richthofen, Lothar Frhr. v. 13-5, 37, 42-5, 54-60, 64, 81-7, 91-3, 128-30, 143, 146	Steinhäuser, Lt. W. 71, 91-4, 105, 123-6, 147
Kullmer, Vfw. 146	Murray, Lt. P. W. 151		Stewart, Lt. D. J. 152
Küppers, Lt. K. 146	NATHANAEL, Offz. Stellv. 78		Stock, Lt. K. 147
LANSDALE, Lt. E. C. 150	Neckel, Lt. U. 131-3, 146	Richthofen, Oswald Frhr. v. 143	Stock, Lt. W. 70, 147
Laumann, Lt. A. 126-7, 131-3, 146	Newton, 2/Lt. R. F. 155	Richthofen, Praetorius Frhr. v. 143	Stoy, Lt. 147
	Niederhoff, Lt. 67-8, 71-2, 146		Strecker, Uffz. 147
Lautenschlager, Vfw. 69, 85, 146	Niemz, Vfw. A. 146	Richthofen, Wolfram, Frhr. v. 101, 105, 113-4, 123-5, 133, 146	Stuart, Capt. J. 149, 153
Leach, Lt. J. O. 59	Niess, Vfw. 146		Stumpf, Vfw. 74, 147
Le Boutillier, Capt. 111-3, 117	Nitsche, Fl. 146	Rickenbacker, Capt. Ed. 132	Suck, Lt. H. 147
Lechner, Vfw. 131, 146	Nöldecke, Lt. W. 141, 146	Ridgway, Gnr. G. 115	Summers, Capt. 130
Leckler, Lt. A. M. 152	Noltenius, Prof. H. 132	Riehm, Lt. K. 146	
Leefe-Robinson, Capt. 46	Noltenius, Lt. F. 132-3, 146	Riensberg, Fl. 91, 146	TAYLOR, 2/Lt. J. B. 155
Leffers, Lt. G. 38, 79	Notzke, Lt. 24	Rieth, Lt. Dr. 146	Taylor, Lt. M. S. 111-2
Legarde, Maj. M. 64	Nungesser, Lt. 38	Rist, Oblt. 90	Tetu, Lt. 23
Leggat, 2/Lt. M. 155		Rödiger, Lt. O. 146	Theiller, Lt. R. 79
Lehmann, Lt. W. 123, 146	O'BEIRNE, 2/Lt. J. I. M. 152	Rolff, Lt. 131, 146	Thelen, Herr 160, 168
Lewis, Lt. C. A. 59	Oesein, Maj. 138	Römer, Lt. 146	Thomsen, Maj. H. 17, 24, 27, 64
Lewis, 2/Lt. D. G. 102, 104, 155	Ohlrau, Lt. 78, 146	Rosencrantz, Lt. 38	
Lewis, Lt. S. H. 102	Osten, Lt. v.d. 66, 71, 78, 81, 93, 141, 146	Rousselle, Lt. O. 93, 146	Todd, Fl. Lt. A. S. 37, 151
Lidsey, 2/Lt. W. J. 152		Rudenberg, Vfw. 146	Tollervey, Sgt. A. 153
Linsingen, Lt. v. 71, 92, 141, 146	Osteroth, Lt. 21	Ruppecht, Crown Prince 14, 16, 28	Townsend, Capt. P. T. 154
Lischke, Oblt. K. 105, 146	Otersdorf, Fr. K. 68-9		Trollope, Capt. J. L. 97
Loerzer, Oblt. B. 131	Otto, Lt. H. 125, 141, 146	Russell, Lt. W. O. 153	Tutschek, Oblt. Ritter v. 78, 90, 190
Loewenhardt, Lt. 66, 78-81, 91, 93, 96-9, 103, 123-130, 146	PALFYN, JAN 78	SANTUZZA (horse) 12	
	Parschau, Lt. O. 23, 38, 79	Schaefer, Lt. Hugo 123-4, 146	Tüxen, Lt. 85, 93, 147
Lossberg, Gen. v. 73	Pascoe, 2/Lt. F. J. 154	Schaefer, Lt. K. E. 36, 39, 46, 48, 52-3, 56	UDET, Lt. E. 98-101, 124-138, 137, 147, 182
Lübbert, Lt. F. 71, 93, 146	Pastor, Lt. 85, 146		
Ludendorff, Fd. Mrsl. 61, 86, 97, 129	Patermann, Vfw. 70, 146	Schaffen, Vfw. 123, 146	
	Pearson, Lt. A. J. 42, 152	Scheele, Lt. 27	VIEHWEGER, Oblt. 28
Lyncker, Lt. v. 22	Pechmann, Lt. P. v. 41	Scheffer, Oblt. 38, 147	Voss, Lt. W. 45, 74-5, 78-82, 147, 190
	Peiler, Lt. M. F. 102	Schibilsky, Lt. K. 147	
MACGREGOR, Flt. Sub-Lt. 81	Pfeiffer, Lt. H. 38, 79	Schiemann, Lt. 147	WALZ, Hpt. 32, 38
Mackensen, Gen. v. 18	Pierson, Gnr. H. 153	Schilling, Oblt. H. 38, 79	Warneford, Lt. W. J. 118
Mackensie, 2/Lt. K. I. 153	Platz, Reinhold 180, 188	Schlegel, 90	Warren, Lt. P. 46, 152
Mackenzie, Lt. W. J. 113, 123	Plüschow, Lt. W. 38	Schliewen, Lt. 147	Watt, 2/Lt. G. M. 152
MacLean, Cpl. 115	Popkin, Sgt. C. B. 116, 120	Schmidt, Lt. 147	Wawzin, Vfw. 147
MacLenan, Lt. J. E. 40, 151	Porter, 2/Lt. W. 97, 155	Schmidt, Sebastian 142	Wedel, Oblt. v. 124, 127-8, 131, 135, 147
Madge, 2/Lt. J. B. C. 154	Powell, Lt. J. C. 152	Schmutzler, Sgt. 93, 124, 147	
Maletsky, Lt. 146	Power-Clutterbuck, 2/Lt. 154	Schneider, Lt. K. 78	Wegener, Prof. 62
Mannock, Maj. E. 33, 57, 133	Praetorius, Samuel 142	Schoenebeck, Lt. v. 81, 84, 141, 147	Weigand, Oblt. 78, 81-2, 147
Manschott, Vfw. F. 79	Praetorius, Tobias 142		Weiss, Lt. H. 101-2, 105, 113, 123-4, 147
Marc, Lt. 44	Püttkamer, Lt. v. 146	Scholz, Vfw. 71, 98, 102, 105, 113, 123, 147	
Marion, Lt. R. J. 123			Welch, 2/Lt. E. A. 153
Markgraf, Lt. 128, 146	QUICKE, Sgt. S. H. 152	Schröder, Lt. (J.G.I) 147	Wense, Lt. v. d. 130, 147
Marquardt, Vfw. 70, 146	Quinlan, Lt. J. 115	Schröder, Lt. 67-9	Wentz, Lt. v. d. 130, 147
Martens, Uffz. 146		Schubert, Herr 160	Wenz, Lt. A. 147
Mather, E. 102	RACZEK, Lt. v. 146	Schubert, Fw. Lt. 71, 93, 147	Wenzel, Lt. P. 93, 123, 130, 147
Matthies, Lt. 146	Rademacher, Lt. 146	Schulte, Lt. A. 79	Wenzl, Lt. R. 105, 113, 147, 130, 133
Matthof, Lt. 38	Raffey, Vfw. v. 93, 141, 146	Schulte-Frohlinde, Lt. 131, 147	
Matzdorf, Lt. 146	Ransom, Lt. H. W. 155	Schultze, Paulas 142	Werkmeister, Uffz. 82, 147
Mason, Lt. C. J. 123	Rautter, Lt. v. 66, 101, 125, 146	Schulze, Lt. 90, 147	Weston, Gnr. R. F. 116
Maushake, Lt. 93, 133, 146	Raymond-Barker, Maj. 104, 155	Schumacher, Sgt. 123, 147	Whatley, Sgt. H. A. 154
May, 2/Lt. W. R. 112-9	Reading, 2/Lt. V. J. 155	Schüz, Oblt. Hans 79	White, Lt. W. W. 132
Mayberry, Lt. R. A. 72-4	Redgate, Capt. A. W. 111-3	Schweinitz, Lt. v. 147	Whiteside, Sub. Lt. R. C. 151
Maxwell, Lt. G. 59	Rees, Lt. T. 29, 150	Seccull, Bdr. J. S. 116	Whitham, Lt.-Col. J. L. 115
McAfee, Lt. A. R. 111	Reeve, Lt. A. 99	Serno, Maj. 28	Wilberg, Maj. 66
McCudden, Maj. J. B. 37, 81-2	Reid, Lt. W. 151	Severs, 2/Lt. A. C. 40	Wilde, Lt. 147
McDonald, 2/Lt. D. P. 152	Reimann, Lt. 26	Sherbrook-Walker, Lt. 45	Wilhelm II, Kaiser 10, 16, 76
McLeod, 2/Lt. A. A. 99-100	Reimann, Vfw. 28-9	Siddall, Lt. 112	Williams, 2/Lt. C. P. 154
McRae, Lt. T. D. 151	Reimers, Uffz. 146	Siegert, Maj. 17, 20	Wilson, Capt. 31
Meintjes, Capt. H. 59	Reinhard, Oblt. W. 68, 71, 78-81, 91-3, 101, 122-7, 134, 146	Siemelkamp, Lt. 101, 147	Wilson, Lt. C. E. 153
Meise, Lt. 146		Sienz, Lt. 147	Winterfeld, Lt. v. 147
Mellersh, Capt. F. 111-4, 117	Reinhardt, Lt. 130, 133, 146	Simon, Lt. G. 51, 141, 147	Wintgens, Lt. K. 38, 78
Melville, Lt. W. B. 59	Reventlow, Count 108	Simpson, Lt. T. L. 113	Wolff, Lt. J. H. 78, 92-3, 101-2, 105, 113, 123-4, 147
Menzke, Fl. 45	Rhode, Fl. 146	Sinclair, Col. T. 118	
Meyer, Lt. 70, 80, 93, 124, 146	Rhys-Davids, Lt. A. F. P. 59, 82, 108	Skauradzun, Lt. 93, 147	Wolff, Lt. Kurt 36-9, 50, 67, 70, 78, 81, 85, 147
Meyer, Hpt. W. 90		Skowronski, Lt. 147	
Meyer, Marine Flgmtr. 38	Richthofen, Maj. A. Frhr. v. 9, 11, 13, 37, 54-6, 67, 106, 143	Smart, 2/Lt. G. O. 152	Wolff, Lt. (III) 93, 131, 147
Millett, 2/Lt. J. M. L. 154		Smith, Lt. C. 45	Wood, Lt. M. H. 149, 153
Mohnicke, Lt. E. 38, 59, 66, 69, 71, 80-1, 93, 128, 131, 145	Richthofen, Bolko, Frhr. v. 10, 11, 90, 109-10, 142-3	Smith, 2/Lt. J. 152	Woodbridge, 2/Lt. A. E. 67
		Smith, Capt. S. P. 102, 155	Wuehlisch, Lt. v. 23
Mölders, Oberst, W. 136-8	Richthofen, Ernst, Frhr. v. 143	Sowerbutts, Pte. G. 116	Wüsthoff, Vfw. K. 69, 70, 74, 80-1, 90, 93, 125, 136, 147
Möller, Gefr. 123, 128, 145	Richthofen, Frieda v. 143	Sparks, 2/Lt. H. J. 94, 154	
Moody, F/Sgt. R. J. 151	Richthofen, Friedrich Frhr. v. 143	Sperrle, Generalmajor 143	
Moore, Capt. G. B. 103, 155		Squire, Lt. A. P. 111	ZANDER, Hpt. 28
Morgan, 2/Lt. J. P. 132	Richthofen, Hartmann Frhr. v. 143	Stall, Lt. G. 150	Zander, Oblt. 147, 195
Moritz (dog) 83-4, 104-5		Stapenhörst, Lt. E. 75, 81, 91, 139, 147	Zastrow, Oblt. H. v. 31
Morris, Lt. L. B. F. 29, 150	Richthofen, Baroness K. v. 110, 142-3		Zeumer, Lt. 19-21, 64
Müller, Oblt. 146		Stark, Rudolf 90, 184, 201	Zwitzers, Lt. 147
Müller, Lt. H. 79			